Library of
Davidson College

O'Neill's Shakespeare

THEATER: Theory/Text/Performance
University of Michigan

Editorial Board
  Ruby Cohn, University of California, Davis
  Michael Goldman, Princeton University
  Timothy Murray, Cornell University
  Austin E. Quigley, Columbia University
  Thomas R. Whitaker, Yale University
  Katharine Worth, University of London

Around the Absurd: Essays on Modern and Postmodern Drama
  edited by Enoch Brater and Ruby Cohn

Tom Stoppard and the Craft of Comedy: Medium and Genre at Play
  by Katherine E. Kelly

Performing Drama/Dramatizing Performance: Alternative Theater and the Dramatic Text
  by Michael Vanden Heuvel

Tragicomedy and Contemporary Culture: Play and Performance from Beckett to Shepard
  by John Orr

The Plot of the Future: Utopia and Dystopia in Modern Drama
  by Dragan Klaić

Shaw's Daughters: Dramatic and Narrative Constructions of Gender
  by J. Ellen Gainor

How Dramas End: Essays on the German Sturm und Drang, *Büchner, Hauptmann, and Fleisser*
  by Henry J. Schmidt

Critical Theory and Performance
  edited by Janelle G. Reinelt and Joseph R. Roach

The Actor's Instrument: Body, Theory, Stage
  by Hollis Huston

Acting as Reading: The Place of the Reading Process in the Actor's Work
  by David Cole

Presence and Resistance: Postmodernism and Cultural Politics in Contemporary American Performance
  by Philip Auslander

Ionesco's Imperatives: The Politics of Culture
  by Rosette C. Lamont

The Theater of Michel Vinaver
  by David Bradby

Rereading Molière: Mise en Scène from Antoine to Vitez
  by Jim Carmody

O'Neill's Shakespeare
  by Normand Berlin

O'Neill's Shakespeare

Normand Berlin

Ann Arbor
THE UNIVERSITY OF MICHIGAN PRESS

Copyright © by the University of Michigan 1993
All rights reserved
Published in the United States of America by
The University of Michigan Press
Manufactured in the United States of America

1996 1995 1994 1993   4 3 2 1

Library of Congress Cataloging-in-Publication Data

Berlin, Normand.
    O'Neill's Shakespeare / Normand Berlin.
      p.   cm. — (Theater—theory/text/performance)
    Includes bibliographical references and index.
    ISBN 0-472-10469-1 (alk. paper)
    1. O'Neill, Eugene, 1888–1953—Knowledge—Literature.
2. Shakespeare, William, 1564–1616—Influence. 3. American drama—
English influences. 4. Drama—Technique. 5. Literary form.
I. Title. II. Series.
PS3529.N5Z567 1993
812'.52—dc20   93-31593
                                                                    CIP

A CIP catalogue record for this book is available from the British Library.

For Barbara, without whom . . .

Acknowledgments

Portions of my "Tragedy" chapter were published earlier in the following journal articles: "The Beckettian O'Neill," *Modern Drama* 31 (March 1988): 28–34; "O'Neill and Comedy: *The Iceman Cometh*," *Eugene O'Neill Newsletter* 12 (Winter 1988): 3–8; "Ghosts of the Past: O'Neill and Hamlet," *Massachusetts Review* 20 (Summer 1979): 312–23. I am grateful to the editors for permission to reprint here.

I offer a special thank you to the former dean of humanities and fine arts here at the University of Massachusetts, Murray M. Schwartz, and to the former chair of the department of English, Robert Bagg, for the award of a Humanities Research Fellowship, which gave me the opportunity to write much of this book.

To the students, both past and present, in my classes on Shakespeare and O'Neill I owe a teacher's debt. It was in my discussions with them and my lectures at them that ideas about these two giants of drama germinated and expanded.

My notes acknowledge the many O'Neill and Shakespeare scholars and critics whose work guided me throughout. To them, my abiding gratitude.

Finally, these "family" dramatists, O'Neill and Shakespeare, have made me ever aware of the preciousness of family feeling. My wife Barbara and our sons, Adam and David, inform this book in ways both they and I will never be able to articulate. To Barbara I owe most—for her ideas, her support, her love.

Contents

Introduction   1

Part 1

1. The Sea   11
2. Black and White   27
3. The Family   57

Part 2

4. Comedy   115
5. History   135
6. Tragedy   165
7. Tragicomedy   225

Notes   255

Index   265

Introduction

Here is how I came to write this book. I've been teaching and writing about Shakespeare for almost all the years I've been in the profession, and for about the last twelve years I've been teaching and writing about O'Neill. My book on O'Neill (*Eugene O'Neill* [Macmillan, Grove, St. Martin's, 1982]), like many books on O'Neill, brought in Shakespeare here and there, but in that book I, like most commentators before me, considered Strindberg and Nietzsche to be the most important influences on O'Neill, with O'Neill himself acknowledging the influences both publicly and privately. In addition, it was clear that other writers, like Ibsen and Conrad and Euripides, were also important sources throughout O'Neill's development. I continue to believe that all those mentioned, and many others, must be confronted in any discussion of O'Neill's dramatic art. When I finished that book, I gave no thought to writing another book on O'Neill, but incrementally—through the years that I was teaching both Shakespeare and O'Neill, with the classes often coming back to back (either Shakespeare before O'Neill, or O'Neill before Shakespeare, depending on the whim of the scheduling officer)—I became increasingly aware that I was saying, and the students were discussing, surprisingly similar things in both classes. That is, I was not able to break away from Shakespeare when I taught O'Neill, and I was often thinking about O'Neill when I taught Shakespeare. Then—I don't know exactly when it happened but "something happened," to use an O'Neill phrase—I realized that Shakespeare and O'Neill couldn't break away from each other. However, another thought quickly accompanied this realization. Would a "connectedness" not have been established had I been teaching any two great dramatists back to back? Suppose I were teaching Chekhov and Beckett, or Euripides and Racine, or Shaw and Brecht. Wouldn't similar ideas and methods cling to these combinations also? The answer, I believe, is yes. There would be a sharing, a relationship, especially because we are dealing with writers engaged in the same dramatic art, in the same "tradition," so to speak, and also because they are treating essential aspects of "human nature." (More later on the reason for the use of quotation marks.) Still, as I began to follow the track of my own observations on the relationship of O'Neill and Shakespeare, I came to the conclusion that the connection between the two—more than the connection between the others in the pairs I cited—was essential, basic, even natural when we consider O'Neill's nurture, while at the same time more mysterious, surprising, and provocative. On the face of it, the plays of Shakespeare and O'Neill are so different; on the face of it, the two dramatists seem worlds apart. In my classes, however, they converged, and when I called attention to the convergence I found that my students benefited from the observation. It seemed to me that insights into the art and minds of both dramatists could be gained by paying attention to their connectedness. When I came upon a specific Shakespeare allusion in O'Neill or when I heard the faintest Shakespearean echo, I asked myself such obvious critical questions as, why this allusion or echo at this point in the play? how much pressure does it put on the play? what set it off in O'Neill's mind? And these questions led to larger questions about O'Neill's conscious or unconscious use of Shakespeare's methods, the technical aspects of Shakespeare's medium, which inevitably led me to recognize that the "vision" of O'Neill—a big word suggesting big ideas—touched the "vision" of Shakespeare more often than I would have expected. In sum, following the track of my thoughts, spurred on by class discussions and perhaps by my initial puzzlement that dramatists so far apart in almost every way (Shakespeare, whose "personality" is forever elusive, O'Neill the man we seem to know so well, in almost every biographical detail; Shakespeare, whose plays have a political, religious, and social framework far different from the plays of O'Neill; Shakespeare the "objective" poet-dramatist, O'Neill, the relentlessly "subjective," often autobiographical, dramatist; and so on) somehow became bedfellows, lodged together in my mind in a way that could not be explained merely by reminding myself of the fact that Shakespeare is in every literate person's mind. So I decided to confront the relationship head-on, resulting in this modest book, which tries immodestly to link two very large figures—the giant of all English-speaking drama and the most important American dramatist. Inevitably, what I present in this book sometimes overlaps what I have written before on these two dramatists separately, but directly confronting their relationship has opened up some interesting avenues of evaluation for me and has afforded me a deeper understanding of O'Neill's creative process. I have followed O'Neill's career chronologically. This has forced me to keep close to O'Neill's development as an artist, an approach that makes clear O'Neill's developing interest in, and use of, Shakespeare. Also, the chronological approach provides me with a kind of anchor, a measure of stability, in a book containing many soundings that may seem provisional or rough. And I have divided the book into two parts—the first examining what I call O'Neill's "first career," with *Mourning Becomes Electra* as the crowning achievement; the second discussing his "second career" in the light of the classifications of genre traditionally used to describe Shakespeare's plays—an arrangement that provides a revealing perspective on the O'Neill-Shakespeare relationship.

Of course, it would have been impossible for O'Neill not to have been influenced by Shakespeare. All writers of the English language who came after him have been influenced in one way or another, for better or worse, by him. That "Shakespeare is still our model" is for Peter Brook an "infuriating fact,"[1] but a fact nonetheless. Marjorie Garber provides a convincing and lively account of the ways that Shakespeare has come to haunt Western culture, calling him "the superego of literature," a ghost we do not seem to be able to give up.[2] That ghost entered O'Neill's life very early. The father who greeted his newborn son on 16 October 1888 was the famous romantic actor, James O'Neill, who probably had some appropriate Shakespeare quotation to mark the arrival of Eugene Gladstone O'Neill. Born in a hotel room on Longacre Square (now Times Square), in the heart of New York City's Broadway, O'Neill was in every respect a child of the theater. Born to that father, the boy Eugene, together with his older brother Jamie, would hear Shakespeare whenever James O'Neill found an opportunity to quote, and if we can judge from the autobiographical *Long Day's Journey Into Night,* many an opportunity was found. Shakespeare was part of O'Neill's voracious reading of books in his father's library. He took a course on Shakespeare during his one year at Princeton University. A wager with his father prompted him to memorize the entire part of Macbeth. For George Pierce Baker, in whose class at Harvard O'Neill studied playwriting for a year, Shakespeare was a god. O'Neill saw productions of Shakespeare's plays, and was especially enthusiastic about John Barrymore's portrayal of Hamlet. He even ends a love letter to a woman whose name is Jessica by quoting the words of Lorenzo in *The Merchant of Venice:* "Fair Jessica shall be my torch bearer."[3] Phrases from Shakespeare dotted his speech and his letters. In short, Shakespeare was tied up with the daily life of O'Neill's family and with his growth and education. And, as we all know, whatever happened in his life O'Neill intensely personalized and dramatized. Shakespeare is part of what happened, and Shakespeare, I shall attempt to demonstrate, in countless ways prodded O'Neill's creative imagination, enriching his dramatic art.

But Shakespeare was never acknowledged by O'Neill himself as an important presence in his life or art. During his six-month stay at Gaylord Farm Sanatorium, where his tuberculosis was being treated, he read, O'Neill tells us, "everything I could lay hands on: the Greeks, the Elizabethans—practically all the classics—and of course all the moderns. Ibsen and Strindberg, especially Strindberg, [who] first gave me the vision of what modern drama could be."[4] He often gave special credit to Strindberg and Ibsen, and to Nietzsche later on, but about Shakespeare he was silent, not even listing him separately when he mentioned reading the Elizabethans at Gaylord Farm. Perhaps it was merely a matter of not mentioning the obvious. Shakespeare may have been so much a part of him that no special acknowledgment was necessary or even came to mind. We rarely acknowledge the air we breathe. Perhaps O'Neill chose to minimize the importance of Shakespeare because he connected Shakespeare with a father he rejected time and again. Perhaps Harold Bloom's "anxiety of influence" was at work,[5] an idea that needs some further discussion when applied to O'Neill. I believe that Bloom's ideas on the nature of influence in regard to poets are richly suggestive in an examination of the O'Neill-Shakespeare relationship. Bloom's belief that poetic history is really a story of how poets have suffered other poets, directly paralleling how each person suffers his own family, casts a revealing light on O'Neill the dramatist and O'Neill the son. (How well chosen are the titles of Louis Sheaffer's splendid biography: *O'Neill: Son and Playwright; O'Neill: Son and Artist.*) Freud's "family romance," which points to the origins of "anxiety of influence," strongly applies to O'Neill as "son" of Shakespeare and James O'Neill, who also happens to be a Shakespearean actor. Bloom is acutely persuasive in maintaining that poets are not autonomous egos, that even the most solipsistic poet is "caught up in a dialectical relationship (transference, repetition, error, communication) with another poet or poets."[6] O'Neill is a strong *self* "caught up" in such a relationship with Shakespeare, a powerful presence as both precursor dramatist *and* father image, with the "family romance" as intense as it could be, intense even though O'Neill seems to be untroubled by the fact of Shakespeare in his past, seems to be unselfconscious about his own relationship to Shakespeare. If Bloom is correct in asserting that "criticism is the art of knowing the hidden roads that go from poem to poem,"[7] then a discussion of Shakespeare's influence on O'Neill requires us to travel the hidden roads—and many roads not so hidden—that go from Shakespeare to O'Neill. What must be emphasized, in response to those who believe that independent poets can be simply themselves and that the critics who travel those hidden roads are usually pedants and mere analogy seekers, is Bloom's large point that "poetic influence need not make poets less original," that it can, in fact, make poets more original. He quotes Kierkegaard's maxim that supports this idea: "If the young man had believed in repetition, of what might he not have been capable? What inwardness he might have attained!"[8] But Bloom insists—and this is an insistence that challenges all commentary on any influence on O'Neill, whether that influence be Strindberg or Ibsen or Nietzsche or dozens of others—that poetic influence cannot be reduced to mere source study or tracing image patterns or offering a comparative history of ideas. A discussion of influence can include, perhaps should include, such scholarly and critical activity, but it cannot remain on the road not hidden. Something more profound, deeper, more mysterious, less verifiable is going on. The "family romance" of O'Neill and Shakespeare takes in all of O'Neill's life and art; it is the focus of my attention.

At the outset it is important to emphasize Bloom's point that the creative mind desperately wishes to insist on its own priority, that the strong poet—in our case, the strong dramatist—must free himself of the agonizing belief that he is in debt to previous writers, that the poetic son must deny or repress his poetic father before he can be his own man, that he needs room for his seemingly unique and distinctive contribution. But an air of melancholy surrounds the latecomer's search for uniqueness. Eventually, if he is fine enough, he will openly acknowledge the dead master of the past, and his own achievement will be greater for it. In fact, the work of the dead master will itself be changed somewhat by his son's accomplishment. The present is always directed by the past—a truism absolutely applicable to O'Neill—but in this respect, additionally, the past is directed by the present. I believe that O'Neill finally acknowledged the greatness of Shakespeare in *Long Day's Journey,* especially at that moment when Edmund Tyrone says that he, Edmund, has only "the makings of a poet," that he merely stammers. *The* poet, the one who does not stammer, is Shakespeare, not only a presence in that late play, but a ghost that seems always to be saying to O'Neill, "Remember me." In the remembering O'Neill uses Shakespeare, absorbs Shakespeare, internalizes Shakespeare. The influence of Shakespeare on O'Neill is my subject, but perhaps, along the way, we may feel Shakespeare's drama somewhat differently because O'Neill's plays give us another perspective on it.

This word *influence* is troublesome; it always has been. Studies of influence sometimes are little more than what Bloom calls "the wearisome industry of source-hunting" and "allusion-counting,"[9] and his belief that this industry will soon pass from scholars to computers has already proved correct. But the service to scholarship of such studies must be acknowledged. They often clear a path to the larger generalizations about a writer's creative imagination. The idea of influence, however, points to more visceral pressures; it is an emotional and intellectual residue that can be tapped in both conscious and unconscious ways because it is there, within the later writer. Whether the influence is transmitted by way of ideology or style or psychology, it comes, if it is important enough, from deep within, so that we are dealing not only with borrowing—which is usually a conscious act—but also with a relationship so organic that the word *borrowing* seems too calculated. The basic meaning of the word influence is "a flowing in," and we should keep that meaning before us at all times. Only by confronting the deep response of one writer to another can we begin to approach the later writer's creative process. I believe that an examination of the Shakespeare that is *within* O'Neill—both plays and man—will allow us to understand more clearly how O'Neill's artistry works.

A discussion of influence must of necessity touch the idea of *tradition*, both words indicating that something *before* is affecting something *later*. One writer feeds the other; the other eats, willingly or not. Even as I write, tradition as a critical idea is being vigorously challenged, especially because tradition has carried with it gender and economic and racial biases that must be examined vigilantly. Even though tradition depends on changes and on modifications of what seems essentially stable, it remains a status quo phenomenon; it suggests stability, the kind of stability that comes when the past influences the present, which then becomes the past again. I believe there's no getting around the truth of such an idea. And I have no doubt that Eugene O'Neill, iconoclast though he was and bold experimenter in dramatic forms, was cognizant of the dramatic tradition, ever aware of the history of drama, closest—in ways even unknown to him—to the center of that tradition, Shakespeare. O'Neill's Shakespeare, like the Shakespeare of all of us, was the dramatist with the most comprehensive soul. O'Neill's Shakespeare was the playwright who, along with the ancient Greeks, produced the highest achievements in the dramatic tradition. Of course, Shakespeare, and even the more recent O'Neill, has accumulated many layers of signification as part of the mythmaking process verbalized by Roland Barthes,[10] and we must be aware of that process. No doubt, we must forever acknowledge that we are all conditioned by time and place, and that criticism, whether dramatic criticism or literary criticism, must recognize its own historicity. And, of course, human nature is not absolutely fixed; it changes under the pressure of time and place. But I believe that human nature, as we observe it through the ages in places far and wide touched by Western culture, does display continuities, does force us to confront a sameness, a connectedness, that we can describe with such words and phrases as "tradition" and "human nature." When Eric Bentley uses such a phrase as "human essence,"[11] or when Francis Fergusson writes about "the theater of human life,"[12] or when Bert States asserts that "the stage [is] directly plugged into life,"[13] they are recognizing that poets and dramatists throughout time, questioning what it is to be human, have touched an essence that allows one to talk about the human condition, about human nature. That is why Homer and Sophocles and Dante and Shakespeare and O'Neill and Beckett—although privileged in any way we may wish to interpret that word—speak to us directly, despite those added layers of signification and regardless of time and place. Humanity seems to hold some things in common, and we, like the listeners to Homer's poetry, or the witnesses to Oedipus's plight, or the gazers at Hamlet's skull or Mary Tyrone's wedding gown, continue to puzzle over some fundamental questions that touch Love and Death and Family Relationships and Nature and God. All people everywhere and in every time seem destined to confront the inexplicable mystery at the center of the most important *human* concerns. I believe, as did Samuel Johnson before me, that Shakespeare's characters are "the genuine progeny of common humanity, such as the world will always supply, and observation will always find."[14] His statement can be applied to O'Neill too, with some qualifying discussion. And I believe, along with one of our finest Shakespeare critics, Norman Rabkin, who takes his cue from Levi-Strauss, that "consciousness changes enormously from one age to another; yet ... certain facts about our interaction with the world remain eternally true, and it is with those facts that much of the most enduring literature deals."[15] Of course, each age refashions Shakespeare after its own image. Shakespeare changes as we change, and each performance of his play is a re-presentation, a reinterpretation, a new realization. This must have been true for the performances in Shakespeare's time too, with Shakespeare himself perhaps looking on as stage manager. Still, any reinterpretation of a Shakespeare play in any age or place has at its core something fixed (despite the text's openness to many and different interpretations), something that an eighteenth-century interpreter and a twentieth-century interpreter will recognize as a center, fluid enough not to be merely a fixed historical entity, but stable enough to be recognized as a text on which the specific interpretation or performance depends. In all cases, I see the dramatist as the authorizing consciousness of the text, and no matter how one may wish to decenter discourse, or change *author* to *author-function,* or demythologize and de-idolize the Bard, or assert that the particular text is the "product of collective negotiation and exchange,"[16] or modify the text's sense of the world, there is still, I believe, that Shakespearean center, creative and unique, that should be acknowledged, and in that center is lodged those unavoidable "human essence" issues.

Shakespeare and O'Neill, like all great writers, reveal "truths" about the human condition, display an understanding of the human individual, that transcends time and place. This is what makes them our contemporaries, what makes each the contemporary of the other. The purpose of my inquiry is to discover and discuss the exact nature of the connection between O'Neill and Shakespeare. The danger built into such an inquiry is that my case could be overstated. There is always the critical tendency to push a thesis too far, and I must admit to a special attentiveness that such a study as this provokes. (After all, I am anxious to hear those Shakespearean echoes.) My awareness of the danger probably has not prevented me from finding some connections that may seem too tenuous. Often I use the word *perhaps*—Beckett's favorite word in conversation. Perhaps I didn't use it enough. On the other hand, some readers will find that I neglected some connections, that more could have been found and more discussed. Of that I have no doubt. But what I'm presenting is not a collection of quotations or allusions or echoes, not a listing of connections or analogues, not a cataloging of parallels and sources. I have not attempted to be thorough. This is the first book-length study of a relationship that I'm sure will be examined by others through the years. My approach, it will be obvious to any reader, is personal and partial, and my hope is that my aim, which is driving me, does not distort the uniqueness of the plays under discussion. Throughout I posit an identity for the dramatist, so when I say *Shakespeare and O'Neill* I mean the artist in authority, the playwright who intends to arouse specific emotions, to elicit specific effects, whether or not he succeeds in doing so for all audiences at all times and in all places. And, finally, can there be any doubt about Shakespeare's power to influence those who came after him? Whether that influence takes the form of blatant imitation or subtle emotional kinship, whether that influence includes direct quotation and allusion or unconscious echoes, whether that influence touches thematic or tonal affinities, the generative power of Shakespeare's influence needs no lengthy discussion. What does need examination is how a specific dramatist "uses" Shakespeare. A discussion of the nature of the relationship between the later dramatist and the most influential of dramatists, between the son and the "father," may bring us closer to understanding the son, and perhaps even the father. When we examine the work of Eugene O'Neill, we encounter at every turn his firm belief, stated by Mary Tyrone, that "the Past is the Present." When O'Neill uses Shakespeare, consciously or unconsciously, the past becomes the present all over again.

Part 1

Chapter 1

The Sea

At first glance, O'Neill's first performed play, *Bound East for Cardiff,* seems to be as far from Shakespeare as one can get. The new playwright gave the Provincetown Players the kind of play it was waiting for, the play that made them what they became, one of the two most important amateur theater companies in New York City. *Bound East for Cardiff* is a realistic one-act play that avoids the trappings of conventional drama, the trappings of Shakespearean drama, especially plot and strong conflict. O'Neill, by means of realistic staging, forces the audience to enter the claustrophobic forecastle of the SS *Glencairn* as it slowly makes its way through a thick fog, bound east for Cardiff from New York City. One of the sailors, Yank, is lying on his bunk, dying of injuries from a fall. He talks to his friend Driscoll about life at sea, about the bad and good old times. He then dies, and the fog lifts.

O'Neill's little play belongs to a different time and a different world from Shakespeare's plays. The obvious differences can be pinpointed easily; in fact, mentioning them probably is not necessary. But it's important in a study of this kind to be clear at the outset about some unequivocal differences between O'Neill and Shakespeare. Both playwrights, like almost all playwrights, wish to give us characters who come to life on the stage; for both, the creation of illusion is important. For Shakespeare, however, the illusion need not be produced by the realistic presentation of life's surface. For O'Neill, certainly in his early and late plays but even in his experimental middle period, such a realistic presentation seems essential. He criticized plays that offer mere kodak-camera realism—"we have endured too much from the banality of surfaces"[1]—but his stage trappings and action and language were clearly realistic, as we have come to use that term. The realistic forecastle of the tramp steamer *Glencairn* contains *things* (bunks, benches, lamp, oilskins, pail with dipper, seaboots, and so on). Its sailors, representing different countries and speaking in different dialects, are sitting, snoozing, talking, smoking, doing what sailors do in their time off the watch. The sense of realistic life on O'Neill's stage is enhanced, of course, by the separation of the stage from the audience because of the proscenium arch and artificial lighting, producing, in fact, a kind of moving photograph. The modern audience, an eavesdropping audience, witnesses a scene that is rooted in the tangible, that is staged solidly, that seems to be tied very closely to the external world. How different from the Shakespearean platform stage, that unlocalized playing area, jutting out into the audience, where actors and audience seem to touch, where the afternoon light of a London day provides the lighting, where the props are few, where words and gestures must do almost all the work—where, in short, the realistic (flesh-and-blood actors, mimesis, sound and gesture) is able to touch the symbolic more easily. O'Neill will forever try to get *behind* the surface of life, *behind* the "thing" reality that his twentieth-century stage seems to demand; he will always want to touch what he will call the "real reality" of our lives. But he, like most modern dramatists who have inherited a solidly staged world, will find it a more difficult challenge than the Elizabethans to get access to that real reality, to offer a mimesis that is realistic and symbolic and psychological. In his experimental middle period O'Neill will find seemingly direct access to the symbolic and psychological through the use of masks and interior monologues, an access that Shakespeare already has at his disposal with the convention of the soliloquy, but O'Neill's strength will reside in reaching those hidden "behind life" places in an essentially realistic framework. The technical resources of the modern stage are there for O'Neill's use, techniques that can create the illusion and atmosphere of authentic surface life. And the stage language that O'Neill's characters use is close to the way people speak. He is usually not successful when he attempts to be too poetic or lyrical. Shakespeare, both a poet and dramatist—a poet-dramatist with no equal—uses his stage language, both blank verse and prose, to get his audience close to his character's *character* without attempting to duplicate the way the character might speak in "real life," although Shakespeare's language is often more naturalistic than is usually suggested. Both Shakespeare and O'Neill, although tied to different theaters and different conventions, are poets of the theater, effectively controlling the theatrical means that their times allow. Both depend upon *words* as their primary means to present drama. Shakespeare, however, is a poet *in* the theater, using words so masterfully, so remarkably connecting his words to the stage action, that no valid comparison with O'Neill or anyone else in relation to language is finally possible. O'Neill has the "makings" of a poet; Shakespeare is *the* poet. We must judge O'Neill's stage language on its own terms, on how it *works* in his plays, preferably in performance. The idea of performance must be stressed because most of the time we are *reading* O'Neill. We are usually reading Shakespeare too, but Shakespeare can be read as drama more easily than we can read O'Neill. Shakespeare's words are themselves dramatically potent; he seems to think in three dimensions. Reading O'Neill, we must strenuously think of his prose as spoken by actors on a stage, an imaginative task not always easy to accomplish, even with the help of his many detailed stage directions. Shakespeare does not need stage directions; the verbal action and the stage action seem one.

The basic and obvious differences I have pinpointed—and other basic differences, like the world picture and the nature of the audience, that I have not mentioned—should not prevent us from acknowledging that both O'Neill and Shakespeare wish to root their plays in realism—a different realism for each, a realism connected to their different conventions—even as they attempt to transcend realism. They wish to present life as we see it *and* what is behind life, the unseen. They offer drama that is both literal and figurative, worlds that are outer and inner, with the boundaries between more rigid in O'Neill than in Shakespeare because O'Neill inherited a less fluid theater with less fluid conventions. Shakespeare's characters can soliloquize whenever he wants them to, calling no attention to the vehicle itself; it is a convention. When O'Neill wants to go inside his characters, his interior monologues work *against* convention, thereby making *Strange Interlude,* for example, a cause célèbre.

Bound East for Cardiff is primarily, almost exclusively, realistic. A one-act play, a slice of sailor life, presenting a solidly staged world, it has no connection to the kind of melodrama and escapist comedy that O'Neill and the Provincetown Players consciously were rebelling against—except, of course, that we are dealing with *theater,* that is, with an audience watching actors on a stage. It also seems to have no relationship to the Shakespeare who came before the nineteenth-century kind of theater represented by O'Neill's father, a theater and father that O'Neill was rejecting, but a theater, incidentally, that featured Shakespeare as a vehicle for star performances. And yet, and yet, this little sea play, which O'Neill claimed contained the "germ of the spirit" of his future work, contains elements and displays a method and projects a tragic idea that seem to reach for a symbolism that we could perhaps call, with some qualifying discussion, Shakespearean. I am stating this idea tentatively because critics usually find what they are looking for, just as painters paint what they want to see. What is tentative here in O'Neill's beginnings will emerge more clearly and more certainly as his work develops, but what we have here in *Bound East for Cardiff* is worth looking at. O'Neill is presenting something new to American drama in 1916, but he is circling around what has been there before in many and different ways.

I begin with O'Neill's use of the monologue to reveal character, a vehicle he will exploit and perfect throughout his development. The dying Yank reveals himself to the audience by exposing his inmost thoughts to his best friend Driscoll. Driscoll is the only possible audience for him *on stage* because the two sailors have shared the same life; in many ways, they are one, they are related, they are family. But Yank would never have revealed himself to Driscoll—and by a reverse extension, to himself—if he were not dying. He is in a boundary situation, between life and death, and he must talk. When he does, the long monologue, interrupted by Driscoll's easy agreement or consoling words, has the pressure of a Shakespearean soliloquy, with Yank figuratively alone on stage, uttering his thoughts aloud, giving us information about his anxieties, his desires, revealing his state of mind at a crucial moment in his life. (Even physically, he seems terribly alone from the play's beginning, lying in the farthest bunk, in the narrowest section of the forecastle, while the stage is crowded with seemingly uncaring sailors, and raucous sounds fill the air.) With Shakespeare the soliloquy is a *convention,* the most important Elizabethan device to reveal what is within. When O'Neill uses this seemingly outdated convention more obviously in *Strange Interlude,* it will seem bold but artificial. In this early play, *Bound East,* the monologue, containing all the force of a soliloquy, doing what a soliloquy does, seems more natural, more plausible for a modern audience, because an almost-mute listener is on stage, reacting in a realistically appropriate but subdued way. Yank's dying monologue gracefully fits into this one-act realistic play. As O'Neill's career continues, one of his most effective devices will be the monologue that is really a soliloquy, and with the passing years the monologue will seem even closer to the soliloquy because the speaker will go ever deeper into self. Of course, I am referring to the monologue-soliloquy as a vehicle for presentation of character; I make no mention of the quality of language in that monologue. As already stated, the Shakespearean soliloquy, wherever found in Shakespeare, has been composed by a poet, by *the* poet. O'Neill's monologues reveal a different quality of excellence, a prosier expression, more mundane, less lyrical, but eminently stageworthy. Yank's monologue reveals a Shakespearean pressure of frustration, and sometimes the repetitions sound a poetically plaintive note. Listen to Yank:

> This sailor life ain't much to cry about leavin'—just one ship after another, hard work, small pay, and bum grub; and when we git into port, just a drunk endin' up in a fight, and all your money gone, and

then ship away again. Never meetin' no nice people; never gittin' outa sailor town, hardly, in any port; travelin' all over the world and never seein' none of it; without no one to care whether you're alive or dead.[2]

This is the language of feeling. Like Shakespeare's soliloquies, O'Neill's monologues, here and throughout his development, are intimate and powerful instruments to present feeling and thought in his modern theater. O'Neill, without directly using the Shakespearean device in his early and late plays (but experimenting with it more directly in his middle plays), achieves the effect of the soliloquy, as we hear the deep conflicts in the minds of his usually doomed, and often inarticulate, characters. (I'm thinking, as obvious examples, of Yank Smith's monologue to the gorilla, of Ephraim Cabot's lamentation to a nonlistening Abbie, of Ezra Mannon's appeal to a closed-eyed Christine, of Erie Smith's storytelling to a somewhat dead night clerk, of Jim Tyrone's anguished revelation to the maternal Josie.)

By means of the monologue, O'Neill, like Shakespeare, wanted to get within his characters and, like Shakespeare, he wanted the play's outer action to reveal the inner person. So too, like Shakespeare, O'Neill wanted to get "behind life," to touch, Lear-like, "the mystery of things."

I'm always, always trying to interpret Life in terms of lives, never just lives in terms of character. I'm always acutely conscious of the Force behind—Fate, God, our biological past creating our present, whatever one calls it—Mystery certainly—and of the one eternal tragedy of Man in his glorious, self-destructive struggle to make the Force express him instead of being, as an animal is, an infinitesimal incident in its expression.[3]

One obvious way to touch that mystery, for Shakespeare and O'Neill, was to present the supernatural on stage. A less obvious way, but perhaps more potent at times, was to allow the natural and the literal to blend into the supernatural and symbolic. In Shakespeare they seem to come together all the time; that's the nature of his theater, as already noted. It's a theater of verbal metaphor.[4] O'Neill must strain toward Shakespeare's freedom to present both the real and the symbolic at the same time. (The strain is often too strongly felt in the middle experimental plays; the melding is more gracefully achieved in the early and especially the later plays.)

In *Bound East for Cardiff* we get a touch of the supernatural and symbolic in "a pretty lady dressed in black," seen by Yank just before he dies. Having expressed his guilty feelings because he killed a man in a drunken brawl in self-defense, having requested that Driscoll buy Fanny the barmaid "the biggest box of candy yuh c'n find in Cardiff" because "she's been good to me," the sailor, whose language is always direct and simple, uncharacteristically uses a metaphor, but for him an appropriate one: "It's hard to ship on this voyage I'm goin' on—alone!" This clichéd metaphor of death, coming after the sentimentality of his words on Fanny, leads easily to his personal vision of death, "a pretty lady dressed in black," his last words before "*his body writhes in a final spasm, then straightens out rigidly,*" according to O'Neill's stage directions. Merely a touch of the symbolic here at the end of a short realistic play, but enough to allow the atmosphere to be charged with death both natural and supernatural, a strong enough charge to withstand the heavy irony of Cocky's words, "The fog's lifted," and to support the stage picture of a silent Driscoll on his knees, moving his lips "*in some half-remembered prayer*" (1:198).

The fog, of course, is what keeps the SS *Glencairn* from getting to Cardiff in time to save the dying Yank. The fog whistle is heard throughout the play, a sound that seems to bring together the fog and the sea and death, so that the fog too can be considered symbolic, as it usually is in O'Neill (where, for example, the fog is "the ghost of the sea,") and sometimes is in Shakespeare (where, for example, the "fog and filthy air" first mentioned by the Witches is more than a mere physical description of the ambiguous condition of Macbeth's world).

But the most important and most natural symbol in this sea play is the Sea itself. The sea, so important a part of O'Neill's life, will be felt in many of O'Neill's plays, even those that are landlocked. O'Neill's closeness to the sea seems to have been a necessity, both a physical and a spiritual need. Biographers tell of his prowess as a swimmer and of his habit of swimming farther from shore than seemed possible, returning spent and satisfied. Always "a little in love with death," O'Neill even talked about ending his life by swimming out to sea until he drowned. His lifelong search for a "home" usually led him, Ishmael-like, to the sea. He lived in Cape Cod, Bermuda, Sea Island, Georgia, and Marblehead, Massachusetts, all near the ocean. When he had no home in his early years of manhood he lived along the waterfront. And he spent his boyhood summers in the New London, Connecticut, summer home of his parents, located near the Thames River. A well-known photograph of the boy O'Neill captures him sitting on a rock with sketchbook in hand, looking at the river with an intensity he never lost.

His sixteen months at sea (in 1910 and 1911) as an apprentice and then an able-bodied seaman provided the great adventure of his life, always recalled in his personal life and in his art. Those seemed to be the happiest days for the dark playwright. Carlotta Monterey, his third wife, complained that she took him all over the world to see all the interesting places, but that his response to his travels was never as enthusiastic as when he talked about his months at sea. His sea days were his most pleasing memory. They came at an important time in his life, allowing him to live the unconventional life of a sailor that he seemed to need—escape from family, freedom to roam, the chance to be both alone and with others, drinking and sexual bouts, closeness to the element that gave him his most transcendental experiences, and perhaps most important, the element that provided him with ideas and emotions and characters for his future work as a dramatist.

In 1910 he shipped on a Norwegian square-rigger called the *Charles Racine,* bound for Buenos Aires from Boston. This two-month trip helped to inspire his sea plays and gave him the mystical experiences that Edmund Tyrone—who is O'Neill's portrait of himself as a young man—relates to his father in *Long Day's Journey Into Night.* After living the life of a bum on the waterfront in Buenos Aires, sleeping on benches, scrounging for alcohol and food, he sailed home on the SS *Ikala,* which was the model for the SS *Glencairn* in the early sea plays. He returned to America in 1911 to live in a waterfront saloon on Fulton Street in New York City, called Jimmy-the-Priest's, where a drink of whiskey was a nickel and a room cost three dollars a month, a "hell hole," to use O'Neill's phrase. Then he shipped out again, now as an able-bodied seaman, to Southampton, England, on an American liner, the SS *New York,* and returned home on the SS *Philadelphia,* both trips giving him more material for his sea plays and allowing him to meet the stoker Driscoll, who appears in the *Glencairn* plays and will eventually become Yank Smith in *The Hairy Ape.*

When in 1912, during his six months of recuperation in a sanatorium for tuberculosis, O'Neill made the important decision "to be an artist or nothing," he had behind him experiences at sea that would feed his creative imagination for all the years to come. His mind was seadrenched, so that even so late a play as *The Iceman Cometh,* set on land in a bar in New York City, will go to the sea for its informing metaphor. Larry Slade, the only awake character in Harry Hope's saloon, describes the place with these words:

> It's the No Chance Saloon. It's Bedrock Bar, The End of the Line Café, The Bottom of the Sea Rathskeller! Don't you notice the beautiful calm in the atmosphere? That's because it's the last harbor. No one here has to worry about where they're going next, because there is no farther they can go. (3:577–78)

And O'Neill's emotional closeness to the sea is most clearly revealed in this statement of Edmund Tyrone, found in the late autobiographical *Long Day's Journey Into Night:* "It was a great mistake, my being born a man. I would have been much more successful as a sea gull or a fish. As it is, I will always be a stranger who never feels at home, who does not really want and is not really wanted, who can never belong, who must always be a little in love with death" (3:812). Both *Long Day's Journey* and *The Iceman Cometh,* O'Neill's two finest plays, reveal the deep connection between the sea and death, O'Neill's two main motifs throughout his career.

It is important to realize that the sea is the element that provided the setting for two of O'Neill's favorite writers, Joseph Conrad and Herman Melville. Because of his dissolute life as a young man, because of his many world experiences, it is easy to forget that O'Neill was always a voracious reader, devouring books from early boyhood. O'Neill was a literary writer, and echoes of his reading can be traced throughout his career. Certainly, in writing his sea plays, O'Neill's dramatic imagination fed on Conrad's *Nigger of the Narcissus,* in which Conrad graphically describes life in the forecastle of a sailing ship, a life shared by men who are connected with one another *and* connected with that elemental force, the sea. Certainly, in writing his sea plays, O'Neill felt the pressure of Melville's melting-pot crews and Melville's insistence on the ambiguity of the sea and the ambiguity of human nature.

Small wonder, then, that O'Neill, in 1928, when planning an autobiographical play, decided to call it *Sea Mother's Son;* it would be, he said, "the grand opus of my life." (The play was never written, but elements of it can be found in *Days Without End* and *Long Day's Journey.*) O'Neill was very much his mother's son, and biographers have not neglected to discuss his Oedipus complex, his constant search for a mother, his guilt feelings connected with his mother's dope addiction, caused by his birth. The idea of mother in O'Neill's plays has been exhaustively examined by scholars and critics. That O'Neill sees his relationship to the sea as the relationship of a son to a mother powerfully expresses the sea's importance to him on a personal level. The sea, like everything else that was personal to O'Neill, is transformed into an artistic preoccupation, with approximately half of his forty-five plays taking place on or near the sea, and with almost all his plays offering some kind of sea symbolism. In the sea plays that begin O'Neill's career, O'Neill dramatizes the relationship between men and the sea, men bound to the sea as children to a mother—with all the positive and negative aspects of such a relationship. The sea functions as a realistic environment, but at the same time it assumes a larger metaphysical dimension, connected with the "inscrutable forces behind life" that O'Neill said it was his ambition to present in his plays. It is to this fluid combination of realism and symbolism in O'Neill that I wish to pay brief attention because it reflects Shakespeare's characteristic method of presentation.

The sea, for O'Neill and for most writers, is an open-ended symbol, meaning different things in different plays and sometimes different things in the same play. In *Bound East for Cardiff* it is the setting for a dying sailor's last words that relate the struggles connected with sea life. On the positive side, it is what binds Yank and Driscoll together, in fact, what binds the family of sailors together, for worse or better. It is a destroyer and a preserver, the element in which the dead Yank will be buried, much to his regret, claimed finally by the sea that gave him his life experience. In *The Moon of the Caribbees,* the play that the new playwright O'Neill favored most because it was the least conventional of the *Glencairn* plays, the sea points more hauntingly to the mystery of things. The sailors once again are bound together because of their connection to the sea, but their various conflicts and desires, presented realistically, seem trivial against the backdrop of the still sea and the sound of the chant coming from a nearby island, a sound described by O'Neill as *"the mood of the moonlight made audible."* (1:544). The chant and the moon and the sea meld together (just as the fog and sea meld together in *Bound East)* to represent what man cannot understand, what is essentially mysterious and disturbing, what points to the secret truth of things. The sound of the chant in *Caribbees* touches a supernatural symbolism, large and wide, of a different quality than the symbolism attached to the sound of the fog whistle, that man-made sound in *Bound East,* heard intermittently as the SS *Glencairn* travels slowly east while a dying Yank travels west to death. Throughout O'Neill, the sea, a powerful and all-encompassing force and symbol, washes along with it other elements of nature that are also symbolic—like fog and moon—with the specific quality of the symbol dependent on the specific play, the artifact.

That the sea controls all of O'Neill's early one-act sea plays perhaps can be most clearly demonstrated in a play that takes place not on the sea but on land, in a waterfront bar. *The Long Voyage Home* dramatizes the pitiful plight of the seaman Olson, who has saved his hard-earned pay for two years in order to return home to his farm in Sweden and to his aged mother. Here we have many of the trappings of melodrama in a carefully constructed realistic play, but displaying as well the kind of irony that O'Neill with time will transform into the dark inevitability that characterizes his later work. The vicious "land" people in the bar drug and rob Olson, and then place him on a rotten ship sailing round Cape Horn. They serve as the unwitting instruments of the sea, the mother who will claim her own, the home that Olson can never leave, O'Neill's sailors forever bound to the dark mysterious force.

In short, early in O'Neill's career he is already functioning as both realist and symbolist, the one sliding into the other, displaying a theatrical fluidity that characterizes Shakespearean drama. Shakespeare's treatment of the supernatural and the symbolic more than three hundred years earlier may have given the new playwright who came along to transform American drama a classic model for emulation. Of course, more immediate models were the modern playwrights, like Strindberg and Ibsen, whom he read and absorbed during his stay in Gaylord Sanatorium, when he decided "to be an artist or nothing." In fact, in Strindberg, the dramatist he most openly acknowledged as an influence, O'Neill was able to appreciate both a realist and an expressionist. But it is with Shakespeare, I suggest, that the seeds for such a combination of different modes were already planted.

As we would expect, the sea—surrounding that island England and naturally a source for poetic symbolism—is an important part of Shakespeare's mind and art. What we know about Shakespeare the man comes from documentation that deals with the mundane events of life: marriage, birth of children, church entries, various litigations, estate matters, a will. We have no direct knowledge of his personal life, as we do of O'Neill's, and therefore can only speculate about his personal encounters with the sea. It is sufficient to note that the lad Shakespeare grew up near the Avon River, which ran through his town of Stratford; the Avon was an unavoidable presence on his walks to his relatives, to the neighboring villages, to his Holy Trinity Church, which was built on the banks of the Avon. The river supplied fresh water and was a means of communication. It was to this river that he returned yearly when he journeyed back to Stratford from London, and it was by the banks of the Avon that he finally decided to retire. Through London flowed the Thames, probably not so "sweete" a river as Spenser poetically suggests, and surely not as sweet as the Avon, but an important presence for the playwright Shakespeare, whose audience would use the river to reach his Bankside theater, whose company would traverse the river to offer court performances at Greenwich or Whitehall. The Thames was the highway for the tall merchant ships that unloaded their cargoes along its docks. And, of course, Shakespeare, like his contemporaries, was ever mindful of England as an island—"this sceptred isle," "this precious stone set in the silver sea"—ever aware of the vast ocean surrounding England as the means to a great expansion, with the Atlantic and the New World the focus of dispute between England and Spain. In short, we need no specific documentation to realize that the literal sea affected Shakespeare's personal life, and even a cursory reading of his plays reveals the importance of the sea to his art. Many a Shakespeare character goes on a sea voyage, both literal and figurative, with the two modes often blending, and with the sea acting as both destroyer and preserver. Perhaps the most obvious voyage of this kind is the one forced upon Prospero and Miranda in *The Tempest,* the circumstances of which Prospero, looking into "the dark backward and abysm of time," haltingly tells his daughter in the play's beginning. His enemies placed him and his infant on a rotten boat "to cry to th' sea, that roared to us" thinking that he and she would die, but the sea and the winds seemed to pity them, doing them "loving wrong," casting them on an island. The sea was both threatening and loving, what it continues to be in the play's present, when Prospero's enemies, also on a sea voyage, are forced by the tempest to land on Prospero's isle. The sea voyages and the storm are natural events, but as the play develops we realize they have meanings that go beyond the natural. At play's end, Gonzalo, the noble old councillor who had provided Prospero with the books he valued above his dukedom, pinpoints the various separations and reconciliations in the play:

> Was Milan thrust from Milan, that his issue
> Should become kings of Naples? O, rejoice
> Beyond a common joy, and set it down
> With gold on lasting pillars: in one voyage
> Did Claribel her husband find at Tunis,
> And Ferdinand, her brother, found a wife
> Where he himself was lost; Prospero, his dukedom
> In a poor isle; and all of us, ourselves,
> When no man was his own.
>
> (5.1.205–13)[5]

We lose in order to find; we suffer to gain. "Though the seas threaten," even the young Ferdinand understands, "they are merciful."

The Tempest, Shakespeare's last play as sole author and because of this his most tantalizingly autobiographical play, is, like the garments worn by those characters thrust by the storm on to the isle, "drench'd in the sea." Everyone in the play seems to "suffer a sea-change," words that come from Ariel's song to Ferdinand about his father Alonzo's "death" by drowning.

> Full fadom five thy father lies,
> Of his bones are coral made:
> Those are pearls that were his eyes:
> Nothing of him that doth fade,

> But doth suffer a sea-change
> Into something rich and strange.
> Sea-nymphs hourly ring his knell:
> > Ding dong.
> Hark now I hear them—ding-dong bell.
>
> (1.2.397–405)

The sea, as presented here in Ariel's song, gives death a precious and welcome quality, almost desirable. That O'Neill's most-quoted words on death, Edmund Tyrone's statement that he "must always be a little in love with death," come immediately after Edmund relates his memories, "all connected with the sea," reaffirms the potency of the sea-death connection and perhaps suggests O'Neill's absorption of Shakespeare's last play.

In addition to *The Tempest,* Shakespeare's *Pericles* and *The Winter's Tale,* both romances, also contain sea voyages that destroy and preserve. In each play the literal sea melds into the symbolic sea in an easy relationship to which the Elizabethan audience was conditioned. But the sea's symbolic tragicomic rhythm can be found in plays other than romances. In *Twelfth Night,* for example, Viola's brother, Sebastian, like Viola herself, is not drowned at sea; he held "acquaintance with the waves," and landed safely in Illyria to provide the miracle that unties all the play's knots. In tragedy, Hamlet goes on a sea voyage to death, which becomes a death voyage for Rosencrantz and Guildenstern, with Hamlet returning "naked" to Denmark. When we see him in the graveyard he seems to have suffered a sea change; he has become a patient avenger, but given the paradoxical nature of tragedy, he will be forced to act almost immediately. And the play that is so conveniently lodged in Shakespeare's development between the tragedies and romances, *Antony and Cleopatra,* is washed by the sea, the place of battles where the world is lost to the general Antony, but also the element in which we view Antony, in Cleopatra's splendid imagination, rising dolphinlike above his element.

The sea, for the metaphoric Shakespeare, is a "sea of troubles" *(Hamlet)* but could also be a "sea of joys" *(Pericles).* It could describe the passion of an Othello (whose "bloody thoughts" are like "the Pontic Sea, / Whose icy current and compulsive course / Nev'r feels retiring ebb") or the youthful urges of a Romeo (whose "bounty is as boundless as the sea," who will go on his death-marked voyage for rich merchandise, Juliet). It could inform the fated declaration of a Brutus who insists that "there is a tide in the affairs of men," but who mistakenly thinks that he is now afloat "on such a full sea" when he is, after all, really "bound in shallows and in miseries." Because the sea, in all its manifestations, is ubiquitous, because other "sea" influences on O'Neill—like Conrad and Melville, who also had Shakespeare behind them—helped to shape O'Neill's mind and art, perhaps the preceding discussion of Shakespeare and the sea, however brief, seems superfluous. I merely wish, at this juncture, to suggest a possible connection between O'Neill and Shakespeare in the way they treat the sea. My next point, however, isolates more clearly the O'Neill-Shakespeare connection. Although O'Neill's *Bound East for Cardiff* touches the supernatural, and in it the sea represents a force both natural and supernatural, the first time we find the supernatural in more than symbolic suggestion occurs in the last one-act sea play that O'Neill wrote, *Where the Cross Is Made,* not part of the SS *Glencairn* series.

Where the Cross Is Made (1918) is little more than a melodramatic exercise for O'Neill, who never took it seriously, it seems, but in it O'Neill presents ghosts on stage for the first time. The play's main character, Nat Bartlett, wishes to have his father, Captain Isaiah Bartlett, committed to an asylum because he insanely awaits the arrival of his ship carrying treasure, a ship that was sunk three years before. Nat hates his father, who forced him to go to sea, where he lost his arm to become "the broken thing I am!" (1:703), but his main reason for hating his father is that the Captain filled him with the mad dreams of a buried treasure that he, like his father, knows to be an illusion, but he, like his father, continues to believe—"And that's mad—mad, do you hear?" (1:705) Perhaps committing his father and burning the map of the island on which the treasure is buried will destroy the mad dream. But then the *Mary Allen,* "loaded with gold," is sighted by the Captain (1:707), who excitedly descends the stairs from his post at the top of the house to inform his son. Both father and son "see" the vessel, although Nat's sister, Sue, cannot. Then O'Neill gives us this stage direction:

> *The sound of the wind and sea suddenly ceases and there is a heavy silence. A dense green glow floods slowly in rhythmic waves like a liquid into the room—as of great depths of the sea faintly penetrated by light.* (1:709)

Sue tries to explain the light in a rational way—"Only the moonlight, Nat." Then she tries to explain the sounds that father and son hear: "A shutter in the wind. . . . Only the rats running about. It's nothing, Nat." But then the ghosts of Silas Horne, Cates, and Jimmy Kanaka "*rise noiselessly into the room from the stairs,*" carrying chests of gold. Here is part of O'Neill's stage direction:

> *Water drips from their soaked and rotten clothes. Their hair is matted, intertwined with slimy strands of seaweed. Their eyes, as they glide silently into*

> the room, stare frightfully wide at nothing. Their flesh in the green light has the suggestion of decomposition. Their bodies sway limply, nervelessly, rhythmically as if to the pulse of long swells of the deep sea. (1:710)

It seems that here we have ghosts that are figments of the shared imagination of father and son, ghosts that the audience sees but that Sue Bartlett cannot see. O'Neill said he wanted the audience to "go mad too," that is, the audience now shares the sight of the ghosts with the two mad characters on stage, Nat and Captain Bartlett. Whatever his playful purpose in presenting the ghosts—resulting in the death of Captain Bartlett from a heart attack and the replacement of Captain Bartlett by his son, who will now and forever watch the sea for the return of the gold-bearing ship—for the first time O'Neill is using a powerful Shakespearean device, which he will use less playfully and more importantly in plays to come.

A ghostly apparition, that is, a "live" ghost appearing on stage, is as Shakespearean a device as the soliloquy that O'Neill also appropriated. When Shakespeare uses a ghost it is to show the *other* world, beyond death, which has a profound effect on what is happening to the protagonist in *this* world. When ghosts appear on stage in Shakespeare, those visited will soon die. The early ghosts of Shakespeare who appear in mechanical fashion at Bosworth Field in *Richard III,* the ghost of Julius Caesar appearing to Brutus, the ghost of Old Hamlet giving his son a deadly mission, the ghost of Banquo sitting in Macbeth's seat—all bring death on stage, all forebode the deaths of the protagonists. In Shakespeare these ghostly figures are strongly connected to the important Elizabethan theme of revenge. O'Neill's sea-dripping ghosts in his early play, *Where the Cross Is Made,* do not belong to such a revenge tradition. They are closer to O'Neill's abiding interest not only in death, but also in the power of illusions, the power of dreams. O'Neill may have been playing with his audience, treating it as insane, but he was boldly using a seemingly old-fashioned Shakespearean device to dramatize one of his most important interests throughout his career, the power of the life-illusion. When he uses ghosts again two years later in his highly successful *The Emperor Jones,* the ghosts will be part of a serious experiment in expressionism and will, in addition, touch the idea of revenge. And when in his later plays he hearkens ghosts of the past who do visibly appear on stage, the Shakespearean model will be felt in more interesting ways and more intensely.

Where the Cross Is Made contains one other element that is both an O'Neillian preoccupation and an abiding interest in Shakespeare: the family. We can consider the sailors on the SS *Glencairn* "family," bound together by the sea, children of the Sea-Mother, but a more conventional family can be found in *Where the Cross Is Made,* if *conventional* is the right word for the illusion-obsessed, mad, troubled Bartletts—or, for that matter, for *any* O'Neill family. Autobiography, in *Cross* as in almost all of O'Neill's plays, puts its distinctive pressure on the dramatist's presentation. Louis Sheaffer's belief that the ship's name in *Cross,* the *Mary Allen,* named after Captain Bartlett's dead wife, is too similar to O'Neill's mother's name, Mary Ellen, to be mere coincidence, correctly pinpoints the play's "private symbolism," with O'Neill and his father and brother hoping for the return of a lost, dope-filled mother to normalcy, paralleling the desire of Nat and Captain Bartlett for the return of the ship.[6] (Ella O'Neill went off morphine in 1914, four years before *Cross* was written, but her "return" may have seemed tentative to O'Neill even in 1918.) Michael Manheim makes the interesting suggestion that Captain Bartlett, separated from his family because of his madness, represents O'Neill's mother and anticipates Mary Tyrone, who also has a special room from which pacing is heard.[7] And, of course, the anxious concerns of children for a parent and the alienation of a parent from children touch the situation of the O'Neill household.

But more important than the specific autobiographical trappings is the simple and clear fact that the *family* is the focus of O'Neill's attention in *Cross,* as it will be in O'Neill's powerful later plays, like *Mourning Becomes Electra* and *Long Day's Journey Into Night.* The family, of course, is also the important focus of Shakespearean drama. We rarely examine, or even pay attention to, the autobiographical basis of Shakespeare's plays, Shakespeare always the "objective" dramatist, whereas O'Neill seems so "subjective" that he is reading over our shoulders or sitting next to us in the theater. Whereas Shakespeare seems invisible, O'Neill seems always there. But there can be no doubt that Shakespeare invested *himself* more deeply in his plays than any other dramatist, including O'Neill. In order to write the way he did, he must have felt and suffered greatly. C. L. Barber sensitively discusses the quality of Shakespeare's personal commitment in his plays, convincingly arguing against T. S. Eliot's idea that there is a separation between the man who suffers and the mind that creates. Barber speculates about what shaped Shakespeare's sensibility, pinpointing the infantile bond to the mother, the birth of a brother, the adolescent's observation of his father's failure.[8] I shall return throughout this book to Barber's important ideas on Shakespeare's temperament and his "whole journey" because they uncannily touch O'Neill's temperament and journey, but for now, acknowledging but putting aside the autobiographical elements that may have put pressure on Shakespeare's art, I merely wish to state that Shakespeare, like O'Neill, is preoccupied with family, with family ties. He, like O'Neill, places the highest value on kinship.⁹ The variations that Shakespeare plays on the idea of family lead directly to considerations of genre—the fearful implications in Shakespearean tragedy, where the family bonds are tightest, the more joyous bondings in Shakespearean comedy, and the important connections between family and state in the history plays. The variations that O'Neill plays on the idea of family also lead to considerations of genre, but O'Neill, because of inclination and temperament, will characteristically be writing in the tragic mode, where family holds the hand of terror.

Chapter 2

Black and White

We find terror without reference to family but importantly connected to ghosts and the soliloquy in the first important O'Neill play that contains strong echoes of Shakespeare, *The Emperor Jones* (1920), although O'Neill never mentioned Shakespeare as a source. O'Neill's acknowledged sources for *The Emperor Jones* are many, as are the unacknowledged sources that O'Neill scholars have noted and examined. The idea for this landmark of American drama, so different from any American play that came before it, came to O'Neill from different directions, demonstrating how absorptive O'Neill's mind was to what he experienced personally and what he read. Louis Sheaffer's splendid biography of O'Neill succinctly pinpoints the various sources. We learn that O'Neill himself said that the idea for *The Emperor Jones* came to him from a friend, a circus man who traveled with a tent show in the West Indies, who told him that the late Guillaume Sam, president of Haiti, boasted that his enemies would never kill him with a lead bullet but that if he were overthrown he would kill himself with a silver bullet. O'Neill made a note of this story of the black ruler and the silver bullet, fascinated enough by the idea to give the title "The Silver Bullet" to the play he was later to write and name *The Emperor Jones*. The idea of a deposed ruler fleeing through the woods came to him later, and later still, reading a book about religious feasts in the Congo, he learned of the use of the drum at such festivals, with the drumbeat beginning at a normal pulse beat and then intensifying until the heartbeat of everyone present corresponds to and is affected by the drumbeat. "There," O'Neill said, "was an idea and an experiment. How would this sort of thing work on an audience in a theater."[1] Other nonfiction reading affected O'Neill's conception, especially Gordon Craig's *The Theater Advancing*, which advocated the use of masks, pantomime, and dance, and Charles Sheeler's book of photographs on African sculpture. Also influencing O'Neill were such works of fiction as Joseph Conrad's *The Heart of Darkness* and Jack London's *The Call of the Wild*. The dramatists Strindberg and Ibsen, always feeding O'Neill's creative imagination, also helped to form the play, the former in the expressionism of *The Dream Play*, the latter in *Peer Gynt*, for Travis Bogard "the primary source of O'Neill's play" in its form and theme.[2] Of course, as always, O'Neill's personal experiences influenced his conception of the play. He knew about the power of forests to affect the imagination from his gold-prospecting days in Spanish Honduras, but closer to home his walk from Old Snail Road to Peaked Hill in Cape Cod, Massachusetts, where he had a cabin, passed through a heavily wooded area, called "the dark place" by Provincetowners, dark and spooky enough to remind him of his nights in the tropical forest of Honduras.[3] People with whom he was personally acquainted also played their parts in forming the play in O'Neill's mind. In New London, O'Neill knew a black man named Adam Scott, who was both a Baptist church deacon and a bartender, a strongly built man who was religious on Sundays but the rest of the week, like Brutus Jones, put his "Jesus on de shelf." During his Greenwich Village days O'Neill knew a black man named Joe Smith, a gambler, who provided him with some of the phrases that come from the mouth of Jones and who introduced O'Neill to other blacks in Greenwich Village. And O'Neill already had known some Jamaican blacks who were part of the crew of the *Charles Racine* during his sea days.

In short, much went into the making of this short play whose theatrical effects—especially the beating of the tom-tom, the ever-darkening forest, the shooting of the bullets—startled audiences into recognizing a new playwright whose play introduced expressionism to America. One source, however, is rarely mentioned in discussions of the play containing the first important black character in American drama, the first black character to approach tragic status. That source is Shakespeare's *Othello*. In fact, in the thematic analogues, in the use of ghosts and soliloquies, in the concept of character, in specific stage details, not only did *Othello* exert pressure on O'Neill's creation but so too did other Shakespeare tragedies. In the early *The Emperor Jones,* as throughout O'Neill's career, Shakespeare's ghost hovers, unacknowledged but potent.

I begin with the Shakespearean elements I discussed in the previous chapter. Whereas the ghosts in *Cross* are presented as part of a playful experiment in making the audience mad, the ghosts in *Jones* are an important part of O'Neill's serious venture into expressionism. In his flight through the Great Forest in the play's six middle expressionistic scenes (framed by the realistic scenes 1 and 8), Brutus Jones, increasingly filled with terror—his own heartbeat increasing with the increasing beat of the tom-tom, as the night's darkness increasingly encloses him—encounters the ghosts of his personal past and his racial past. O'Neill uses the old-fashioned Shakespearean device of ghosts in a bold theatrical experiment, and he combines that device with another Shakespearean technique, the soliloquy, in *Jones* closer to the Shakespearean soliloquy than in *Bound East* because Jones is alone on stage even though the stage is peopled as well by the figments of his fearful imagination. That is, the expressionism that O'Neill uses allows an effective use of *both* the Shakespearean ghost and the Shakespearean soliloquy, combined in scenic images of strong theatrical power, echoing the remarkable compression Shakespeare achieves in his ghost scenes in *Julius Caesar* and *Hamlet* and *Macbeth*. In scene 3, for example, Jones sees the first ghost of his personal past, Jeff, the dice-shooting Pullman porter he killed. The clicking sound of the dice that Jeff is throwing mechanically, like an *"automaton,"* mingles with the beating of the tom-tom, with Jones alert to both sounds. When he sees the apparition, he *"stands transfixed,"* terrified:

> Who dar? Who dat? Is dat you, Jeff? *(starting toward the other, forgetful for a moment of his surroundings and really believing it is a living man that he sees—in a tone of happy relief)* Jeff! I'se sho' mighty glad to see you! Dey tol' me you done died from dat razor cut I gives you. *(stopping suddenly, bewilderedly)* But how you come to be heah, nigger? *(He stares fascinatedly at the other who continues his mechanical play with the dice. Jones' eyes begin to roll wildly. He stutters)* Ain't you gwine—look up—can't you speak to me? Is you—is you—a ha'nt? *(He jerks out his revolver in a frenzy of terrified rage.)* Nigger, I kills you dead once. Has I got to kill you ag'in? You take it den. *(He fires. When the smoke clears away Jeff has disappeared. Jones stands trembling—then with a certain reassurance)* He's gone, anyway. Ha'nt or not ha'nt, dat shot fix him. (1:1048)

The sounds and Jones's words and the sight of the ghostly mechanical Jeff, who seems both real and unreal, combine to present a scene of strong sensual appeal, allowing the audience to enter Jones's agitated, terror-filled mind. The emotional involvement of an audience with the *mind* of a protagonist is exactly what Shakespeare aims for and more successfully achieves because his language is that of a poet. Take, for example, Macbeth's sight of the dagger that draws him toward the murder of Duncan. Macbeth's heated imagination is working, and his *words* allow us to "see" the dagger that O'Neill would *show* us in an expressionistic scene, both playwrights playing on "Nothing is but what is not," words that come from Shakespeare but that describe the images expressionistically presented by O'Neill. Jones's eyes, like Macbeth's, "are made the fools o' th' other senses," to use Shakespeare's words; Jones, like Macbeth, sees what is not there but what is in his "heat-oppressed brain." At the end of his dagger soliloquy Macbeth hears the bell which invites him to the killing of Duncan, pushing him into the darkness of hell. At the end of scene 3 the shot from Jones's gun, killing Jeff again, reassures Jones for the moment, but the sound of the tom-tom, ever louder, pushes him deeper into forest and night.

Just as Macbeth later sees a more terrible vision when the ghost of a gory Banquo sits in Macbeth's place at the feast, so too the ghostly visions continue for Jones and produce increasing terror in his soul. However, whereas Macbeth cannot sit in the chair of state he killed for, Jones, in his mind's re-creation of his racial past, can sit in a ship with other slaves coming to America from Africa. In this bold scene O'Neill gives up words entirely. In the scenes in which Jones kills a white prison guard and shoots an auctioneer and a planter during a slave sale in the South, Jones talks to the apparitions of his personal and racial past; in the ship scene Jones acts out a mime, the soliloquy abandoned for a stage picture only. But we do have sounds. Here is O'Neill's extended stage direction, describing the figures seen by Jones and by the audience:

> *They are sitting in crumpled, despairing attitudes, hunched, facing one another with their backs touching the forest walls as if they were shackled to them. All are negroes, naked save for loin cloths. At first they are silent and motionless. Then they begin to sway slowly forward toward each other and back again in unison, as if they were laxly letting themselves follow the long roll of a ship at sea. At the same time, a low, melancholy murmur rises among them, increasing gradually by rhythmic degrees which seem to be directed and controlled by the throb of the tom-tom in the distance, to a long, tremulous wail of despair that reaches a certain pitch, unbearably acute, then falls by slow gradations of tone into silence and is taken up again. Jones starts, looks up, sees the figures, and throws himself down again to shut out the sight. A shudder of terror shakes his whole body as the wail rises up about him again. But the next time, his voice, as if under some uncanny compulsion, starts with the others. As their chorus lifts he rises to a sitting posture similar to the others, swaying back and forth. His voice reaches the highest pitch of sorrow, of desolation.* (1:1055–56)

The visual and aural aspects of the scene overwhelm the verbal. The verbal articulation of feeling by the main character is not necessary here, not possible here. The stage image and Jones's howl joined with the cries of his fellow slaves are enough to produce the desired audience experience, an experience that can only be known in performance. I would say the same is true for the Macbeth banquet scene. Macbeth uses words—as usual with Shakespeare, remarkably effective words heard by an audience that still possessed an aural imagination—but much of the power of the scene depends on what he sees and his confusion when he sees it. Macbeth is getting to know his world by the sights he sees in his frenzied imagination. Because of what he sees, because of what his "eyes" tell him, he can acknowledge that "the time has been, / That when the brains were out, the man would die, / And there an end" (3.4.77–79). But this is not that time. He complains that there's no use burying the dead these days if "our graves must send / Those that we bury back" (3.4.70–71). O'Neill cannot give such words of awareness to his inarticulate hero, Brutus Jones, but like Shakespeare, O'Neill gives us a potent stage image and a poetry of cries and howls, producing a feeling of haunting despair, as in *Macbeth*. I am not suggesting that O'Neill had Shakespeare specifically in mind when creating his slave-ship scene in *Jones*—and, again, we notice that O'Neill, like Shakespeare, cannot get too far away from the sea—but I am suggesting that Shakespeare's mode of presentation, his remarkable use of visual imagery and wordless sounds, allowed O'Neill to realize the possibilities of a poetry *of* the theater (to use Cocteau's phrase) in addition to a poetry *in* the theater that we all highly value in Shakespeare. O'Neill has only "the makings of a poet" when we have as our model the Shakespeare who writes such verbal poetry as we find in *Macbeth;* however, O'Neill, like Shakespeare, was a poet of the theater, with more than the mere makings, effectively using sight and sound, even in so early a play as *Jones,* to produce important thematic reverberations. The Shakespearean "ha'nts" that Jones sees—and that expressionism allows an audience to see on stage—gives O'Neill's play a rich dimension. At the end of the slave-ship scene, Jones joins the slaves of his racial past, fearfully accepting their plight as his plight, it seems, before utter darkness descends and he moves on, sleepless and haunted, to go even deeper into his racial past, with O'Neill taking us further back into the dark abysm of time. At the end of Macbeth's banquet scene, Macbeth cannot "sit" among his subjects and guests, the seat occupied by the ghost of Banquo, suggesting that Banquo's descendants will occupy the throne of Scotland, as the witches predicted. The guests leave in disorder, and Macbeth, sleepless and haunted, will go on, "young in deed," wading deeper into blood because to return "were as tedious as go o'er." For both Jones and Macbeth the roads they travel lead relentlessly to death.

When we turn to O'Neill's portrayal of his black character, Brutus Jones, we cannot avoid thinking about Shakespeare's Othello. The very blackness of both characters—let alone O'Neill's great familiarity with Shakespeare, particularly Shakespeare's *Othello*—pushes us to a consideration of the relationship of Brutus Jones to Othello, especially when we realize that a black man as the main character on the American stage of 1920 was a rarity, forcing audiences to think back to whatever black character of importance they knew, and that character would be Othello. It is not surprising that reviewers, seeing the fine performance of Paul Robeson (who replaced the original Jones, Charles Gilpin) suggested that Robeson should now try to play Othello.[4] In addition to the blackness of the main characters there are many other connections between *Jones* and *Othello*, each perhaps tenuous when we wish to find a direct influence, but all together allowing me to assert with some assurance that Shakespeare's tragedy of love and jealousy puts its distinct pressure on a play that treats neither love nor jealousy. Both *Othello* and *Jones* have tight structures, the latter shorter and tighter than Shakespeare's play, taking less than one day, although Shakespeare's play takes only one day and a half from the time we arrive in Cyprus. Both plays offer an admirable simplicity of design, easily grasped by audiences. In both plays a place—in *Jones* the Great Forest, in *Othello* Cyprus—represents more than a place; it's a process in which things happen to the main character, forcing him to be stripped of his outer layers of civilization. In both plays the moon is connected to the madness of the main character. In *Jones* we *see* the moonlight; in *Othello* we *hear* of its power: "It is the very error of the moon, / She comes more nearer earth than she was wont, / And makes men mad" (5.2.109–11). Perhaps most important, both plays deal with "high" men of great self-assurance who fall into barbarism as they journey toward death, a regressive progress by both characters that points to the abiding qualities of human nature that transcend the idea of blackness even as they contain it.

In Shakespeare, the first important image we get of Othello comes from Iago's contemptuous words, spoken to Brabantio: "an old black ram / Is tupping your white ewe." But when we see Othello for the first time, he is grand, calm, as sure of himself as a man can be. Listen to his words when he learns from Iago that Brabantio will try to sever his ties to Desdemona:

> Let him do his spite;
> My services which I have done the signiory
> Shall out-tongue his complaints. 'Tis yet to know—
> Which, when I know that boasting is an honor,
> I shall [provulgate]—I fetch my life and being
> From men of royal siege, and my demerits

May speak, unbonneted, to as proud a fortune
As this that I have reach'd; for know, Iago,
But that I love the gentle Desdemona,
I would not my unhoused free condition
Put into circumscription and confine
For the sea's worth.

(1.2.17–28)

And a little later, when a fight is about to break out, the experienced professional soldier, so calmly in control, need merely say: "Keep up your bright swords, for the dew will rust them." Othello is secure in his accomplishment, in his reputation; he has a strong sense of self. The first important image we get of Brutus Jones comes from a man who hates him, the *"cowardly and dangerous"* white man, Smithers. When he learns from the old woman in scene 1 that the natives on the island have run to the hills in revolt against their "emperor," Smithers says: "Serve 'im right! Puttin' on airs, the stinkin' nigger! 'Is Majesty! Gawd blimey! I only 'opes I'm there when they takes 'im out to shoot 'im" (1:1033). When we first see Jones, he, like Othello, is marvelously self-assured, grand, in control. O'Neill's stage directions pinpoint Jones's *"self-reliant confidence"* which *"inspires respect."* His costume, as described by O'Neill (and perhaps an example of racial stereotyping on O'Neill's part), is gaudy, with its heavy gold chevrons, gold braiding, brass spurs, and pearl-handled revolver. *"Yet,"* O'Neill asserts, *"there is something not altogether ridiculous about his grandeur. He has a way of carrying it off"* (1:1033). Jones's idiom, of course, is worlds away from the music of Othello, but the Othello assurance is there: "Talk polite, white man! Talk polite, you heah me! I'm boss heah now, is you fergettin'?" (1:1034).

The high sense of self that each character possesses belongs to an image of the romantic hero in each. That is, each sees himself as a romantic hero in a story of his own life that each relates. Othello is the storyteller beyond comparison; his adventures, told in a large poetic idiom, filled with specific exotic detail, captivated Desdemona, as it captivates the Venetian court. For the story he told, Desdemona gave him "a world of sighs; / She swore, in faith 'twas strange, 'twas passing strange; / 'Twas pitiful, 'twas wondrous pitiful" (1.3.159–61). The Duke tells Brabantio, "I think this tale would win my daughter too." Throughout the play Othello seems to see himself as the main character in a story, and in his death he plays out his romantic part in that story—ending with a speech that some critics consider to be too self-dramatizing, but however evaluated, a speech that ends with a self-inflicted mortal wound ("I took by the throat the circumcised dog

/And smote him—thus") and a dying kiss, a satisfying romantic and tragic end to Othello's story of self. Brutus Jones also plays the romantic hero, sans love, in the story that he creates, a story of the silver bullet that captivates the "bush niggers," that even affects the snickering Smithers, and most important, seems to impress Jones himself.

> I has de silver bullet moulded and I tells 'em when de time comes I kills myself wid it. I tells 'em dat's 'cause I'm de on'y man in de world big enuff to git me. No use'n deir tryin'. And dey falls down and bumps deir heads. (*He laughs.*) (1:1036)

Jones, like Othello, dies in his own romantic story, but his weapon is not a sword; it is a silver bullet, the bullet he shoots at the crocodile after making a large statement about his past, his racial past: "What—what is I doin'? What is—dis place? Seems like I know dat tree—an' dem stones an' de river. I remember—seems like I been heah befo'" (1:1057). Jones, like Othello who told the story of the Venetian who killed the Turk, reaches into the past to conclude his story, which also concludes his journey. In short, both Jones and Othello romanticize self and both die within that romanticization, both achieving a fitting end, aesthetically satisfying and morally satisfying.

The Christianity of both protagonists is an important ingredient throughout both their stories, but especially at the end. Othello's act of killing Desdemona, that rich pearl he threw away "like the base Judean," denies him any possibility of heaven. His words to the dead Desdemona reveal that he knows his destination after his "journey's end." "When we shall meet at compt, / This look of thine will hurl my soul from heaven, /And fiends will snatch at it" (5.2.273–75). His ending, informed by the large idea of justice—with Othello recognizing himself as the barbarous Turk whom the Venetian killed—touches important Christian ideas. He knows he cannot be redeemed in the afterlife; his judgment on himself—a Christian killing the Turk in him—is the right judgment, and he knows that devils will "roast" him "in sulphur," wash him in "liquid fire." Judgment day is a Christian concept; he is the Judas who brought Jesus (Desdemona) to death. At the same time, Othello is a pagan Moor, the barbarous villain that the Christian must destroy. That Othello always had both Christian and pagan tendencies is evident throughout the play. His speeches are filled with Christian references, especially touching heaven and hell, but the superstitious pagan side of his character comes out strongly in his description of that remarkable handkerchief, the play's most important prop, the handkerchief that has "magic in the web." His belief in that magical handkerchief somewhat qualifies our attitude toward Othello's earlier dismissal of Brabantio's idea that Othello used witchcraft to win Desdemona. His telling of his own story, he insisted, won the heart of Desdemona, but the story he lives on stage contains elements that touch witchcraft, that is, magic and mystery, in addition to Christianity, which has its own magic and mystery. Othello is a richly conceived, mixed character—Christian and pagan, Venetian and Turk, in control at first (secure, at ease, impressive), disintegrating as the play progresses (insecure, disturbed, mad), regaining control once more at the end, dying with nobility.

At first, Brutus Jones seems to wear his Christianity lightly. He doesn't disagree with Smithers's accusation that he hasn't paid much attention to the Baptist church since he arrived on the island. "I've 'eard myself you 'ad turned yer coat an' was takin' up with their blarsted witch-doctors, or whatever the 'ell yer calls the swine." Jones vehemently asserts: "I pretends to! Sho' I pretends! Dat's part o' my game from de fust. If I finds out dem niggers believes dat black is white, den I yells it louder 'n deir loudest. It don't git me nothin' to do missionary work for de Baptist Church. I'se after de coin, an' I lays my Jesus on de shelf for de time bein'" (1:1042). The vehemence with which he delivers his words suggests that Smithers touched something that needs explaining. Jones declares that he's still a good Baptist, that his professed belief in witchcraft is only a game to fool the natives, that he is much different from them. But in the course of his journey through the play he becomes more and more terrified by visions, by "ha'nts." As he strips his emperor's clothes, he increasingly becomes the kind of superstitious "bush nigger" he talked about with such contempt. His soliloquies are dotted with references to the "Lawd," and he recalls the Baptist parson who told him there are no such things as "ha'nts" even as he chastizes himself for seeing them—"Is you civilized, or is you like dese ign'rent black niggers heah? Sho'? Dat was all in yo' own head" (1:1049). (Talking of himself to himself is what Othello often does in Shakespeare's play.) What is in Jones's head, expressionism allows us to see. And Jones's visions, produced by a superstitious mind, touching dark thoughts, eventually lead him to a more genuine Christianity—"Lawd Jesus, heah my prayer. I'se a po' sinner, a po' sinner! I knows I done wrong, I knows it! . . . Lawd, I done wrong! And down heah whar dese fool bush niggers raises me up to the seat o' de mighty, I steals all I could grab. Lawd, I done wrong! I knows it! I'se sorry! Forgive me, Lawd! Forgive dis po' sinner!" (1:1052). The conflict of paganism versus Christianity finds its most powerful scenic representation at the climax of Jones's story, at the end of the journey in scene 7, when Jones, farthest back in his past, sees a witch doctor whose dance becomes *"a narrative in pantomime,"* according to O'Neill's full stage directions:

> *He flees, he is pursued by devils, he hides, he flees again. Ever wilder and wilder becomes his flight, nearer and nearer draws the pursuing evil, more and more the spirit of terror gains possession of him. His croon, rising to intensity, is punctuated by shrill cries. Jones has become completely hypnotized. His voice joins in the incantation, in the cries, he beats time with his hands and sways his body to and fro from the waist. The whole spirit and meaning of the dance has entered into him, has become his spirit. Finally the theme of the pantomime halts on a howl of despair, and is taken up again in a note of savage hope. There is a salvation. The forces of evil demand sacrifice. They must be appeased.* (1:1058)

When the witch doctor calls to *"some God"* within the depths of the water, a crocodile appears, perhaps a god of evil, a god of power, perhaps representing Jones's own sinfulness and pride and evil, certainly a mysterious *"implacable deity demanding sacrifice,"* to use O'Neill's words (1:1058). At the moment of this obviously pagan vision, Jones calls out to his Christian god, "Mercy, Oh Lawd! Mercy! Mercy on dis po' sinner." As Jones and the crocodile crawl toward one another, Jones cries out: "Lawd, save me! Lawd Jesus, heah my prayer!" As if *"in answer to his prayer"* the thought of his silver bullet comes to Jones. He fires at the crocodile, who *"sinks back behind the river bank."* The witch doctor disappears. *"Jones lies with his face to the ground, his arms outstretched, whimpering with fear as the throb of the tom-tom fills the silence about him with a somber pulsation"* (1:1059). A stunning theatrical moment, but more than this, an effective conclusion to the pagan-Christian rhythm throughout the play—with Jones in the position of a cross, having called upon Jesus, but whimpering with fear like the superstitious natives he exploited, as his mind forces him to confront his savage self. His shooting the crocodile with the silver bullet is a form of suicide in the expressionistic scene, melding into the killing of Jones by silver bullets in the concluding realistic scene when Lem's soldiers "cotch" Jones, with the beating of the tom-tom abruptly ceasing when Jones's heartbeat ceases.

The Emperor Jones, like *Othello*, concludes with the death of a black man who gave the impression of strength and grandeur in the play's beginning, but whose weakness forces him to become "low," only to stir himself to a just action, connected with sacrifice, at play's end, an action resulting from recognition of self within a Christian-pagan context. Both black protagonists are assaulted from the outside—Othello by Iago, Jones by Lem and his soldiers. But both ultimately are destroyed from *within*. Shakespeare gives us words, often glorious words, to allow us to discover and understand that within. And he gives us the inarticulate ravings of an essentially poetic man who loses his bearings in the course of his journey downward. And he gives us some compelling stage images, like the one found at the end of the temptation scene, act 3, scene 3, when both Othello and Iago are on their knees in a kind of mock marriage, punctuated by Iago's words, "I am your own for ever." In O'Neill we get some words—ordinary, colloquial, dialectal words, and ravings too from a man who loses his bearings—to help us understand what is within Brutus Jones, but we also *see* the within because of O'Neill's effective use of expressionism. Again, O'Neill, a poet *of* the theater, is reaching for effects remarkably achieved by Shakespeare, the poet both of the theater and in the theater. O'Neill, whether consciously or not, seems to be following the pattern of Shakespeare's play.

Of course, the black-white opposition is significant to both plays, creating similar problems when one confronts the racism of Shakespeare and O'Neill. To state the obvious, there was color prejudice in Shakespeare's time, as there is in our time, O'Neill's time. Blacks, for the Elizabethans—and it should be stated that all dark-skinned people were lumped together so that there were no clear distinctions between words like *Moor* or *Ethiope* or *Negro* or *blackamoor*—blacks, for the rather insular Elizabethans, were ugly and sinful and barbarous. For them, Satan was black, and, to quote the King of Navarre in Shakespeare's comedy, *Love's Labor's Lost,* "Black is the badge of hell, the hue of dungeons, and the school of night." Shakespeare, writing *Othello*—and presenting Aaron the Moor in his early tragical melodrama, *Titus Andronicus,* and the Prince of Morocco in his comedy, *The Merchant of Venice*—deals with this color prejudice, but it must be acknowledged from the outset that this is not the main focus of his tragedy. Although the important idea of Othello's color difference from those around him must never be lost, in *Othello* Shakespeare dramatizes the vulnerability of men to fearful thoughts that poison judgment and force us to perform terrible deeds. Shakespeare is a man of his age who had acquired the prejudices of his age, but in *Othello* the color prejudice comes from characters who are evil (Iago) or foolish (Roderigo) or distraught (Brabantio). That is, like all great writers, Shakespeare tests the assumptions of his age, something he does with the Elizabethan attitude toward Jews, I believe, in *The Merchant of Venice.* In that play, in which Shakespeare is calculatingly playing with values, we get this line from a disguised Portia: "Which is the merchant here? and which the Jew?" In

Othello, perhaps a similar question can be asked. "Who is black and who is white?" The fact that Shakespeare calls his onstage whore Bianca (white) suggests he wants us to consider such a question. Bianca, we notice, in her jealousy reflects the black man Othello, reflects the mistaken image that the black man has of his pure wife Desdemona, reflects in her genuine concern for Cassio the white woman's love for her black husband. White reflects black and white!

Othello is a black man, once a slave, from an exotic past who marries a white Venetian woman. As we already noticed, our first image of him and his wife comes from Iago: "an old black ram is tupping your white ewe." He refers to Othello as "the devil," tells Brabantio that his daughter is "cover'd with a Barbary horse" and that the newly married couple is "making the beast with two backs." But even before we get these color and animal references Roderigo had referred to Othello as "the thick-lips." Brabantio is genuinely puzzled that his daughter rejected "the wealthy curled darlings of our nation" in order to run to "the sooty bosom" of Othello, someone "to fear, not to delight!" Brabantio believes that Othello used witchcraft to win her, that he "practic'd on her with foul charms," a natural thought coming from a conventional man who is contemplating for the first time not only a daughter's disobedience but the power of an exotic black man, stereotypically connected with magic and mystery. After listening to Othello's story about how he won Desdemona—appealing music coming from the lips of the soldier who said he's "rude" in his speech—the duke tries to console Brabantio with the words, "Your son-in-law is far more fair than black," thereby supporting the black stereotype even as he tries to excuse it. However, the blackness of Othello is emphasized not only by Iago, Roderigo, and Brabantio. Othello himself, worked on by Iago, becomes obsessed by it. He believes he doesn't have "those soft parts of conversation that chamberers have" because he is "black." His poisoned thoughts make him believe that Desdemona "is now begrim'd and black / As mine own face." And, ominously, with Iago in complete possession of Othello toward the end of the brilliant temptation scene, Othello shouts out, "Arise, black vengeance, from the hollow hell!" (3.3.447). This is the vengeance that drives him steadily onward—like the Pontic (black!) Sea, to use Othello's allusion—to smother Desdemona at play's end. (Uttering these words, James Earl Jones as Othello in a 1964 New York production beat his chest, King Kong style, reverting to the savage, a stage action that calls to mind the primitive regression of the *Emperor* Jones who becomes *Brutus* Jones, with the Brute part of that name functioning. James Earl Jones, like Paul Robeson before him, played both O'Neill's black man and Shakespeare's.)

Othello's blackness helps us to better appreciate the courage of Desdemona in making her fateful choice of husband, even as it allows us to better gauge Iago's cleverness in using that blackness to weave his plot. And Othello's blackness, because it is connected to mystery and witchcraft, to primitive darkness, allows us to understand his passion when he "discovers" his wife's infidelity. In his diseased mind, her sinfulness destroys his self-esteem, pollutes him and all mankind. She must be eliminated. He must perform "black vengeance," which takes in more than mere revenge. It hearkens primitive sacrifice; it necessitates a ritual of appeasement to some pagan gods, with Othello both priest (witch doctor) and executioner—even as Othello, as previously discussed, operates at the same time in a Christian framework. (With the words, "Arise, black vengeance," Laurence Olivier tore the very conspicuous cross from his neck.)

Blackness, of course, is at the very core of *The Emperor Jones,* with Jones himself not only a black man but an American black man who epitomizes the progress and/or regress of his race. The stereotype is crudely present—Pullman porter, crapshooter, razor carrier, murderer, prisoner, slave, superstitious, fearful, a speaker of dialect. When he enters the play, O'Neill's stage directions tell us this: *"He is a tall, powerfully-built, full-blooded negro of middle age. His features are typically negroid, yet there is something decidedly distinctive about his face—an underlying strength of will, a hardy, self-reliant confidence in himself that inspires respect."* (The "yet" reveals O'Neill's residual prejudice.) Smithers in the first scene, like Iago in his first scene, pinpoints Jones's blackness in meanspirited terms—"stinkin' nigger!"—but Jones himself has nothing good to say about the "bush niggers," the "low-flung woods' niggers," whom he rules as emperor, has nothing but contempt for their obedience to him—"And dere all dem fool bush niggers was kneelin' down and bumpin' deir heads on de ground like I was a miracle out o' de Bible. Oh Lawd, from dat time on I has dem all eatin' out of my hand. I cracks de whip and dey jumps through" (1:1036). As the play progresses, he calls himself "fool nigger," and his actions mirror the fearful actions of the blacks he holds in contempt as he too bumps his head on the ground. In his journey backward he, like Othello, contemplates the barbarian within himself, meeting a witch doctor of his own imagination, ready to offer himself as a sacrifice in expiation for his sins, with the pagan sacrifice also touching Christianity, as in *Othello.*

In both plays the black man emerges superior to the white man, with Iago and Smithers displaying interesting similarities, although Smithers does not come close to being the extraordinarily rich and haunting character that Shakespeare created. Each white man begins his respective play. Smithers's character note is struck immediately in his treatment of the old black woman whom he handles roughly, raising his whip to her "*threateningly,*" and just stopping himself from reaching for his revolver to shoot her. His color prejudice is revealed immediately in his attitude toward the natives and toward Jones, who for Smithers is merely "the stinkin' nigger" who puts on airs, acting the emperor. O'Neill's stage directions have already described Smithers as a white man with a "*pasty face*" that is "*sickly yellow*" and with an expression of "*unscrupulous meanness, cowardly and dangerous.*" When Smithers talks with Jones, whose manner reveals a man of "*grandeur,*" he seems a sniveling malicious coward. Interestingly, at play's end, after Jones's death by the silver bullet, it is Smithers who pays Jones a grudging but admiring compliment: "Gawd blimey, but yer died in the 'eight o' style, any'ow!" The curtain falls on his ever-contemptuous attitude toward the natives—"Stupid as 'ogs, the lot of 'em! Blarsted niggers!" This in response to Lem's silence when Smithers asks the question: "And I s'pose you think it's yer bleedin' charms and yer silly beatin' the drum that made 'im run in a circle when 'e'd lost 'imself, don't yer?" (The play's first book publication by Boni and Liveright in 1921 contains these last words of Smithers.) Smithers remains Smithers, shallow, mean, unable to fathom the mystery connected with the power of blackness, and certainly incapable of ever making the kind of journey taken by that black man Jones, whose imagination is as powerful as his body, whose journey led to sacrifice and awareness. If not a tragic hero, Jones is certainly a big man whose large fears, formless as well as formed, touch depths that the small white man Smithers will never experience, making Smithers's color prejudice seem sordid.

Iago's words and actions in the whispered beginning of *Othello* reveal a malicious white man, like Smithers in a position of subordination to the black man and equally envious and resentful, the perennial loser expressing contempt for a winner. He immediately reveals his color prejudice, as we have noticed, but his cynical view of Othello and Desdemona as the "old black ram" and the "white ewe," the first "view" we get of them, is canceled out when we see the loving couple in the next scene. Essentially a coward, Iago calls out to Brabantio under the cover of darkness. How different from the grand Othello, who will face his adversary openly, gaining our respect. The passionate savagery of Othello, a victim of himself as well as of Iago, touches depths of character and nobility that the more evil, because rational, Iago can never reach. At play's end, with the tragic bed heavily laden because of his actions, Iago speaks no word. Like the crocodile in *Jones,* also representing a mysterious power, a force of evil, Iago, who will always remain Iago, cannot be killed. Like Smithers, Iago has the last word because his silence speaks volumes—about himself and about the tragic Othello. Every director of *Othello* must make an important decision about Iago's silence at the end of the play. Does Iago look at that tragic bed of love and death with a feeling of triumph? with amazement at his own accomplishment? with contempt for the man he duped? with some realization that the black man was a high figure indeed? with no expression, thereby heightening the mystery? Whatever the last gesture, Iago, whose color prejudice, like Smithers's, by play's end seems merely base and ignoble, remains alive, like Smithers. The living white men are clearly inferior to the dead black men, who have given their names to the titles of their respective plays. And both black men finally represent all men, entangled in a "forest," stripping themselves of the outer clothing of civilization, reaching the darkest parts of themselves, displaying fearful imaginations, finally claimed by darkness. If this last sentence is accepted as true for both Othello and Jones (and we must acknowledge the representative name of O'Neill's hero) then it is also true for King Lear, another high man who strips himself to become unaccommodated man, the thing itself, another journeyer to darkness, and for Macbeth, another "emperor" whose powerful imagination forces him to see his own fall *down*. *Othello* exerts an important, if perhaps unconscious, influence on *The Emperor Jones,* and the other Shakespeare tragedies put some pressure on O'Neill's early play too. (I parenthetically add that the first name of Jones, Brutus, calls to mind another Shakespearean high man who kills an "emperor" and kills himself.)

The foregoing discussion notwithstanding, the question of the racism of both Shakespeare and O'Neill remains debatable. The theater history of *Othello* provides too many examples of directors wanting to make Othello "whiter" than he is in order to make him more acceptable to white audiences. Of course, this says more about the interpreters and audiences of Shakespeare than about Shakespeare, who makes his black man a noble and sympathetic character. As late as 1943, when Paul Robeson played Othello, the mere portrayal of Othello by a black actor was a "racial event of the first magnitude."[5] The theater history of *The Emperor Jones* is not a long one, but from the very beginning the "racism" of the play was challenged by the remarkable black actor who created the part of Brutus Jones, Charles Gilpin. Even though the play offers the first important part for a black actor in America, even though Gilpin made theater history with the boldness of his performance in that part, becoming an instant success, a star, still, in the course of its early runs, Gilpin, a proud black man, began changing the word "nigger" to "Negro" or "colored man," and made other changes in the dialogue.[6] O'Neill balked at Gilpin's liberties, even threatening to "beat the hell" out of him if he made any changes, and eventually had Gilpin replaced by Paul Robeson, who also became a big success in the part. Gilpin seemed to believe he had the right to tone down the play's "racism" because he completely identified with the role to the point where he played "emperor" all over Harlem and even said, after seeing Robeson in the part, "I created the role of the Emperor. That role belongs to me. That Irishman, he just wrote the play."[7] Paul Robeson, on the other hand, applauded O'Neill for creating Brutus Jones. "O'Neill has got what no other playwright has—that is, the true, authentic negro psychology. He has read the negro soul, and had felt the negro's racial tragedy."[8] Years later, talking about the film version of *The Emperor Jones,* Robeson said in an interview that O'Neill "dug down into my racial life and has found the essence of my race. Every word he wrote for 'The Emperor Jones' is true to the Negro racial experience."[9] Robeson, who also played Othello, made no comparable statements about Shakespeare's black man, probably because Shakespeare was not so directly dealing with the black racial experience, but Robeson did insist on Othello's racial identity and played Othello as a great "Negro warrior" operating in an alien culture that eventually destroys him.[10] (I parenthetically add that Robeson said that playing Othello took enormous energy, "only Emperor Jones, twenty years before, had involved a comparable effort.")[11]

Controversy about the residual racism in both *Jones* and *Othello* will continue to flourish, especially when the plays are put on stage. I believe that *Jones* is not performed very often precisely because it may offend sensibilities, and no discussion like mine, pointing out the black man's representative quality and his superiority to the white man in the play, will squelch the discussion of racism in this time of heightened awareness. (Although no discussion of racism greeted Louis Gruenberg's operatic version of *Jones,* which opened at the Metropolitan Opera in January 1933, NBC, in 1952, shelved plans to produce the opera because of perceived racism.) Each audience, each reader, will decide whether Brutus Jones and Othello offer stereotypes that are objectionable, supporting racist beliefs, despite the sympathetic treatment of each black man by each dramatist. After Othello, Shakespeare presented no more black characters. (The closest he comes in color is the tawny Cleopatra, one of his greatest creations.) After Brutus Jones, O'Neill plunged even more deeply into the problem of black-white relationships with his *All God's Chillun Got Wings* (1923). Not surprisingly, *Othello* once again is part of the underpinning of a play about a black man married to a white woman. But before he wrote *Chillun* he gave the American public another play, without a black man, a play that provides an important transition from *Jones* to *Chillun*—*The Hairy Ape.*

The Hairy Ape, O'Neill's important expressionistic play after *Jones,* was written in 1921, with the realistic *Anna Christie* (written 1920, produced 1921) sandwiched in between. *Ape* and *Jones* have many characteristics in common, the most important being the combination of realism and expressionism, and the dramatization of the journey of a representative man (with Smith, like Jones, a representative name) in eight scenes, a journey toward the primitive and toward death. Its differences, however, are profound, not the least of which is Yank Smith's inability to reach back into a past, something Jones was able to do, because Yank has no past.[12] Everything is present with him, now, and his search to *belong* to that present leads him to think about his condition, with his thinking eventually leading him to death. Yank's position in various scenes in the attitude of Rodin's *The Thinker* emphasizes this idea. The repetition of a visual image to the point that it takes on a symbolic dimension is a Shakespearean technique, used brilliantly, for example, in the kneeling of Lear throughout his play. The cause of Yank's thinking is a woman named Mildred Douglas. Yank was secure in his world of the stokehole; he was the center of that world, sure of himself, a man who belonged. Then down comes a woman into that furnace world, calls him a "filthy beast," and chaos comes. What I wish to suggest in this brief discussion of *Ape* is that O'Neill has both *Jones* and *Othello* in mind ("mind" may be too strong a word here in respect to *Othello*) when he writes this realistic-expressionistic play about a white man's attempt to belong to a society that rejects him. In any play about alienation in America the idea of minorities, especially blacks, comes easily but appropriately to mind. In *Ape,* I wish to suggest, O'Neill gives us a white man who is a "black" man who is finally both black and white, that is, everyman. In doing so, Shakespeare's black man, like O'Neill's black man, Jones, is not too far below the surface of O'Neill's presentation.

Our first view of Yank and the other firemen in the crowded, claustrophobic forecastle of an ocean liner is that of Neanderthal men, with stooping postures, having *"long arms of tremendous power, and low, receding brows above their small, fierce, resentful eyes."* They act like beasts in a cage, with the cage serving as O'Neill's important metaphor throughout the play, presented both realistically and expressionistically, leading to Yank's realization at play's end that his cage is spiritual as well as literal. In the stokehole of scene 3 the white men feeding the furnace *"are outlined in silhouette in the crouching, inhuman attitudes of chained gorillas."* In scene 4 the firemen, even after scrubbing their faces with soap and water, still have coal dust around their eyes, dust that *"sticks like black make-up."* Yank, in this scene, has not washed, so he stands out *"a blackened, brooding figure."* In scene 5, the Fifth Avenue scene, Yank still has *"the black smudge of coal dust"* sticking around his eyes *"like makeup."* And from the moment that Mildred Douglas calls him a "filthy beast" in scene 3, which in the following scene Paddy changes to a "hairy ape," Yank is obsessed with that idea, finally visiting the gorilla in his cage in the last scene, only to be crushed to death. The ape kills the ape, a form of indirect suicide that should remind us of Jones's indirect suicide when he shoots his silver bullet at the crocodile. The play is filled with references to, and noises from, the jungle, but Yank's journey through the scenes of the play does not lead him to such a realization as Jones's "seems like I ben heah befo'." Yank, the white man in black makeup, seems less fortunate than the black man who went back to his roots. Yank is a marginalized man, rootless, a stranger alienated completely from society.

Much of what I said about the pressure of *Othello* on *Jones* applies to *The Hairy Ape* too. Yank Smith, like Jones and Othello, begins his play as a man sure of his position. He belongs to the stokehole world; he is respected for his power and strength. He, like Jones and Othello, goes on a journey leading to awareness, but his awareness is more devastating than Jones's, because Jones was able to call on Jesus and Jones at least recognized a place. Yank is completely lost, between heaven and hell, a midposition that he now believes might indeed be hell, a recognition that gives him, I believe, a tragic status.

> I ain't on oith and I ain't in heaven, get me? I'm in de middle tryin' to separate 'em, takin' all de woist punches from bot' of 'em. Maybe dat's what dey call hell, huh? (2:162)

The words come from an inarticulate man, forever groping with words, learning how to think—"Tinkin' is hard"—but a man displaying existential frustration, a man who sees himself in that same hell that Othello, the remarkably articulate hero, verbalizes so powerfully but does not necessarily feel more strongly.

Of course, the most important element in *Ape* that was not present in *Jones* and that points more directly to *Othello* is the presence of a woman, the "cause" of the devastation. Yank Smith, before Mildred Douglas comes along or comes down, like Othello before Desdemona, was of a "free condition," to use Othello's phrase. He had his place, he excelled at his job, he did not have to "think," nor did he think, about matters foreign to him. Then a woman appears who changes one's condition. In Othello's case, a white woman who was captivated by his talk, by his "mind," she says, perhaps by his difference, perhaps by his physicality, as so much of the play's subtext suggests. In a "black" Yank Smith's case, a white woman—"*like a white apparition*" in her white dress—who is horrified at the sight of him, "*her whole personality crushed, beaten in, collapsed, by the terrific impact of this unknown, abysmal brutality, naked and shameless"* (2:137). She looks at his *"gorilla face,"* calls him a "filthy beast," and faints. Her reaction to him seems excessively strong, with O'Neill uncharacteristically keeping the root cause of it unexpressed. Because the scene is sexually charged immediately before Mildred's arrival—one need only listen to Yank's words as he feeds the furnace, like making violent love to a woman—her "horror" at Yank's physicality indicates a new experience for her, perhaps an unconscious yearning for the primitive. Whatever the reason for Mildred's strong emotion, it is Yank's reaction to her that propels the play. And the same can be said about Othello's reaction to Desdemona. Both proud men feel themselves deeply insulted by the behavior of the women who have entered their lives. Both lose their self-assurance, think about their deficiencies, feel mocked by the new circumstances, are lost in a darker forest, it seems, than Jones was. And both seek revenge on the women who changed their "free condition." Again, Yank's language is not Othello's, but his bewilderment and desperation, and his barbarism just below the surface of his blackened skin, are close to that of Shakespeare's hero.

> I'll fix her! I'll tell her where to get off! She'll git down on her knees and take it back or I'll bust de face offen her! *(shaking one fist upward and beating on his chest with the other)* I'll find yuh! I'm comin', d'yuh hear? I'll fix yuh, God damn yuh! (2:143)

Yank ends the scene with these words: "She done me doit! She done me doit, didn't she? I'll git square wit her! I'll git her some way! Git offen me, youse guys! Lemme up! I'll show her who's a ape!" (2:143). Yank's apelike beating of his chest is O'Neill's appropriately designated stage action. The stage action would be equally appropriate to Othello, as it was when James Earl Jones performed the part when he utters "Arise, black vengeance, from the hollow hell! / Yield up, O love, thy crown and hearted throne / To tyrannous hate! Swell, bosom, with thy fraught, / For 'tis of aspics' tongues!" (3.3.447–50). The gesture, I believe, belongs to each protagonist: frustrated, illusions shattered, desperate, seeking justice, asserting power, ready to destroy the "cause," the woman who sullied one's self-image, who hurt one's pride. It should be no surprise, therefore, that Paul Robeson, during the year he was performing Othello in London (1930–31), played Yank Smith in a short-lived revival of *The Hairy Ape*. His performance of that part on the London stage gave the idea of *belonging* a more obvious racial dimension, and perhaps made the play a more clear indictment of American society. Certainly it allowed the *Othello* echoes to enrich

O'Neill's story of a "black" man and a white woman and the tragic consequences of their meeting.

Having portrayed a black man's journey through memory and time in *Jones*, having added a woman to another man's journey to death (this time a blackened white man) in *Ape*, O'Neill in *All God's Chillun Got Wings*, his next realistic-expressionistic play, makes the image of a black man and a white woman the center of his conception. The play, in addition to being a psychological study of two disturbed people, is a study of race relations, perhaps more didactic than O'Neill wanted it to be or thought it was. In fact, the play can mechanically be split in two, the division of its acts, with the first act emphasizing race, the second act psychology, although race, of course, is important in the second act as well. The controversy surrounding the presentation of *Chillun* has been documented fully.[13] In 1924, when *Chillun* was performed at the Provincetown Playhouse in New York City after having been published in *The American Mercury*, America was not ready for the dramatization of the marriage of a white woman to a black man. Violence was threatened by the Ku Klux Klan, O'Neill received death threats, the play was almost canceled, and the play's reception by both whites and blacks included venomous attacks. Hatred and prejudice filled the air surrounding its presentation, but the production went forward, with the audience "generous with applause."[14] Reviewers and critics were usually cool toward the play, although very warm toward Paul Robeson's performance as Jim Harris, the black man who adores the shallow, racially prejudiced, white woman, Ella Downey, to the point of self-sacrifice. All the reviewers, of course, mention the issue of race prejudice and miscegenation in the play, some considering the play a kind of treatise, others—taking their cue from O'Neill himself—claiming that O'Neill is not advocating a thing in this play, that "the racial factor is incidental. The play is a character study of two human beings."[15] Still others insisted that the play transcends the race question, with O'Neill going "much deeper" than sociology, offering, in fact, "tragedy."[16] My own view is that *Chillun* is both a treatise on race relations and a clinical study of "two human beings," with the play almost cleanly split into two parts, and with a different Shakespeare play informing each part.

Act 1 accentuates the race idea; act 2 concentrates on the sanity-insanity of its two protagonists. The Shakespeare of the first part is the Shakespeare who wrote *Othello,* as we would expect in a play about a black man wedded to a white woman; the Shakespeare of the second part, less predictably, is the Shakespeare who wrote *Macbeth*. That O'Neill had his own family situation in mind when writing the play has been convincingly suggested by a number of scholars.[17] Jim and Ella are the names of O'Neill's father and mother, and the relationship between the two characters offers specific parallels to the relationship of James O'Neill and Ellen Quinlan. Ellen Quinlan's feeling that she married beneath her, that she was a social outcast because of her marriage to an actor, her desire to stay away from people, and her dope addiction that allowed her to retreat to girlhood, are very close to Ella Downey's feeling of superiority over her husband, her shame and self-consciousness because she married a black man, her desire to be alone, her eventual insanity that brings her back to childhood. James O'Neill, who raised himself above the poverty level and had high ambitions to be a great Shakespearean actor, only to be thwarted by latching on to that great money success, *The Count of Monte Cristo,* in part for the sake of his wife and her needs, touches the life of Jim Harris, who raises himself from his dire circumstances to eventually take the bar examination, only to be thwarted by failing the exam, in part because of his wife's needs. Both men believe they married above them; both adore their wives. Both wives have a love-hate relationship with their husbands. Perhaps these parallels do not take us very far in trying to understand what happens in the play, but they do point to the important fact that O'Neill, in *Chillun,* is drawing heavily on his own family history, something he did not do in *Jones* or *Ape,* but what he will do from now on. But one part of his personal family life does have an impact on his artistic presentation, I believe—the fact that his father often quoted Othello's famous speech on his marriage to Desdemona, "Most potent, grave, and reverend signiors." Sheaffer speculates that James O'Neill perhaps "unconsciously felt a kinship with the blackamoor" because Desdemona was "attracted to the Moor by the romance of his strange and dangerous past," just as Ellen Quinlan was attracted to the glamorous figure of the theater, James O'Neill.[18] This is a fine insight, touching the important idea that the marriage relationship of James O'Neill and Ellen Quinlan had a black-white quality to it, mirroring the situation in Shakespeare's *Othello* and the situation in O'Neill's *Chillun.* From *Long Day's Journey* we know that *Othello* was very familiar to the three men of the O'Neill family and that Othello was the role James O'Neill played better than Edwin Booth, the role to which he seemed most attached. What happened in O'Neill's own family gives *Chillun* its emotional coloring, informing not only the black-white relationships in act 1, but also the psychological instabilities of his main characters in act 2. Certainly O'Neill, from this point on in his career, will present many plays that have *family* as the important focus, and in this respect O'Neill's closeness to Shakespeare will become stronger as O'Neill's career progresses because Shakespeare was a member of the family and because Shakespeare invests much of his artistic energy on the family and the values connected with the idea of family. The O'Neill-Shakespeare family connection will be more obviously clear in O'Neill's next important play, *Desire Under the Elms,* but in *Chillun* O'Neill's own family situation puts pressure on the play, perhaps less easily measurable, but certainly there. Now that his brother Jamie had recently died—one year after his mother's death, three years after his father's, so that O'Neill's immediate family, the family he was obsessed with throughout his development, was now all gone—O'Neill seems to be more free to write his family into his plays. In *Chillun* some family sparks are flying, as I already suggested; with the years ahead the heat of a more steadily burning fire will be felt.

Taking my lead from Louis Sheaffer, I believe one other element colored O'Neill's presentation of the black-white marriage in *Chillun*. Because O'Neill stored in his mind, and in his notebooks, ideas and stories that could eventually be used in his plays, I have no doubt that O'Neill, a fan of boxing, paid close attention, when he was a reporter in New London in 1912, to the sensational story of the suicide of Etta Johnson, the white wife of the black heavyweight champion, Jack Johnson. Sheaffer records the words she uttered a few weeks before she shot herself: "I am a white woman, and am tired of being a social outcast. I deserve all of my misery for marrying a black man. Even the Negroes don't respect me; they hate me. I intend to end it all."[19] Etta Johnson commits suicide; Ella Downey Harris in her insanity retreats to childhood; Ellen Quinlan O'Neill in her dope addiction attempts to commit suicide and often reverts to girlhood. (Ella Downey's white husband, before she marries Jim Harris, is a boxer.) Characteristically, O'Neill's creative imagination seems to be working on everything that comes within its grasp, and this includes the Shakespeare who dramatized a black-white marriage in *Othello,* the play his father forever quoted.

Act 1 of *Chillun* heavily treats race relations, with expressionism helping O'Neill to dramatize the racial situation. The first three scenes of the four in act 1 show us a corner in lower New York where "*three narrow streets converge.*" O'Neill's stage directions tell us, "*In the street leading left, the faces are all white; in the street leading right, all black.*" It is spring and the blacks are "*participants in the spirit of Spring,*" whereas the whites are "*awkward in natural emotion.*" The laughter "*expresses the difference in race*" (2:279). And that's what O'Neill stresses in all the street scenes, the racial difference, with the blacks appearing more vital, more genuine, more natural than the whites, the difference particularized, as the play progresses, in the portraits of Jim and Ella. (*White* is not a positive idea in O'Neill. Take, as examples, the white Smithers and the white Mildred, already discussed, pointing ahead to the white meetinghouse of Puritanism in *Mourning Becomes Elec-*

tra.) The children of the first scene, including the white Ella and the black Jim, play marbles together, unaware of racial differences. By the second scene, nine years later, the differences have had a profound impact on the relationship of Ella and Jim, and in the third scene, five years later, we learn that Ella has already been married to Mickey, the boxer, whom she has left, and that they had a child, now dead. In this scene Ella condescendingly asserts that Jim is "the only white man in the world! Kind and white" (2:291), and at the end of this scene Jim declares his love for Ella, saying that he'll "serve" her and lie at her feet "like a dog," that he will become her "slave," as he sinks down to his knees and "*in a frenzy of self-abnegation . . . beats his head on the flagstones*" (2:294). At this moment it is easy to recall Brutus Jones's words about the bush niggers "kneelin' down and bumpin' deir heads on de ground." The "slave" idea will persist, and the kneeling will be an important repetitive gesture. The staging of the marriage that takes place in scene 4 is relentlessly symbolic, with "*two racial lines*" forming on each side of the church gate, as Jim, dressed in black, and Ella, dressed in white, pass between the two lines, which are "*fixed and immovable*" (2:295, 296), producing the same sense of rigidity as the marionettes in the expressionistic scene 5 of *The Hairy Ape*. The scene and the act end with Jim's hysterical words expressing "hope" as he looks at the sky and says, "We're all the same—equally just—under the sky—under the sun—under God—sailing over the sea—to the other side of the world—the side where Christ was born" (2:296). The Christ that he mentions at the end of this act will be hearkened again at play's end, and the sky he looks at here will be the heaven he will reach for later, for only in heaven do all God's children have wings.

The first act offers almost no character portrayal, merely images and ideas in rather quick succession that highlight racial differences. O'Neill's expressionism allows for little character analysis here; it is not the expressionism that gives us the mind of a character on a racial journey, as in *The Emperor Jones*. It is closer to the expressionism of the German dramatists, like Kaiser, who wish to make a comment on society. O'Neill, in act 1 especially (but also throughout) is commenting on racial antagonism in America. He did not want to be considered a didactic dramatist, but there's little doubt that in *Chillun* he wishes to confront racial intolerance. He is not advocating mixed marriages, but he is placing the black-white marriage in a social context that highlights racial prejudice, thereby indirectly appealing for racial tolerance in general. The expressionism gives us the distinct social lines, and when the characters speak, the black man's status in the white world becomes crystal clear. Mickey, for example, says that Ella "hates the sight of a coon," the kind of sentiment that brings us close to the attitude of Iago and Roderigo and Brabantio toward Othello, someone "to fear," according to Brabantio, that is, someone who is frightening. In *Othello,* however, the white woman courageously loves the black man and is attracted to him because of his "mind," perhaps because of his exotic qualities, his blackness. In *Chillun,* the insecure white woman is attracted to the black man because he appears to her to be "white," which for Ella, not for O'Neill, is a positive idea.

In the three scenes of act 2, more psychological than social, O'Neill probes his characters more deeply, and he does so in a single setting, one room, a room in which the walls shrink with each passing scene. This mechanical narrowing of the play's physical world mirrors the ever-diminishing conditions and resources of the human beings within that room, in fact, mirrors the classical tragic condition, although the play, I feel, falls short of tragedy. In *Othello* too the larger outside orderly world of Venice becomes the more ominous and darkly constricted world of Cyprus, eventually narrowing to a tragic bed, the center of Othello's diseased imagination. A similar narrowing can be felt in *Macbeth,* the play that emerges as an important source of Shakespearean echoes in act 2 of *Chillun.*

The first scene of act 2, two years after the marriage of Jim and Ella, gives us two additional characters of importance, Jim's mother, an old-fashioned *"mild-looking, gray-haired Negress,"* and Jim's sister Hattie, whose *"defiant face"* indicates her militancy and her pride in being black. It also gives us two important props. The first is a colored photograph in a heavy gold frame of Jim's father, *"an elderly Negro"* wearing the kind of *"outlandish"* uniform, adorned with medals and sashes, that reminds us of Brutus Jones who, like Jim's father, also became successful by "white" standards. The other prop, the very opposite of anything white, is *"a Negro primitive mask from the Congo,"* a beautiful work of art, *"conceived in a true religious spirit,"* the wedding gift of Hattie to Jim and Ella. The mask seems to dominate the room because it has a *"diabolical quality,"* in contrast to the other, more mundane furnishings in the room (2:297). O'Neill is rather obviously extending his black-white symbolism, with "black" once again emerging as an indicator of a superior system of values. In the scene's very beginning, we hear a Macbethian echo. Hattie, assuring her mother that she won't "kick up a fuss" about Jim's marriage to Ella, which she deplores, says, "What's done is done," words used by Lady Macbeth to assure Macbeth that their dark deed of murder is behind them (2:297). Later, the same Lady Macbeth will say, "What's done cannot be undone," a more accurate description of the way things are. For Hattie, the marriage of her brother to the white woman whom she knows to be a racist is an accomplished fact. The marriage, as she evaluates it, will be as devastating to her brother as Macbeth's deed is to him. Later, Hattie will attempt to undo the deed by having Jim send Ella to a sanatorium, but she will not succeed. For Jim and Ella, what's done cannot be undone.

Hattie's quotation from *Macbeth,* perhaps too fleeting to be noticed in performance, points ahead to a more sustained echo in scene 2, where we find Jim in the ever-narrowing room, studying for the bar exam. O'Neill describes his state of mind: *"his attention wanders, his eyes have an uneasy, hunted look, he starts at every sound in the house or from the street."* He can't concentrate on his studies, *"slams the book shut,"* opens the window and *"sinks down beside it, his arms on the sill, his head resting wearily on his arms, staring out into the night"* (2:305–6). Jim's weariness, his desperation, the fact that every sound disturbs him, his looking into the night—all touch the condition of Macbeth. We needn't recount the sounds that Macbeth hears after he murders Duncan, but it is interesting to note that the last sound that disturbs Jim Harris was previously heard during the expressionistic wedding scene concluding act 1, when the single stroke of the church bell signaled the forming of the two racial lines, and then another single clang stopped the organ grinder's "Old Black Joe" and awakened Jim *"from a trance."* In *Macbeth* too the sound of a bell profoundly affects Macbeth; it is the signal from Lady Macbeth for Macbeth to do the deed—"I go, and it is done; the bell invites me." (This "done" points ahead to Macbeth's "I have done the deed," and to Lady Macbeth's "What's done is done.") And it is the sound that a sleepwalking Lady Macbeth hears in her nightmarish recreation of the murder: "One—two—why then 'tis time to do't." Perhaps these Shakespearean echoes, connecting Jim's disturbed mind to Macbeth's, seem dim, even after Hattie's previously stated "what's done is done," but the ensuing dialogue between Jim and Hattie about Ella's mental state should leave no doubt that Shakespeare is hovering over O'Neill's play.

When Hattie asks, "What did the doctor tell you, Jim?" Jim answers, "The same old thing. She must have rest, he says, her mind needs rest— *(bitterly)* But he can't tell me any prescription for that rest—leastways any that'd work" (2:306). In Shakespeare's play the doctor tells Macbeth that Lady Macbeth is "troubled with thick-coming fancies, / That keep her from her rest." Like Ella's doctor, Macbeth's doctor cannot "minister to a mind diseased." Both Jim Harris and Macbeth recognize the ineffectuality of doctors; both bitterly must accept and live with the mental agony of their wives. And both protagonists, like their wives, lack sleep, in all of Shakespeare's plays the balm for a troubled mind. Jim's words to Hattie pinpoint his psychic restlessness: "If I can only hold out! It's hard! I'm worn out. I don't sleep. I get to thinking and thinking. My head aches and burns like fire with thinking" (2:307). (Thinking, we recall, drove Yank Smith to his gorilla-death, to his ultimate sleep.) Thinking prevents Jim from "the season of all natures, sleep," to use Lady Macbeth's words—and she should know. Ambition is what drives both Macbeth, who wishes to be king and to stay king, and Jim, who says, "I've got to prove I'm the whitest of the white!" (2:309). Jim tells Hattie that he must prove to Ella that he's "a real man!" Macbeth dares "do all that may become a man," and, in fact, it is Lady Macbeth's attack on his manhood that prompts him to do his bloody deed. But the connection between Ella and Lady Macbeth does not stop there. O'Neill—after presenting the sleepless and disturbed Jim and after Jim's talk with Hattie about Ella's mental sickness—offers us his version of Lady Macbeth's sleepwalking scene. Ella enters the room *"noiselessly,"* wearing

> *a red dressing-gown over her night-dress but is in her bare feet. She has a carving-knife in her right hand. Her eyes fasten on Jim with a murderous mania. She creeps up behind him. Suddenly he senses something and turns. As he sees her he gives a cry, jumping up and catching her wrist. She stands fixed, her eyes growing bewildered and frightened.* (2:310)

Ella tells Jim she was "having a nightmare"; she doesn't know how she got there. "I have such terrible dreams, Jim." And then she reverts to childishness: "I'll be a little girl—and you'll be old Uncle Jim who's been with us for years and years—Will you play that?" (2:310). (The moment points five years ahead to the ending of *Strange Interlude.*) Of course, Jim will "play" to the very end of the play, forever feeling pity for his fragile wife. The image of a mentally disturbed woman, estranged from her world-weary husband, walking a nightmare, must bring into view Lady Macbeth. So too the knife Ella is carrying brings to mind the dagger Lady Macbeth perhaps would have used on Duncan, had he not looked like her father, had she not seen him with "the eye of childhood." It also brings to mind the daggers she does hold when she takes them from her terror-stricken husband immediately after the murder of Duncan. And when Ella in the next scene—still wearing her red dressing-gown, still in her bare feet—talks in soliloquy to the Congo mask, which represents everything she despises, her words clearly point to Lady Macbeth's sleepwalking scene: "Black! Black! Black as dirt! You've poisoned me! I can't wash myself clean!" (2:312). Her soliloquy is Shakespearean in its intense presentation of inner thoughts *and* in its placement at the point of structural necessity. Two mad women seem to be coming together in O'Neill's imagination—one he creates in *Chillun,* one created for him by Shakespeare, both reflecting a dope-filled mother who often seemed to be sleepwalking, childlike, destructive.

In the play's last scene Ella does use the knife—on the Congo mask!

Elated that Jim did not pass the bar exam, which seems to verify her white superiority over her black husband, she plunges the knife into the mask with a sense of triumph, as if she is destroying Jim's *blackness*. Her frenzied action brings out the only moment of anger toward his wife that Jim displays: "You devil! You white devil woman! *(in a terrible roar, raising his fists above her head)* You devil!" Ellen's *"bewildered cry of terror,"* "Jim!" is enough to recall Jim to himself (2:313–14). Ella continues:

> It's all right, Jim! It's dead. The devil's dead. See! It couldn't live—unless you passed. If you'd passed it would have lived in you. Then I'd have had to kill you, Jim, don't you see?—or it would have killed me. But now I've killed it. (2:314)

Ambiguity surrounds Ella's destruction of the devil mask, which is an act of madness, of course, but the mask does have a *"diabolical quality,"* we have been told. Ella herself, momentarily in Jim's eyes, is the devil, which seems to be whatever cannot be understood or explained. Indeed, mystery and madness cling to the climax of the play. Perhaps, as Philip Kolin believes, the supernatural quality of the witches in *Macbeth* puts its distinctive pressure on the play. Kolin relates the Congo mask in *Chillun* and the witches in *Macbeth* to "the tragic operation of fate."[20] I would not take the Macbethian echo that far. I see the mask as closer to the "magic in the web" of Othello's handkerchief, both potent symbols of mystery, representative of the black protagonist, his past, his culture, but not pointing to the strong fatedness we find in tragedy. When Ella, originally fearful of the mask, plunges the knife into the mask, a line from *Macbeth* comes to mind: "tis the eye of childhood / That fears a painted devil." This is Lady Macbeth's line when she tries to arouse the courage of her husband. Ella at this moment is a child fearful of a painted devil, and it is as a child that Jim recognizes her. When she asks, *"like a child,"* "Will God forgive me, Jim?" Jim's answer provides his finest insight: "Maybe He can forgive what you've done to me; and maybe He can forgive what I've done to you; but I don't see how He's going to forgive—Himself" (2:314). But Jim's moment of genuine and justified disappointment is quickly subdued by his great love for Ella, who is now his "little girl," as she thinks back to their childhood of the first scene when they could play together with no awareness of black and white. Jim goes to his knees again—a repetitive stage action that accentuates his "slave" status—and looks up, saying:

> Forgive me, God—and make me worthy! Now I see Your Light again! Now I hear Your Voice! *(He begins to weep in an ecstacy of religious*

> *humility.)* Forgive me, God, for blaspheming You! Let this fire of burning suffering purify me of selfishness and make me worthy of the child You send me for the woman You take away! (2:315)

He ends the play, after the child Ella tells him to "Come and play!" with these words: "Honey, Honey, I'll play right up to the gates of Heaven with you! *(She tugs at one of his hands, laughingly trying to pull him up from his knees as The Curtain Falls.)*"

I find this to be a troublesome ending, one that considerably diminishes the stature of Jim, and makes him seem small when compared to Othello and Macbeth. Granted, few modern characters can come too close to the remarkable creations of Shakespeare, and one could say that Jim, like Othello, loves "not wisely but too well," that his powerful, self-sacrificing love for Ella, like the love of Othello for Desdemona, heightens him. But there is no largeness to Jim Harris in his last moments. Jim's "slave" status (he is kneeling again) and his empty words asking forgiveness of the God he previously blasphemed place him in a nontragic position. In this play about race relations, Jim seems to be *accepting* the racism of his wife and the comforting illusions associated with Christianity. Jim seemed so clear-sighted when he spoke of God having difficulty in forgiving Himself, seemed so right in his fine mocking speech when he learned he did not pass the bar exam:

> Pass? Me? Jim Crow Harris? Nigger Jim Harris—become a full fledged Member of the Bar! Why the mere notion of it is enough to kill you with laughing! It'd be against all natural laws, all human right and justice. It'd be miraculous, there'd be earthquakes and catastrophes, the seven Plagues'd come again and locusts'd devour all the money in the banks, the second Flood'd come roaring and Noah'd fall overboard, the sun'd drop out of the sky like a ripe fig, and the Devil'd perform miracles, and God'd be tipped head first right out of the Judgment seat! (2:313)

His self-sacrificing resignation at play's end seems the empty gesture of a man almost as neurotic as his child-wife. This would be true, I believe, even without the Othello-Macbeth analogues, but Shakespeare's tragedies, even as they enrich specific moments in *Chillun,* work against the acceptance of the play as tragedy. *Chillun* is a fine play about race relations, much ahead of its time; it portrays two vulnerable people caught up in the problem of black versus white; it contains some stunning theatrical moments, especially the expressionistic church scene and the scene in which

Ella kills the Congo mask (both emphasizing the black-white idea). The play forces us to say with Othello, "The pity of it." But the intensity and terror and universality of tragedy escape it, I believe, a view not held by T. S. Eliot, who wrote that O'Neill in *Chillun* is "more successful than the author of *Othello*, in implying something more universal than the problem of race—in implying, in fact, the universal problem of differences which create a mixture of admiration, love, and contempt, with the consequent tension."[21] Unavoidably, Shakespeare's play about a black man comes to mind when discussing *Chillun*, as it comes to mind when discussing *Jones* and to a lesser extent *Ape*. (That Paul Robeson played Othello and Jim Harris and Brutus Jones and Yank Smith provides an interesting passing comment on the relationship of these characters.) Shakespeare's *Othello*, I have attempted to demonstrate, has a clearer and more important relationship to *Jones* than to *Chillun*, even though the later play mirrors the marital situation in *Othello* more closely. *Chillun*, on the other hand, comes closer to Shakespeare's *Macbeth* when we concentrate on the psychological states of Jim and Ella, their agony in act 2. It is *All God's Chillun Got Wings*, the play about people of a family in conflict, not *The Emperor Jones* or *The Hairy Ape*, plays about the journeys of single men, that seems to touch O'Neill's deepest personal interest, if we can judge from the plays he will go on to write. People in conflict, usually within a family, usually with the man in tragedy merging himself with a woman, is also Shakespeare's deepest interest.[22]

Chapter 3

The Family

Desire Under the Elms, written and performed in 1924, is a breakthrough play in O'Neill's development, resembling neither the realistic-expressionistic plays that came before it nor the experimental plays that succeed it. It came to O'Neill in a dream, he stated, and although one can look back to his own earlier farm play, *Beyond the Horizon,* and to his one-acter, *The Rope,* to find some suggestions of what is to come, although one can go to the bookish O'Neill to discover the Greek-drama underpinning, although one may even want to insist that he was more than a little influenced by Sidney Howard's *They Knew What They Wanted,*[1] and, most important, although every one of O'Neill's plays is part of the pattern of his whole development (so that, as with Shakespeare, to fully appreciate any one play we should know all the plays), still the fact remains that O'Neill said he dreamed the play. This idea must be stressed because in *Elms* for the first time we feel strongly the subjective impulse that will be a touchstone of O'Neill's finest work. What he dreamed was a play about a family, his family, and the dream came at an important time in his life. (The only other play he dreamed was his comedy *Ah, Wilderness!,* about a family that he *wished* he had.) O'Neill's father had died in 1920, his mother in 1922, his brother in 1923, and the play he dreamed in 1924 worked out some of his deepest feelings about the family now gone, especially about his mother. One need not be too committed a Freudian to assert with assurance that in *Elms* O'Neill dramatizes his Oedipal feelings. This is a convenient place to confront O'Neill's denial of Freudian influence on his work. O'Neill was correct, of course, in insisting that the best dramatists are "intuitively keen analytical psychologists";[2] this is what Freud himself asserted, and, in fact, he put this belief into practice by going to Sophocles' great play and to *Hamlet* to illustrate his Oedipus complex. Freud's insights were there before Freud, of course, but in formulating them, especially in formulating his Oedipus complex as a rudimentary obsession in human nature, Freud met and continues to meet resistance. We seem to wish to deny the Oedipus complex in ourselves but are usually not altogether unwilling to describe Oedipus or Hamlet by using Freud's insights. What I find interesting about O'Neill is that he was willing to admit his own Oedipus complex. After some sessions with the psychiatrist Gilbert V. Hamilton, O'Neill was told he had an Oedipus complex, and that this complex caused not only feelings of guilt but also O'Neill's excessive drinking. According to O'Neill's friend, Jimmy Light, as recorded by Louis Sheaffer, "Gene kidded about it when he told me that after much probing and questioning, Hamilton found he had this complex. 'Why, all he had to do,' Gene said, 'was read my plays.'"[3] He could admit to a close friend, kiddingly perhaps, that the complex was found in his work, but later on he was clearly unwilling to admit Freudian influence on his creativity. "To me," O'Neill insisted, "Freud only means uncertain conjectures and explanations about truths of the emotional past of mankind that every dramatist has clearly sensed ever since real drama began.... I respect Freud's work tremendously but I'm not an addict!" And he adds, as I return to *Elms,* "Whatever of Freudianism is in *Desire* must have walked in 'through my unconscious.'"[4] Well, whether consciously or unconsciously, Freud—and certainly the Oedipus complex—walked in. Biographers and most commentators on O'Neill's work have offered detailed comments on this important idea, and I will touch some of the main aspects of the idea in the following discussion, but at the outset and in connection with the thesis of this book I wish to make the observation that the play in Shakespeare's canon that is the breakthrough play for Shakespeare, which deals with family, which dramatizes Oedipal feelings, is *Hamlet,* the play one feels Shakespeare had to write, the play written right after the death of Shakespeare's father, when Shakespeare was probably the age of O'Neill when he wrote *Elms,* thirty-six—an age when, according to Ernest Jones, "a highly significant change ... took place in Shakespeare's personality."[5] *Hamlet,* I will demonstrate, allows us to see *Elms* more clearly. Shakespeare's ghost play informs O'Neill's ghost play, perhaps no surprise because Shakespeare and O'Neill—and, for that matter, Freud—possess a tragic sense of human destiny and recognize the pain that arises from powerful instinctive desires operating within family situations. In addition, I believe a close examination of *Elms* will reveal that Shakespeare helped O'Neill discover or strengthen some of his dramaturgical techniques.

Although used freely, the source that is unequivocal and clearest must be acknowledged first—Euripides' *Hippolytus.* The story of Hippolytus and Phaedra and Theseus offers the strongest literary underpinning to *Elms,* although the Oedipus legend gives the play—and probably Euripides' story too—its rich psychological coloration. O'Neill may have dreamed the plot ingredients of *Elms,* but it is a story he had already confronted in his waking hours, one that became readily available to him when his psyche was searching for a container for his deepest thoughts. The Hippolytus story has the haunting resonances of an archetypal event in man's life. A young man spurns the passionate advances of his stepmother, Phaedra, who takes revenge by accusing him of having attempted to dishonor her. The young man's father, Theseus, curses his son, who is killed when a bull emerges from the sea to frighten the horses of his chariot. The archetypal story has its parallels in the account of Bellerophon in *The Iliad* and in the biblical story of Potiphar's wife. Of course, the Oedipal myth lurks in the background, this time in reverse, with a mother loving a son. The incest motif and the forbidden fruit idea and the attractions of sin and sexuality are built into a tale possessing high dramatic potential. In *Elms* O'Neill follows the mythic account, but with significant variations. O'Neill's father, Ephraim Cabot, brings a new wife, Abbie Putnam, home to his New England farm. She, Phaedra-like, is attracted to her stepson Eben and makes advances toward him. Eben, like Hippolytus, spurns Abbie at first, but eventually, unlike Hippolytus, succumbs to her desire and his. In their sexual union the Oedipal echoes strongly resonate. Eben's love for Abbie is bound up with his love for his mother, who plays an important part in O'Neill's story, perhaps *the* important part, although she never appears on stage. She was the second wife of Ephraim; his first wife was the mother of Simeon and Peter. Ephraim, like Theseus, is a possessor of many women, but his is not a Theseus-like philandering nature. On the contrary, Ephraim embodies a New England Puritan tradition that is biblical and oppressive; he is the stern apostle of a hard, demanding God. Theseus's curse on Hippolytus in the mythic story becomes Eben's curse on his and Abbie's son in O'Neill's story, with the instrument of death not a bull from the sea but Abbie herself. O'Neill's play ends with Ephraim, like Theseus, alone, and with Abbie and Eben leaving the stage together, hand in hand, on the way to their deaths as murderers of the infant.

O'Neill successfully manages to place the Hippolytus story in an American historical context, New England in 1850. The changes he brings to the traditional story point to his own need to dramatize his family situation—son against father, son loving mother—and in doing so he presents a play of largeness and depth. What seems most Greek about O'Neill's treatment are not the elements of the traditional story but his emphasis on determinism, not the determinism associated with Greek gods, of course, but a Freudian determinism that is older than the Greek gods. Necessity hangs over the play like the elms of O'Neill's opening description; in fact, the elms point directly to the play's determinism.

> Two enormous elms are on each side of the house. They bend their trailing branches down over the roof. They appear to protect and at the same time subdue. There is a sinister maternity in their aspect, a crushing, jealous absorption. They have developed from their intimate contact with the life of man in the house an appalling humaneness. They brood oppressively over the house. They are like exhausted women resting their sagging breasts and hands and hair on its roof, and when it rains their tears trickle down monotonously and rot on the shingles. (2:318)

Whatever happens in the play seems to be controlled by the "sinister maternity" represented by the elms. Mother, in all the forms of that powerful idea, must be acknowledged in order to understand the play's movement and meaning. Mother is the female principle, Mother is the demands of the past, Mother is avenging spirit, Mother is lover. In human form, Mother is Ephraim's second wife, soft, good-natured, worked to death by Ephraim, and Abbie, who takes Eben's mother's place in the home and in his affections, and Min, the prostitute shared by father and son. In animal form, Mother is the cows that Ephraim must visit when he needs warmth. In the form of nature, Mother is the elms, darkly rooted, maternally protective and oppressive, creating shadows and hidden corners, informing the play's action.

The ghost of Eben's mother haunts the play, as important an agent of retribution as Hamlet's ghostly father. The son in each play is heeding the command, "Remember me!" the words spoken in *Hamlet* and implied in *Elms*. Each son seems always to be remembering the dead parent, with memory prompting revenge and feelings of guilt in Hamlet.

> This is most brave,
> That I, the son of a dear father murthered,
> Prompted to my revenge by heaven and hell,
> Must like a whore unpack my heart and words,
> And fall a-cursing like a very drab,
> A stallion. Fie upon't, foh!
>
> (2.2.582–87)

In Eben memory prompts the feeling that he didn't appreciate his mother when she was alive, but that now he will act in her behalf:

It was on'y arter she died I come to think o' it. Me cookin'—doin' her work—that made me know her, suffer her sufferin'—she'd come back t' help . . . come back t' bake biscuits—come back all cramped up t' shake the fire, an' carry ashes, her eyes weepin' an' bloody with smoke an' cinders same's they used t' be. She still comes back—stands by the stove thar in the evenin'—she can't find it nateral sleepin' an' restin' in peace. She can't git used t' bein' free—even in her grave. (2:324)

The son's actions are triggered by revenge for the dead parent, with both sons born to set things right. Hamlet believes he must attempt to cleanse the world, for "the time is out of joint." Eben's world is smaller, a family farm that he believes was taken from his mother. The enemy in both plays is a father—the stepfather-uncle Claudius in *Hamlet,* the natural father Ephraim in *Elms.* And the son's attachment to the mother controls his actions and emotionally colors each play. That is, in *Hamlet* and *Elms* the two important themes are revenge and woman, with family relationships, connecting both themes, of the utmost importance. Each son is acting in a play that a dead parent wrote, but, significantly, each son does not play the part to the full extent because the idea of revenge, the motivating trigger to the action, becomes in the course of each play less important than another large idea: in *Elms* love, in *Hamlet* determinism. The difference between these ideas tells us much about the difference between our protagonists: one, a young man filled with desires of all kinds, who instinctively grasps for life's meaning and finds it in the love of and for his stepmother; the other, a young man who is an intellectual, who is able to place his feelings within a larger frame of reference, who thinks about large philosophical matters like divinities that shape our ends. For Eben, as for Yank Smith, "Tinkin' is hard"; for Hamlet it is his life's blood. But the bond between Eben and Hamlet—so strong a connection in this as in other respects that I believe *Hamlet* underpins *Elms* more strongly than does Euripides' *Hippolytus*—is that each is a son haunted by the ghost of a parent, and each must confront a mother.

Hamlet, from the moment we first see him, is filled with father and mother, not only the father who is now dead but the father who now occupies the throne and shares his mother's bed. Even before he learns of his father's murder Hamlet is sick at heart—because his father is dead and, perhaps more important, because mother seems not to be troubled by that devastating fact. Hamlet has returned from school in Wittenberg to find his mother with that other man, his father's brother but no more like his father, Hamlet insists, than a satyr to Hyperion. In his first soliloquy, perhaps the most important soliloquy in the play because it reveals Hamlet's tortured mind *before* he is given his heavy task of revenge, he is puzzled by and disappointed with his mother's behavior. He recalls his parents' past togetherness. His father was "so loving to my mother / That he might not beteem the winds of heaven / Visit her face too roughly." His mother would "hang" on his father "As if increase of appetite had grown / By what it fed on" (1.2.140–45). There is a profound difference, without Hamlet being consciously aware of it, in the kind of detail Hamlet chooses to describe his parents' loving relationship. His father's behavior toward his mother seems naturally affectionate and warm and pleasant and caring; the words used to describe his mother's behavior are clearly sexual, revealing a woman who seems to need a man, perhaps any man. Hamlet ends his soliloquy with these words of sexual disgust:

Within a month,
Ere yet the salt of most unrighteous tears
Had left the flushing in her galled eyes,
She married—O most wicked speed: to post
With such dexterity to incestuous sheets.

(1.2.153–57)

Eben Cabot does not have the ability to verbalize his agony in such potent terms. Whatever sexual disgust he feels, and it is not great, is attached to Ephraim's roaming the country for a bride at his old age. Eben's deep love for his dead mother prods the hatred he feels for the husband who abused her. His love for mother also blends into his desire for his father's new wife, who allows him to act out the Oedipal triangle. His attitude toward both parents is presented in a straightforward manner to his stepbrothers early in the play: "I hain't his'n—I hain't like him—he hain't me!... I'm Maw—every drop o' blood!" (2:322). Eben possesses some fine inner qualities, a sensitivity that cannot be revealed effectively in words but that the audience immediately perceives. The play opens with Eben looking at the sunset, saying "God! Purty!" O'Neill, in his stage directions, says Eben looks at the sky with *"puzzled awe."* Eben is tapping into something large, but he has no effective way to express his feelings. Something larger than himself seems to be driving him throughout the play: at first, the ghost of his mother drives him toward revenge, but increasingly important is a more mysterious force, call it nature, that drives him toward Abbie. Abbie knows it will happen.

Ye been fightin' yer nature ever since the day I come—tryin' t' tell yerself I hain't purty t' ye. *(She laughs a low humid laugh without taking her eyes from his. A pause—her body squirms desirously—she murmurs languorously)* Hain't the sun strong an' hot? Ye kin feel it burnin' into the earth—Nature—makin' thin's grow—bigger 'n' bigger—burnin' inside ye—makin' ye want t' grow—into somethin' else—till ye're jined with it—an' it's your'n—but it owns ye, too—an' makes ye grow bigger—like a tree—like them elums—*(She laughs again softly, holding his eyes. He takes a step toward her, compelled against his will.)* Nature'll beat ye, Eben. Ye might's well own up t' it fust 's last. (2:341–42)

This nature, this desire, this passion, is working along with what he believes to be his mother's ghostly wish: revenge on Ephraim. Eben fulfills this combination of desires in mother's parlor in the play's most sensational scene, climactic in every sense of the word.

In the course of *Elms* Eben and Abbie move from desire to love. Eben desires the farm (his mother's farm, as he sees it) and the land and, of course, revenge against a father who abused his mother. Abbie's desire is for a home, the only reason she, thirty-five years old, married the seventy-five-year-old Ephraim Cabot. These desires of both the younger protagonists—Eben is twenty-five—are darkly tied to sexual desire, a desire each has for the other, satisfied in the parlor scene (part 2, scene 3). The parlor is Eben's mother's room, the room where she was laid out when she died, never occupied since her death. O'Neill gives the room a supernatural significance. Abbie, whose desire for the house *includes* that room, the only room she has not possessed as yet, summons Eben to court her there. When she enters the room, she is frightened. She tells Eben: "When I fust come in—in the dark—they seemed somethin' here." Eben instinctively says, "Maw." Abbie continues: "I kin still feel—somethin'." Eben again says, "It's Maw" (2:353). This word "somethin'" has been sounded before by O'Neill; it's one of those vague words that can take on meaning and force only from the dramatic context. In the play's second scene Simeon, responding to Eben's charge that Ephraim killed his mother, makes this statement: "No one never kills nobody. It's allus somethin'. That's the murderer." And a few lines later, Simeon again: "It's somethin'—drivin' him—t' drive us!" Vengefully, Eben shouts out, "Waal—I hold him t' jedgment! . . . Somethin'! What's somethin'?" (2:322–23). The "somethin'" becomes a mysterious force behind the actions and thoughts of the characters. That "somethin'" is what Abbie feels in the parlor, and Eben feels it too. In the parlor scene it clearly is connected with Mother, whose presence almost becomes tangible, hovering over the lovers, as the elms hover over the play. In fact, Mother becomes Abbie before the scene is over, or, to put it another way, Abbie becomes the mother to the child Eben—pointing ahead in O'Neill's development to the eternal Mother played by Josie Hogan in *A Moon for the Misbegotten,* forever protecting her child, pointing ahead in *Elms* to the tragic irony of Abbie as Mother killing her own infant. When Eben says Maw was murdered by the hardness of Ephraim, he begins to sob.

> *Abbie. (both her arms around him—with wild passion)* I'll sing fur ye! I'll die fur ye! *(In spite of her overwhelming desire for him, there is a sincere maternal love in her manner and voice—a horribly frank mixture of lust and mother love.)* Don't cry, Eben! I'll take yer Maw's place! I'll be everythin' she was t' ye! Let me kiss ye, Eben! *(She pulls his head around. He makes a bewildered pretense of resistance. She is tender.)* Don't be afeered! I'll kiss ye pure, Eben—same 's if I was a Maw t' ye—an' ye kin kiss me back 's if yew was my son—my boy—sayin' goodnight t' me! Kiss me, Eben. (2:354)

The restrained kiss of mother and son leads to the passionate kisses of lovers. Abbie declares her genuine love for Eben; Eben believes that what is now happening is his mother's "vengeance on him [Ephraim]—so's she kin rest quiet in her grave!" Abbie: "Vengeance o' God on the hull o' us! What d'we give a durn? I love ye, Eben! God knows I love ye!" And the scene's curtain falls on Eben's "I love ye!" as the lovers' lips *"meet in a fierce, bruising kiss"* (2:355).

The parlor scene is filled with changing and complex emotions—desires that are lustful, natural, Oedipal, revengeful—displayed within a ghostly atmosphere. The next scene finds the previously closed parlor shutters flung back; the sun and air will now enter that room of death which has become a room of love. "Maw's gone back t' her grave. She kin sleep now," says Eben, believing that the act of vengeance was the very act of sleeping with his father's new wife (2:356). But the play continues, the plot thickens, and Maw seems not to have gone back to her grave. In fact, it is Ephraim who strongly feels her presence when he says, in part 3, scene 1, "Even the music can't drive it out—somethin'. Ye kin feel it droppin' off the elums, climbin' up the roof, sneakin' down the chimney, pokin' in the corners! They's no peace in houses, they's no rest livin' with folks. Somethin's always livin' with ye" (2:363). Somethin' again, it's always somethin'. Whatever that "somethin'" is—and it's obvious that O'Neill is calculatingly touching mystery when he uses the word—one aspect of it is Mother's presence, her ghost, her "sinister maternity." Mother seems to be controlling the play's crucial scenes; she is the "somethin'" that must be reckoned with. Her role in *Elms* is similar to the role of the Ghost in *Hamlet*.

My belief that Shakespeare's Ghost is lurking in the corners of O'Neill's imagination when he is writing *Elms* cannot be firmly substantiated, but it is worth noting, at the least, that *Hamlet* begins with the question, "Who's there?" that when Horatio appears on the scene, he asks, "What, has this *thing* appeared again to-night?" that Bernardo, after the Ghost leaves, asks the previously skeptical Horatio, "How now, Horatio, you tremble and look pale. Is not this *something* more than fantasy?" (1.1.53–54; emphasis added). The Ghost, like Eben's Mother, hovers over the play and triggers the action and prods a son to become an avenger; the Ghost, like Eben's Mother, will not be able to rest until the revenge is negotiated. And the revenge idea in *Hamlet,* as in *Elms,* will be absorbed by and connected with other, perhaps more potent, ideas and emotions that will lead to the death of the son. In both plays a son enters a mother's room in which a ghost seems present and comes to terms with Mother in that scene; in each play that scene is climactic.

In the closet scene in *Hamlet*—I almost said parlor scene—Hamlet is able to purge himself by expressing those thoughts that he had to keep *within* up to that point: "But break, my heart, for I must hold my tongue." The sexual disgust he felt in his first soliloquy—in his mind's eye watching his mother and Claudius rushing to those "incestuous sheets"—here comes vomiting forth, as he chastizes his mother for her lustful behavior: "Nay, but to live / In the rank sweat of an enseamed bed, / Stew'd in corruption, honeying and making love / Over the nasty sty!" (3.4.91–94). Hamlet seems so obsessed with his mother's sexuality that we cannot avoid going to Freud to explain his actions and words, nor should there have been such a negative critical clamor when Laurence Olivier's film, concentrating on the individual psyche within a family situation, emphasized the Oedipal attraction of Hamlet to Gertrude, always in low-cut gowns, with the closet scene a veritable love scene between son and mother. It is precisely the Oedipal emphasis that allows me to connect O'Neill's parlor scene in *Elms* to Shakespeare's bedroom scene in *Hamlet*. (I parenthetically note that O'Neill did not like the Olivier film. Did he find it too Oedipal?) Eben is a Hamlet who can, in fact, have his mother because Abbie isn't his mother, although, at the same time—through O'Neill's clever manipulation of ideas and emotions—she is. Hamlet, less fortunate, can only see his mother with that other man, the new father, and what he sees both disgusts him and fascinates him. Telling his mother what *not* to do, he dwells on the image of their togetherness.

Let the bloat king tempt you again to bed,
Pinch wanton on your cheek, call you his mouse,

> And let him, for a pair of reechy kisses,
> Or paddling in your neck with his damn'd fingers,
> Make you to ravel all this matter out,
> That I essentially am not in madness,
> But mad in craft.
>
> (3.4.182–88)

Eben can have his father's wife, thereby acting out the Oedipal wish *and* exacting his revenge by means of that very sexual act. Hamlet seems not to be able to kill the man who has taken his father's place (and his place) in mother's bed, although he does passionately kill Polonius, believing him to be Claudius, for who else would be in mother's bedroom? Well, someone else *is* there, and for the only time in the play the Family is together—Mother, Father, Son—but mother can't see father. Whether or not the Ghost is a figment of Hamlet's imagination in this scene—just as whether or not the ghost of Eben's mother is present in the parlor—the atmosphere in a mother's room (closet or parlor) is charged with dark sexual undercurrents, forces behind, the supernatural, "somethin'." And in each scene a son feels more free because of his encounter with mother in her room. After the closet scene, Hamlet runs around Elsinore, playing hide-and-seek with a dead body, using wild words, playing mad and perhaps touching madness. Eben, after the parlor scene, *"seems changed,"* according to O'Neill's stage directions. *"His face wears a bold and confident expression, he is grinning to himself with evident satisfaction"* (2:355).

I believe that the appearance of Mother's ghost in *Elms,* the possibility that she is the "Force behind" or has a strong relationship to that force, marks an important development in O'Neill's dramatic art. For the first time O'Neill is tapping his subjective resources, his own psyche, in a creative way. Using classical underpinnings, he is writing out his own story in a tale of greed and desire set on a farm in New England in 1850. We observed that he had already written his family into previous plays, but with *Elms*—now that all members of his family are dead—he seems more able to effectively dramatize those powerful interior "family" feelings that will be tapped again and again in his best plays to come. Discussing Shakespeare, C. L. Barber makes the important point that when the Ghost of Hamlet appears on the Elizabethan stage we have in Shakespeare's development "a new kind of dramatization of the hero—in relation to the hero's need and the need Shakespeare brings to his art."[6] A fine insight. Barber, like Ernest Jones before him, sees Hamlet as a turning point in Shakespeare's development; for both Barber and Jones, Shakespeare's tragic period begins with *Hamlet.* I am suggesting that *Elms* marks a comparable turning point in O'Neill's development. O'Neill is also bringing a need to his art, and that need, that powerful subjective impulse that remarkably comes through in objective drama, is the hallmark of his art. O'Neill's plays, like Shakespeare's, met personal needs in the man who wrote the plays, perhaps a truism for all great writers, but a fact more strongly felt in O'Neill, and strongly felt in Shakespeare once we attempt to see him through his work, to find the man who suffered to create, something that does not seem necessary to do with Shakespeare because he is so supreme an objective artist. With O'Neill it is more necessary to do because his art is closer to his neurosis and because he is more intrusive, offering full stage directions, reading over our shoulders, so to speak, or sitting next to us in the theater. O'Neill in *Elms,* like Shakespeare in *Hamlet,* is offering a new kind of tragic experience in his art; in both plays the investment of the dramatist in the family situation is intense, plumbing deep feelings in the playwrights themselves, producing powerful emotions in the audience. Contributing to these emotions in our reception of O'Neill's play, I wish to suggest, is Shakespeare's play—ghosts prodding ghosts.

That Eben Cabot is O'Neill's self-portrait seems clear from the first description of Eben—"*tall and sinewy,*" "*good-looking,*" his expression "*resentful and defensive,*" and especially the "*defiant dark eyes,*" the last almost a direct pointer (2:319). (Most people who met O'Neill personally seem compelled to mention those dark eyes.) Eben, like O'Neill, is the "spittin' image" of both his father and mother; he is both stubborn and sensitive. He hates his father, greedy for land (as James O'Neill was greedy for real estate); he loves his mother, who was abused by the father. And Eben possesses, as I've already indicated, O'Neill's Oedipus complex, with O'Neill dreaming the play that allows his alter ego to engage sexually his father's wife. Even the murder of the infant in the play replays the death of Edmund O'Neill, the dead child whose name Eugene takes in the most directly autobiographical of his plays, *Long Day's Journey Into Night.*

In the scheme just presented, Ephraim Cabot is James O'Neill, the father-rival, tyrannical, greedy, parsimonious, abuser of those closest to him, yet finally perhaps a sympathetic character, someone to be forgiven (as James O'Neill is forgiven in *Long Day's Journey).* But there is more to O'Neill's portrayal of Ephraim Cabot, and I take my cue from O'Neill himself, who said, "I always have loved Ephraim so much! He's so autobiographical!" Louis Sheaffer correctly sees Ephraim as another O'Neill self-portrait—for O'Neill too scorned whatever was "easy" ("one of the most damning words in O'Neill's lexicon"), and O'Neill too was "a difficult, demanding husband and an inadequate father," and O'Neill also "suffered from an abiding sense of isolation, of being misunderstood by those closest to him."[7] Ephraim Cabot is the most complex character in *Elms* and the most interesting. Surely, part of this complexity comes from O'Neill's ambivalence toward him, with O'Neill the dramatist presenting himself as *both* father and son, both legitimate lover of mother and forbidden lover of mother, as both prideful Puritan—as stony as the God he represents—and lonely, vulnerable parent and husband. Ephraim Cabot has considerable height and is the most memorable character in the play, perhaps in all of O'Neill. To give us Eben Cabot, O'Neill went to Hamlet, as I have attempted to demonstrate; to give us Ephraim Cabot, O'Neill went to *King Lear*.

I'm not the first to discuss the Ephraim Cabot–King Lear relationship. Emil Roy sees many connections between *Elms* and *King Lear,* and he has pinpointed these in a tight six-page article.[8] Although I do not completely accept his argument—he strains too hard, I believe, to make an Abbie-Cordelia connection and an Eben-Lear connection—I find that he is convincingly insightful in his appreciation of the similar qualities in Ephraim and Lear ("stubborn dignity, unimpeachable egoism and lonely desperation") and of their similar situations (victims of filial ingratitude, rejected by children, forced to speak to themselves or to the elements, reliance on gods). I wish to expand some of these Ephraim-Lear connections, and in doing so I shall place the emphasis where I believe it belongs: both *Elms* and *King Lear* are essentially dramatizations of the relationship between parents and children. *King Lear,* like *Hamlet* and *Hippolytus,* is a literary source for *Elms,* but it, like those two plays, is also part of O'Neill's "unconscious biography."[9] And it is also part of O'Neill's conscious biography, because O'Neill's Ephraim Cabot already allows us to "hear" the favorite quotation of James O'Neill, coming from *King Lear,* that James Tyrone proclaims to his son Jamie in *Long Day's Journey:* "How sharper than a serpent's tooth it is / To have a thankless child!" (1.4.288–89). This is not an unusual feeling for a father, although few fathers can capture the emotion in such effective words. It is precisely because such an attitude is commonplace, pointing to *family situations* not significantly altered by time or place, that *King Lear* and *Long Day's Journey* and *Hamlet* and *Elms* seem so representative, touching the experiences of all of us. Of course, the specific trappings of tragic drama—violence, murder, adultery, incest—belong to unique families only, those special "houses" from Greek tragedy through Elizabethan-Jacobean tragedy to (and to a lesser extent) modern tragedy, but basically we are witnessing what happens in broken families, incomplete families—where are all the missing mothers and fathers in Shakespeare? why do the missing parents in O'Neill exert such influence?—families that are recognizable and representative. On the most important and concrete level,

Lear, king though he is, is a father; part of his problem is that he confuses his position of king (with its godlike overtones) with that of father. Basically, Ephraim Cabot is a father; part of his problem—and much of his height—is that he confuses his patriarchy with that of a stony God. Both men must learn to "see better," Kent's warning to Lear. Ephraim Cabot, as O'Neill's stage directions tell us, has eyes that are *extremely near-sighted, blinking continually in the effort to focus on objects, their stare having a straining, ingrowing quality* (2:335).

Both King Lear ("fourscore and upward") and Ephraim Cabot are old men (Cabot's seventy-five years is close to the age of James O'Neill when he died), but both are remarkably vigorous and active. Both are physically robust men who seem gigantic—one, able to endure a terrible storm, both outside and inside; the other, able to whip a son fifty years younger, able to outdance and outjump and outhoot any of the play's meanspirited younger country folk in one of the play's finest scenes, the celebration of the birth of "his" son (actually his grandson, Eben's child). Both men come to symbolize the Nature they are part of—Lear *is* storm and rain, *is* weeds and flowers; Ephraim *is* stone, *is* the land, *is* the God he follows. In both plays the concept *nature* is significant, widening the plays' horizons, with the word itself, and all variations of the word, punctuating the plays' physical and emotional atmospheres. Both old men endure beyond the time they should—King Lear finally dying, Ephraim ready to confront again his immense loneliness, "*his shoulders squared, his face stony,*" as he "*stalks grimly toward the barn*" (2:377).

In *King Lear* what we witness in the play's middle, after Lear's earlier gross mistakes in judgment regarding members of his family, is a Lear who roams on a heath with no boundary, a dark territory, so dark that it seems both a terranean reality and a subterranean reality, a landscape of the demonic. In fact, this landscape is *all* boundary, where Lear is living at life's edge, forced to look at himself and at the world as he never did before, forced to ask the big questions about man's condition. Life at the edge is terrible for Lear, as it is for all tragic figures, and it is richly complex. His experience on the boundary brings out the best and the worst in this old man—his newly acquired selflessness, his new awareness of man's needs, his understanding of true love, but also his fierce anger and rage, his gross denial of love and justice, his sexual nausea (so repellent that it exceeds Hamlet's and forces us to believe it belongs to Shakespeare himself). In short, the experience of Lear on the heath is passionate and inclusive—positive and negative, mad and sane, full. Because his experience is full, the kind of fullness that can only come from such a genius as Shakespeare, it is no revelation to suggest that part of that experience touches the experience of Ephraim Cabot in O'Neill's play. Ephraim is a giant of a man, like Lear, but a more limited man, perhaps closer to that other father, Gloucester, who also touches Lear's experience but does not have Lear's large capacity to feel strongly and express powerfully all that happens to him. What I wish to stress here, because it points clearly and directly to Ephraim Cabot, is Lear's need for the maternal.[10]

Lear's fatherhood in many and important ways defines him, and his paternal mistakes lead to the agony of his family (just as Gloucester's mistakes as father lead to his family's problems). But Shakespeare seems to insist throughout—again, the emphasis is on family—that Lear is also a child. We hear from Goneril that "Old fools are babes again." The more gentle Cordelia, returning from France, says that the mad old man is "child-changed." (How limiting are the glosses on this rich phrase in most editions of Shakespeare's plays, insisting that Lear is changed *by* his children, when he is both changed *by* them and changed *to* a child.) In the play's beginning, we hear Lear, the autocratic king and father, giving orders, demanding love and loyalty from his children. We hear a different note when, after disowning Cordelia, he says that in his "unburthen'd"(!) crawling toward death he would like to have been nursed by his favorite daughter Cordelia. ("I loved her most, and thought to set my rest / On her kind nursery.") If I were to use O'Neillian terms (and here, perhaps, O'Neill allows us to see Shakespeare more clearly just as throughout I'm suggesting that Shakespeare allows us to see O'Neill more clearly), I'd say that Lear, "a little in love with death," wished to crawl toward the warmth of a woman, an earth mother, death. (Lear says, "So be my grave my peace.") The Fool, in his characteristically handy-dandy way, mocks Lear by saying Lear made his daughters his mothers, thereby touching a truth that transcends the mockery. And, of course, the mad Lear seems very close indeed to that infant he describes to the blind Gloucester in their excruciating meeting when he says, "we came crying hither. / Thou know'st, the first time that we smell the air / We wawl and cry" (4.6.178–80). But the scene that most powerfully demonstrates the need of Lear, that infant-father, for a mother comes after his deep sleep, after new garments are put on him (clothing a naked babe for the first time?), while the music is playing, during a scene that is nothing short of a rebirth, as he awakens to see "this lady" who is "his child, Cordelia," the daughter who becomes at this precious moment the mother to a dependent child, caring for him, soothing him, nursing him to recognition. A remarkably affirmative scene (act 4, scene 7) in a play that touches despair, because here we forget about the abuses of fatherhood, the ingratitude of children, the family as a broken vessel, shattered, unrestorable; here we have the warm togetherness of mother/daughter and infant/father. If only the play ended here! But it doesn't. At play's end, we witness with pain and wonder the agony of the father Lear with the dead child Cordelia in his arms, and we are forced to think of the Pietà with the roles reversed (handy-dandy?), with the son holding the mother, because we recall the reconciliation scene where father was child and child was mother. In the play's beginning, Lear the father made great demands on his children; in the end, Lear the father loses all—the three daughters dead *on stage,* with Lear paying attention to one only, the important one, the one whose voice was ever soft, in fact, the one who said "Nothing." Lear loses all after realizing his own basic need, the need of a child for a parent, and now recognizing that need in his own child, now fully appreciating the love of the daughter-mother now lost. That love, with its core in family relationship, is the most potent positive reality in a play that borders on sheer darkness.

Ephraim Cabot throughout O'Neill's play possesses the harsh paternalism of the King Lear who begins Shakespeare's play. He is a hard and difficult father whose sons detest him. Two run away from him and his farm; one remains to exact revenge. Ephraim is the archetypal (and typically O'Neill) father against whom a son must revolt, and who, of course, is the son's rival in the Oedipal triangle. Nor is Ephraim better as a husband, having worked to death two wives. As autocratic as Lear, although no king, Ephraim sees himself as the only true follower of a hard God; in fact, he seems to be that very God, stony and lonely. Although Abbie and Eben—in their desires, in their love, in Eben's need for revenge—move the play along, the dominant figure is Ephraim, the stone around whom the play flows, the old man who boastfully upholds a Puritan tradition that represses life, who has piled up the stones around the farm and around himself, who asserts with utter conviction that "God's hard, not easy! God's in the stones!" (2:349). In his hardness he acquires mythic proportions. Just as that terrible old man Lear seems to become part of the nature he addresses throughout the storm scenes, so too Ephraim Cabot becomes the stones, the farm, the God he reveres. (Whereas Eben, looking up to the sky and admiring the sunset, seems very small within that large context, Ephraim seems to encompass all the land and landscape.) Yet, like Lear, Ephraim—this father, this husband—has needs that go beyond his fierce desire to hold on to the farm, to control his sons and wives. He, like Lear, needs warmth and companionship, and most important, I believe, he, like Lear, needs a mother—and this is what makes him so complex and interesting a character, this is what makes him similar to his son Eben ("spittin' image") in a play in which Mother lurks in every corner of the house, overhangs the farm itself in the form of elms.

O'Neill gives Ephraim a poignant speech (part 2, scene 2) in which he expresses his deepest thoughts and frustrations to his new wife Abbie, who is not listening, who in fact is looking through the wall of the bedroom to Eben's bedroom while Eben, in his room, is looking through the wall at her. The wall between bedrooms seems transparent as the lovers' *"hot glances"* meet; the wall between Ephraim and his wife, who is positioned next to him on the bed, is stone, like the walls around the house. Ephraim tells the unlistening Abbie about his two previous wives who "never knowed" him; he tells her about the stones that he made into walls, about his hard God who is "in the stones," about his "lonesomeness," about "the voice o' God cryin' in my wilderness" in the spring, telling him to "seek an' find!" With passion he turns to Abbie: "I sought ye an' I found ye!" But her expression is blank; her attention is elsewhere; she, like his previous wives, doesn't know him. Angrily, after threatening her that he wants a son (which she promises him), *"he pulls on his trousers, tucking in his night shirt, and pulls on his boots,"* according to O'Neill's stage directions.

> Abbie. (*surprised*) Whar air ye goin'?
> Cabot. (*queerly*) Down whar it's restful—whar it's warm—down t' the barn. (*bitterly*) I kin talk t' the cows. They know. They know the farm an' me. They'll give me peace. (*He turns to go out the door.*)
> Abbie. (*a bit frightenedly*) Air ye ailin' tonight, Ephraim?
> Cabot. Growin'. Growin' ripe on the bough.
>
> (2:350)

He *"plods off toward the barn,"* while Abbie and Eben continue to *"stare at each other through the wall."* Then Abbie goes to Eben's room, tells Eben to court her in his mother's parlor, which leads us to the next scene, the parlor scene, where Mother, as I have already discussed, controls the actions of both Abbie and Eben, and where we have our climactic scene of Oedipal love.

In his confession to his wife, Ephraim had said—just before he decides to go to the cows in the barn—that the house is cold, that "they's thin's pokin' about in the dark—in the corners." The things poking about become the "somethin'" in the parlor scene. It seems that Mother lurks in all the rooms, and Mother, we come to realize, is what Ephraim needs, without being conscious of it. That is why he goes to the cows, conventional symbols of maternity, the perfect animals (perfect because they belong naturally and realistically to the farm, perfect because of their obvious symbolism) to indicate Ephraim's need for the warmth of Mother and female. "It's wa'm down t' the barn—nice smellin' an' warm—with the cows" (2:344).

That is why, when the call of God came in the spring, he sought and found the buxom Abbie, herself a kind of earth mother, always invoking the forces of Nature, full of natural desire and passion and vitality, representing the Dionysian urges that clash against the Puritan stoniness of the man, who found her and gave her a "hum." Ephraim Cabot's bond to the cows is strong and necessary. Stone though he may be, the old Ephraim Cabot, like the young Stephen Dedalus—and like the old King Lear and the young Hamlet, and like Oedipus, like all men—must meet a "moocow" on the road of life.

Lacking King Lear's large capacity for pain and understanding which leads to his recognition of love after his initial denial of it, Ephraim Cabot seems a less sympathetic character than Lear but still sympathetic. Certainly, the idea behind "Ripeness is all," a phrase that we find in *King Lear,* clings to O'Neill's hard man who is "growin' ripe on the bough." Both Shakespeare and O'Neill meet the difficult challenge of having an audience sympathize with an old hard man who should be wiser and who causes terrible pain, sinning as well as sinned against. Their age, and the endurance that comes with it, helps to give them height. King Lear's new awarenesses and Ephraim Cabot's renewed commitment to his old values earn them respect. Lear dies with his daughter (mother) in his arms, a daughter he finally pays very close attention to—"Look on her! Look, her lips, / Look there, look there!" Ephraim walks toward the barn to be with the cows (mother), but he too, although unable to fathom the deep love of Abbie and Eben at play's end, is able to appreciate, grudgingly perhaps, the heroic gesture of Eben who chooses to die with Abbie—"Purty good—fur yew!" (2:377)—finally paying close attention to his son. Both old men have come a long way, not only in coming *to* their old age but *in* their old age. They invoke their gods along the way, but despite the Christian trappings and larger frames of reference in both plays, we come down to the terrible happenings within a *family,* the dark urges and consequent conflicts of all-too-human fathers and children. Both dramatists, of course, are tapping a common human source that can be discussed in psychological and archetypal terms, but O'Neill, as I'm suggesting throughout, fortunately has behind him the Shakespeare whose art gave these family matters their most effective dramatic representation.

In my discussions of Eben and Ephraim as Hamlet and King Lear figures, I have concentrated on *Elms* as family drama, as the product of deep psychological pressures within O'Neill. I am suggesting that Shakespeare, whose similar pressures led him to the writing of *Hamlet* and *King Lear,* has been absorbed by O'Neill, that Shakespeare is an important part of O'Neill's inner biography in addition to being a literary or bookish influence, that Shakespeare, in fact, helps O'Neill write a breakthrough tragedy that allows us to feel the subjective impulse more strongly than ever before in O'Neill's career. At the risk of finding Shakespeare behind every O'Neillian bush—where he probably is!—I merely mention in passing that O'Neill's emphasis on sexuality in *Elms*—the many references to "hard," the "growin'" speech by Abbie, the parlor scene, Min, and so on—combined with the powerful desire called possessiveness in relation to the farm makes one think of another Shakespeare tragedy that brings together sexual desire and material desire, that contains a possessive woman, a woman who mocks her partner's manhood, who sometimes seems his mother, and who talks of killing the infant she gives suck to. And Abbie and Eben, like Lady Macbeth and Macbeth, are being driven by forces they cannot control, the "Force behind" that leads tragic characters to their deaths.

I wish to pursue one speculative idea pertaining to O'Neill's title, *Desire Under the Elms*—O'Neill is very careful with titles—because it will lead me to a discussion of other, more technical, aspects of Shakespeare's influence on the play. *Desire Under the Elms* is a superb title, interesting in itself because it catches one's attention, and succinctly pointing to what happens in the play. The play is filled with Desire (desires of all kinds, as we have noticed), and whatever happens in the play happens *under* the elms—physically under them, as the stage directions insist, and symbolically under them, as they represent Nature and Mother. What the title does not do is inform us who is the play's main character, which is the function of many of O'Neill's other titles and, for that matter, the function of all the titles Shakespeare uses for his tragedies. A play's title, when it is the name of a character, almost always indicates the person on whom a dramatist wishes the audience to focus its attention. That is why the shared titles in Shakespeare—*Romeo and Juliet*, *Antony and Cleopatra*—force us to consider *both* lovers as the important tragic figures; that is why the title *Macbeth* confirms for us the isolated importance of Macbeth himself despite the powerful presence of his wife; and that is why the title *Julius Caesar* gives us so much trouble—we expect Caesar to be the protagonist, but Brutus fills that role (or should we reconsider this idea precisely because the play's title is *Julius Caesar*?). O'Neill's titles, when he gives us the names of the protagonists, offer no problems—*The Emperor Jones, Anna Christie, Marco Millions, The Great God Brown, Mourning Becomes Electra*—and, in fact, help us to interpret a play by allowing us to know where O'Neill wanted to place his emphasis. The title *Anna Christie*, for example, forces us to consider Anna as the main character, even though Chris Christopherson is so important and memorable a figure. (In an earlier version of the play the title was *Chris Christophersen,* but O'Neill changed his emphasis and changed his title.) That O'Neill named his late and probably best one-acter *Hughie* allows us to focus on the dead clerk as the center of attention even though he never appears on stage. How helpful, then, it would have been if O'Neill called *Desire Under the Elms Eben and Abbie* or *Ephraim Cabot* (or *The Great God Cabot).* What we have in the title that O'Neill gives us is the possibility of multiple protagonists or the family as protagonist—exactly what we have, in fact, in those late great plays, *The Iceman Cometh* and *Long Day's Journey Into Night.* We are not sure who is the main character in *Elms* because we split our attention between the characters or, perhaps more precisely, we allow our attention to absorb all the "main" characters at the same time. Is it the story of Eben and Abbie, adulterous lovers who, at play's end, walk hand in hand into the sunrise and death? Is it the story of Ephraim Cabot, terribly alone, who walks to the barn and his cows? Is it the story of a family, racked by desires, the members so closely connected that what happens to one affects what happens to all? Perhaps these questions need not be answered (or asked?) since the play will affect us emotionally at whatever level it can. But one point I wish to make is that an unclear protagonist or a group protagonist requires ensemble acting of the highest order. If balances are to be maintained no starring role should emerge, something difficult to achieve given the nature of performance. It's clear, for example, that in the original stage production of *Elms* in 1924 Walter Huston's acting seemed to make *Elms* Ephraim's play; it's equally clear that in the unbelievably bad movie of 1958 Burl Ives's portrayal of Ephraim seriously diminished the part, and allowed a young Sophia Loren to make Abbie the most interesting character. However, a more important point is that a dispersed protagonist inevitably leads us to consider O'Neill's ambivalence toward his characters—in essential respects his ambivalence toward himself, with his own personality, his own psychological urges, absorbed by the characters he presents—an ambivalence that informs his thinking and feeling. O'Neill, like Larry Slade in *The Iceman Cometh,* is compelled to see two sides to every situation. This ambivalence points to, perhaps produces, some of the most salient characteristics of his method of presentation, his dramatic art. O'Neill wants us to see juxtaposed stage images; he wants us to feel conflicting emotions; he wants us to be as divided, it seems, as the characters he presents (and as the playwright who creates them). To accomplish his purpose he orchestrates his material in ways that must remind us once again of that supreme master of orchestration, Shakespeare. Take, as an obvious example, the conflicting emotions we feel in the parlor scene already discussed, in which the sexual union of Eben and Abbie takes place in an atmosphere of lust and incest and Oedipal desire *and,* at the same time, in an atmosphere of natural and genuine love between two sympathetic characters. An unnatural union seems naturally consummated. O'Neill has given a dark psychological and physical moment dramatic life, calculatingly troubling his audience in a turbulent scene that produces mixed emotions. His method, and perhaps his accomplishment, I wish to suggest, is not of a different order of significance than, to take one example, the troublesome praying scene (3.3) that Shakespeare gives us in *Hamlet.* At the moment when Hamlet, sword in hand, is ready to exact revenge on the kneeling, unknowing Claudius, Hamlet seems a bloody insensitive murderer, whereas the murderous Claudius—praying, asking for forgiveness but intellectually honest enough to know that his prayers are meaningless because he still wants to hold on to the fruits of his murder, his crown and queen—seems a sympathetic and vulnerable man. Shakespeare here produces mixed emotions, playing with his audience's sympathies.

Both O'Neill and Shakespeare seem to thrive on ambiguities, inconsistencies, shifting perspectives. Kenneth Muir, discussing this quality in Shakespeare, offers the following quote from Strindberg about "the singularity of Shakespeare": "Shakespeare describes people, in all their facets, as inconsistent, as contradictory, as torn—and tearing themselves to pieces—as aggressive and as incomprehensible as the sons of men really are."[11] The words apply to O'Neill as well, and, not surprisingly, to Strindberg himself, O'Neill's most acknowledged influence. Ephraim Cabot, for example, that man of stone, rigid in his Puritanism, representing everything that denies the natural, the Dionysian, in human behavior, needs the warmth of the cows, as we have seen, but also is most Dionysian—drinking, singing, dancing—in the remarkable scene of jubilation celebrating the birth of his new heir. In this scene O'Neillian ironies prevail, combined with a highly effective depiction of meanspirited, tight, county folk, but surely much of the scene's power depends on our witnessing a different Ephraim, filled with exuberance, no stone at all, in fact closer to the free and natural Indians whose war dance he is imitating. While he cuts his grotesque capers, he chastizes those around him: "Ye're a sickly generation! Yer hearts air pink, not red! Yer veins is full o' mud an' water! I be the on'y man in the county! Whoop! See that! I'm a Injun! I've killed Injuns in the West afore ye was born—an' skulped 'em too!" (2:361). Notice that he's both Injun and killer of Injuns, just as he's both a natural man and a stone. Inconsistent, contradictory, complex, Ephraim Cabot, like so many of O'Neill's (and Shakespeare's and Strindberg's) characters, repels and attracts, is divided himself and divides us.

The divided nature of O'Neill's characters can be found throughout his work, but in *Elms,* for the first time, the dividedness (perhaps the result of strong autobiographical impulses) stems from a rich ambiguity attached to a mode of vision that forces the audience to hold on to two opposing attitudes, one playing against the other, causing the audience perspective to shift as the play progresses, and not necessarily allowing the audience to come to a satisfyingly conclusive opinion or feeling. Thesis and antithesis, but not necessarily synthesis. How *should* we feel at the end of *Elms*? Two lovers, hand in hand, have found true love, and this love has caused them to find death. A solitary man, never understood and never understanding others, carries on alone, the farm his and his alone, but what price ownership? A sheriff, *"looking around at the farm enviously"*—the last a carefully chosen word in O'Neill's stage directions—gives us the last words of the play: "It's a jim-dandy farm, no denyin'. Wished I owned it!" (2:378). The sheriffs words bring to mind all the desires of the play that inevitably led to the love-death of Eben and Abbie, to the stark aloneness of Ephraim. The irony attached to the sheriff's words gives us a little distance from the three important protagonists, but not enough to squelch the powerful tragic effect. O'Neill is playing with our emotions, and the ambivalence allows for no easy audience satisfaction—which seems right, for we know how much O'Neill detested whatever was easy. *Elms,* I suggest, offers the same kind of mixed-reaction conclusion that we find in Shakespeare's tragedies. O'Neill's complementary vision of the world, so similar to Shakespeare's,[12] shapes our reaction to his endings. The same kind of questions we ask about the ending of *Elms* can be asked about the endings of Shakespeare's tragedies. (I am not suggesting, of course, that the plays of Shakespeare share the same problems or complementarities as O'Neill's plays or that any one Shakespeare play emphasizes the same problems or complementarities as any other Shakespeare play.) At the end of *Hamlet* how *should* we react to Fortinbras as the prospective king of Denmark? Does he deserve Hamlet's "dying voice"? With Hamlet dead, having negotiated his revenge, going to "the rest" that is "silence," do we share Hamlet's concern for the state? How closely *is* the play's political dimension connected to the the personal dimension? (How much *did* we lose in the Olivier film when he omitted Fortinbras?) In *Hamlet,* as in *Elms,* "love" leads to death, but how emotionally important is it that someone called Fortinbras will own the "jim-dandy farm" called Denmark? At the end of *Othello* we witness a tragically loaded bed—again with love leading to death—but we also look at the silent man looking at the bed, perhaps smiling at the destruction he helped to cause, and at that moment, I suspect, our emotional reaction is split between deep pity for the tragic lovers and deep fear for the inexplicable evil that Iago represents. At the end of *King Lear* we have many mixed reactions—which

I will discuss later, especially in relation to Lear's carrying on stage the dead Cordelia—but surely the easy consolation that Edgar will "sustain" the "gored state" rubs against everything we have experienced in the play. Edgar is a worthy successor; he has witnessed and suffered and endured; we have observed him throughout becoming riper and wiser. But in the world of *King Lear* we know that ripeness is not all, and our emotions are mixed because the gesture toward tragic reconciliation doesn't seem more than a mere gesture. At the end of *Macbeth* we seem to be on more firm ground because Macbeth the "butcher" is dead and Malcolm gives every indication of becoming a better ruler than his gracious father, so that we may be able to hold on to the possibility—perhaps stronger here than in the other tragedies—that Scotland will be healed, that its gored state will be sustained. But even here the dominant rhythm of the play, the dizzying seesaw effect of its movement and language, the power of ambition, the darkness that lodges within the souls of all men and women, force us to be wary and complicate our emotions. (Roman Polanski's brilliant ending to his movie—in which Donalbain, witnessing the crowning of his brother Malcolm, immediately rides to the cave of the witches, so that we know there's no end to ambition and desire, that it goes on—beautifully captures the play's dialectic and rhythm, although it takes liberties with Shakespeare's script.) O'Neill, while writing *Elms,* need not necessarily have had in mind the endings of Shakespeare's tragedies, but he certainly shared Shakespeare's fondness for the ending that disturbs our emotions, and since, as I have tried to demonstrate, Shakespeare seems present in so many other ways, I believe that O'Neill's ending, built upon ambivalence and complementarity, may have been influenced by Shakespeare's tragic endings, also offering shifting perspectives.

Now, the most available, most mechanical, dramaturgical instrument for presenting clear oppositions is the juxtaposition of visual images or spoken statements, the technique of counterpointing, of which Shakespeare, here as in every other respect, is the master. Jean Howard has convincingly pinpointed various aspects of Shakespeare's "orchestration," making the important point that Shakespeare deliberately divides the visual and aural attention of his audience, forcing what she calls "psychic fragmentation" in an audience which, because of this fragmentation, becomes a participant in the drama.[13] We can go almost anywhere for examples of Shakespeare's use of asides as a contrapuntal technique to bring two opposing views to an audience. (One obvious example: "A little more than kin, and less than kind," the first aside of Hamlet, in fact the very first words of Hamlet in the play, the aside a perfect vehicle for the inner man who is opposed to and commenting on the rotten world around him.) So too we find many examples of visual juxtaposition in Shakespeare, the most obvious early example being the two tents on stage at the end of *Richard III*, with ghosts in stilted mechanical fashion wishing long life to Henry Tudor, then death to Richard III. Shakespeare was fortunate in his platform stage, of course, which allowed for such easy juxtapositions, and was fortunate in the Elizabethan convention of aside and soliloquy, which allowed for verbal juxtapositions. The fluidity and flexibility of the Elizabethan platform stage gave Shakespeare the opportunity to control naturally the rhythm of his plays, and the soliloquy and aside are conventions that allowed him to display the inner person. O'Neill had no such possibilities for fluidity or innerness because he was working with the fourth-wall convention and within a realistic acting tradition. But he was forever striving to get close to what he considered "the one true theatre, the age-old theatre, the theatre of the Greeks and Elizabethans," the theater that he called "imaginative" theater.[14] To achieve this goal he often tried to use the dramaturgical resources of that "true" theater. I've already discussed his use of the Shakespearean soliloquy and the supernatural ghost in his early plays, in some of which the mode of expressionism allowed him to get within the minds of his characters. In the nonexpressionistic *Elms* we find an effective variation on the Shakespearean ghost because the ghost of Mother is present but not seen, thereby fitting neatly into O'Neill's inherited realistic tradition. So too in *Elms* we get to the inner character by means of soliloquy uttered within a realistic play with no hint of expressionism. How natural, for example, are Eben's thoughts, spoken aloud, at the end of part 1, scene 2, as he looks up to the sky and gets ready to go to Min, the prostitute that his brothers and his father before them already slept with.

> Waal—thar's a star, an' somewhar's they's him, an' here's me, an' thar's Min up the road—in the same night. What if I does kiss her? She's like t'night, she's soft 'n' wa'm, her eyes kin wink like a star, her mouth's wa'm, her arms're wa'm, she smells like a wa'm plowed field, she's purty . . . Ay-eh! By God A'mighty she's purty, an' I don't give a damn how many sins she's sinned afore mine or who she's sinned 'em with, my sin's as purty as any one on 'em! (2:326)

Eben's thoughts are not part of a soliloquy convention, but they do comprise a soliloquy that fits easily and effectively into O'Neill's realistic framework. The sensitive Eben always seems to be looking at the sky; in fact, his first words, the first words of the play, are "God! Purty!" as he, alone on stage, sighs in *"puzzled awe"* at the New England sunset. And his thoughts in this Min soliloquy fit naturally into the Oedipal scheme because in having Min he is the rival of his father, who first had Min; soon he will have his father's new wife, Abbie. Of course, Eben's soliloquy comes from the lips of an inarticulate man, certainly a speaker infinitely less articulate than any of Shakespeare's speakers. Eben Cabot is a kind of Hamlet without the intellect and without the language. What I am stressing here is O'Neill's effective appropriation of a Shakespearean convention for his own purposes. O'Neill's characters, even when they *are* articulate in his later plays, do not have the verbal range or depth of Shakespeare's characters, but O'Neill is able to use the Shakespearean device within the realistic theater he inherited without calling attention to that device.

Shakespeare's brilliant use of repetition to highlight a theme (like the string of words that touch the idea of seeing in *King Lear)* or to color emotionally the atmosphere of a play (like the fair-foul combinations in *Macbeth*) may have made O'Neill bold in offering his many repetitious phrases and words throughout his career. For example, that first "Purty!" coming from Eben, immediately followed by the "Purty" of his brother Simeon, who, lacking Eben's sensitivity, stares "dumbly up at the sky," is the first in a string of "purtys"—describing sunsets and sunrises, describing Min and Eben's mother and Abbie, describing the farm, describing the infant murdered by Abbie. In Shakespeare the implications widen as the words are repeated; in O'Neill the repetitions do not resonate so effectively, but they serve important purposes. In *Elms,* Eben's first words and last words—looking at sunset in the beginning and sunrise at the end—contain "Purty," allowing us to come full circle and forcing us to realize what a long way Eben has come, traveling from sunset to sunrise (which, paradoxically and tragically, is death). It is a brilliant stroke on O'Neill's part to have Ephraim Cabot, having learned that Eben is willing to die with Abbie, say to his son with "*grudging admiration*": "Purty good—fur yew!" This "purty" has a different meaning and quality from the other "purtys" in the play, but it recalls the others, placing Ephraim closer to his son even as they say "goodbye."

Although O'Neill in *Elms* is highly effective in his use of such Shakespearean devices as the soliloquy and the repetitive word or phrase, his fourth-wall convention did not allow him to achieve the Shakespearean fluidity and flexibility that the Elizabethan platform stage made possible. I suggest that it is precisely because he was *reaching for* the Shakespearean ideal that he hit upon the bold stage technique of using removable walls in *Elms,* which allowed the action to move swiftly from inside to outside, from room to room, and allowed the audience to see more than one setting. A leaflet that publicized the play proudly asserted: *"Desire Under the Elms* strips away the fourth wall of life."[15] The Cabot farmhouse, with the elms overhanging and the stones surrounding, is the single setting for the entire play. When the action takes place in a particular room, an exterior wall is removed; when the action takes place in more than one room, then more than one wall is removed. The device allows O'Neill to contrast indoor and outdoor scenes, or to contrast two or more indoor scenes. This method of staging remains realistic, but it allows for fluidity of presentation and it produces highly effective juxtapositions, as, for example, in the scene in which we see the country folk in the kitchen having a good time at the expense of Ephraim *and* we see Ephraim alone outside on the porch after his vigorous dancing *and* we see Abbie and Eben together upstairs near the cradle of their child. This scene alone testifies to O'Neill's creative theatricality. And it achieves the kind of counterpointing that Shakespeare realizes in his orchestration of stage patterns on his platform stage. Shakespeare's inherited unlocalized playing area gives him a rich opportunity to divide his audience's attention, supporting a mode of vision that thrives on complementarity. O'Neill had the more difficult task of working with a localized realistic playing area, but he found a remarkably effective solution, one that allowed him enough flexibility to orchestrate juxtapositions and enough fluidity to cut down on scene changes. (Concerning the latter, there can be little doubt that he remembered the awkwardness and the time-consuming quality of the scene changes in *Beyond the Horizon,* his other farm play, produced four years earlier.) O'Neill's use of removable walls allows him—in the counterpointing, in the rhythm of presentation, in the combination of realism and stylization—to be Shakespearean within the strict confines of his inherited realistic stage. It is interesting to note that this distinctive stage design was discovered by O'Neill himself, not by his brilliant designer-director Robert Edmond Jones, as most critics assumed at the time.[16] Also interesting to note, by way of concluding these remarks on O'Neill's stage technique in *Elms,* is that when the play was revived in 1963 on an arena stage, the reviewers complained about the awkwardness of the staging. The power of O'Neill's play, like the power of Shakespeare's plays, is bound up with its scenic method of presentation. *Elms,* in which O'Neill emulates Shakespeare's freedom of presentation, demands the multiple setting of a proscenium stage, and nothing else will do, it seems.

When America went to see *Desire Under the Elms,* probably for the wrong reasons (since the play had great notoriety because of censorship), the audience saw what was up to that time America's finest tragedy. Obviously, the audience of the time did not know it was a breakthrough play in O'Neill's development—nor did O'Neill. In *Elms* O'Neill settled into the realistic mode that would be the source of his greatest artistic strength and, as I have attempted to demonstrate, this "dream" play, written after the deaths of father, mother and brother, unconsciously allowed him to give the subjective impulse freer reign without being obtrusive, an impulse which included the Shakespeare he did not acknowledge as a source of creativity, the Shakespeare who was part of his conscious and unconscious biography. O'Neill did not offer his eager American audience a tragedy of comparable value until *Mourning Becomes Electra* was staged by the Theatre Guild in 1931. He worked approximately three years on that ambitious play—an enormous labor that made him wonder why he ever attempted "the damn thing"—and in the five years before that (that is, for five years after *Elms* was produced) he feverishly experimented with his artistic medium, wishing to give his audiences plays different from any they had experienced before. But this restless five-year activity produced plays that strain for largeness and depth, achieving results far different and less successful than those achieved when O'Neill gracefully combined realism and symbolism, as he did in *Elms* and as he would do again in *Mourning Becomes Electra,* the tragedy that in so many ways, including its Shakespearean echoes and characteristics, is a companion piece to *Elms*. The path from *Elms* to *Electra* seems clear and direct, and my discussion of the later play could follow at once from my discussion of *Elms*. But other plays in between O'Neill's two Greek-based and Shakespeare-influenced tragedies have an important bearing on O'Neill's writing of *Electra*. They must be confronted, if only briefly, not only to indicate O'Neill's artistic restlessness, but to suggest how his heightened experimental activity helped to shape the writing of the best plays to come.

Some big ideas lay behind the creation of the five experimental plays—Marco Millions, The Great God Brown, Lazarus Laughed, Strange *Interlude, Dynamo*—that O'Neill wrote between the two realistic tragedies, *Elms* and *Electra,* ideas that were intrinsic to the vision of a "theatre of tomorrow" as propounded by Kenneth Macgowan in a book of that name. Macgowan's views, which both O'Neill and Robert Edmond Jones shared, insisted on a return to the religious spirit of plays of the past even as they recognized and applauded the discoveries of the new psychology. That is, the "tomorrow" movement—to use O'Neill's *Iceman* phrase—really was a "yesterday" movement. The new, which depended on the momentous probings of Freud and Jung, was expected to capture what the old Greek and Elizabethan dramatists already possessed, a spiritual reality, call it an inner reality, that transcended surface reality by going deeper within and by going further beyond or behind. Macgowan and O'Neill and Jones—eventually forming the triumvirate that would produce its own plays for a few years—favored a new realism that demanded a new stagecraft, the kind of stagecraft that Adolph Appia and Gordon Craig and Max Reinhardt had already championed in Europe. Macgowan's words clearly indicate the purpose of the new drama:

> It will attempt to transfer to dramatic art the illumination of those deep and vigorous and eternal processes of the human soul which the psychology of Freud and Jung has given us through study of the unconscious, striking to the heart of emotion and linking our commonest life today with emanations of the primitive racial mind.[17]

This new drama, based on the insights of Freud and Jung, somehow would evoke a communal religious spirit that was already there before these psychological insights were verbalized. As Leonard Chabrowe asserts, "The Theatre of Tomorrow was to be a modern equivalent of what the theater had been in Elizabethan England and Athens."[18] Now, this idea, that the new is essentially a recapturing of the old, must give us pause. It comes very close to Mary Tyrone's statement, in a context worlds apart from the polemics of Macgowan: "The past is the present, isn't it? It's the future, too." For O'Neill, it seems to have been a belief he lived by, and it's one that was with him even before he met Macgowan or was acquainted with Macgowan's ideas. After all, didn't George Cram Cook, whose ideas fascinated O'Neill and certainly influenced him, insist back in the Provincetown days that a new theater was needed to capture the Dionysian spirit that infused great drama from the very beginning? And didn't Nietzsche, whose *The Birth of Tragedy* strongly influenced O'Neill's views on drama, also champion a kind of primitivism, a Dionysian realism that aimed for psychological depths and spiritual heights? "The Greek dream in tragedy is the noblest ever!" wrote O'Neill himself.[19] Here is one of O'Neill's most quoted statements about his ideals for an imaginative theater:

> But what do I mean by an "imaginative" theatre—(where I hope for it, for example, in the subtitle of *Lazarus Laughed:* A Play for an Imaginative Theatre)? I mean the one true theatre, the age-old theatre, the theatre of the Greeks and Elizabethans, a theatre that could dare to boast—without committing a farcical sacrilege—that it is a legitimate descendant of the first theatre that sprang, by virtue of man's imaginative interpretation of life, out of his worship of Dionysus. I mean a theatre returned to its highest and sole significant function as a Temple where the religion of a poetical interpretation and symbolical celebration of life is communicated to human beings, starved in spirit by their soul-stifling daily struggle to exist as masks among the masks of living![20]

The statement has behind it the vision of Nietzsche and Cook, the credo of Macgowan and Jones. The truly new—the deep, the significant, the necessary—must capture the spirit of the old, must avoid the easy realism of "show-shop" theater, must get "behind life," the oft-quoted phrase that O'Neill used in the playbill for *The Spook Sonata,* which was the first play produced by the triumvirate of O'Neill and Macgowan and Jones, the play written by Strindberg, who was for O'Neill the "precursor of all modernity in our present theater." It is in the context of these large ideas about theater that O'Neill writes his experimental plays. The Greek ideal seems always to be in his mind, as it was in the minds of Nietzsche and Cook and O'Neill's associates in the Experimental Theater. Yet, interestingly for my purposes, notice that Elizabethan drama enters O'Neill's thoughts. His "age-old" theater is the theater of both the Greeks *and* Elizabethans, as if the Elizabethans had a spiritual, communal, Dionysian theater experience, as if going to the Globe was going to a "Temple." (Notice too that Chabrowe's comment on the Theater of Tomorrow includes Elizabethan England.) Macgowan, in his *Theatre of Tomorrow,* even as he seems to place greater emphasis on music and design and movement than on words, still thought of soliloquy and aside as vehicles to be used by the new playwrights. "The soliloquy," he states, "will return again as a natural and proper revelation of the mind of a character."[21] He is thinking here of Shakespearean drama, not Greek drama. And even Nietzsche, who offers his provocative contrast between the Dionysian and Apollonian spirits in the context of Greek drama, mentions Hamlet as a Dionysian man; that is, for Nietzsche, Hamlet and Oedipus and Prometheus are all masks of Dionysus. Nietzsche's *The Birth of Tragedy,* we can never forget, was "a seminal book devoured and repeatedly debated by Cook and O'Neill."[22] When O'Neill writes his much-quoted *Memoranda on Masks* in 1932 to explain publicly his use of masks in the plays already behind him, he goes to *Hamlet* and *Julius Caesar* to answer his own question: "Why not give all future Classical revivals entirely in masks?" O'Neill is discussing masks, the device of Greek drama, but he, like Nietzsche and Macgowan, also has Shakespeare in mind. For all these theoreticians of the new drama, the old classical drama is a model and guide, an old drama that includes the Elizabethans, especially Shakespeare, even in contexts that seem exclusively Greek. Shakespearean drama offers the kind of realism that allows for an awareness of what is "behind life"; it is not surface realism, it accommodates the potent combination of the literal and symbolic; it is imaginative theater. O'Neill's mind may have been concentrating on the remarkable accomplishment of the Greeks—and that he used Greek myth and drama in both *Elms* and *Electra,* that he went to masks and choruses as theatrical devices, testifies to this—but lurking in the corners of his creative imagination was the accomplishment of the Elizabethans, especially of Shakespeare.

Although Shakespeare can be felt in *Elms,* no clear Shakespearean echo sounds in the play O'Neill put aside to write *Elms* and then immediately returned to after *Elms, Marco Millions* (1925, produced in 1928), the first Theatre Guild production of an O'Neill play, the beginning of a fruitful and long relationship between the most important commercial producing company in America and America's most important dramatist. The Guild had the necessary technical resources to meet O'Neill's ever-expanding needs. *Marco Millions,* certainly O'Neill's most blunt criticism of American materialism, covers a wide expanse of space and a long duration of time, as did his earlier historical romance, *The Fountain* (1922, produced 1925), which dramatized the life of Juan Ponce de Leon. It was bold of O'Neill to attempt biting satire within an historical pageant, and at times the satire against Marco Polo, O'Neill's historical version of Sinclair Lewis's Babbit, hits the mark, especially in the context of America in the twenties. O'Neill's theatrical boldness certainly tested the ability and imagination of the designer Lee Simonson who considered the play "a scene designer's holiday." However, O'Neill's insistent presentation of Nietzschean mystical messages, usually from the lips of Kublai Khan, mutes the satire and eventually collapses the play. Surprisingly, in the light of my discussion of *Elms,* which O'Neill was writing at about the same time as *Marco Millions,* the play has no autobiographical interest whatsoever, as if O'Neill is consciously taking a step away from himself, thereby neglecting one of his great strengths as a dramatist. He also takes a step away from Shakespeare, unless we wish to consider that the play's very expansiveness, its many characters and scenes, its spacial and chronological arrangement, reflects O'Neill's attempt to emulate the expansiveness of Shakespeare. O'Neill does ask for a divided stage that allows for counterpointing, and this seems Shakespearean, although the scenes are handled too confusedly to produce the kind of effective juxtapositions that *Elms* displayed with its removable walls, or that Shakespeare was able to negotiate on his less-cluttered platform stage.

Like *Marco Millions, The Great God Brown* (1925, produced 1926) also attacks American materialism in the person of William Brown, but the real interest in this play clings to its psychological dimension. In writing *Brown* O'Neill's ambition is as large as ever, his need to experiment theatrically as intense as ever, but rather than aiming for the horizon and beyond, rather than traveling with a Marco Polo or a Ponce de Leon over the expanse of the known and unknown world, he decides to travel deeper within the individual, piercing the psyche, and this leads to his use of masks and his genuine excitement about his "new" theatrical device. Here, as we have already noticed, the new points to the old. Tragic masks were used in Greek drama, heightening the stylized and symbolic nature of the characters. And masks were used in the primitive rituals that Kenneth Macgowan described in his *Masks and Demons,* a book O'Neill read. In using masks, O'Neill seems to be hearkening after the kind of mystery we associate with religious ritual and religious drama, but in reality he was examining another kind of mystery, that which is lodged within the mind of a single person. Travis Bogard accurately pinpoints the difference between the usual use of masks "to conventionalize the human individuality, to idealize man or to typify him" and O'Neill's use in *Brown:* "to reveal the human individuality as directly and profoundly as possible."[23] In this respect, O'Neill's use of masks *was* new, as new, in fact, as the provocative ideas of Freud and Jung. Explaining his use in *Memoranda on Masks,* O'Neill claims that masks are "the freest solution of the modern dramatist's problem as to how—with the greatest dramatic clarity and economy of means—he can express those profound hidden conflicts of the mind which the probings of psychology continue to disclose to us."[24] In the same paragraph that contains these words, O'Neill states his aim of presenting an "inner drama" in his work, "a drama of souls." This aim is prodded, as he fully realizes and asserts, by "the new psychological insight into human cause and effect," which is nothing less than "a study in masks, an exercise in unmasking." The mask as "a symbol of inner reality" seems to be a "new convention" for O'Neill. Granted, but the problem with his use of masks in *Brown* is not only the confusion resulting from too exuberant and too complex a use (which led to his need to explain himself publicly by writing *about* his use), but also his overly ambitious aim of making the play "mystical and abstract" as well as "psychological." It's difficult enough for the mask to reveal nothing less than the human soul, finally an impossible task even when the soul is seemingly confronted directly and cleanly, but O'Neill then muddies the psychological waters with the jetsam and flotsam of Nietzschean messages, all within a realistic framework featuring "recognizable human beings." The play is an artistic failure, I believe, but it is also a remarkably interesting attempt to extend drama beyond the limits of the old surface realism, mystifying to its original audiences but still able to hold their attention for 283 performances. Writing *Brown,* O'Neill seemed more interested in his *use* of masks than in the *characters* wearing the masks. The mask covers no interesting face; the frozen facial gestures correspond to no beating heart. The audience witnesses a literal exercise in unmasking, but the interest is in the exercise itself. Questions abound, which on first consideration may suggest interesting or suspenseful or deep theater, but the search for answers is carried on in the mind only, as if the only way to get to the heart of the mystery of psyche is for the *mind* of the audience to confront the *mind-masks* of characters. This procedure squelches O'Neill's unique strength as a dramatist, his appeal to the emotions. Admittedly, there are moments in the play when the autobiographical impulse exerts enough pressure to make the play interesting—moments connected to O'Neill's portrait of the poet-artist Dion Anthony, whose qualities touch O'Neill himself: alone, sensitive, unable to reveal his true self to the world, ever aware of the masks people wear to protect themselves from others and from themselves, always in need of a mother (both Cybel and Margaret), "born with ghosts in your eyes," as Cybel tells Dion—but these are precious few moments. Still, as we think of O'Neill's development as a dramatist, *Brown* is an important play. In it we see O'Neill struggling to stage the *inner* character, excitingly aware of the duality in man, the ambivalences, certainly offering too theatrical a dramaturgy of dialectics, but locating his play where it seems to belong, in the fragmented self, which we call man, in an essentially realistic framework. O'Neill is traveling within, perhaps by the circuitous route of theatrical devices that call attention to themselves, but his indirections will find directions out. His desire to go deeper within may fleetingly remind us of Shakespeare's accomplishment in this respect—his amazing grasp of psychology (without the benefit of Freud and Jung)—and O'Neill's restless experimentation, his need to extend the limits of his dramatic medium, may suggest to us the Shakespeare who was forever exploring and revivifying his medium, but we find very little Shakespeare in *The Great God Brown*. O'Neill had Shakespeare (as well as the Greeks and Nietzsche) in mind when writing his explanatory *Memoranda on Masks*, as we already observed, but he did not tap that fruitful source when writing his bold but bewildering play.

Masks were again used by O'Neill in his next play, *Lazarus Laughed* (1926), but here he reverts to their conventional use, allowing them to represent character types. Here too he returns to the expansiveness of setting that we found in *Marco Millions*. That is, instead of remaining with his exploration of inner reality, what he attempted to do in *Brown*, he casts his eyes toward the horizon again, making up in scenic effects and stage groupings and sheer pageantry what he significantly loses in psychology. He called *Lazarus Laughed* "A Play for the Imaginative Theatre"; by writing it he wished to return the theater to "a Temple where the religion of a poetical interpretation and symbolical celebration of life" is offered to soul-starved human beings. It's an ambitious aim, and *Lazarus Laughed* is the most theatrically ambitious play ever written by an American, but O'Neill stretches his medium so far that he leaves drama behind. It is exciting to witness O'Neill's imagination captured by the sheer possibilities of a massive theatrical event—lavish use of music and movement, hundreds of actors, about four-hundred costumes, about three-hundred masks—but theater without drama, philosophy (especially Nietzschean affirmative musings taken insistently from *Thus Spake Zarathustra*) without psychology, spectacle without interesting characters in action, mutes the excitement. In attempting to present nothing less than a religious myth on the grandest scale possible—or should I say grandest scale impossible because it has never been tested by professional performance—O'Neill abandoned his powerful ties to realistic theater, and seems to have abandoned his search for the "inner life" of his characters, the "drama of souls." *Lazarus Laughed* contains much laughter—from the characters, not the audience—but the laughter never strikes to the heart of emotion. Lazarus has returned from the dead, affirming life in his laughter, but he reveals no inside, suffers no loss, feels no frustration. The audience never feels the truth of his affirmative message because his highly poeticized words and prophecies, his relentless aphorisms, come from no believable (I almost said living) character. Not only does this affirmative, mystical, panoramic pageant betray the genuine feelings of O'Neill's basically dark self, but it also, for all its theatrical trappings, works against his basic dramatic instincts, which combined theater and *character* to produce a drama of emotions. Nietzsche and the Bible put considerable pressure on this play; Shakespeare is nowhere to be found.

It seems clear that O'Neill, moving from *Marco Millions* to *The Great God Brown* to *Lazarus Laughed,* is progressing by fits and starts, latching on to a method of presentation or a unique device and then leaving it or subduing it, becoming excited about something old-new and then losing the excitement, always making another fresh start. If we were living during those heady experimental years of the late twenties, we would say that O'Neill is a restless playwright, lashing about to find new ways to present drama, perhaps too anxious to be a pioneer, perhaps too quickly abandoning a new idea before its potential is exhausted. From our vantage point in time, surveying O'Neill's entire development, we know that the theatrical devices and methods of these experimental years—and, in fact, of *all* his years, including the earlier ones that gave us the realistic sea plays and the expressionistic *Jones* and *Ape* and *Chillun*—were transformed or absorbed in his later plays. Not much was wasted, a generalization we can make with equal assurance about the early work of Shakespeare. In this respect—and getting him ready for *Mourning Becomes Electra* and the great late plays to come—probably the most important play of this experimental period is *Strange Interlude* (1927, produced 1928), which took him from a biblical past to contemporary America, from romantic extravaganza to domestic drama, from theatrical expansiveness to an exploration of the thoughts of individual characters. Here, as in *Brown,* O'Neill returned to an essentially realistic theater and returned to a dramatization of the inner life, attempting to touch the mystery of the soul within, but instead of using masks to project the hidden conflicts of the mind, his new exercise in unmasking relied on audible interior monologues or asides or soliloquies, in fact, the very devices that Macgowan predicted for his theater of tomorrow, as we already noticed. Macgowan was thinking of the revival of the old Shakespearean convention, but for most commentators on O'Neill's use of the soliloquy, the novel comes to mind. Travis Bogard, for example, says that in *Strange Interlude* O'Neill availed himself "of a novelist's privilege of permitting his characters to express unspoken thoughts."[25] The play had the popularity of a novel when it was published, and O'Neill's own statements about the play suggest that we should look to the novel as the source of his new method of presenting drama. Certainly, the audience, because it has knowledge of both the character's outer self (words spoken to others in dialogue) and inner self *(thoughts* spoken aloud), is able to obtain a rather full portrait of the character, the kind of fullness usually available in the novel. James Joyce's *Ulysses,* a novel that O'Neill greatly admired, comes easily to mind here because Joyce, with his stream-of-consciousness method, offers the reader what O'Neill offers his audience, a continuous flow of inner commentary. The difference is that O'Neill's spoken thoughts are more orderly, more directly relevant to what is being said to other characters on stage, than is Joyce's more accurate rendition of the usually jagged thought process. Observing what is happening in *Strange Interlude,* we, like Charlie Marsden (the novelist *in* the play), can say, "What a plot for a novel!" and we can agree with Peter Egri's claim that *Strange Interlude* "incorporates the form of the novel in the pattern of the drama."[26] Louis Sheaffer's belief that there was in O'Neill's playwriting "for all his instinctive theater . . . a novelistic strain" rings true.[27] It seems that O'Neill, in writing *Strange Interlude,* was aiming for the depth and scope and complexity that is available to the novelist, with the soliloquy as the key device in achieving this aim. But the fact remains that the soliloquy was, after all, that old device used by the Elizabethan dramatists to project the inner thoughts of characters in a *play.* We should not dismiss too quickly that remarkable Elizabethan convention as a spur, at least, to O'Neill's creative imagination, especially in the light of Macgowan's comments, Nietzsche's references to Hamlet, and O'Neill's references to Shakespeare in his *Memoranda on Masks.* Even a cursory look at the Shakespearean soliloquy makes clear its affinities to O'Neill's *Interlude* technique.

Shakespeare's purpose in presenting a soliloquy was generally twofold:

to define clearly the character speaking the soliloquy, revealing his innermost thoughts, strengthening the character's reality, *and* to give the actor an opportunity to share a private emotion with the audience, offering his feelings, which in turn affect the feelings of the audience. We can go almost anywhere for examples in Shakespeare. Take Prince Hal's "I know you all" soliloquy in *1 Henry IV*. Hal has just bantered with Falstaff, the audience enjoying the fun and companionship of this odd couple, a lean young prince of the royal household and a fat old debaucher. The dialogue between them establishes some of the important characteristics of their relationship, with the strain of criticism in Hal's words somewhat concealed in humor. Then Hal is alone on stage, telling us directly that the comedy we witnessed was part of the calculating role he was playing, that he stands on firm responsible ground, that his reputation belies the integrity of his character, and that when the right time comes the world will know the true self called Prince Hal. The soliloquy *gives* us that self, defining Hal for us, allowing us to *hear* what he thinks and feels, thereby influencing our attitude toward him *from now on*. Hal becomes a more full character for us because Shakespeare's convention allows us to experience his inner life in the most natural way, natural, that is, because we know that the soliloquy is a convention of Shakespeare's theater. As we already observed in the *Elms* discussion, we are closer to the inner Hamlet because of his remarkable first soliloquy, "O that this too too sallied flesh . . . " Hamlet's many soliloquies and asides bring us very close to this inner man, although some residue of mystery always remains whenever we think about Hamlet.

    This having been said, it remains obvious that Shakespeare's soliloquies, which do what O'Neill's audible thoughts do in *Strange Interlude*—reveal inner motives and feelings, define character, offer a deeper reality—have a strength and effectiveness that O'Neill's soliloquies rarely achieve. The reason—outside of the essential difference in the brilliance and suggestiveness of the language—is that Shakespeare prepares for his soliloquies. They do not offer an ongoing stream of inner revelation, as do O'Neill's audible thoughts. They *mean* more, or take to themselves a higher importance, because they do not occur often. Hamlet's first soliloquy is heard immediately after a crowded and noisy court world leaves the stage. The solitary figure in black, now alone, even more alone when we consider the bare platform stage of the Elizabethans, begins to speak to us—and his aloneness, the space around him, the tumult and talk that preceded this moment, and his spoken, deeply felt thoughts all work together to concentrate our attention on his character. O'Neill's spoken interior monologues in *Strange Interlude* allow for no such concentration. His realistic modern stage is cluttered with furniture, his characters are not often alone, the spoken thoughts are competing with the spoken dialogue, a give-and-take that allows for some dramatic excitement, perhaps, but does not allow for the kind of intensity and concentration established by Shakespeare. O'Neill is using the old Shakespearean convention in a new way, and he is attempting, without unqualified success, to achieve the same inner-life effect that Shakespeare achieves. I have no doubt that O'Neill had the novel in mind when he used his interior monologue device, but how could the Shakespearean soliloquy, a conventional device used in a play, not have exerted its own special influence?

Let me add one other point of comparison between O'Neill's soliloquies and Shakespeare's: they seem to present exactly what the character is thinking. Bernard Beckerman writes that Shakespeare's art gives us "positive reflection," that is, "the poetic expression mirrors exactly the inner state of an individual." He says that in *King Lear,* for example, "whatever anguish Lear experiences, he expresses. There is proportion between the force of his images and the passion he feels." Even when Shakespeare presents a villain, Beckerman asserts, "Shakespeare does not stress the face-mask syndrome. Differences between the villain's mask and his true face are given facts of the narrative, but in the midst of a villain's scheming Shakespeare does not play upon the tension between what a villain says and what he feels."[28] In *Strange Interlude,* when O'Neill uses the soliloquy, which is functioning as the face behind the mask, we have Shakespearean positive reflection. The words of O'Neill's characters exactly mirror their thoughts, and although there is considerable conflict between the spoken dialogue and the spoken inner thoughts, although O'Neill is presenting continuous contradiction and counterpoint, there is surprisingly little tension between word and thought. The relationship between word and feeling is too clear, too direct, too efficient. We *did* feel tension when O'Neill's inarticulate characters (like Brutus Jones and Yank Smith) tried to express their deep feelings, but beginning with the experimental period and extending into his late plays O'Neill, like Shakespeare before him, gives us "positive reflection."

Outside of the soliloquy there seems at first glance to be little else in *Strange Interlude* that is Shakespearean. But a second glance reveals some connections that should be mentioned. In *Strange Interlude* O'Neill offers the kind of antitheses and counterpointings that we associate with Shakespeare's dramaturgy. Its most obvious manifestation, perhaps too obvious and occurring too often, is the simple contradiction uttered by a single character. For example, Ned Darrell's words when Nina asks him to stay for lunch: "(*struggling—shakenly*) No, I think I'd better—(*thinking desperately*) got to go!... can't go!... got to go!" (2:727). More interesting is the counterpointing of ideas spoken by the same character. Here is Nina on God the Mother vs. God the Father: "I am living a dream within the great dream of the tide... breathing in the tide I dream and breathe back my dream into the tide... suspended in the movement of the tide, I feel life move in me, suspended in me... no whys matter... there is no why... I am a mother... God is a Mother..." (2:715). "Strange interlude! Yes, our lives are merely strange dark interludes in the electrical display of God the Father!" (2:817). This antithesis is somewhat analogous to the two natures in *King Lear,* Edmund's goddess who stands up for bastards versus Lear's goddess, whom he asks to *suspend* her legitimate and natural purpose in order to make his daughter barren.

Most interesting is not only the counterpointing of character *feelings* but also the more complex antithesis of realism and something that goes beyond realism, like the tableau O'Neill presents at the end of act 6. The three men in Nina's life—Sam Evans, her husband; Ned Darrell, her lover; Charles Marsden, a father figure—*"mechanically"* sit down in silence while Nina remains standing, *"dominating them,"* according to O'Neill's stage directions (2:754). Each man speaks his hidden thoughts, as allowed by O'Neill's soliloquy device. Then Nina speaks her thoughts:

> My three men!... I feel their desires converge in me!... to form one complete beautiful male desire which I absorb... and am whole... they dissolve in me, their life is my life... I am pregnant with the three!... husband!... lover!... father!... and the fourth man!... little man!... little Gordon!... he is mine too!... that makes it perfect!... *(with an extravagant suppressed exultance)* Why, I should be the proudest woman on earth!... I should be the happiest woman in the world!... *(then suppressing an outbreak of hysterical triumphant laughter only by a tremendous effort).* Ha-ha... only I better knock wood... *(She raps with both knuckles in a fierce tattoo on the table.)* before God the Father hears my happiness! (2:756)

Then she kisses each man differently—Sam *"as she might kiss a big brother,"* Charlie *"as she might her father,"* Ned *"lovingly on the lips as she would kiss her lover"* (2:757). This scene approaches Shakespearean complexity. We cannot reduce what is happening to any single statement, and we cannot explain the exact nature of its impact on us, but it does move us. What is happening on stage is both realistic and nonrealistic, challenging our emotions. As a comparable Shakespearean example, we might turn to Gloucester's fall from the imaginary cliff at Dover. His despair, the result of spiritual regret and physical blinding, brings him to thoughts of suicide.

The trickery of his good son Edgar, counterpointing the trickery of his evil son Edmund, allows him to endure life a little longer, to wait for a death less desperate. We don't know what exactly to make of Gloucester's imaginary leap from despair to hope, from the heights of a Dover cliff but actually a couple of feet on the Shakespearean platform stage, a troublesome stage action that can lead to either laughter or tears. The jump is both real and not real, comical and terrible, true and not true. I am not claiming that O'Neill was thinking of this particular Shakespeare scene or any similarly complex one when writing his "my three men" scene. But Shakespeare's mode of presentation, so rich in suggestiveness, so difficult to clearly articulate, may have taught a valuable lesson in playwriting to an eager and ever-restless student of the drama.

The play's title, both as a title and as a phrase used within the play, stresses the importance of time, a theme essential to both O'Neill and Shakespeare. O'Neill, through the lips of Nina Leeds, makes explicit what the title suggests: "the only living life is in the past and future ... the present is an interlude ... strange interlude in which we call on past and future to bear witness we are living!" (2:784). The ghosts of Nina's past—especially the ghost of her lover, aviator Gordon Shaw, who was killed in World War I before she was able to marry him, thanks to her father whom she never forgives, and before she had sexual relations with him, thanks to Gordon's own sense of honor—haunt and frustrate her present desires. Her life is fulfilled only when she dominates her three men, it seems, but hers is a short-lived happiness; in fact, as the years go by, she becomes "sick of the fight for happiness." And the years do go by! The play stretches over a five-hour period, in which the audience witnesses the characters' physical aging and spiritual changes, with Nina beginning the play at age twenty and ending it at age forty-five, "beyond desire," resting comfortably in the arms of her "father" Charlie (now sixty), and falling asleep as "the evening shadows" close in around them. Life is a dying process, and the persistent consciousness in O'Neill of the tragic consequences of the workings of time, of the temporal nature of man, of mutability, brings him close, in theme and conviction, to Shakespeare's emphasis in his tragedies. Not that *Strange Interlude* is a tragedy. By no means, especially because O'Neill is dramatizing what Frederic Carpenter correctly labels "the dead average of human experience,"[29] but O'Neill is getting in the mood. The play reveals the darker side of O'Neill, his essential side, what *Marco Millions* and *Lazarus Laughed* did not do, and what *The Great God Brown* did not sustainedly or successfully do. Death, connected with time and determinism, plays its part in producing the effect of *Strange Interlude,* but it does not become the kind of tragic condition that propelled the action of *Desire*

Under the Elms or that will comprise the entire atmosphere of *Mourning Becomes Electra*.

Although O'Neill presents Nina Leeds as a middle-class heroine in a domestic drama, he uncannily makes her portrait mythic as well as personal. She seems to be a woman and Woman. With the passing years she plays every role associated with the idea of woman—daughter, whore, wife, mistress, mother, child. (All the roles pertain to her relationships with men, which, along with the play's mechanical Freudianism, helps to date the play.) Her personal desires seem insatiable, to the point where she could be called neurotic, but the desires she arouses in the men in her life are equally intense. The long play allows her to display a wide range of emotions, from sexual and spiritual frustration to peaceful contentment. But O'Neill pushes the emotional personal Nina toward the symbolic Nina by giving her "strange, devious intuitions," expressed for the most part, but not always, through her soliloquies. These intuitions allow her to raise the provocative idea of God the Mother, whose birth pains created life, who is the source of all that is natural in life, including death. Nina's Mother God stands in stark contrast to the usual conception of God "the Boss," "the male God that makes life so perverted." (We are reminded, of course, of the hard male God of Ephraim Cabot.) By play's end, in the mythic battle of the gods, the Father God is the winner, as Nina clearly recognizes: "Strange interlude! Yes, our lives are merely strange, dark interludes in the electrical display of God the Father!" However, along the way—and it's a long way—Nina herself takes on the Mother God characteristics in that she represents Woman in all her complex facets, filled with womanly frustrations, feeling a woman's emotional needs, relishing her temporary power over men, inevitably becoming resigned to the dominance of the male. Hers becomes the peace that stems from such resignation. She asks Charlie: "Will you let me rot away in peace?" (2:815). And at play's end, regressing into childhood, united with her "father" in the person of Charlie Marsden—for Freudians a confirmation of her Electra complex—she wishes "to die in peace! I'm so contentedly weary with life!" (2:817). Nora's is both a personal and mythic struggle against time and God the Father. In her various roles she is a woman who holds an audience's interest even as she holds the interest of the men in her life.

The closest Shakespeare analogue to the kind of portrait O'Neill gives us in Nina Leeds is Cleopatra. The comparison may seem farfetched and subjective in the extreme because middle-class, representative Nina and the exotic queen Cleopatra occupy worlds remarkably different, but it is interesting to note, at least, that both women play various roles, both are the sources of enormous interest for the men in their lives, both occupy personal and mythic territory, both are real and not real. (Concerning the last, for example, how effectively Shakespeare first gives us an artificial Cleopatra on the unbelievable barge, and then immediately presents a woman who must catch her breath as she runs along the Egyptian streets. Cleopatra is both "statue" and "breather.") Nina may not have the characteristics of a *femme fatale,* an epithet synonymous with Cleopatra, but she does have a strong sexual dimension. Charles Marsden in act 2 offers this spoken thought: "I suppose every single damned inmate has fallen in love with her!... her eyes seemed cynical... sick with men... as though I'd looked into the eyes of a prostitute" (2:654). Ned's spoken thought: "How much need I tell him [Charles Marsden]?... can't tell him the raw truth about her promiscuity" (2:663). Marsden again: "She's hard!... like a whore!... tearing your heart with dirty finger nails!... my Nina!... cruel bitch!" (2:668). This approaches the Roman view of Cleopatra—"strumpet," "whore," "triple-turned whore." Nina may not have the overpowering seductive charm of Cleopatra, as Shakespeare describes her, but listen to Ned Darrell, her lover: "she always had strong physical attraction for me... that time I kissed her... one reason I've steered clear since... take no chances on emotional didos... need all my mind on my work" (2:704). Later, Ned again: "touch of her skin!... her nakedness!... those afternoons in her arms!" (2:720), and "got me where she wants me!... her body is a trap!... I'm caught in it!... she touches my hand, her eyes get in mine, I lose my will!" (2:728). Later still: "came back because I love her!... sound of her voice... seemed to burn inside my head... God, I'm licked! ... no use fighting it... I've done my damnedest... work... booze... other women... no use... I love her!... always!... to hell with pride!" (2:746). And eleven years after those words: "our love!... well, whatever it is that has bound us together, it's strong!... I've broken with her, run away, tried to forget her... running away to come back each time more abject!... or, if she saw there was some chance I might break loose, she'd find some way to call 'me back... and I'd forget my longing for freedom, I'd come wagging my tail" (2:760). Admittedly, Ned is a prosaic Antony, but his dilemma (the conflict between love and profession), Nina's Cleopatra-like pull on him, even some of the specific details of his inner utterance, all are echoes of Shakespeare's mature romantic tragedy. For Antony, who wanted to keep his mind on his duty—the only one who responsibly remained in the marketplace, not rushing with everyone else to see Cleopatra approach on her remarkable barge—Cleopatra is the trap he cannot avoid. He, like Ned, is struck by many a "Roman thought," and says, "These strong Egyptian fetters I must break." He is always drinking; he marries another woman but must return to Cleopatra because he can never forget her; she is part of him. Even when she leaves the battle at sea, he "flies after her," not wagging his tail like a dog, as does Ned, but comparably, "like a doting mallard," losing his pride. Antony, like Ned, realizes the strength of the bond of love and attraction:

> Egypt, thou knew'st too well
> My heart was to thy rudder tied by th' strings
> And thou shouldst tow me after. O'er my spirit
> Thy full supremacy thou knew'st, and that
> Thy beck might from the bidding of the gods
> Command me.
>
> (3.11.56–61)

Even Ned's reference to Dido, the only time Dido is mentioned in any O'Neill play, recalls the one reference to Dido in *Antony and Cleopatra,* that glorious moment when Antony, thinking Cleopatra is dead, says, "I will o'ertake thee, Cleopatra," and then,

> Stay for me!
> Where souls do couch on flowers, we'll hand in hand,
> And with our sprightly port make the ghosts gaze.
> Dido and her Aeneas shall want troops,
> And all the haunt be ours.
>
> (4.14.50–54)

Of course, no moment in O'Neill's play comes close to approaching the richness of this moment in Shakespeare, but Ned Darrell is a reflection, pale though it may be, of the Antony caught in a trap, in love and lust with a woman of infinite variety. Cleopatra, Shakespeare makes clear, is more than lover and mistress. She is the daughter "descended of so many royal kings." She is a "wife" to Antony in the end, saying "Husband, I come!" when she thinks of joining him in death. She is a mother not only to her own children, only briefly mentioned, but to the asp that will suck the nurse to sleep. And she is a goddess, displaying the natural fecundity of Nina's God the Mother. Her last words, as she begins the sleep of death, suggest the contentment Nina feels at the end of *Strange Interlude:* "As sweet as balm, as soft as air, as gentle—O Antony!" In short, Nina and Cleopatra, like Ned and Antony, share similar qualities. I state this rather gingerly, with the hope that my comparisons do not appear too subjective. I do not claim that *Antony and Cleopatra* was a source for *Strange Interlude,* but the two plays have much in common. The connections I have pinpointed may be merely coincidental, and they touch general human concerns, but Shakespeare is so much a part of O'Neill and the soliloquy is so obviously a Shakespearean device that it is difficult not to see Shakespeare casting his shadow on O'Neill's *Strange Interlude.* (That Shakespeare is in O'Neill's mind when he writes the play can be discerned from a sentence found in the second scenario. Ned Darrell is filled with worry about Nina when she's in the sanatorium. As O'Neill states it, Darrell "tries to throw it off—'What is Hecuba to him?'" *Hamlet* seems always to be with O'Neill, but the sentence does not appear in the final playscript.)

Autobiography enters *Strange Interlude* in various ways, with Nina the "first real portrait" of O'Neill's mother, according to Travis Bogard,[30] with Nina, according to Michael Manheim, a changed-sex portrait of O'Neill himself,[31] although Ned Darrell also displays many of O'Neill's characteristics. O'Neill's Oedipus complex and his first encounter with a prostitute come into play with Charlie Marsden's thoughts. (Charlie, in fact, is the character O'Neill said he liked most, after Nina.) And O'Neill's affair, during his Greenwich Village days, with Louise Bryant, the wife of his friend Jack Reed, gives the Darrell-Nina-Evans triangle a biographical interest. O'Neill saw his own life—all our lives—as a "strange interlude," and he allowed pieces of that life to enter his play in disguised fashion, but his autobiography does not put the kind of emotional pressure on the play that we found in *Elms* or that we will find in *Mourning Becomes Electra.* *Strange Interlude* was the most celebrated play of the twenties, enormously successful commercially because of the novelty of the soliloquy device, because of its great length, necessitating a dinner break (another novelty), because of its popularization of Freud's ideas, allowing the audience to get its Freud the easy way, and because it was censored for obscenity. Evaluating it as part of O'Neill's entire development, I would say it is successful because O'Neill had come "home" to a realistic setting, to an exploration of the inner person, to a more characteristically dark attitude toward life. Nevertheless, *Strange Interlude* remains a dated play with obvious flaws, a theatrical experiment that is more important for what it anticipates than for what it is.

Even more flawed is the next and last experimental play O'Neill writes before he begins to concentrate on *Electra. Dynamo* (written 1928, produced 1929) was on O'Neill's mind for a few years, originally thought of as part of a trilogy dealing with religion. Fortunately, the trilogy never materialized, although its second part, entitled "Without Ending of Days," eventually became *Days Without End,* written in the thirties. O'Neill, ambitious as ever, had a "big subject" in mind when he composed *Dynamo,* as we learn in a letter he wrote to George Jean Nathan. His aim was to

> dig at the roots of the sickness of Today as I feel it—the death of the old God and the failure of Science and Materialism to give any satisfying new One for the surviving primitive religious instinct to find a meaning for life in, and to comfort its fears of death with. It seems to me anyone trying to do big work nowadays must have this big subject behind all the little subjects of his plays or novels, or he is simply scribbling around on the surface of things and has no more real status than a parlor entertainer.[32]

For this "big work" he decided to use the soliloquy device again, not as often as in *Strange Interlude* but still perhaps more often than necessary to establish the roots of Reuben Light's psychological problem—his disillusionment with a father whose God denies life, and his victimization by a possessive mother. O'Neill also uses the *Elms* device of allowing the audience to see both interior and exterior scenes simultaneously, and he even goes further back, to *The Hairy Ape,* for his use of sounds as a dramatic motif, especially the sound of the dynamo. Reuben's worship of the dynamo as a substitute God blends into his incestuous desire for the dynamo as a substitute mother, to whom he finally returns in his death when he incestuously electrocutes himself. Again, the autobiographical O'Neill is dramatizing some primal family betrayals and struggles and psychological complexes, with the Mother-God idea—an idea he seemed unable to avoid during his experimental period—producing its most bizarre manifestation in the "maternal" machine. And again, O'Neill in *Dynamo* is experimenting with many and different theatrical devices, but unfortunately these are put in the service of a mechanical melodramatic plot and a vague philosophical idea. Shakespeare does not find his way into this play, except, of course, for the leftover *Interlude* and *Elms* devices, but a *Hamlet* phrase can be found in his notes on the casting of *Dynamo.* O'Neill knows it will be difficult to find the right actress for Mrs. Fife, one of O'Neill's large earth mothers, in fact, the mother for whom Reuben Light displays incestuous longings at play's end (since his Oedipal desires encompass flesh as well as machine). O'Neill writes" "Ah, here's the rub—the fattest (in more ways than one!!) part in the play and the hardest to cast."[33] This seems to be the only touch of humor connected with the entire dismal affair called *Dynamo.*

It's clear that in the five experimental plays produced between *Desire Under the Elms* and *Mourning Becomes Electra* O'Neill was trying to be both expansive (reaching for the horizon) and deeply introspective (reaching for the soul). He saw himself, with great justification, as the breaker of new dramatic ground. When he won the Nobel Prize for Literature in 1936, he wrote to his friend Russel Crouse that "my pioneering had busted the old dogmas wide open and left them [American playwrights] free to do anything they wanted in any way they wanted."[34] Having written the five plays I have discussed briefly, O'Neill himself became "free" of his pioneering restlessness (with one exception, *Days Without End*), "free" to return to realism, the source of his greatest strength as a dramatist. In three of those plays *(Brown, Strange Interlude, Dynamo)* what he literally presented on stage by means of masks and soliloquies—the thoughts and feelings of his characters—now were able to return to the dialogue and to the subtext. What was hidden would have to become known in ways that didn't disrupt the realistic structure of narration. The masks and soliloquies allowed for too mechanical, perhaps too easy, an articulation of feelings, leaving little room for audience participation. Shakespeare's convention, the soliloquy, gave him direct passage to the inner life of his characters, but it was Shakespeare's *convention* and it was used sparingly. O'Neill's experiments displayed the strain that must come when a modern dramatist on a modern stage attempts to present realistic characters in a style that is nonrealistic, that calls attention to itself *as style*. Still, these experiments were important to O'Neill because his large ambitions and specific new/old devices got him closer to the "drama of souls" he was determined to present on the modern stage. These devices were absorbed in his later realistic plays, beginning with *Mourning Becomes Electra*. Is it not possible to say that O'Neill in his experimental period is searching for Shakespeare's flexibility and fluidity, for Shakespeare's ability—because of his genius, but also because of his stage and the conventions of his theater—to reach that *innerness* which produces realistic *character*? Can we not say that O'Neill was searching for what Shakespeare already had? And I do not mean language, which O'Neill knew was a lost cause for him. O'Neill wrote to Joseph Wood Krutch, "Oh, for a language to write drama in! For a speech that is dramatic and isn't just convention! I'm so straight-jacketed by writing in terms of talk!... But where to find that language?"[35] He could also have written, "Oh, for the kind of convention that Shakespeare had, like the soliloquy and aside, to allow me to get inside my characters! Oh, for the kind of platform stage that Shakespeare had, to achieve maximum fluidity and flexibility!" Knowing that he did not have "poetic" gifts, knowing too that he had a sure, perhaps instinctive, grasp of stage effects—after all, he was his father's son—O'Neill was bold in his theatrical experimentation. Searching for his own dramatic language, he thrashed about, trying everything, including devices that we associate with Shakespeare, but there is not much in these plays, outside of such devices, that we can discuss with some confidence as Shakespearean, what we were able to do when examining *Jones* and *Chillun* and *Elms*. With *Mourning Becomes Electra* (written 1929–31, produced 1931) the frenzied experimentation is over. O'Neill will attempt to present "unreal realism," but he'll do so in a realistic play that absorbs and makes less obtrusive the experiments that came before. He will take much time to write *Electra,* perhaps because the subject was a big one as he competes with the Greek dramatists he so much admired, perhaps because he now has achieved domestic security in his third marriage, to Carlotta Monterey, perhaps because he's ready to settle down within himself, returning to familial feelings of guilt and compassion, to a reliance on straight talk from the heart, to a dependence on the actor as the main conduit for emotion. With *Electra* he returns as well to Shakespeare.

In a 1929 letter to Kenneth Macgowan, that is, while he is composing *Electra,* O'Neill clearly reveals his attitude toward the theatrical devices he used in the experimental plays: "No more sets or theatrical devices as anything but unimportant background—except in the most imperatively exceptional case where organically they belong."[36] A look at his work diary for *Mourning Becomes Electra* (which begins with a brief notation in 1926 and ends with a September 1931 entry) indicates that he was thinking about masks and interior monologues, but finally, by July 1930, he decided that they "now seem entirely unnecessary." In his 21 September 1930 entry, O'Neill offers this interesting comment:

> Scheme for revision and final version—in spite of labor on this stylized conception am glad I did it—time not wasted—learned a lot—stylized solil. uncovered new insights into characters and recurrent themes—job now is to get all this in naturally in straight dialogue—as simple and direct and dynamic as possible—with as few words—stop doing things to these characters—let them reveal themselves—in spite of (or because of!) their long locked-up passions, I feel them burning to do just this![37]

He seems to be insisting to himself that he must be "direct" and that he must allow the characters to reveal *their* own feelings directly. Still, notice that he doesn't regret the time he spent on his "stylized conception" because he "learned a lot." Certainly, between the realistic *Elms* and the realistic *Electra* his stylized experimental plays taught him a lot, bringing him closer to the *inner* person, so close that his characters can now reveal themselves directly. No obtrusive theatrical device, he feels, must get in the way of the direct expression of a character's needs. At times, however, the play's psychology is too direct, too clinical, with the characters offering their own Freudian explanations of behavior. Here, for example, are Christine's words to Lavinia: "You've tried to become the wife of your father and the mother of Orin! You've always schemed to steal my place!" (2:919). Or, as another example, here is Orin talking to the dead Adam Brant, his mother's lover, whom he has just killed: "If I had been he I would have done what he did! I would have loved her as he loved her—and killed Father too—for her sake!" (2:996). This is psychological determinism so directly stated, so explicit, that it gives little opportunity for an audience to work at its own investigation of the character's innerness or motives. O'Neill successfully eliminated the *literal* theatrical devices that revealed the inner person, but at times he does not allow a subtext to remain subtext, at times he is too anxious to put everything into the direct speech of his characters. Still, for the most part, *Electra* powerfully reveals the inner agony of its characters. Here, even more than in *Elms,* O'Neill worked down to his own emotions, and he allowed those emotions to spill out on the page more directly than ever before without neglecting the discipline always connected to his dramatic art; he, after all, *controlled* those characters who were "burning" to release their "locked-up passions." Even a cursory reading of his work diary reveals the problems that the *craftsman* O'Neill confronts in order to present what for him was his biggest project ever. But he seems to be taking more time and more pains to offer his audience *realistic* drama, which for O'Neill means a "sense of the unreal behind what we call reality which is the real reality!"[38] In short, in *Electra* he gets closer to that "drama of souls" than ever before, even as he gets closer to his private feelings, to himself.

It is strikingly interesting, I believe, that in order to get to that "real reality" in *Electra* O'Neill went, as he did in *Elms,* to Greek drama and legend. Autobiographical as these plays are, O'Neill cannot as yet offer his past, his feelings, directly—as he will come close to doing in *Long Day's Journey*—but must submerge himself in the Greek story. That he went to the Greeks suggests that here, as always, O'Neill was challenging himself; he was vying with the best. As he wrote to Joseph Wood Krutch in 1929, after criticizing modern American playwrights who present no "big themes," who are merely "success-chasers": "Well, no one can find fault with me on these lines on what I'm setting out to do now. It's an idea and dramatic conception that has the possibilities of being the biggest thing modern drama has attempted. Far the biggest! You have to go back to Greeks and Elizabethans to tie it."[39] O'Neill's biggest challenge, stated repeatedly in his work diary, is presented in the very first entry in 1926, when *Electra* was merely an idea: "Is it possible to get modern psychological approximation of Greek sense of fate into such a play, which an intelligent audience of today, possessed of no belief in gods or supernatural retribution, could accept and be moved by?" He would use the Greek story of Electra to present his modern—read Freudian—approximation of Greek fate, with Aeschylus's *Oresteia* trilogy as the predominant underpinning for the narrative structure. He follows Aeschylus closely in the first part *(Homecoming)*, somewhat closely in the second part *(The Hunted)*, rarely in the third part *(The Haunted)*. Electra does not even appear in Aeschylus's third play, *The Eumenides*; in O'Neill's trilogy Electra (Lavinia) is the focus of attention throughout. The play is hers, although she shares it at times with Christine Mannon and Orin Mannon and Ezra Mannon. She is the prime mover of the play's action; her last moments absorb all the previous action in the play. In *Electra,* as in *Elms,* O'Neill uses a classical story as it suits his purpose. Of course, he changes much, easily pinpointed and perhaps too easily criticized by those, like St. John Ervine, who wish to assert the superiority of the ancients, wondering how O'Neill "dares comparison with Aeschylus."[40] He changes much, but he keeps what is essential to tragedy, death and determinism. What he keeps and how he modifies what he keeps allows me to connect him with Shakespeare in this play that marked the climax of what could be called O'Neill's first career, the play that clearly pointed the direction he would take in the late great plays of his second career.

However strong the case may be for Shakespeare's influence on *Electra,* it is clear that from O'Neill's point of view—and in the light of his use of Aeschylus, his entries in the work diary, his private comments on his "big" play that will compete with the Greeks—Greek drama is his primary inspiration. We should not forget this even as we notice that when he wrote about "the one true theatre" he yoked together "the theatre of the Greeks and Elizabethans," even as we notice that in the letter to Krutch he states that "you have to go back to Greeks and Elizabethans" to find what he is attempting in *Electra.* The Greeks are most important, but the Elizabethans are very much on his mind too. (I add parenthetically that in a letter to George Jean Nathan, written in 1929, that is, while he is working on *Electra,* O'Neill mentions that he saw his first "talkie" and that its technique "could set me free in so many ways I feel still bound down—free to realize a real Elizabethan treatment and get the whole meat out of a theme." He goes on to say he is not impressed with the objection that the talkies will "do away with the charm of the living breathing actor," because for him "the play's the thing," and the play may be even better served by the new medium.)[41] I do not believe, as do Horst Frenz and Martin Mueller, that in *Electra* we have "more Shakespeare and less Aeschylus,"[42] but I do wish to claim that in *Electra*, as in *Elms* with which it has obvious affinities, Shakespeare puts his distinctive pressure on O'Neill's creative imagination.

The *Oresteia* trilogy has basic affinities with the play that is the most important Shakespearean source for *Mourning Becomes Electra*, the play that served a similar purpose for *Elms*, the play that was most internalized by O'Neill (and perhaps by all who are reading this book)—Hamlet. Aeschylus's trilogy, O'Neill's, and *Hamlet* have revenge as the main theme. A crime of the past causes a protagonist in the present to act and to suffer. The past in Aeschylus and O'Neill goes back farther than the past in *Hamlet*, it seems. In Aeschylus it all started with the Atreus-Thyestes relationship, in O'Neill with the Abe Mannon-David Mannon relationship, but in Shakespeare it starts with the death of the protagonist's father, nothing immediately behind that event, as in Aeschylus and O'Neill. (However, one must state parenthetically that Claudius's act, which is the act of Cain on Abel, has "the primal curse" connected with it, and so may reach back even farther than the Aeschylus and O'Neill curses.) Still, the main action for the three playwrights focuses on a child who must avenge a father's death. In Aeschylus we have a daughter who prods a son to revenge, but the son, Orestes, is the unequivocal center of the play, the dilemma and act of revenge his and his alone, the entire trilogy named after him. In *Electra* we witness two children who have the choice of revenge, Lavinia and Orin. In *Hamlet*, we concentrate on the one son, Hamlet, but there's another son, Laertes, who seeks revenge for *his* father's death, and still another avenging son, Fortinbras; in fact, we may wish to see Ophelia as another daughter who, like Lavinia, has lost a father but who plays no active part in avenging that father's death, although her madness and death prod her brother to action. The protagonist's choice of allegiance to either father or mother is important to the three playwrights, although in Aeschylus the conflict of patriarchy versus matriarchy takes on a high religious dimension, resolved in nothing less than a divine court trial where gods must decide, and where Orestes is finally absolved of his crime. In the more secular *Electra* and *Hamlet*, absolution does not seem possible and death triumphs, although Shakespeare allows the last minutes in his play to soften Hamlet's guilt and crimes—Laertes forgives him, Horatio will report his cause "aright," "angels" will sing him to his "rest." No such softening for Lavinia in *Electra*.

O'Neill follows the main features of the Aeschylus plot, but in doing so he seems to be following the plot features of *Hamlet* even more closely than those found in the *Oresteia*. I have no way of verifying my intuition that O'Neill had *Hamlet* in mind without realizing it, but notice, at least, that the murder of Ezra Mannon, like the murder of Old Hamlet—and unlike the murder of Agamemnon—comes by way of poison. Notice that the father in both plays reveals the murderer to the avenging child, Ezra pointing "an accusing finger" at Christine while Lavinia is in the room (2:946), the Ghost revealing the specifics of his death to Hamlet (1.5.35–79). When Lavinia enters that room, the *bedroom* of Ezra and Christine, she says, "I had a horrible dream—I thought I heard Father calling me" (2:946). The Ghost literally calls Hamlet, an event we witness on a haunting midnight stage. (And again, later, the Ghost appears in the bedroom where the family is together for the only time in the play, but mother doesn't see father, who may be in Hamlet's "dream.") Both fathers are ghostly presences throughout the plays—Old Hamlet literally a ghost, Ezra Mannon a portrait and a dead body—putting enormous pressure on the minds of the avengers. In both plays the fathers, like the mother in *Elms,* demand revenge and force their children into the role of avenger. The deed of murder in both plays—as opposed to the murder of Agamemnon—is a dark secret that the avenger must expose, and both avengers, Lavinia and Hamlet, must use indirections to find directions out. Both fathers, returning from the dead, tell harrowing tales—Old Hamlet offering the specific details of his poisoning, and describing as well his purgatorial condition in the "undiscovered country from whose bourn" this traveler returned; Ezra Mannon returning from the war that, as he describes it, is a return from the discovered country of the dead. Both Lavinia and Hamlet have stubborn memories; they cannot carry on as usual after their fathers' deaths; they cannot cast off their nighted color. Mourning becomes them both, and both are "born to set things right" in family tragedies that acquire mythic dimensions.

Each avenger must confront a mother's betrayal and a mother's sexuality, but here the complex and rich (should I say Shakespearean?) Hamlet must be split to give us two O'Neill characters, Lavinia and Orin. (Still, we will find that Lavinia has her own split complexity; she is both her father and her mother—"I'm only half Mannon.") Again, as in *Elms,* O'Neill's Oedipus complex must be acknowledged as he works his way toward his deeper self and as he uses the play that allowed Shakespeare to work toward his self. Both Lavinia and Orin, like Hamlet (and like O'Neill), must confront a "guilty" mother, but their feelings about that mother are lodged in very different personalities. Lavinia, acting out an Electra complex (which, for our purposes and O'Neill's, is merely an Oedipus complex with the sexes reversed—"daddy's little girl" rather than "mama's little boy"), is filled with hatred and rage against her adulterous mother: "How can you be so vile as to try to use me to hide your adultery?" "You vile—! You're shameless and evil! Even if you are my mother, I say it!" (2:916). Michael Manheim sees Lavinia's attitude as a reflection of "O'Neill's recurrent hostility toward his mother for her addiction."⁴³ This seems right. Of course, the experience of betrayal by a mother is what breaks the heart of Hamlet. What somewhat complicates the issue in *Electra* is Lavinia's love for Adam Brant, who looks like her father and her brother—after all, he's part of the "family," with O'Neill's "mask-like" faces insisting on family resemblance and, as a consequence, insisting on the idea of incest. Lavinia sees her mother as a rival in *all* her relations with the men in her life. Only when she is ready to acknowledge—because of a Freudian slip—that she *did* love Adam Brant and that her revenge against mother had a motive additional to the fact that her mother killed her father can Lavinia meet her true self. Love of "father" in all its manifestations triggers her behavior, making her a cold avenger, a kind of *"tragic mechanical doll"* (2:974), according to O'Neill's stage directions.

Orin's relationship with his mother is straightforwardly Oedipal. He, unlike his model Orestes but exactly like his model Hamlet, can only *speak* daggers to his mother. He, like Hamlet, can't picture his mother with that other man—whether it be her husband Ezra, the father he detests (echoing the Eben-Ephraim relationship and pointing ahead to the son-father relationships in the later plays), or her lover Adam Brant, who looks like his father and who looks like him, Orin. "Mother!... I could forgive anything—anything—in my mother—except that other—that about Brant!" (2:971). His homecoming encounter with his mother is heavy with incestuous words and gestures. He admits that he, like his mother, is glad that his father is dead; if it weren't for Brant, his mother would be his alone. Killing Brant, he feels, frees his mother for him: "I'll make you forget him! I'll make you happy! We'll leave Vinnie here and go away on a long voyage—to the South Seas" (2:1001). But Brant's death leads to Christine Mannon's suicide, to Orin's bitter agony and self-reproach, eventually to his death by suicide after his incestuous advances are repulsed by his sister, who has now become his mother. Death, he believes, is "an island of peace" where "Mother will be waiting for me" (2:1042). (This idea clearly looks forward to O'Neill's last play, *A Moon for the Misbegotten*.) The incest motif, so powerfully present in *Hamlet,* less so in the *Oresteia,* pervades *Mourning Becomes Electra,* and Orin the tentative, vacillating, passionate, somewhat mad, bookish, sensitive, Oedipal avenger seems to have come from the same womb as Shakespeare's Hamlet.

Orin shares another important character trait with the melancholy Dane, and in this he and his sister (and O'Neill) are one. They are all, to use Edmund Tyrone's words, "a little in love with death." Just as Freud's ideas on the Oedipus complex inform *Electra,* as they did *Elms,* so too Freud's beliefs about the death instinct charge the atmosphere of *Electra*—

and in this respect *Electra* seems different from *Elms*. (Perhaps the experimental plays in which O'Neill dealt with time and death led to this preoccupation with death in *Electra,* as if laughing Lazarus, having returned from the realm of the dead, must travel back there again.) Orin and Lavinia are Mannons, and Mannons have always been related to death. As Ezra tells Christine, Mannons "went to the white meeting-house on Sabbaths and meditated on death. Life was a dying. Being born was starting to die. Death was being born" (2:937–38). Orin, returning from the war, shares his father's death obsession. He gives a graphic account of his "heroic" deed of killing a man, and then killing another: "It was like murdering the same man twice. I had a queer feeling that war meant murdering the same man over and over, and that in the end I would discover the man was myself" (2:977). Sometimes—and here the death idea and the Oedipal idea connect—the face of the murdered man was his father's. And when he visits the body of his dead father in act 3 of *The Hunted* he realizes that "Death becomes the Mannons." Christine's evaluation of Orin, returned from the war, is the correct one: "He's still sick! He's changed! He's grown hard and cruel! All he thinks of is death!" (2:974). The words could be describing Hamlet, returned from Wittenberg, changed, growing hard, thinking only of death. Orin, like Hamlet, contemplates suicide; unlike Hamlet, he finally commits suicide, not a noble death, rather a way to end the self-torture, a way to gain the "felicity" that a union with mother will allow.

Lavinia, also death marked and death obsessed, is made of different mettle than her brother. She is the heroic tragic heroine; the trilogy belongs to her. Like Hamlet, she wears black, and her actions up to and including the killing of Adam Brant are prodded by revenge for a father's death and disgust with a mother's behavior. Her passion has a Hamlet-like intensity, and when she talks to the portraits of the Mannons in the sitting room, or to the portrait of her father (in the robes of a judge) in his study, we may hear an echo of the Hamlet-Ghost exchanges. Her emotions, dark and deep, lead her down the path of revenge and murder. In the trilogy's beginning she, like Hamlet, identifies completely with the father; however, unlike Hamlet, she confronts her mother almost immediately. (Hamlet must hold his tongue until his cathartic scene in mother's bedroom.) Like Hamlet, Lavinia controls the action of the play, uncovering a crime by "indirections"; also like Hamlet, she is controlled by fate—she could have said, with Hamlet, "my fate cries out!" She too was "born" to her condition—"O cursed spite!"—which makes her a victim as well as a victimizer. She tries but she cannot escape the cage of family and self. "Always the dead between!" she realizes at trilogy's end, and it's the large realization of a determined tragic heroine. But it's also a realization that is tinged with poignancy because Lavinia thought that once justice was done, once the claims of family and the dependence of brother were eliminated, she could lead a normal life as the wife of Peter Niles. After all, she knew that life had other possibilities than living in the Mannon house, described as a "sepulchre," a "tomb." She experienced the South Sea islands, she lived a freer life, she wants to feel love, she can order flowers for the Mannon house—and in this respect she is "half Mannon" because her mother is part of her nature too. The cold calculating "tragic mechanical doll" called Lavinia is like her father, whose portrait—the picture of a judge—hangs over the play and hangs over all her actions. But the woman who begins *The Haunted*, the woman who had the island experience, whose body has *"filled out,"* (2:1014), who now wears the green of her mother, who seems *"sure of her feminine attractiveness"* (2:1014), wants to put ideas of death and judgment behind her. She tells the guilt-ridden Orin—who now has acquired *"the statue-like quality"* (2:1014) of his father (and of the earlier vengeful Lavinia)—that the past is altogether behind them: "The dead have forgotten us! We've forgotten them!" (2:1015). ("What's done is done," we can almost hear her say.) Like Eben in *Elms*, Lavinia is the "spittin' image" of both father and mother, but God the Father (to borrow an *Interlude* phrase) prevails. Freud's death instinct is more powerful than all that seems positive and alive in Lavinia's nature. And a Freudian slip brings Lavinia back to reality: "Want me! Take me, Adam!" (2:1052). Having said "Adam" instead of "Peter," she realizes that the dead, after all, cannot be driven away, that her love for Adam Brant (who resembled her father) helped to prod her hatred of mother and her revenge. "Always the dead between!" (2:1052). ("What's done cannot be undone.") Becoming the judge of her own actions, she must now punish herself. Her last moments depart drastically from the Aeschylus source—which does not at all deal with Electra, which allows Orestes to be free of the Furies who hounded him—and also from the alleged Shakespeare source—in which a successful avenger goes to the "felicity" of death and to a "rest" that is "silence." Lavinia, facing the fact of fate, the fact that she was born a Mannon, acknowledging a guilt that can only be punished by the Mannons—and she's the last Mannon—courageously walks into the Mannon tomb, containing all the ghosts of the past, in order to confront the dead. The shutters are closed with a bang, the door closed behind her, the curtain descends on the trilogy.

Lavinia's final act haunts the mind. It is unquestionably the best ending O'Neill wrote up to that time. The act itself seems to absorb everything that led to it, the inevitable culmination of all the foreboding entrances to and exits from that awesome house. But now there's no exit from. The curtain seals Lavinia's doom. At this moment Lavinia resembles Sophocles'

Antigone more than any Electra of the Greek dramatists and more than Hamlet. Antigone also inherited her condition, is filled with both hate and love, travels a narrowing path to death, enters her cave alone and resolute, despite the terror within. But as Hamlet *approaches* his last moment, he and Lavinia, avenging children, have a distinct family resemblance. Hamlet, in the play's last scene—that is, after killing Polonius, after disgorging his sexual nausea in mother's bedroom, after sending Rosencrantz and Guildenstern to death, after contemplating the skull of Yorick (which emblematizes the death he was looking at throughout the play), after his leap into Ophelia's grave (foreshadowing the leap to come)—is able to tell Horatio, "There's a divinity that shapes our ends, / Roughhew them how we will." Hamlet at the end, like Lavinia at the end, has discovered the terrible truth of man's determined existence. Hamlet, like Lavinia, seems calmer as he faces the prospect of death, the fact of fate. He realizes that there is no escape from the condition to which he, like Lavinia, like all of us, was born. Hamlet and Lavinia have such different personalities—Lavinia hasn't the wit or imagination or playfulness or fullness of that remarkable Renaissance prince—but they both project high intensity of emotion, they both come to similar philosophical awarenesses, they both are creatures of death (mourning becoming to them both), and they both are examples of the extraordinary psychological power of the dramatists who created them.

Whatever objections one may have to my linking together two such different characters as Lavinia and Hamlet, no one will dispute, I believe, that *Mourning Becomes Electra* is O'Neill's death play, just as *Hamlet* is Shakespeare's death play. Hamlet, seeing the ghost of his father, contemplating the skull of Yorick, negotiating revenge, Lavinia, looking at the portraits of the dead, talking to her dead father, negotiating revenge—both protagonists are death obsessed, and each belongs to a play in which death is the most important condition of the experience of all the characters. The plays' atmospheres are charged with death. All of Denmark is finally a graveyard; all corpses are rotten even before they enter the graves; all the characters, not just Hamlet, finally must look at the skull of death. The Mannon house is itself a "sepulchre," but the darkness of death pervades the atmosphere of the entire trilogy. In exterior scenes, if the sun is not setting, then the moon is casting its eerie light. In interior scenes, if candles are not flickering in dark rooms, then the lighted lamp is "turned low." Shadows are always falling on the gray walls of the Greek-style house. *Electra* offers a wide context of death, just as in *Hamlet* we find that not only is Elsinore rotten but all of Denmark is rotten. When *Electra* begins, the Civil War has just ended, but O'Neill dwells on the deaths it has caused, not the peace that has come. When Ezra Mannon comes home, he reminds us of the death of Lincoln, and takes no joy in the victory of the North: "All victory ends in the defeat of death. That's sure. But does defeat end in the victory of death?" (2:932). We have already noticed Orin's emphasis on "murdering the same man over and over" in war, that man finally himself, the victor essentially the loser, the dead one. In the one scene that could possibly give us relief from the Mannon atmosphere of death, the scene that O'Neill pinpoints as the "center" of the trilogy (*The Hunted*, act 4), on the stern of Adam Brant's clipper ship, we find there's no escape from death after all. An old chantyman sings "Shenandoah" mournfully, and tells of the good old days, now gone forever. He says: "Everything is dyin'! Abe Lincoln is dead. I used to ship on the Mannon packets an' I seed in the paper where Ezra Mannon was dead!" (2:987). (And we already *saw* the dead body of Ezra Mannon on stage in the previous scene.) Then the chantyman sings "Hanging Johnny," which triggers this reaction from Brant: "Damn that chanty! It's sad as death!" (2:988). And in this scene— remember, a scene *away from* the Mannon "temple of death," as Ezra Mannon called it—we witness the onstage murder of Brant, who, as Orin discovers, looks like Ezra Mannon: "I've killed him before—over and over" (2:996). I stress the climate of death in a scene that could possibly provide some welcome relief because it reminds me that Shakespeare in *Macbeth* does allow for some relief from death and terror when he moves his audience to England for one scene only (act 4, scene 3), away from a sick Scotland, to suggest some possibility of healing. Obviously, a more relentless O'Neill wishes to offer no such relief.

The context of death is social as well as historical, for New England Puritanism, like war, brings death, death of the spirit. That is why going to the meetinghouse on Sabbaths, as Ezra tells Christine, meant "meditating on death." The repressions of a Puritan society affected Ezra's relationship with a wife he now wishes to win over. He now realizes what Christine knew all along—and what Lavinia will later proclaim when she tells Peter, "I hate what's warped and twists and eats into itself and dies for a lifetime in shadow" (2:1043)—that Puritanism deadens the soul, distorts love, sets up a wall between people.[44]

It is clear, then, that in *Mourning Becomes Electra,* as in *Hamlet,* death is the most important condition of the felt experience of the characters and of the audience. In both plays, death is tightly bound up with determinism, and both death and determinism are closely connected to Freud's family romance. O'Neill undoubtedly chose Aeschylus's *Oresteia* as his Greek source because it dwells on intense and dark family relationships within a larger context of fate, the same reason he chose Euripides' *Hippolytus* as his Greek source for *Elms.* (And the most important "family romance" Greek play, Sophocles' *Oedipus Rex,* provides additional underpinning for both *Electra* and *Elms.*) O'Neill, I maintain, less consciously, perhaps unconsciously, chose Shakespeare's *Hamlet* as a source for the same reason. And Shakespeare, we must remember, was closer to O'Neill's own family situation than were the three great Greek dramatists. In his most autobiographical play, *Long Day's Journey,* the portrait of Shakespeare takes center stage; O'Neill's father, the Shakespearean actor, quotes Shakespeare; Shakespeare provides the focus for some family discussion. In *Mourning Becomes Electra,* less autobiographical than *Long Day's Journey* but still highly personal, the Shakespeare presence is less obtrusive. The portraits are those of dead Mannons and of Ezra Mannon, the father as judge. It's clear that O'Neill is working through to some of his deepest feelings about his relationship with his father. Ezra Mannon is a man who could easily be hated—stern, repressive, bullying his son into going to war, distorting his wife's love to make it seem like lust, working to death the sailors on the ships he owned, a "skinflint" without a heart, according to the chantyman. Still, there's another side to him that prevents an audience from judging the judge too harshly. That is, he has a complexity that demands full attention, the kind of complexity that we observed in Ephraim Cabot, another New England, stern, stubborn, parsimonious, Puritanical husband-father who tries in vain to touch his wife's understanding (a wife who has also taken as lover someone in the family), the kind of complexity that the autobiographical James Tyrone also possesses. The three fathers—Ezra, Ephraim, Tyrone—hateful in so many ways, genuinely seek love from wives who repulse them. The emotions that they feel, the understanding that they desperately need and do not get, temper the hardness of their portraits. O'Neill's deep need to be reconciled with his father—like Shakespeare's deep need to be reconciled with his father, as the father-son relationship in *Hamlet* darkly demonstrates[45]—provided a remarkably strong creative impulse in O'Neill's career, beginning with and intensified in *Electra.*

The imaginative impulse that O'Neill's relationship with his mother triggered has already been confronted in my discussion of *Elms* and in this discussion of *Electra.* What seems clear to me is that O'Neill in *Mourning Becomes Electra,* by drawing on his Greek and Shakespeare sources, is getting closer than ever before to those family secrets, to his own past, to his innermost feelings. O'Neill, like Hamlet, is both Orin and Lavinia. Orin, in *The Haunted,* returns to the Mannon house from the South Sea islands in order to face his ghosts (an idea repeated by Lavinia and introduced comically by the chorus of townspeople in the first scene). Much to Lavinia's regret and great consternation, Orin is doing so by *writing* a history of the family, a story of crime and punishment. These are Orin's words:

"I've tried to trace to its secret hiding place in the Mannon past the evil destiny behind our lives!" (2:1029). Like Orin, O'Neill is also writing about his past in order to locate that "secret hiding place"; he is attempting to go "behind life." Lavinia will face her ghosts more directly, it seems, by entering that house of the dead. Like Lavinia, O'Neill has marched heroically into his dark room of the past to confront his family ghosts. What I find particularly interesting about O'Neill's creation of characters who are doing in the play what O'Neill is doing *writing* the play is this: as he is working through to his deepest self in *Electra,* as he is composing during those excruciating months of work recorded so precisely in his work diary, he is thinking about but finally discarding those extra theatrical trappings, like *Brown* masks and *Interlude* interior monologues. He is stripping *down* to his own feelings even as he is stripping *away* whatever seems superfluous to the realistic mode that is his greatest strength. The work diary gives us a blow-by-blow account of a stripping process that resulted in a marvelous confluence of method and aim. He wishes finally to achieve a simplicity and directness that would most effectively allow his *characters* to "reveal themselves." He feels that they are "burning to do just this!" Read: O'Neill is burning to reveal himself. With *Mourning Becomes Electra* he approaches that goal.

Of course, discarding the obvious techniques he used in the experimental plays does not mean he has abandoned technique. In *Electra,* as in *Elms,* he will continue to orchestrate the emotions of his audience by means of (Shakespearean?) counterpointing and juxtaposition; he will use exterior and interior scenes; he will rely, as usual, on repetitive actions and echoing words and phrases (even an echoing song, like "Shenandoah," and an echoing of character in family resemblances). In *Electra* he will allow the direct speech of the characters—with its relentless probing, with its high emotional pitch—to reveal what is within, which means he will give us the intensity and revelation of the Shakespearean soliloquy without using the formal soliloquy. (At times, in *Electra* as in *Elms,* a variation of the formal soliloquy is used—as when Orin, alone in his father's study, addresses the dead body of his father, or when Lavinia, alone with the portraits of the Mannons, talks to them directly.) And the complementarity and shifting perspectives and dividedness of character that we associate with Shakespeare we find in *Electra*. In short, O'Neill, in this tragedy of death and determinism, continues to aim for an Elizabethan fluidity and flexibility, even as he offers a realistic play whose underpinning is Greek drama, whose guiding inspiration is Freud, whose subtext is unconscious biography. Shakespeare, I wish to stress, is part of this biography, even as Shakespeare's methods of dramatic presentation affect O'Neill's methods.

I add one other O'Neillian technique that calls to mind Shakespeare's dramaturgy. The chorus scene that introduces *The Haunted*—in which the townspeople talk about the Mannon house as haunted ("The graveyard's full of Mannons and they all spend their nights to hum here" [2:1008]) and in which one of the townspeople enters the house on a wager and comically yells in terror as he runs away from it—gives us the kind of comic relief provided by the gravedigger scene in the last act of *Hamlet*. In each case, comedy lowers the play's emotional tension, but the theme of the play is not lost, death remaining the abiding issue. That is, in each play relief is emotional, not thematic, the audience always aware of the O'Neillian and Shakespearean center of interest. This is a good example, I believe, of a conscious Greek convention, the chorus, combining with what may be a less conscious Shakespearean technique to produce an effective O'Neillian scene.

For most contemporary observers, *Mourning Becomes Electra* marked the climax of what could be considered the first career of Eugene O'Neill. It was critically and commercially successful, having received admirable direction by the Theatre Guild's Philip Moeller, a memorable set by Robert Edmond Jones, and superb acting by Alla Nazimova as Christine and Alice Brady as Lavinia. In fact, the play received the most enthusiastic reviews that O'Neill would read in his lifetime, and it further solidified his already secure reputation as America's most important dramatist, giving him a big push toward his Nobel Prize of 1936. When Lavinia Mannon enters her house at the end of *Mourning Becomes Electra,* O'Neill is entering his own house, ready to face his personal past, his family, more directly. In that house, confronting his dead, O'Neill will write some of his most enduring plays, in what could be called his second career. In that house, the portrait of Shakespeare hangs prominently.

Part 2

Chapter 4

Comedy

It is appropriate, I think, that O'Neill's second career begins with a play that provides comic relief for O'Neill himself. He had behind him the agony of creation connected with *Mourning Becomes Electra,* and he was struggling with the recalcitrant autobiographical material of *Days Without End* when, according to his own statements, he dreamed *Ah, Wilderness!*. He awoke on the morning of 1 September 1932, with the play "fully formed and ready to write," and he wrote it in a six-week burst of activity.[1] It was, to use O'Neill's words, "crying to be written!" Only once before did O'Neill "dream" a play; that was *Desire Under the Elms,* which, like *Electra,* was unconscious biography. In *Ah, Wilderness!* he approached his biography more directly, even though it was dreamt. Travis Bogard puts the matter succinctly: "In creating the Miller sitting-room, O'Neill made his first direct incursion on the autobiographical substructure of his life. He entered with joy, colored by nostalgia."[2] Bogard makes this statement after reporting that O'Neill visited the New London Monte Cristo house with Carlotta when they returned from Europe, a disappointing physical visit to the house that was the center of O'Neill's creative imagination, the house that would become, with some changes in wallpaper and furniture, the setting for *Long Day's Journey*.

"Nostalgic comedy" is what O'Neill labelled *Ah, Wilderness!* in his work diary, and in another statement he calls it "nostalgia for a youth I never had."[3] Later still, he says, "The way I would have liked my boyhood to have been."[4] These comments force us to see the play as wish fulfillment, what a dream often is. Still, O'Neill's biographers and commentators have convincingly argued that O'Neill in 1906, when *Ah, Wilderness!* takes place, was happier than O'Neill in 1912, the year of both *The Iceman Cometh* and *Long Day's Journey*. However colored by wish-fulfilling dream, the play offers direct autobiography but, as in a dream, the characters are split, with O'Neill's father becoming both Nat Miller and Sid Davis, with O'Neill's mother becoming both Essie Miller and Lily, with O'Neill's brother becoming both Sid and Arthur's friend, Winton. The main character in the dream is the dreamer, O'Neill, who appears unsplit as Richard Miller, the portrait of the playwright as a young man. Incidents in the play reflect what happened to O'Neill in 1906 and later, and in this sense the play is direct autobiography, but the reflection is colored by wish and dream fantasy, which tends to soften the impact of some of the real events in O'Neill's life. (I'm thinking especially of Richard's encounter with Belle, "*a typical college 'tart' of the period*" (3:51), in a bar, only the palest reflection of O'Neill's devastating first encounter with a whore, an experience that Sheaffer calls "traumatic.")[5] In what O'Neill called his "comedy of recollection," he is recollecting—less dreamily than in the recollection of his personal life, more directly and accurately—a particular time and place in American history. This is what O'Neill clearly planned to do, as the following quotation indicates:

> My purpose was to write a play true to the spirit of the American large small-town at the turn of the century. Its quality depended upon atmosphere, sentiment, an exact evocation of the mood of the dead past. To me, the America which was (and is) the real America found its unique expression in such middle-class families as the Millers, among whom so many of my own generation passed from adolescence into manhood.[6]

Raleigh and Bogard clearly demonstrate that O'Neill does indeed offer an "exact evocation" of a dead past—middle-class, New England, America in the beginning of the new century—when the Fourth of July was an important secular celebration, when a system of family values was shared and understood, when the world (between a Civil War and World War I) seemed sunnier.[7] In bringing vividly and accurately to life a specific time and place, O'Neill offers realistic drama, filled with the exact room furnishings, the appropriate songs and holiday sounds and atmosphere, the authentic aura of domesticity within a middle-class home, the mundane everyday talk, the family jokes, and, pointing more directly to the plot, the usual dilemma of an adolescent in love and in rebellion against a complacent family. Once again, O'Neill is confronting family life, what seems to be the main focus of most of his plays, but the Millers, of course, are worlds apart from the Mannons and even from the Tyrones, whose living room they seem to share. Most commentators would agree with Frederic Carpenter's assertion that the "backdrop" of the "nostalgic 'paradise'" presented in *Ah, Wilderness!* is really the "wilderness" we find in *Long Day's*

Journey—"the dark underworld of alcoholism, prostitution, and spiritual despair."[8] The bright *Ah, Wilderness!*, like the dark *Long Day's Journey*, is a realistic play, and we may wish to see both plays as "two sides of the same coin," as the Gelbs suggest, since O'Neill is treating the same family, one caught in a pleasant dream, the other caught in a terrible reality. One can easily list the similarities between the plays, but each similarity seems to point to a difference. In both plays the members of the family love one another. (But in one play the love is mixed with hatred, in the other the love is steady and warm.) In both plays parents are worried about their children. (But how differently is that concern expressed, and in *Long Day's Journey* the problems of the children are caused by the problems of the parents.) In both plays, a son gets drunk and has a relationship with a prostitute. (But what a difference between the adolescent Richard and the debauched Jamie, between Belle and Fat Violet.) In both plays a young man quotes from his favorite authors, who write about forbidden and dark things. (In one, these quotations are in books hidden in the young man's bedroom, something to hide from parents in typical adolescent fashion; in the other, the books are on display in the sitting room, providing a source of deep contention between father and son.) In each, an outside sound punctuates the play's atmosphere. (In one, an ominous foghorn; in the other, the firecrackers of a Fourth of July celebration.)[9] The differences, of course, are what separate comedy from tragedy, and I would like to pay close attention to this generic separation in my discussion of *Ah, Wilderness!*. The play need not be examined through a lens provided by *Long Day's Journey*, a play that will be written a few years later; it should be looked at as what it is, a rather pure comedy. This is a difficult task because O'Neill is the dark brooding playwright as tragedian, a fact we can never erase from our minds, a fact that triggered the surprised reactions of reviewers and audiences when *Ah, Wilderness!* was first performed. Who would have thought O'Neill had such humor in him? The reviewers discovered that Eugene O'Neill is just plain folks after all; he *can* write a bright comedy; he *can* offer pleasurable entertainment.[10] Obviously, O'Neill was getting out of the shadows he himself created, temporarily doffing his mourning garments. His psyche demanded relief; a dream provided it; the writing of a comedy was the result. And throughout this process O'Neill seems pleased to be doing something different, perhaps seeing himself as the experimenter he always was. In writing to Macgowan about the straightforwardly realistic *Ah, Wilderness!* and the play he was struggling with at this time, *Days Without End*, he says: "These two plays will, I know, set you to wondering what a change has come over me." In the same letter, he says that with *Mourning Becomes Electra* he had gone "as far as it was in me to go along my old line."[11] O'Neill is clearly suggesting that he will now be going along a new line, which allows me to think of his plays since *Electra* as comprising his second career. Certainly, with his only full-fledged comedy, *Ah, Wilderness!*, it is clear that a sea change *has* come over him. The Shakespearean phrase fits perfectly, I believe. Found in the song that Ariel sings to Ferdinand about his supposedly dead father, lying "full fadom five" below the sea, death caused his father to suffer a "sea change / Into something rich and strange." Death is transformed into something else, something precious. O'Neill seems to insist on this sea change in a remarkably revealing letter to Laurence Langner, discussing *Days Without End:* "this play, like *Ah, Wilderness!* but in a much deeper sense, is the paying of an old debt on my part—a gesture toward more comprehensive, unembittered understanding and inner freedom—the breaking away from an old formula that I had enslaved myself with, and the appreciation that there is their own truth in other formulas too, and that any life-giving formula is as fit a subject for drama as any other."[12] The key words here are "truth" and "life-giving." A dreamy wish fulfillment though it is, a respite from O'Neill's characteristically dark vision, *Ah, Wilderness!* is the product of a dramatist's desire to write another kind of play, a comedy which has its own truth and proceeds according to its own life-giving formula. And that's the way we should confront it. With *Ah, Wilderness!* O'Neill is writing an authentic comedy for the only time in his career—although comedy is an important ingredient of many plays throughout his development—and when he writes his only comedy he has as his model, I believe, the greatest writer of romantic comedy in our language. Of course, *Ah, Wilderness!* is not Shakespearean comedy, but I am suggesting that O'Neill's nostalgic or sentimental or domestic comedy has as its inspiration the comedy of Shakespeare.

The obvious differences between O'Neill's realistic *Ah, Wilderness!* and Shakespeare's romantic comedy are easy to pinpoint. The most basic difference is the one that separates—to use a strictly Elizabethan context—Ben Jonson from Shakespeare. Jonson's comedies offer the atmosphere of realism; they try to stick close to ordinary existence, everyday life. They are usually satirical, certainly intellectual, and they conclude with the sense that society's values or the values held by the dramatist will be maintained. They usually obey the Aristotelian unities, and, like all comedy, they end happily. Shakespeare's romantic comedy makes no attempt to offer realistic illusion, has no obvious connection to ordinary life, the plots improbable, the stories bordering on the fantastic. They usually range in place and time, with Shakespeare positing what Northrop Frye calls the "green world" in which changes take place that lead to the happy ending. Their thrust is not satirical, usually; their main purpose seems to be sheer entertainment. Although Jonsonian comedy, modeled on the New Comedy of Plautus and Terence, often deals with a young man's pursuit of a woman, his obstacles along the way—usually his father—and his eventual victory, it does not offer the heavy atmosphere of *love* produced by romantic comedy. That's why *romantic* is the proper descriptive adjective for Shakespeare's comedy. Its main theme is love, "the course of which never did run smooth," but eventually "Jack shall have Jill; / Nought shall go ill"—both quotations coming from *A Midsummer Night's Dream*. But romantic though they are, these comedies, as C. L. Barber correctly insists, "almost always establish a humorous perspective about the vein of hyperbole" connected with romance.[13] Not a deeply satiric—or Jonsonian—perspective, merely "a humorous perspective," a more gentle mocking of a love connected with springtime, connected with a holiday spirit and a contagious festivity.

Obviously, *Ah, Wilderness!*, a play that attempts to present an "exact evocation" of a particular time and place, depends on the illusion of realism; it is closer, in this respect, to Jonsonian comedy than to Shakespearean comedy. It dramatizes ordinary, everyday experience in a setting that is domestic, comfortable, bourgeois, filled with the furnished things that make up a real room, filled with the ordinary concerns that make up a real day. And that O'Neill's theater is a modern theater—fourth-wall convention, authentic props and furnishings—makes *Ah, Wilderness!* even more realistic than Jonson's plays, places them even further away from the fantastic worlds of Shakespearean comedy. What, then, allows me to push my thesis into so seemingly unwelcome a comedy as *Ah, Wilderness!*?

Although O'Neill's comedy is realistic for all the reasons stated, it displays the customary pattern of romantic comedy, and it approaches the tone and holiday atmosphere of Shakespearean comedy—always excepting, of course, the differences in verbal presentation, O'Neill never approaching the remarkable range and depth of Shakespeare's wordplay. When Nat Miller, in the play's last scene, tells his wife, "From all reports, we seem to be completely surrounded by love!" (3:101), he is placing the emphasis where it belongs—the play is filled with love of all kinds, but most important, the young love of Richard Miller (soon to be seventeen; O'Neill is seventeen and a half in 1906) for Muriel McComber, the course of which is not running smooth because of a conventional blocking agent, Muriel's father. Having discovered love letters from Richard to Muriel—filled with heated Swinburne quotations—McComber ("*a thin, dried-up little man . . . dressed with a prim neatness in shiny old black clothes*" [3:19]) brings the letter to Nat Miller and accuses Richard of attempting to corrupt his daughter. Nat defends his son to an angry McComber, who will not allow his daughter to see Richard again. Nat himself is not pleased with the passionate letters—those are not the kind of letters, he believes, that a boy sends to "a decent girl"—but a confrontation with his son eases his mind, because Richard insists that he loves Muriel, that he wants to marry her, that his thoughts are chaste (even though his choice of quotation suggests otherwise). Feeling betrayed by Muriel because his letters should have been secret and because a letter she sends him (through her father) indicates they can't see each other again, Richard plays the scorned lover—"I hate her! . . . I want to be alone!" (3:25–26). When we next see Richard, "*his face wears a set expression of bitter gloom; he exudes tragedy,*" says O'Neill in his stage directions (3:31). Richard tells Lily that "Life is a joke!"; he proudly declares, "I'm a pessimist!"; "*with an air of cruel cynicism*" he denounces Muriel and women in general (3:32). That his father, later in the act, refers to Richard as "Melancholy Dane" is singularly appropriate. Richard, in a dark Hamletian mood, continues to inveigh against women—"all women love to ruin men's lives!"—and is ripe for his encounter with the prostitute Belle in the next scene, which takes place in a dingy, dimly lighted bar (which contains a nickel-in-the-slot player piano blaring out popular tunes), that is, takes place away from the domestic comfort of the Miller home. An inexperienced and naive young man, Richard gets drunk, but not drunk enough to accept Belle's sexual advances, which shock him. He gives her a five-dollar bill, recites poetry, and is kicked out of the bar when he tries to accost Belle's new friend, a salesman. Returning home sick from his drink, he promises never to touch the stuff again, and stoically (and again, Hamlet-like) says, "I'll face—my fate." A letter from Muriel asks him to meet her that evening, and once again O'Neill takes Richard away from home, this time to a moonlit beach, with the sounds of a live orchestra heard faintly in the background. (The two scenes away from the Miller home—bar vs. beach—are clearly juxtaposed in every respect—atmosphere, music, types of woman.) After a long soliloquy by Richard—in which he declares his warm and chaste feelings for Muriel (whose letter he kisses), in which he recalls Belle ("she was just a whore . . . she was everything dirty" [3:87]), in which he praises the beauty of the night—the lovers meet, with Richard continuing his tragic pose for a while: "I wanted to die. I sat and brooded about death. Finally I made up my mind I'd kill myself" (3:92). Then, genuinely succumbing to the moment, he kisses Muriel "*tremblingly.*" "The moon is beautiful, isn't it?" (3:96), asks Muriel. With the moon shining on the young couple, Richard becomes the poet again, staring at the moon, quoting Swinburne, then Kipling because he'd rather go "on the road to Mandalay" than to Niagara Falls, Muriel's choice for a honeymoon. A soft scene of young love, its passion a little foolish because that's what love is—"Lord, what fools these mortals be!"—but not so foolish that we discount its value to the young lovers involved. The Richard-Muriel relationship gives us our main love story, containing many of the trappings of Shakespearean comedy, including the emphasis on chastity. The lovers are blocked at first by an older generation, but their triumph seems secure by play's end. They travel to a green world for one scene, a moonlit beach where their love is affirmed. (Notice that O'Neill, even in a seemingly landlocked comedy, cannot get far from the sea. So too in Shakespearean comedy and romance the sea is a strong presence.) The moon—symbol of romance, of chastity, of love-madness—shines over their togetherness. And music fills the air. Stated in this bare way, we have in *Ah, Wilderness!* what we have in *A Midsummer Night's Dream.* That Richard late in the play is called "Love's Young Dream"—and that O'Neill dreamed the play—reenforces this connection. (More tenuously, perhaps, the word *puckish* appears only three times in all of O'Neill, all in this play, describing Sid.) The *Hamlet* allusion and echoes do not dampen the comedy: they highlight the pose of the adolescent lover who is the object of gentle satire, the kind of gentle satire that Shakespeare gives us. (Think of the melancholy Orsino or the impetuous Orlando, lovers who must be seen, as Richard is seen, from a humorous perspective.)

Richard and Muriel are not the only lovers in *Ah, Wilderness!* As in Shakespearean comedy, the music of love is played on many strings, with counterpointing, in both Shakespeare and O'Neill, the important reflective device. I need not rehearse the various reflections on love that we find in *A Midsummer Night's Dream*—with each of the four worlds (Theseus and Hippolyta, the Athenian lovers, the fairies, Bottom and mechanicals) juxtaposed to every other world—or in *Twelfth Night,* in which Shakespeare contrasts the different kinds of love felt by an Orsino, a Malvolio, a Sir Andrew Aguecheek, and a Viola. So too in *Ah, Wilderness!* two other couples are played off against the young, foolish, heartfelt, adolescent love of Richard and Muriel—Sid and Lily, Nat and Essie. The relationship of Sid and Essie adds both humor and melancholy to the play. Each is a stereotypically comic character—the drunken uncle (a joker in every respect) and the spinster aunt—but their sixteen-year relationship, in which Lily always rejects a Sid who will never change his drinking and womanizing habits ("He's just Sid") adds a strand of genuine melancholy to the play. The love-hate dynamic that we find in O'Neill's darker plays makes itself felt in this comedy through the relationship of Sid and Lily, but it is muted by the play's comic, amiable atmosphere and by the fact that sixteen years of such a love-hate dynamic produces a comfortable equilibrium and changelessness, an acceptance of the way things are, a confirmation of the status quo, in short, a condition that seems to belong to the genre of comedy. Nat and Essie's relationship is another variation of the status quo. At times solicitous of one another, at times mildly irritated with one another, Nat perhaps a trifle condescending toward Essie, Essie sometimes making jokes at Nat's expense, their marriage is prosaic, comfortable, lacking passion, their lives absorbed by the needs and antics of their children. In both O'Neill and Shakespeare the strings of love make different sounds.

In romantic comedy love leads to marriage; certainly, when Jack gets Jill the expectation is that the marriage bells will chime. Shakespeare stops his comedies at that point, and we can say, daring not to think further about it, "they lived happily ever after." (Shakespeare's Rosalind gives us the proper perspective on this idea when she tells Orlando that "men are April when they woo, December when they wed; maids are May when they are maids, but the sky changes when they are wives.") In O'Neill's comedy, we have Richard and Muriel, the young lovers who maintain their idealism, who woo under moonlight and look forward to those wedding bells, all in the Shakespearean mold, but we also have an older, sadder couple realizing that marriage can never come for them, and another older couple who are married, but the idealism and foolishness and passion are no longer there, the word *happily* needing some qualifiers connected with the idea of friendship or shared responsibility or family feelings. At first glance, the older couples seem out of place in a romantic comedy, but they too point to the presence of Shakespeare in *Ah, Wilderness!*. First, we have the obvious comic laughter caused by the drunkenness of Sid, the intoxicated uncle (like Sir Toby Belch) who is the play's only ostensibly comic character; Sid is like the Shakespearean clown (remember, he's the puckish one), *and* like the Shakespearean fool (remember, he's the "wise" one, "the kid who wrote the book!"). Second, we have the older couples partaking of the general holiday atmosphere more joyously than the young Richard (who, asserting his own independence, shouts out against the sham of the Fourth of July) and the young Muriel (who, after all, is locked in her room for the day). When Nat and Sid return from the Fourth of July picnic, we find "Uncle Sid's soused again" (as little Tommy reports) and Nat not drunk, "*just mellow and benignly ripened*" (3:37) (as O'Neill's stage directions tell us). Sid, Nat reveals, "was the life of that picnic! . . . He ought to be on the stage" (3:38). (O'Neill here, as often, giving us those self-reflexive comments that remind us, as Shakespeare often does, that we're seeing a play.) The entrance of the intoxicated Sid, wearing his "Puckish" grin, allows the holiday dinner to begin, and here O'Neill, pulling out all stops, gives us the play's most comic scene, with the laughter coming at the expense of Nat Miller too because of his supposed aversion to bluefish and because of his oft-repeated story about Red. The comic release that comes from the holiday occasion informs the scene, as it does the play. The workaday world is put aside on this holiday occasion, with the Fourth of July, that distinctly American holiday—and not a bad holiday for an Irishman like O'Neill, who, like Richard, understands the hypocrisy behind the notion of independence in American society but who surely appreciated the defeat of the British—providing the kind of ritual festivity (without the fantastic or supernatural) that Shakespeare gives us in his midsummer nights or his twelfth nights or his May days. The Fourth of July, the folk ritual of America, is a festive and social time, a time for "cakes and ale," a time exuding a general sense of well-being. *Ah, Wilderness!*, in its realistic mode, exactly evoking a particular time and place, beautifully captures the holiday mood, helped considerably by the play's music. Songs of all kinds fill the air, sung in the Miller home, blaring in the bar where Richard is almost seduced, filtering through the moonlit beach scene. Although they genuinely join in the holiday festivities, the older couples nevertheless remind us that holidays cannot last, that time does exact its price on youth and idealism and passion. They help to establish a tone for *Ah, Wilderness!* that is very close to that produced by Shakespeare in *Twelfth Night*, the last of his romantic comedies, the play he is writing at about the same time he's writing *Hamlet*, which may have some influence on the tone of the comedy. O'Neill too, even in his only full-fledged comedy, cannot cast aside the "Melancholy Dane" that Richard is called, that O'Neill himself is.

Time is a big theme in all of O'Neill's plays, as it is in Shakespeare's plays, but I believe that nowhere in the work of either dramatist does it play as important a part in the evocation of *mood* than in *Ah, Wilderness!* and *Twelfth Night*. The dazzling comic complications in *Twelfth Night* need time (and the entrance of Sebastian) to bring matters back to normal, if normal is the right word to describe the "Feast of Fools" affairs in Illyria. Viola, coming out of the sea, brings a fresh breeze to the love world of Illyria. But her disguise causes many of the plot complications, and at one point she seems overwhelmed by events. She forthrightly asserts: "O time, thou must untangle this, not I, / It is too hard a knot for me t'untie" (2.2.40–41). And time does untangle the knot here, as in all of Shakespeare's comedies and romances. But time has another dimension as well; it makes us realize that another process, alien to comedy, is at work. Feste captures its essence in his song, "O Mistress Mine," voicing the traditional *carpe diem* theme in its second stanza:

> What is love? 'Tis not hereafter;
> Present mirth hath present laughter;

> What's to come is still unsure.
> In delay there lies no plenty,
> Then come kiss me sweet and twenty;
> Youth's a stuff will not endure.
>
> (2.3.47–52)

Comedy, the genre itself, is "present mirth" and "present laughter." But the sense of time passing affects both comedy and love, certainly youthful love. The fool who sings this—a man "wise enough to play the fool," we hear from Viola—is himself growing old. Sad and wistful, he observes and knows the world around him. In most productions, his singing of "O Mistress Mine" brings tears to the eyes of Sir Toby and Sir Andrew, comic characters (also older than the young people around them) who seem to realize the truth of the sentiments expressed. But they return to present mirth, singing and dancing, making too much noise for that stolid "virtuous" man in black, Malvolio, who cannot abide a "cakes and ale" world.

Another song by Feste, in the play's most poignant scene, touches death. Act 2, scene 4 begins with the melancholy Orsino asking for music, as he did in the play's beginning; he relishes songs that have "a dying fall." Before Feste arrives to sing his song, Orsino and the disguised Viola have a beautiful exchange about love, in which Orsino asserts: "For woman are as roses, whose fair flow'r / Being once display'd, doth fall that very hour." Viola/Cesario agrees: "And so they are; alas, that they are so! / To die, even when they to perfection grow!" (2.4.38–42). Recognition of the workings of time brings sadness to both lovers, especially to Viola, who must hide her true self behind her disguise. Then Feste enters to sing "Come away, come away, death," a song that welcomes death because love is unrequited, a song asking that flowers not be strewn on the grave, the sad lover wishing for anonymity (what, in fact, is Viola's painful condition). Feste knows what kind of song will please the self-indulgent Orsino, and he feeds his melancholy to obtain a tip. When Feste leaves, the poignant dialogue between Orsino and Viola continues, with Viola/Cesario genuinely affected by the song, coming close to betraying her disguise as she tells Orsino that her sister "never told her love, / But let concealment like a worm i' th' bud / Feed on her damask cheek" (2.4.110–12). The image, of course, returns us to the rose whose beauty is so short-lived. The scene invests love and youth with a fragility that the genre comedy usually cannot sustain. Time can untie the knots of comic complication, making for happy resolutions, but it also can remind us that the "present" of "present mirth" does not last long. It is altogether fitting, therefore, that Feste, who gave us the *carpe diem* song and the song of death, concludes the play with a song that pinpoints the ages of man. The play is over, with the Jill we care for most, Viola, getting her Jack, and with another Jill, Olivia, getting a substitute but eminently worthy Jack, Sebastian. Sir Toby, we hear, has already married Maria as a reward for her part in the "letter" plot which made Malvolio look so "mad," and Malvolio has left the play with ominous words of revenge. Alone on stage, Feste sings of childhood and manhood and marriage and old age, that is, he sings of time's relentless workings, always with the refrain, "For the rain it raineth every day." He reminds us at play's end what he has projected throughout: that the comic vision is limited, that time plays its secret part in life's play, that when the play is over we must return to what *is* rather than "what you will" (the other title of *Twelfth Night*), that the rain, a spring shower in a comic world, may become the downpour of a storm in a tragic world. *Twelfth Night* is a remarkable festive comedy, but its tone is darker than that of any of the other romantic comedies because the pressure of time, real world time, is always felt. Feste's last song ends with these lines: "But that's all one, our play is done, / And we'll strive to please you every day." The next day, however, Shakespeare will be pleasing his audience not with comedy but with *Hamlet*, and judging from the tone of *Twelfth Night*, we realize it could not have been otherwise.

Ah, Wilderness! is a realistic comedy that always gives us real world time. In fact, O'Neill even obeys the classical unity of time and, as we already observed, painstakingly attempts to evoke the atmosphere of a specific time and place. But the holiday atmosphere connected with the Fourth of July and the dream world of young lovers, a world of music and moonlight, project the kind of timelessness that we associate with romantic comedy. That is, O'Neill's play offers the audience present mirth; its "life giving formula," to use O'Neill's phrase (the formula of comedy and the values that O'Neill seems to admire in the Miller family), allows O'Neill, because he is writing comedy, to celebrate life. But *Ah, Wilderness!*, like *Twelfth Night*, contains darker strains as well, strains that seem much closer to the temperament of the tragic O'Neill, the O'Neill we knew before he dreamt his comedy, his "what you will" wish fulfillment. The pleasant and indulgent comedy contains an underside that sometimes manages to surface, and when it does surface we realize we are in familiar O'Neill territory. His first stage directions, for example, tell us that the Miller sitting room looks "*cheerful in the morning sunlight*," but a doorway in the rear wall leads into "*a dark, windowless, back parlor*" (3:5), a fact he wants us to have although it seems to serve no real purpose except to indicate that some rooms are not cheerful. (A dark back room figures importantly in many of O'Neill's plays.) Other dark features of the play, typically O'Neillian features, are drunkenness and prostitution, but these are softened by the comic atmosphere. Yes, Sid's need for a drink and loose women stop Lily from marrying him, but their long-lasting relationship has its own dimension of warm value, so we do not consider Sid's character terribly flawed. Sid is Sid, as Lily tells us, just as Sir Toby Belch is Sir Toby Belch, jokesters and drinkers and uncles both. Belle the "tart" is a nonthreatening prostitute, pleasant, amiable, even "philosophical" (telling an embarrassed Richard that "even the little flies do it!"—an idea that belongs to a totally different world when King Lear expresses it). When Richard tells his father that Belle "made everything seem rotten and dirty," his Hamlet-like pose reflects more on his adolescence than on Belle's whorishness.

But the comedy contains another kind of darkness, connected with the sadness of lost youth and passing time, a dimension it shares with *Twelfth Night*. *Ah, Wilderness!* is filled with songs, some comical (as when Belle changes one of the lyrics of the popular "Bedelia"—"Bedelia, I'd like to feel yer"—thereby shocking Richard), some highly sentimental and nostalgic.[14] When Arthur, with dripping sentimentality, sings "Then You'll Remember Me," an old favorite, sadness fills the air. Nat Miller, O'Neill tells us, "*gazes before him with a ruminating melancholy, his face seeming to become gently sorrowful and old*" (3:69). Essie's expression becomes "*more and more doleful.*" Lily's face grows "*tragically sad,*" and Sid, who has a hangover and is already filled with "*self-loathing and self-pity,*" is "*about to cry.*" In short, the older couples are strongly affected by a sentimental song of the past; not only its lyrics *about* a former time but the song itself, coming from a former time, their time of youth, fills them with nostalgic sadness. Almost immediately, Arthur sings "Dearie," a popular song not of the distant past but equally sentimental, causing a similar effect. An essentially comic scene remains comic—excessive sentimentality and melancholy produce their own kind of comedy; witness Orsino and Jaques—but the idea of time *passing* and love *remembered* suggest life's darker rhythms.

Even more important than the songs in giving *Ah, Wilderness!* a melancholy atmosphere are the quotations from "The Rubaiyat of Omar Khayyam," which also provides the play's title. O'Neill, we have already observed, took great care with his titles. The title for his only comedy beautifully captures the mood of the play and points to the importance of the poem throughout the play. In act 1, when Essie Miller condemns "those awful books Richard is reading," Richard gives his enthusiastic opinion of each of the writers his mother mentions—Bernard Shaw is "the greatest playwright alive today!"; Ibsen "the greatest playwright since Shakespeare!"; Swinburne "the greatest poet since Shelley!" When Essie refers to "The Rubaiyat," Richard exclaims: "That's the best of all!" (3:16). At which point we learn, to Essie's dismay, that Nat and Sid and Lily all read the poem too. Lily offers the first of the three imporant quotations from that epicurean/agnostic poem:

> The Moving Finger writes, and having writ,
> Moves on: nor all your Piety nor Wit
> Shall lure it back to cancel half a Line,
> Nor all your Tears wash out a Word of it.
>
> (3:17)

Lily quotes these words, according to O'Neill, "*with a sad pathos.*" As well she should, because it offers the truth of her present condition, a truth that O'Neill presents often, most poignantly in *Long Day's Journey,* the other side of *Ah, Wilderness!.* Her awareness of a past that cannot be erased, of time that progresses relentlessly, is verbalized for her by the poem. That is, the poem does what her own prosaic language cannot do; it gives voice to her feelings, tapping a deep sadness. (Previous to her quoting, she seems to be "*in a melancholy dream.*") Richard immediately quotes *his* favorite verses from the poem, verses as appropriate to him in his youth as Lily's to her in her age.

> A Book of Verses underneath the Bough,
> A Jug of Wine, A Loaf of Bread—and Thou
> Beside me singing in the Wilderness.
>
> (3:17)

These are the most famous lines in the poem, and one can understand why its epicurean sentiment, coupled with the idea of love, would appeal to Richard. *Wilderness* is an interesting word here because it harkens a world, a condition, so different from the comfortable domestic scene we are witnessing on stage. Richard—should I say O'Neill?—*omits* the last line of the popular four-line stanza: "Oh, Wilderness were Paradise enow!" He is interrupted by Arthur who sees Old Man McComber approaching the house. The blocking agent in the comedy's love story interrupts not only the relationship of Richard and Muriel but the stanza that capsulizes that relationship, coming from the lips of the young man who is forever quoting from those scandalous poets in his letters to Muriel. But notice that the "Oh" of the line *not* quoted becomes the "Ah" of O'Neill's title. (Could this be why Richard does not quote the last line?) The change from "Oh" to "Ah" seems small, and I may be dangerously close to putting too heavy an academic hand on the change, but the "Ah" suggests a nostalgia, a longing, I would even say a past, that "Oh" does not suggest. Richard does *not* have that past, and therefore does not utter the phrase that gives us the play's title. The past belongs to the older couples, and the title clings to an atmosphere of pleasant sadness. Wilderness, after all, is youth that is paradise, for O'Neill the youth he wished he had, a kind of dream. Art does our dreaming for us. When the dream is a wish fulfillment, we have the comedy called *Ah, Wilderness!*; when the dream is a nightmare, we have a tragedy called *Long Day's Journey Into Night.*

Richard and Lily offer their quotations from "The Rubaiyat" early in the play, in act 1. The play itself treats of Richard's young love for Muriel—bread and wine and verses, the wilderness of youth. The play also suggests, through the older couples and the songs of nostalgia, that the moving finger of the past has written a sad story that cannot be changed. This last sentiment is captured by the third quotation from "The Rubaiyat," appearing at the end of *Ah, Wilderness!* thereby making the poem a framing device. At play's end, all is well with Richard; he has returned from his moonlit moments with Muriel by the sea, still in a daze because the moon is still shining. Nat, watching his son, recalls his own past: "I can only remember a few nights that were as beautiful as this—and they were long ago, when your mother and I were young and planning to get married." Richard's reaction, as O'Neill offers it, is remarkably revealing. He stares at his father

> *wonderingly for a moment, then quickly from his father to his mother and back again, strangely, as if he'd never seen them before—then he looks almost disgusted and swallows as if an acrid taste had come into his mouth—but then suddenly his face is transfigured by a smile of shy understanding and sympathy.*

Richard then says: "Yes, I'll bet those must have been wonderful nights, too. You sort of forget the moon was the same way back then—and everything" (3:105). The words "disgusted" and "acrid taste" momentarily remind us of the Richard who posed as Hamlet, the "melancholy Dane" disgusted with love relationships, here, as in *Hamlet,* the love of a father and a mother. The Oedipal idea persists, even in O'Neill's mellow comedy. Then comes the genuine realization by a young man, seeing his parents freshly, that they too had their midsummer nights, that the moon abides, affirming the continuity of love and nature, the continuity of life itself—and that's the affirmation of comedy. With the moonlight shining on him—as it shone on his son in the beach scene, as it shines on Richard now—Nat Miller puts his arms around Essie, looks at his son, and says, "There he is—like the statue of Love's Young Dream." Then he quotes from "The Rubaiyat": "Yet Ah, that Spring should vanish with the Rose! / That

Youth's sweet-scented manuscript should close!" (3:107). Shakespeare's *Dream* play (about young lovers, foolish, bewildered, in moonlight), Feste's songs and sentiments, Viola's flower—all come together at this precious moment. The "manuscript," of course, brings us back to Lily's quotation about the "Moving Finger" that writes, and the "Ah" allows us to think about the play's title and to recall Richard's "wilderness" quotation on the paradise of youth and love, a paradise that we know lasts, like the rose, for only a moment. Nat's "Ah" takes in the remembrance of spring by an older man—spring, the life-giving time of comedy, the time now past for him but present for his son. He shakes off his melancholy with these words to his wife: "Well, Spring isn't eveything, is it, Essie? There's a lot to be said for Autumn. That's got beauty, too. And Winter—if you're together." Essie's "Yes, Nat" affirms the comic rhythm, the sense of continuity, but it doesn't erase the nagging thought that autumn and winter are not the seasons of comedy, that winter storm is not springtime shower. For this reason, I believe, O'Neill has as his last stage direction these words: "*She kisses him and they move quietly out of the moonlight, back into the darkness of the front parlor*" (3:107). Life's transience and fragility, the workings of time, the precariousness of the comic genre itself—especially precarious for the dark playwright who wrote only one conventional comedy, precarious too, perhaps, for the greatest playwright who abandons springtime with his *Twelfth Night*—these are the ideas that follow Nat and Essie into that darker room as the play's curtain descends.

Ah, Wilderness!, as the only authentic comedy in O'Neill's considerable body of dramatic work, stands out as an aberration, a welcome one if we can judge from its enthusiastic reception when it was first performed (becoming, in fact, next to *Strange Interlude,* O'Neill's most popular play in his time) and if we can judge from its continued popularity through the years (not only on stage but on film). Still, as we have seen, it is based, as Louis Sheaffer says, on O'Neill's "obsession with family life and his own past."[15] It came to him as a dream and allowed him briefly to step out of the shadows created by the indirect biography of *Mourning Becomes Electra* and the more direct biography he was confronting in *Days Without End,* the play he was writing when he had that dream. He needed relief from his writing of *Days Without End* because, according to O'Neill himself, "considering its length I worked harder and longer on this play than on any before."[16] The length was only two hours stage time, but the struggle to write the play seemed momentous. O'Neill went through eight drafts, each changing the play's ending. The first draft, for example, ended with the protagonist's suicide in despair; the last and final version ends with his strong affirmation in faith. Because the play offers much direct biography, it seems clear that O'Neill was struggling with *himself* even as he was struggling with his material. Interestingly, O'Neill has his main character, John Loving, struggle with autobiographical material in the novel he is writing, so that one gets the sense of mirrors reflecting mirrors. The autobiographical material has its own interest in allowing us to witness O'Neill's spiritual gropings, his sense of frustration in a modern world without faith, his personal quest for some affirmative meaning in a God-forsaken world. (The trilogy he planned, which included *Dynamo* and *Days Without End,* would have been entitled "Myth Plays for the God-forsaken.") But the play itself, as drama, deserved the negative reviews it received when it opened in 1934, the negative response it has received from critics through the years. The play lacks movement or action; it is essentially a weak intellectual debate between modern rationalism and religious faith. Certainly the debate idea was an important part of O'Neill's thinking, because the play's subtitle is "A modern Miracle Play." Actually, and strictly speaking, I believe O'Neill must have meant morality play, a distinct medieval genre in which a war of good versus evil is waged for the soul of an Everyman character. The morality plays that contained this psychomachia observed the following pattern: the Everyman character begins the play in a state of innocence and goodness, goes through a period of sinful living with an evil companion by his side (the Vice character), but by play's end recognizes the evil of his ways, rejects the Vice, repents his sins, and is saved. An affirmative Christian ending is the staple of the medieval morality play. The debate of evil versus good is meant to mirror a psychological battle, of course, and this is the agon O'Neill wishes to dramatize in *Days Without End.* As he said in his *Memoranda on Masks,* "Consider Goethe's *Faust,* which, psychologically speaking, should be the closest to us of all the Classics. In producing this play, I would have Mephistopheles wearing the Mephistophelean mask of the face of Faust. For is not the whole of Goethe's truth *for our time* just that Mephistopheles and Faust are one and the same—*are* Faust?"[17] The battle over the soul of man in the medieval morality plays, the two characters who are one in Faust—these are found in *Days Without End,* in which O'Neill gives us John and Loving, who make up John Loving, the Everyman (read O'Neill) character. And Loving, the evil part of John Loving, wears a mask, "*the death mask of a John who has died with a sneer of scornful mockery on his lips*" (3:113). O'Neill in *Days Without End* uses a split-character device, with John Loving played by two actors, a bold experimental technique, and he uses the one literal mask just described, the last time he will experiment with that device. Because of O'Neill's experimentation, *Days Without End* seems a throwback to the period of the late twenties. The play was produced during

O'Neill's second career, and its rather direct autobiographical content allows us to think of it there, but it avoids the directness of realism, it relies on self-conscious stage techniques, and it offers too didactic a religious message (with Catholicism taking the place of the Nietzschean messages of *Marco Millions* and *Lazarus Laughed*). In his protagonist's artificial acceptance of Catholicism at play's end, O'Neill seems to be returning to the Catholicism of his youth. It certainly is tempting to speculate that his struggle with the play (mirroring his protagonist's struggle with his novel and with his faith) and his discontentment with his various nonaffirmative endings, stems from his wish to relieve his personal guilt for having left the Catholic faith. Many Catholics at the time rejoicingly believed that O'Neill had returned to the fold, but this was not the case. In a letter to Sophus K. Winther, he asserts that the affirmative ending to the play was the only one possible, both "psychologically" and "mystically inevitable," given the character of John Loving, and O'Neill insists that the end does not mean he returned to Catholicism. And then he adds: "But I would be a liar if I didn't admit that, for the sake of my soul's peace, I have often wished I could."[18] I find this statement highly interesting. *Ah, Wilderness!* his only comedy, was a dreamed wish fulfillment; *Days Without End*, over which he struggled and which he interrupted to write *Ah, Wilderness!*, presents the return to Catholicism of its protagonist, fulfilling the wish of the man who writes the play. Art fulfills dreams, for the dramatist as well as the audience.

Days Without End, in its experimentation, in its expressionistic technique, seems to belong to a previous career, but looked at in another way, it belongs with *Ah, Wilderness!* as wished-for biography and, allowing for much qualifying discussion, as comedy. Of course, we are dealing here not with the romantic comedy of Shakespeare or the realistic comedy of Jonson but the spiritual comedy of the medieval morality tradition. No matter what sins were committed by the Everyman character, no matter how active a part he played in the sinful tavern world, no matter how forcefully he rejected the "good" character and embraced the "evil" character, he ended with repentance and salvation. The end is what usually controls a genre, and the morality play, because of its ending, was always a comedy, a divine comedy in the same way that Dante's glorious poem, going through hell and purgatory, is a divine comedy because it ends in paradise. The morality structure, I believe, is what made O'Neill think that the affirmative ending was the only one possible. I have little doubt that he knew he was using that structure, because of his subtitle *and* because the play proceeds from a commercial setting (John Loving's office) to a domestic setting (his living room, his study, his wife's bedroom) and finally to a religious setting (the interior of a church)—that is, the play progresses, morality style, toward the personal and inevitably toward salvation. O'Neill said the ending was psychologically inevitable, but I would dispute that. The end for John Loving, judging from what he says throughout the play, could have been accomplished in any one of several ways, in fact, the several ways of O'Neill's various drafts—including suicide because John Loving recognizes the evil "Loving" in his own nature. That he becomes the victor over Loving by embracing his lost faith is inevitable only if some "mystical" need is being fulfilled, in both O'Neill and John Loving, a need that conveniently coincides with the morality-play design. But notice the struggle in O'Neill before he got to that "inevitable" ending, as if his own dark nature, his truer nature, would not allow him to end the play so positively. And notice too the obvious exaggeration of that affirmative ending, as if O'Neill was trying to convince himself. The melodamatic death of Loving, "*his arms outflung so that his body forms another cross,*" John rising from his knees, standing "*with arms stretched up and out, so that he too is like a cross,*" while "*the light of the dawn*" swiftly rises, causing the face of Jesus on the Cross, a life-size figure, to "*shine with this radiance,*" leading to "*an expression of mystic exaltation*" on John Loving's face and to his last words to Father Baird, the Catholic priest: "Life laughs with God's love again! Life laughs with love!" (3:180)—well, this too-muchness reveals the strain of O'Neill's effort to achieve what was supposedly inevitable. This ending does not stem convincingly from the play's middle. Tripling the cross is O'Neill's attempt to make the ending unequivocally optimistic; it seems merely shrill. But the positive ending does force us to categorize *Days Without End* as a comedy, not a traditional comedy like *Ah, Wilderness!* (with its romantic-comedy and realistic-comedy trappings, with its Shakesparean echoes), but another kind of comedy, perhaps closer to Shakespeare's tragicomedies or romances, in which a winter's tale eventually becomes a spring's tale, in which a tempest becomes a gentle fair breeze—but closer only in the sense that something dark and foreboding has become affirmative, only in the sense that the ending is positive, with none of the remarkable modulations of tone that we find in Shakespeare's last plays, O'Neill never coming close in *Days Without End* to a large and convincing vision of life as expressed through *dramatic action.*

John Loving's last words, "Life laughs with love!" force us to recall *Lazarus Laughed,* that overly ambitious play of the experimental period, which also presented the didactic debate of good versus evil, a debate staged within a theatrical spectacle. *Lazarus Laughed* also ends on a positive note, not so unequivocally positive as *Days Without End* but positive enough to consider it another example of spiritual comedy. And we would have to place *The Fountain* (written 1922, produced 1925)—like *Lazarus Laughed* a physically elaborate play depending for its effect on the stage designer and costume maker—in the same category because it offers a positive ending, a mystical affirmation of life, a Nietzschean affirmation rather than a Christian affirmation. Because *Days Without End* and *Lazarus Laughed* and *The Fountain* are all poor O'Neill, artistic failures offering blown-up *positive* ideas that the plays' dramatic actions do not make *true,* it seems clear that spiritual or mystical comedy, whether the source of affirmation is Christianity or Nietzsche, is not a happy genre for O'Neill. Although it gives him some opportunity to present bold theater, it never allows him to present living drama; its ideas work against his basically dark view of life; these ideas seem hollow because they do not belong to an action. On the other hand, when O'Neill stays with straight realism and works within a traditional comic genre (whose greatest practitioner—at the very least an unconscious influence on O'Neill—seems to stress entertainment over ideas, or, to put this more precisely, who offers ideas that gracefully emerge from the entire comic action), then we have the successful comedy called *Ah, Wilderness!,* successful both artistically and commercially.

Comedy, of course, is not the genre we associate with Eugene O'Neill. He is so tragic a dramatist, offering so strong a sense of loss and alienation, so heavy a sense of death, so pervasive a sense of fate, that the subject of comedy seems tangential to his main interests. But to take such a position would be limiting. True, he wrote only one successful authentic comedy and three spiritual "comedies" that were unsuccessful, but throughout his career he ventured into the comic, with some element of comedy found in almost all of his plays. In his development as a playwright, he made progressively greater and more important use of comedy, and in his last plays his essentially tragic view of human nature successfully incorporated comedy to produce works of the largest inclusiveness. I shall discuss the comedy found in these late plays in the following chapters, whose headings (generic labels usually associated with the plays of Shakespeare) indicate where my emphasis will be placed: history, tragedy, tragicomedy. We will find that O'Neill's use of comedy in plays that are clearly not comedies—his mixing of modes, his counterpointing of the tragic and the comic—is both Elizabethan and modern, Shakespearean and Beckettian.

Chapter 5

History

That O'Neill is an historical dramatist—in addition to being America's most important tragic dramatist, with history and tragedy overlapping or absorbing one another—has been convincingly demonstated by some of our finest O'Neill scholars. John Henry Raleigh, with his usual clarity of presentation, places O'Neill's history plays into three groups: (1) "the historical exotics" (*The Fountain, Marco Millions, Lazarus Laughed*); (2) the plays dealing with American history of the nineteenth and early twentieth centuries (among them, *Desire Under the Elms, Mourning Becomes Electra, A Touch of the Poet, More Stately Mansions*); and (3) the plays dramatizing O'Neill's personal history (*Ah, Wilderness! The Iceman Cometh, Long Day's Journey into Night, Hughie, A Moon for the Misbegotten*). He connects O'Neill's work as an historical dramatist to such "retrospective" nineteenth-century novelists as Scott, Hugo, Dickens, and George Eliot,[1] and it is to the novel that Peter Egri and Jean Chothia also go when they speculate about the influences on O'Neill's writing of his American history cycle.[2] There is no reason to disclaim, and every reason to accept, these influences because for O'Neill, as for Shakespeare long before him, whatever he read seems to have become grist for his artistic mill. (O'Neill himself, in a letter to Barrett Clark, mentions the novels *War and Peace* and *Jean-Cristophe* as possible influences.)[3] Of course, the more obvious place to look for influence on O'Neill as a writer of a cycle of history plays is to a *dramatist*, in fact, to the greatest writer of history plays in our language. Certainly, O'Neill conceived plans for a cycle that could have equaled in size and sweep and ambition Shakespeare's two tetralogies, which stretch in historical time from 1399 to 1485, but what O'Neill finally left us was only one complete play, *A Touch of the Poet*, the unfinished *More Stately Mansions* (in third-draft status), and a scenario for *The Calms of Capricorn*. O'Neill realized he would not be able to complete before his death all the plays of the projected cycle—whose overall title was to be "A Tale of

Possessors, Self-Dispossessed"—so he and Carlotta in 1953 destroyed the manuscripts on which he was working exclusively from 1935 to 1939. Carlotta's words reflect the agony of that destruction: "He could only tear a few pages at a time, because of his tremor. So I helped him. We tore up all the manuscripts together, bit by bit. It took hours. After a pile of torn pages had collected, I'd set a match to them. It was awful. It was like tearing up children."[4] (This account is an example of Carlotta's tendency to rewrite experience. The Hotel Shelton room had no fireplace; the building's incinerator was probably used for the destruction of the manuscripts.) Travis Bogard laments the magnitude of our loss with these words: "It was a work of astonishing scope and scale. . . . Nothing in drama, except Shakespeare's two cycles on British history, could have been set beside it. The two plays that have survived reveal something of the power of life that beat in it, but they show only vestiges of what its full plan realized would have provided: a prophetic epitome of the course of American destiny."[5] Bogard goes to the right place to find his comparison. I can think of no dramatist other than Shakespeare who attempted a project of such epic dimension. Of course, as we have come to expect, O'Neill did not acknowledge Shakespeare as a model for his history cycle, but can there be much doubt that the dramatist who undertook so ambitious a theatrical project was not aware of the only other theatrical project of such scope? That O'Neill's notebook of 1928 has a notation that indicates he is thinking of writing a play about "Falstaff-Prince Hal," an idea he refers to again in his work diary of 1933,[6] merely reenforces what seems obvious, that Shakespeare, here as always, is lurking in the corners of O'Neill's creative imagination. *A Touch of the Poet,* the only completed play of the cycle, contains Shakespearean echoes; *More Stately Mansions,* in its unfinished state, touches Shakespeare in many and different ways. The rich connection between family and nation, between individual and historic destiny, is dramatized by both dramatists. Of course, many of the methods and aims, not to speak of the times, of the two playwrights are different, but as dramatists of "history" they reflect each other in both fleeting and significant ways.

Whatever conclusions we can draw about the scope and content of the completed cycle must come from information gleaned from what was not destroyed, which includes O'Neill's notes on the plays and his letters to friends. This raw material—and we must always remind ourselves that nothing remaining is definitive except *A Touch of the Poet*—has received careful scholarly attention, allowing us to construct the main narrative outline of the cycle and to speculate with some assurance about its thematic thrust.[7] Originally planned as a five-part cycle, it expanded to eleven plays in the course of O'Neill's feverish work on it. While writing his drafts and making his plans, O'Neill kept going back in time, trying to find the beginning, the cause, for all the action to follow. Because he, like Mary Tyrone, always felt the past is the present and the future too, he was intent on getting back to some significant starting point, which finally—here the word *finally* is relative, for who knows how far back his retrospective urges would have led him if he continued working on the cycle?—finally rested on the ancestor of the Harford family, Jonathan Harford, an idealist who dreamed of freedom but who was tempted by the desire for land and the desire for an attractive woman. The theme of greed begins with the dilemma of Jonathan Harford, who abandons his dream, stays with the woman Naomi and her three daughters for a while, but eventually returns to a life of freedom in the wilderness. Jonathan Harford comes close to being the cycle's first possessor self-dispossessed, but his flight to the wilderness saves him, although it leaves his son Ethan (later named Evan) in the hands of Naomi and her three daughters, "possessors" all.

The eleven plays would have covered an enormous stretch of American history, from 1755 to 1932. The first two plays would have concentrated on Jonathan Harford, the cycle's first dreamer who had "a touch of the poet," who takes part in America's Revolutionary War, and is killed on Bunker Hill. The third play treats Jonathan's son Evan during the years 1783–94. Evan, an idealist like his father, goes to France to follow Robespierre, eventually returning to America to live alone in a summer house, described by Deborah Harford in *Poet* as a "temple of Liberty," which he builds in the garden of the Harford mansion. He eventually dies in the old uniform of the French Revolution National Guard that he is fond of wearing. In this third play, called "The Greed of the Meek," Evan's three half sisters amass a fortune and even "embrace the profits of the slave trade," according to Deborah Harford in *Poet,* who couldn't help admiring the three sisters, "evil old witches," who had a common bond with her: they all admired Napoleon. (Deborah was forever dreaming she was Napoleon's wife Josephine.) This is a bond shared by Sara Melody, who held it against her father that he fought *against* Napoleon. The fourth play, called "And Give Me Death," taking place in 1806, ends the first subgroup of four plays that O'Neill titled "The Blessed Sisters." It deals with Deborah's marriage to Henry Harford, the son of Evan, a marriage motivated by her desire for his fortune, a desire that eventually dispossesses the evil sisters who fail in their attempt to clutch Deborah with their "aged, greedy fingers." The first four plays of the cycle, we see, contrast the dreams of freedom with the realities of possession, all harping on the important theme of greed that pulses through the entire projected cycle. (Parenthetically, we should note that the three evil sisters, "witches," who seem to possess Evan Harford, his son Henry, and eventually Deborah's son Simon, have at least a passing resemblance to those Shakespearean creatures, the witches in *Macbeth,* prophetic instruments of desire and greed who point to a dark destiny.)

The fifth and sixth plays of the cycle will be discussed later in greater detail. The fifth, *Poet,* was completed to O'Neill's satisfaction; the sixth, *Mansions,* survives in an unfinished, and therefore rather full, state. These two plays O'Neill called "Sara and Abigail"—he later changed the name Abigail to Deborah—plays that look back to "The Blessed Sisters" and ahead to the next group of four plays, called "The Four Brothers." These four plays, that is, plays seven through ten in the cycle, treat the four sons of Simon and Sara Harford, each of whom is an American success story, which for O'Neill means a story of greed, materialistic accomplishment, and thwarted dreams. The proud mother Sara predicts the future of her four sons in the Epilogue of *More Stately Mansions:*

> Fine boys, each of them! No woman on earth has finer sons! Strong in body and with brains, too! Each with a stubborn will of his own! Leave it to them to take what they want from life, once they're men! This little scrub of a farm won't hold them long! Ethan, now, he'll own his fleet of ships! And Wolfe will have his banks! And Johnny his railroads! And Honey be in the White House before he stops, maybe! And each of them will have wealth and power and a grand estate. (3:559)

The seventh play, *The Calms of Capricorn,* for which we have the scenario, is set in the year 1857; it dramatizes Ethan Harford's success-failure with his "fleet of ships," and it displays O'Neill's continuing fascination with the sea.[8] The eighth play, taking place in California in the gold rush days between 1858 and 1860, treats Wolfe Harford's successful bank ventures; the ninth, set in the years 1862–70, deals with Senator Honey Harford; the tenth, from 1875–93, concentrates on the machinations of Jonathan Harford in his seizure of the railroad business. Finally, as a kind of epilogue to the entire cycle, the last play, called "Hair of the Dog," spanning the years 1900–1932, would have dealt with the granddaughter of Honey Harford, who rises to great wealth, with greed the continuing focus, the play suggesting that human nature will not change, that dreams will forever be squelched by man's possessiveness, that America is the world's "greatest failure," to use O'Neill's words, because it has always played "that everlasting game of trying to possess your own soul by the possession of something outside of it."[9]

Even so brief an outline of the cycle suggests that O'Neill's ambition was Shakespearean in its largeness. The projected cycle had great spatial range, including Europe as well as the United States and the seas surrounding, and covered many generations in historical time. On the narrative level, the cycle was tied together by the Harford-Melody family, the union of New England Yankee and Irish immigrant, which is the focus of plays five and six, *Poet* and *Mansions,* dramatizing the relationship of the Yankee Simon Harford, the dreamer who has "a touch of the poet," and the Irish Sara Melody, another possessive woman who changes a man's dreams. In the first four plays we go back to Simon Harford's ancestry; in plays seven through eleven we encounter the Harford-Melody progeny. The Harford-Melody family is meant to reflect American history from before the Revolutionary War through the depression of the early thirties. O'Neill's plan is sketched by the excited playwright in a 1935 letter to Robert Sisk, who handled publicity for the Theatre Guild: "Each play will be, as far as is possible, complete in itself while at the same time an indispensable link in the whole.... Each play will be concentrated around the final fate of one member of the family but will also carry on the story of the family as a whole.... There is a general spiritual undertheme for the whole cycle and the separate plays make this manifest in different aspects."[10] O'Neill's letter to Sisk and his various notes indicate that he's thinking intensely about method, suggesting various techniques to himself, forever aware of the difficulty of presenting complicated family relationships within a wide historical context. This important idea of the story of a specific *imaginary* family through several generations reflecting American history, with *real* historical figures providing a backdrop, serves as a revealing comparison and contrast to Shakespeare's presentation of his history cycles. Shakespeare also connects family to history, with family ties crucially linked to the destiny of a nation, but in Shakespeare the family or families dramatized—royal families—contain real historic figures treated imaginatively by Shakespeare. Shakespeare's history plays seem more closely attached to actual history because they have as their primary focus real figures of history. O'Neill uses such real historic figures as Aaron Burr and Andrew Jackson and Napoleon as a backdrop to his "domestic" history; Shakespeare's "domestic" history of royal families *is* the history of his nation, but he often uses completely imaginary characters as a backdrop to royalty in order to encompass a wider world *and* to reflect the royal world. (In *Henry VI* Shakespeare even uses what for him is an uncharacteristic device of presenting, at the bloody Battle of Towton, an anonymous son who kills his father, then an anonymous father who kills his son, to indicate the terror of civil war, a *national* terror that is essentially *familial.*) Both O'Neill and Shakespeare offer spiritual underthemes; both offer wide canvasses *and* close psychological studies; both use similar techniques—parallel situations, repetition of ideas and images, character development within and between plays, prediction of things to come and remembrance of things past—to unify the particular play within the cycle *and* to unify the cycle as a whole. Each dramatist is passionately involved in his country's history, with both dramatists seeing clearly the dark forces connected with power and human desires and frailties, with both dramatists understanding the terrible human cost of success to family and nation.

Shakespeare wrote ten history plays, eight of which comprise the two tetralogies which offer an epic sweep of English history from 1399 (the end of the reign of Richard II) to 1485 (the ascension of Henry VII, the first of the Tudors). The first group of four plays, the three parts of *Henry VI* and *Richard III,* were written first, although they dealt with the later historical events. The *Henry VI* plays treat the Wars of the Roses, the enmity of two families, the houses of York and Lancaster, and the competing claims for the crown. *Richard III* concludes with the death of the Yorkist Richard at the Battle of Bosworth Field and the uniting of the two houses of York and Lancaster in the marriage of Elizabeth of York to Henry Richmond, beginning the Tudor reign that gave England the Queen Elizabeth who is ruling England *while* Shakespeare is writing his history plays. With the second group of four plays—*Richard II,* the two parts of *Henry IV, Henry V*—Shakespeare goes back to the cause of the civil wars that he already dramatized in his first tetralogy: the deposition of the legitimate king, Richard II. Each of Shakespeare's history plays is distinct and independent, but each is connected to the other plays in the tetralogies, sometimes closely, sometimes only because the country's overall history forces the connection. O'Neill in his history cycle, as we saw, also kept going back and back to find the origins of the problems that ensued. He too deals with the union of two families, and he too projected independent plays that have connections to the other plays in the cycle. This has little to do with influence, perhaps, but it suggests, at least, that the dramatic instincts of our two historical dramatists lead them to search for *causes* that connect events to each other and to a national destiny. What is important, I believe, is the fact that each dramatist ties the fortunes of a nation to the condition of a family.

From his earliest history plays, the first tetralogy, Shakespeare makes the family the image of England's problems. Norman Rabkin convincingly stresses the idea that "the family serves as a model for England's troubles not only because the dissension is in fact within the extended royal family, but more importantly because like the body the family is the traditional image of organic wholeness." Rabkin sees Lord Talbot *and* Joan of Arc, contrasting characters in every respect, as playing out "their conflicting ideals in symmetrical acts of familial commitment."[11] Talbot represents an old order, acting out his insistence that family loyalty and solidarity are important values—values that are dying even as Shakespeare is writing, according to the best historian of the family, Lawrence Stone[12]—and Joan utterly denies the Talbot values. But Shakespeare's treatment of both characters points to the family as a significant focus for an interpretation of a country's history. In Shakespeare, precisely because he is dealing with royal families, the connection between family and nation is tight; he is ostensibly dramatizing the actual history of his country, offering the people of England a view of the past. In O'Neill the family is presented as a microcosmic reflection of a larger national destiny, with O'Neill insistently pushing the thesis formulated by his overall title, "A Tale of Possessors, Self-Dispossessed." Each playwright is holding the mirror up to his country's history, but Shakespeare's mirror directly reflects historical personages who are treated imaginatively, whereas O'Neill's reflects imaginary characters. Both, however, focus on personalities, the psychological makeup of their characters, and in this respect for both dramatists their characters are imaginative creations, with Shakespeare often distorting the facts of history in order to make his historical characters more alive or true to life. This is just another way of saying that Shakespeare and O'Neill are dramatists, treating history on a personal level, offering complex human beings whose thoughts and actions may tell us more about history than the facts offered by scholars. (In fact, some of Shakespeare's most memorable scenes in the history plays are not historical in the factual sense, but highly personal and significant. Take, as examples, Richard wooing Anne in *Richard III,* the dying Henry IV talking to his son Hal, Richard II giving up his crown.) Both dramatists are interested in the divisions within human beings, but the difference between them is that Shakespeare's characters are kings (or prospective or aspiring kings) so that the divided nature in Shakespeare takes on an added historical dimension, because for the Elizabethans a king was both man and God, with special responsibilities—although even in this respect some of O'Neill's proud characters, who see themselves as possessing a kind of godhead in their success, touch the Elizabethan idea of kingship. Of special interest, I believe, is that for both O'Neill and Shakespeare history teaches dark lessons. Almost all of Shakespeare's kings are failures as kings, monarchs whose reigns reflect their personal weaknesses or crimes or sins. Richard II neglects and abuses his country even as he dramatizes himself. Henry IV usually is "this vile politician, Bullingbrook." Henry VI is pure and saintly, but completely ineffectual. Richard III is a destructive usurper and murderer. Henry V is, in one sense, Shakespeare's only success story; in another sense, a flawed human being whose complex character is eminently discussable, and whose depiction stretches over three plays, one of which, *1 Henry IV*, is probably our greatest history play. (The complexity of the Hal-Henry character, made more complex when we try to evaluate his relationship to Falstaff, is what must have drawn O'Neill to him as a possible focus for a play. It is the only time O'Neill mentions a Shakespeare play as source material.) For O'Neill American history offers one continuous lesson in failure, so that he considers American history and American tragedy to be synonymous. In 1922, many years before he even thought about a history cycle, O'Neill said:

> Suppose some day we should suddenly see with the clear eye of a soul the true valuation of all our triumphant brass band materialism; should see the cost—and the result in terms of eternal verities! What a colossal, one hundred percent American tragedy that would be.... Tragedy not native to our soil? Why, we are tragedy, the most appalling yet written or unwritten![13]

Shakespeare's mirror—a larger mirror than O'Neill's because it belongs to the more comprehensive Shakespeare—includes not only the high historical figures but the purely imaginary "low" people who are affected by the actions of the high. The citizens in the streets who complain about a "troublous world" (*Richard III*), the carriers who lament that "this house is turned upside down since Robin Ostler died," (*1 Henry IV*), the common soldiers before the Battle of Agincourt (*Henry V*), the gardeners who wonder why they should take care of their garden when that garden called England is being neglected by their king, Richard II, and, most memorable, the tavern world of Falstaff and company—these representations of an ordinary, workaday, "base string" world provide a rich and revealing commentary on the history produced by the high and the mighty.[14] O'Neill's smaller mirror, reflecting a democratic society, reveals the common man (who usually wishes to be uncommon and whose high desires often make him uncommon), while the high people (presidents and dictators and mythmakers) are reflected fleetingly in the background. Given the nature of American society, it is the common man in O'Neill who provides a commentary on a nation's character and destiny. It is difficult for anyone writing about Shakespeare or O'Neill to avoid using the mirror image to describe their dramatic art. The mirror as both idea and prop has great importance in Shakespearean drama. The very purpose of drama, according to Hamlet, is "to hold as 'twere the mirror up to nature." The mirror is also essential to O'Neill's thinking about himself and his art; its importance is effectively captured by these words of Lazarus: "Tragic is the plight of the tragedian whose only audience is himself! Life is for each man a solitary cell whose walls are mirrors."[15] Which brings me to *A Touch of the Poet*, the only completed play of the unfinished cycle, the play that contains a mirror as its most important prop *and* that is itself a mirror, reflecting not only O'Neill's large purpose in writing his history cycle, but reflecting as well O'Neill himself at a crucial time in his artistic development, when he soon will be working on his great autobiographical last plays. *A Touch of the Poet*, in fact, has often been discussed as one of the late autobiographical plays because its characters closely mirror O'Neill's family.

Lodged between O'Neill's two planned tetralogies, "The Blessed Sisters" and "The Four Brothers," both *A Touch of the Poet* and *More Stately Mansions*, the fifth and sixth plays of the projected eleven, point both back and ahead, thereby validating O'Neill's requirement that each play in the cycle, although distinctive and whole, remain an indispensable part of the larger cycle. *Poet* is a crucial link in the family-nation drama, probably the most crucial link because its important narrative focus is the union of the Yankee Harford and Irish Melody families. Perhaps for this reason alone O'Neill expended his most creative energy on it, eventually *completing* it, something he was not able to do with any of the other plays of the cycle. Perhaps too he was more personally drawn to the emotional center of the play, Major Cornelius Melody, whose relationship with his daughter and wife gives the play its dimension of high value. Con Melody is one of those flawed O'Neill fathers who are not easy to like but who emerge as both likable and sympathetic characters by play's end, clearly reflecting O'Neill's ambiguous attitude toward his father, on whom Con Melody is modeled. Michael Manheim believes that the play is "primarily" about James O'Neill Sr.—"actor, father, and proud Irishman"—and he offers a convincing argument to support this view, as does Virginia Floyd in her discussion of the play.[16] Sara Melody's attitude toward her illusion-filled, deeply flawed father reflects O'Neill's negative attitude toward his father, but Sara, here also reflecting O'Neill, realizes at play's end that a father's life and illusions are inextricably bound with the child's attitude toward self. In *Poet*, as in many O'Neill plays—and in many Shakespeare plays—the father is an important focus of dramatic attention, but the presence of mother is always felt. In *Poet* two mothers make a composite portrait of Ella O'Neill: Nora Melody and Deborah Harford. Nora is the wife as victim, loving, abused by an alcoholic and vain husband, Catholic, guilt ridden, essentially weak (except in her love). Deborah is mother as victimizer, both aloof and assertive, withdrawing into her dream world and therefore hard to touch, but displaying a strong possessive maternity when she returns from that dream world. The two mothers, the peasant Nora and the aristocratic Deborah, have two temperamentally different children, Sara and Simon, but both children finally are O'Neill himself: Sara with respect to her relationship with her father and mother, Simon because of his physical description, some of his political and philosophical ideas, his relationship with his mother and father, *and* because he's the dreamer who has "a touch of the poet." Notice, however, that the phrase that describes Simon Harford and gives the play its title (and recalls one of O'Neill's earliest dreamers, Robert Mayo in *Beyond the Horizon*) attaches to Con Melody too, a dreamer with a touch of the poet, as the play presents him. O'Neill in *Poet* holds up many mirrors to himself and his family; some of these mirrors cannot help but reflect as well the Shakespeare who is part of himself and his family.

Con Melody has a Shakespearean complexity and depth. An Irishman who fought on the side of the British against Napoleon, he achieved some glory as a major at the Battle of Talavera but ruined his military career because of an adulterous affair with a Spanish nobleman's wife, which led to a duel in which he killed the nobleman. He had gone to war leaving behind his young wife Nora and their child Sara. His marriage to Nora was precipitated by their sexual union before their marriage, for which the Catholic Nora feels guilt, and which Con harps on as the big mistake of his life, although he suggests to his daughter that such a sexual union may win her Simon Harford, a marriage opposed vigorously by Simon's Yankee parents. The Melody family comes to America, where Con buys a small tavern a few miles from Boston. He lords it over the Irish laborers who frequent the tavern as well as over his wife and daughter, who work for him at the tavern while he relives his former days as Major Cornelius Melody, usually posing aristocratically before his mirror in full glorious uniform, reciting Byron:

> I have not loved the World, nor the World me;
> I have not flattered its rank breath, nor bowed
> To its idolatries a patient knee,
> Nor coined my cheek to smiles,—nor cried aloud
> In worship of an echo: in the crowd
> They could not deem me one of such—I stood
> Among them, but not of them.
>
> (3:203)

(Byron, like the other Romantic poets, has a Hamlet-like streak of morbidity and a deeply felt alienation from the outside world, characteristics shared by O'Neill himself.) The words of the Byron poem clearly express

Con Melody's attitude toward himself and toward the crowd. Con is a tyrannical braggart, filled with illusions of grandeur, usually drunken and lazy, hot-blooded, filled with self although not really knowing himself, playing a role so insistently, living a lie so fully, that the mirror he gazes into reflects a uniform and a body but not a soul. At play's end, when he is beaten up like any peasant and humiliated in his attempt to have an aristocratic duel with Simon's father (who insulted him by trying to bribe him so that Sara would not marry Simon), Con shoots the beautiful mare to which he was devoted because it represented his glorious past, and he joins the drinking, lowly Irish in his tavern, something Major Cornelius Melody would never have done. Now, with dream dissolved, with pride broken, the Irishman Con Melody, no longer the superior man, will be not only "among them" but "of them." Sara, who forever verbally assaulted her father, wanting him to face reality instead of that mirror which merely reflected the lie of his life, now wants him to return to his romantic illusion because she realizes, as O'Neill must have realized in his relationship with his father, that her father's pride is her pride too. But her father doesn't listen to her—he never did!—and he joins the tavern world as a beaten man. His loving wife Nora remains devoted to him, and Sara, having seduced Simon in the room upstairs, will emerge as one of the cycle's "possessors," although she clearly recognizes the value of love, especially the love of her mother for her father. Simon Harford, the idealist who has a touch of the poet, a young man who wishes to live a life of Thoreauvian simplicity—and a character who is not *seen* in this play—will become a changed man because of his union with Sara the realist. That change will be dramatized in *More Stately Mansions*. In *Poet* the personal victory of Sara over Simon reflects the larger victory of greed and possessiveness over idealism, what O'Neill considers to be the appalling and repeated condition of American history.

When O'Neill presents the dividedness of Con Melody, he is holding the mirror up to nature; when Con looks into his mirror he sees what he *wishes* to see, a grand Byronic hero. However, at play's end, Con sees what is truly in front of him, "a clown in a circus." Con's mirror teases the mind to recall the two mirrors in Shakespeare's history plays. The first is found in Gloucester's first soliloquy in *Richard III,* when he comments on his own deformity and correctly insists that he was not "made to court an amorous looking-glass." But after his successful wooing of Anne—one of those scenes in a history play purely invented by Shakespeare to display the cynical audacity of his villain and the frailty of the lady—Richard elatedly asks, and we ask with him, "Was ever woman in this humor woo'd? / Was ever woman in this humor won?" (1.2.227–28). He ends the wooing scene with this couplet: "Shine out, fair sun, till I have bought a glass, / That I may see my shadow as I pass." The sun of York is shining and the winter of his discontent has changed to sunny springtime because of his changed attitude toward himself. He'll now buy a mirror—"I'll be at charges for a looking glass"—something he never needed or wanted before, because now—Shakespeare insists on the "now" throughout the first act of *Richard III*—now he has "crept in favor with myself," the word "crept" beautifully suggesting that Richard instinctively knows himself. Richard's mirror reveals the truth and reveals what he perhaps likes to think is a new truth. (I say perhaps because with Richard one cannot be sure he is not slyly poking fun at himself.)

But the more interesting Shakespearean mirror appears as a prop that blossoms into an idea. It is found in *Richard II,* the play that begins Shakespeare's second tetralogy, the tetralogy that more strongly prodded O'Neill's imagination. In the deposition scene, another of Shakespeare's imaginary "unhistoric" scenes, Richard is called upon to comply with the formality of giving up his crown "in public view," so that no suspicion of usurpation will fall on the politic Bullingbrook/Henry IV. Richard, forever the self-dramatizing king, plays out this scene to the discomfort of all who are watching him, dwelling on the agony of his loss of kingship and self:

> O that I were a mockery king of snow,
> Standing before the sun of Bullingbrook,
> To melt myself away in water-drops!
>
> (4.1.260–62)

This remarkable image perfectly fits the dramatic situation and precisely describes Richard's deepest feelings. A new sun is shining, the old order is dead, the certainty of divine kingship is gone, and Richard wishes that his own identity were lost. He wishes to disappear, from life *and* from this very scene that he has exploited so effectively. But before he departs he asks for a mirror, a rather startling request, certainly an incongruous request, given the public occasion. Bullingbrook, with little or no hesitation, at this moment acts as Richard's stage manager by saying, "Go some of you and fetch a looking-glass." He, of course, wants this scene to conclude as quickly as possible, and he realizes that it's best to humor the actor who controls the scene. When the mirror comes, Richard stares into it, and here we have the supreme self-reflexive moment:

> Give me that glass, and therein will I read.
> No deeper wrinkles yet? Hath sorrow struck

> So many blows upon this face of mine,
> And made no deeper wounds? O flatt'ring glass,
> Like to my followers in prosperity,
> Thou dost beguile me! Was this face the face
> That every day under his household roof
> Did keep ten thousand men? Was this the face
> That like the sun, did make beholders wink?
> Is this the face which fac'd so many follies,
> That was at last out-fac'd by Bullingbrook?
> A brittle glory shineth in this face,
> As brittle as the glory is the face,
> *(Dashes the glass against the ground)*
> For there it is, crack'd in an hundred shivers.
>
> (4.1.276–89)

Looking at self, Richard recognizes the mirror's beguiling flattery and his lost "glory." His final request, now that he has dashed the self that the glass mirrored, is to ask "leave to go"; having lost the pride of kingship, he no longer wishes to be "the observ'd of all observers," to borrow a phrase attached to another tragic figure "too much in the sun."

I wish to suggest—and suggest is the most I can do—that Con Melody's mirror is made of the same glass as the mirrors of Shakespeare's Richards, that O'Neill and Shakespeare use the mirrors in similar ways. Always "in favor" with himself, Con sees what he wishes to see when he looks in the mirror, the Byronic hero of past days. We know, but he does not, that his brilliant uniform hides whoever is the true or real Con Melody, someone he cannot *see* in his mirror. Adored by his ever-loving wife, still attractive to women—even Deborah Harford temporarily succumbs to his charm—projecting a striking figure in his "emperor's clothes" (and how can we not recall Brutus Jones's uniform before he goes on his forest journey to self discovery), Con Melody allows the mirror to "con" him, to offer an illusion of self that feeds his Byronic ego, to satisfy the aloof tragic actor's best audience, himself. His other audiences, outside of his wife, actually dislike him or hate him. Not only the Irishmen in the bar upon whom he looks down, and the Yankees who look down on him, but also his daughter Sara, who is sick of his self-indulgence and his cruelty to her mother. Sara realizes he's living a life-lie; she wishes that he would "face the truth of himself in that mirror" (3:263). At play's end, after his humiliation at the hands of the Harford servants and the police, after his pride is broken, Con does face the truth, and his last look at the mirror reveals a different self to him. With some of Richard II's mocking tone, Con reports what he sees: "Be Jaysus, if it ain't the mirror the auld loon was always admirin' his mug in while he spouted Byron to pretend himself was a lord wid a touch av the poet" (3:277). He then recites his favorite Byronic lines—"I have not loved the World"—"*in mocking brogue,*" after which he "*guffaws contemptuously*" and says, "Be Christ, if he wasn't the joke av the world, the Major. He should have been a clown in a circus. God rest his soul in the flames av tormint! (*roughly*) But to hell wid the dead" (3:278). Loud noise from the bar makes him turn away from that mirror. The man who was "alone in the hell av pride," as Nora expresses it, will now join the tavern world. "Be God, *I'm* alive and in the crowd they *can* deem me one av such! I'll be among thim and av thim, too—and make up for the lonely dog's life the Major led me" (3:278). After seeing himself as he really is, Richard II went into further solitude, first to prison, then to the solitude of death, becoming a truly tragic figure. In contrast, Con Melody, after seeing himself, joins the world, calling for life, but he also sees himself as a fallen man who has lost his pride—which is Sara's pride too, she tells him. The play's ending offers such mixed emotions that it is difficult to place *A Touch of the Poet* in any generic category. As a history play in a cycle called "A Tale of Possessors, Self-Dispossessed," in fact, as the central play in that projected cycle, it makes its own statement about the death of dreams and poetry, and the triumph of acquisitiveness and trickery. But a history play can be either comic or tragic, and when we reflect on *Poet,* especially on the play as the story of Con Melody, we encounter considerable difficulty in attempting to label it, although once again a look at Shakespeare as a possible influence perhaps may help us.

I mentioned that O'Neill had considered the Falstaff-Prince Hal story as a possible idea for a play, and I've suggested that the mirror in *Richard II,* the first play of the Hal tetralogy, may have been behind Con's mirror in *Poet,* with Con, like Richard, finally seeing himself as he is. The crucial moment in each play is the *seeing* of self, after which Richard progresses toward death and Con Melody toward a kind of death in killing his mare and in killing the Byronic Major Cornelius Melody. But Con also moves toward life as he enters the bar to join the lowly Irish in story and song; in fact, Con says, "I'm alive." That phrase, "I'm alive," coming from a man who often conforms to a comic type, the braggart soldier, a man who is part of a tavern world, surely must figure forth in our minds the Shakespeare character who makes his first appearance in the play immediately following *Richard II* in the tetralogy, *1 Henry IV.* "Give me life," says Falstaff at the Battle of Shrewsbury, where he avoids the action because he will not have "such grinning honor" as the dead Sir Walter Blunt has. Falstaff is the con artist of the *Henry IV* plays, bragging about his accomplishments, seeing himself romantically as one of "the minions of the moon," one of "Diana's foresters," instead of the thief he is, a man who loves his drink and even suggests, when giving a thumbnail sketch of Prince John of Lancaster, that "the young sober-blooded boy" should drink some sack to temper "the cold blood he did naturally inherit of his father" (*2 Henry IV,* 4.3.118). Con Melody displays many Falstaffian characteristics, and he too, in evaluating the character of Simon Harford, believes he's "a bit on the sober side," although he discerns "a romantic touch of the poet behind his Yankee phlegm" (13:205). But Con is not Falstaffian in his attitude toward fighting and war and honor. Falstaff's "discretion" allows him to avoid battle; for him "honor" is merely a word. Con has fought bravely and continues to be belligerent when honor is at stake. His pride propels him to go to Henry Harford with his foolish challenge of a single duel, leading to his humiliation and the death of his pride. In this respect, Con Melody must remind one of Hotspur, who displays bravado, who is "the theme of honor's tongue," who will foolishly fight against great odds, whose pride pushes him toward death. That Con Melody displays aspects of such opposite characters as Falstaff and Hotspur points to his complexity. My belief that O'Neill, when writing *Poet,* had in mind Shakespeare's characters from the second tetralogy cannot be tested, but it is not unreasonable, especially in the light of the Falstaff–Prince Hal notation in his work diary.

Prince Hal, the most important character in the second tetralogy, seems to be missing from *Poet,* but even here I hear an echo of Hal when Con, looking into the mirror, finally rejects his former self, that is, rejects both the Falstaff and Hotspur in himself. And just as Hal's rejection of Falstaff causes the death of Falstaff, as we hear in *Henry V,* so Con's rejection of his former self—Con, like Hal, putting away his former self and returning to the world to which he belongs—causes his death, as we hear in *More Stately Mansions.* The Hostess tells us of Falstaff's death: "The king hath kill'd his heart." Nora Melody's comment on Con's death: "it was the broken heart of his pride murthered him." Hal will figure more importantly in *Mansions* because that play contains the story of a son, Simon Harford, who rejects his father only to become his father; in *Poet* we get portions of the story of Simon, unseen upstairs, from his mother Deborah—and already her comments point us toward the Oedipus complex—but the full presentation of Simon's character, especially his relationship with family, will be found in *Mansions.*

Shakespeare's *Henry V* comes into *Poet,* I believe, with one interesting allusion, although this may appear merely coincidental. The French, just before the Battle of Agincourt, are portrayed by Shakespeare as braggarts who quarrel among themselves, a group of soft, decadent, snobbish aristocrats. The Dauphin is especially offensive in his "braggart soldier" stance, declaring that he has "the best armor of the world" *and* the best horse. He loves his horse, and admits having written a sonnet in praise of his horse, even declaring "my horse is my mistress." More seriously, Con Melody is so attached to his mare that his shooting of the horse is really the destruction of his own pride, a kind of spiritual suicide. But before that happens, the braggart Con, so pleased to declare his Byronic separateness from common men, utters: "To hell with men, I say—and women too! . . . Give me a horse to love and I'll cry quits to men" (3:236). Sara sharply undermines his "blather about lovin' horses," just as those surrounding the Dauphin undermine his comments on his horse-mistress. But perhaps the Dauphin-Con-horse-love connection will be recognized only by those who are especially attentive to such connections.

At the risk of making another such connection, I wish to call attention to an interesting confluence of words that link together *Poet* and *1 Henry VI*, the first history play written by Shakespeare, the play that offers the seminal scene of the picking of the white rose and the red rose to symbolize the differences in the two political factions, differences that lead to the chaotic civil wars dramatized by Shakespeare in the first tetralogy. Warwick makes this prophecy when he witnesses the plucking of the roses, one of Shakespeare's many prophecies in the history plays that must come true, of course, precisely because the "history" is *behind* Shakespeare: "this brawl today, / Grown to this faction in the Temple Garden, / Shall send between the Red Rose and the White / A thousand souls to death and deadly night" (2.4.124–27). The Temple Garden, a garden in the precincts of two of London's four legal societies, the Middle Temple and the Inner Temple, is the location of the important plucking of the roses, probably the most famous scene in Shakespeare's first tetralogy. Perhaps this scene was lodged in a far corner of O'Neill's mind when he has Deborah Harford tell Sara about Jonathan Harford, Simon's great-grandfather (the focus of the first two plays of the cycle). Jonathan Harford, "a fanatic in the cause of pure freedom," disillusioned with the Revolutionary War and a follower of Robespierre, lived in "a little temple of Liberty" that he built in the Harford garden. There is no relationship at all between the two temples, but the garden figures importantly in *Mansions* and throughout Shakespeare's history plays, and the linking of temple and garden in O'Neill may have its unprovable source in Shakespeare's simple place designation connected with history.

Other Shakespeare echoes, not necessarily from the history plays, can be heard in *Poet,* especially from *Macbeth,* which, of course, is a tragedy that easily absorbs the designation *history play*. For example, I hear a verbal echo when Nora Melody—filled with guilt because of the "mortal sin" she committed when she, an unmarried young woman, slept with Con—says: "It's the pain of guilt in my soul. Can a doctor's medicine cure that? No, only a priest of Almighty God" (3:257). This comes close to words uttered by both Macbeth and the Doctor concerning the guilt that Lady Macbeth carries within her. Macbeth to the Doctor: "Canst thou not minister to a mind diseas'd?" (5.3.40). The Doctor during the sleepwalking scene: "More needs she the divine than the physician" (5.1.74). But more interesting, perhaps, is O'Neill's use of an effective and frequent stage sound, the knocking at door or gate. I need not rehearse that remarkable moment in *Macbeth*, so brilliantly described by Thomas De Quincey, when the knocking at the gate, heard immediately after a terrified Macbeth does his bloody deed, interrupts his guilt-filled conversation with Lady Macbeth. The noise appalls Macbeth, bringing him and his wife back to *reality*. The knocking shocks the self-absorbed couple into the realization that they must address themselves to the outside world. In fact, it is Macduff who is knocking, and retribution will come finally from his hands. Shakespeare fully exploits this stage noise by immediately giving us the Porter scene, in which the Porter dwells on the "knock, knock," both a child's game (in a play filled with children and the absence of children) and a reminder that the door of hell awaits Macbeth and Lady Macbeth. This richly conceived sequence of stage action in Shakespeare cannot be—has not been—matched by any other dramatist, but perhaps a connection in *Poet* can be suggested, one that brings us back to the mirror. When Con Melody looks into the mirror he sees an "officer and gentleman," a Byronic figure who has created a world of romantic illusion that he alone occupies, "among them but not of them." In act 1 his daughter Sara appears in the doorway, watching him look at himself, interrupting his self-contemplation. In act 2 Deborah Harford opens the door quietly while Con is looking at himself in the mirror, and when he discovers her presence he is *"shamed and humiliated"* (3:216) because he's been caught in his romantic pose a second time in the same morning. That evening, this time wearing the brilliant uniform of a major in Wellington's army, looking so splendid that even Sara had said earlier, "You look grand and handsome, Father" (3:228), Con looks at the mirror again. With uniform and pose, Major Cornelius Melody is completely absorbed in the role he is playing, wholly belonging to a world of his own creation. Then comes the loud knock on the door which causes him to start *"guiltily"* and step away from the mirror (3:244). It is the curt, cool Nicholas Gadsby, the Harford lawyer, coming to buy off Melody so that Sara will not marry Simon, an action that leads directly to Melody's rage and the idea of a duel, which eventually will bring down Con, stripping him of pose and pride. The knocking at the door here, like the knocking at the gate in *Macbeth,* is the knock of reality and retribution, destroying a world of the character's own creation, highlighting guilt and shame. An important stage sound is shared by Shakespeare and O'Neill. In this connection, one may be reminded of the knocking heard in Shakespeare's *1 Henry IV,* where once again retribution is knocking, this time in the person of a sheriff who interrupts Falstaff's praise of himself in act 2, scene 4. It comes at a crucial moment. Falstaff has declared to Hal, "Banish plump Jack and banish all the world," to which Hal offers what has become a Shakespearean crux, "I do, I will." The knocking represents the outside world making demands on the tavern world, demands that must be answered, by Hal as well as Falstaff, who wants desperately to continue praising himself. This important stage sound, occurring in a history play that provides other Shakespearean echoes, may have been heard by O'Neill when he was writing his history play.

Con Melody, who contains within him aspects of Falstaff and Hotspur and Hal, cannot be formulated in a phrase. He is a complex and attractive presence in a history play that highlights the death of dreams—Con's dream and Simon's dream and the American dream—dreams that point in different directions. O'Neill's concentration on him—and here once again we should recognize the shadow that James O'Neill casts on the play—perhaps reduces the "history" part of this history play, pushing *Poet* closer to the last autobiographical plays. Also, the tragic aspects of American history—especially the triumph of materialism over idealism, the triumph of Sara realism over Simon dream—tend to be softened somewhat, or temporarily forgotten, because of the colorful and comic side of Con Melody's characterization. O'Neill is able to elicit many and different emotions and thoughts in his only completed play of the history cycle. No generic label sticks firmly to the finished product because the audience's point of view seems to shift between comedy and tragedy, complicated by the history dimension. Although or perhaps because the next play in the cycle was left in an unfinished state, we are on firmer ground when we discuss *More Stately Mansions,* in which no Con Melody is present to produce conflicting emotions, in which the atmosphere is darker, the family struggle more intense, and in which the Shakespeare play that exerts the greatest pressure is *Hamlet,* although the *Henry IV* plays continue to prod O'Neill's creative imagination.

Shakespeare, it must be stressed, wrote his history plays before he wrote his greatest tragedies, and in many respects he needed to work through his histories to get at tragedy. When he stopped writing the English history plays, he immediately turned to Roman history with *Julius Caesar,* his first tragedy in the Shakespearean mold. (The distance between *Julius Caesar* and *Hamlet* is much shorter generically than the distance between *Romeo and Juliet* and *Hamlet.*) O'Neill also, it seems, had to work through his histories to get to his last tragic plays. Perhaps it was easier for him to face himself more directly in those last plays precisely because he had worked on the more "objective" history plays. O'Neill was working on his history cycle even as he was thinking about, and very close to writing, his late tragedies, so that we can find many parallels between *Poet* and *Mansions* and *Iceman* and *Long Day's Journey,* with all of these plays autobiographical. And as we've observed, whenever O'Neill dramatizes his own life we seem to feel the presence of Shakespeare's tragedies, especially *Hamlet;* this is certainly true of *Mansions.* Still, *Mansions,* as Jean Chothia correctly insists, displays many devices and manipulates time in ways that remind us of O'Neill's middle period.[17] But even these devices, like the Mary Tyrone soliloquies, seem Shakespearean, as does the sense that a character changes over a span of years, which we find especially in Shakespeare's history plays. (Notice, for example, how much we learn about the usurper Bullingbrook/Henry IV when we move from *Richard II* to *1 Henry IV,* and how much closer we get to Henry IV, that sleepless father, when we get to *2 Henry IV.*)

Whereas the father was important to O'Neill in *A Touch of the Poet,* mother provides the autobiographical pressure in *More Stately Mansions,* especially the relationship of mother and son. But O'Neill's depiction of father in *Mansions* holds high interest too, with the relationship of Simon to his father Henry Harford providing a provocative comparison to that of O'Neill to his father. Henry Harford is an enormously successful businessman who is alienated from wife and family, a businessman who greedily overextends himself and eventually dies bankrupt. His son takes over his father's business, more precisely, absorbs his father's business into his own, becomes even more successful than his father for a time. The autobiographical underpinning here seems unmistakable.[18] James O'Neill was enormously successful as an actor; he extended himself in his moneymaking tours of *The Count of Monte Cristo,* eventually only to feel spiritually bankrupt (and even materially so if we consider his real-estate dealings). His son, in the same field, theater, absorbs his father's theater even as he rejects it, to become a successful and important playwright.[19] I add in passing that Shakespeare too had a father who was successful for a time, who went bankrupt, and whose son brought success to the name of Shakespeare by acquiring the title of gentleman. As C. L. Barber demonstrates, his father's lost success had a strong and lasting effect on William Shakespeare.[20] It could not have been otherwise for O'Neill who often spoke of the effect of his father's empty success on his own attitude toward success.

The father-son relationship in *Mansions,* which mirrors the father-son relationship in O'Neill's life, echoes the Prince Hal–Henry IV relationship in Shakespeare's second tetralogy. (Could this be a possible reason for O'Neill's interest in writing a play about Prince Hal?) A prince rebels against his kingly father—who also feels a kind of bankruptcy, having usurped a crown and always reminding himself of the blood on his hands—only to absorb his father's position and become even more successful than the father. Simon's days in the log cabin, dreaming his Thoreauvian dreams of freedom, divorcing himself from all that his father represents, is close to Hal's days in the Boar's Head Tavern, living his own brand of freedom and wilderness, trying to give himself distance from the court world corrupted by a usurpation, and probably enjoying the youthful thrill of rebelling against a father. Simon, like Hal in his rebellion against a father, is also like Hal in being very much *like* the father, a crafty businessman who will take over the company, just as Hal takes over the kingdom—with both young men successful, but with both paying a price for success. "Banish plump Jack and banish all the world"—a loss for Hal, a loss for Simon. The human cost of responsibility in Shakespeare, the human cost of greed and materialism in O'Neill.

However, unsurprisingly, in the light of our previous discussions of *Elms* and *Electra,* and in anticipation of the late autobiographical plays, it is a son's relationship to a mother that gives *Mansions* its dramatic potency. Deborah Harford possesses many of the characteristics of O'Neill's mother; consequently, in so many ways she directly anticipates the portrait of Mary Tyrone. Deborah's withdrawal to her private world of dreams, to her private garden, hiding away from her son but becoming the domineering mother when she reenters his world—these come very close to Mary Tyrone's withdrawal (in her dope dreams, in her spare room) and to both her absence from and dominance of her family. Michael Manheim's insistence that the fear of his mother's permanent withdrawal is the context of "O'Neill's greatest pain"[21] finds considerable supporting evidence in *Mansions* as well as in *Long Day's Journey.* Simon's relationship to his mother is the driving motive of *Mansions,* with Sara the wife absorbing much of the mother idea (in addition to the idea of whore) within her characterization, reminding us especially of Abbie Putnam's role in *Elms,* but also of the other earth mothers in O'Neill's plays. And when we confront the son-mother relationship in *Mansions* (or in any O'Neill play, it seems), we cannot avoid discussing the Oedipus complex, nor can we avoid hearing the echoes from *Hamlet*.

Simon Harford's crucial meeting (1.2) with his mother in the old log cabin—the cabin that the successful Simon and Sara now own, the cabin that represents Simon's past as a dreamer, when he had a touch of the poet—seems to reveal O'Neill's deepest thoughts about his mother, even as it points to the Hamletian underpinning. A son is puzzled because his mother now seems a stranger; a mother believes her son has changed. "What has happened, Mother?" asks Simon. Deborah's answer is the answer that O'Neill gives in all such contexts: "Why, nothing has happened, Dear, except time and change" (3:322–23). It is an answer that Shakespeare also gives, especially in his history plays and tragedies. Deborah's reference to "revengeful Time," which "lashes" the face with wrinkles, which makes shapeless the body, which—and this is more important, she says—forces the soul to look into the "mirror" of self only to see "the skull of Death" (3:323–24)—these are morbid Hamletian thoughts coming, in this scene, from the mother. In *Hamlet* it is the son who sees and fondles the skull of death, who thinks of mother when he says to Yorick's skull, "Now get you to my lady's chamber, and tell her, let her paint an inch thick, to this favor she must come" (5.1.192–94). In *Mansions* the son will inherit his mother's and the playwright's dark thoughts of death as the play progresses. Here, in 1.2, he is puzzled by his mother's behavior even as he was when a child, unable to distinguish between "the part" mother played and her real self. He is "jealous" because his mother invited his brother Joel to her private garden instead of him. (To be admitted to his mother's garden would be a return to the womb for Simon, fulfilling his continuing Oedipal wish.) Deborah says that Joel, when invited, "looked as astounded as if a nun had asked him to her bedroom," adding that he "stared the flowers out of countenance for half an hour, and then fled!" (3:322–23). The Shakespearean phrase, "out of countenance," nudges us to place the nun and bedroom references in the context of *Hamlet,* I believe. Here, Simon, Hamlet-like, confesses his discontent to his mother, urging her to change and be the way she used to be in her relationship to him. Their meeting even contains the idea of poison, and refers in passing to "peering . . . from behind curtains," what Sara is doing at that moment as she spies upon mother and son, what Polonius did during the mother-son confrontation in *Hamlet*. Here in 1.2, so early in this long unfinished play, Simon's Oedipal feelings are clearly revealed, even as Hamlet in 1.2 reveals his Oedipal feelings.

Simon's incestuous attachment to his mother intensifies as the play progresses, with the Hamlet echo very strongly heard when Simon is *"repelled"* by his mother's suggestion that she could marry again, especially with "Father scarcely cold in his grave" (Joel's words). Simon's disgusted reaction: "It is revolting, Mother!" (3:375). The incest idea thickens with every added suggestion by Simon that his mother and his wife have merged to become one: "you appear as one woman to me. I cannot distinguish my wife from—" (3:401). His confusion persists to the very end of the play, resulting in his complete helplessness, causing Sara to become the mother to the "boy" Simon, as Sara herself realizes in the Epilogue: "I'm your mother now, too." While he was fighting the idea that mother and wife are one, while he was trying to keep them distinct, he played upon the jealousy of both wife and mother, telling Sara in 3.3 that he was thinking of his mother, then telling his mother that he was thinking of Sara. Sara, in an interior monologue, says that he is lying, that "he said that to hurt her," correctly pinpointing the nature of the game Simon is playing, and reminding us of Hamlet's game in the mousetrap scene when he tells his mother that he'd rather sit by Ophelia—"here's metal more attractive." Throughout the play, in his confusion over his relationship with mother and wife, in his growing nihilism, Simon utters Hamletian thoughts—he is "weary" with life, he wishes to "rest in peace," he, like Edmund Tyrone, seems "a little in love with death."

The Hamlet connections that I have presented are suggestive, by no means definitive. They provide a thread, let us call it a subliminal thread, that attaches Shakespeare's play to O'Neill's, widening the range of implication in *Mansions,* even as we penetrate more deeply to O'Neill's private thoughts. Shakespeare's *Hamlet* dramatizes the Oedipal situation, a family relationship, but at the same time we cannot forget the son is the prince of Denmark, the family is royal, the woes of the family deeply interlaced with the woes of the country. In Shakespeare, because of his powerful dramatic *poetry,* we seem to see and feel the poison that Claudius poured in Hamlet's father's ear, the poison that coursed through his body and finally spilled over into all of Denmark. Family is connected to country, the personal connected to history—a situation similar to that found in Sophocles' *Oedipus Rex.* These micro-macrocosm connections seem more muted in O'Neill's *Mansions,* with O'Neill clearly more interested in the personal drama of his characters, but the history is not neglected, nor is his larger purpose of making *Mansions* an important part of the tale of possessors self-dispossessed. (It could perhaps be argued that Shakespeare in *Hamlet* is also more interested in the personal tragedy of a particular son, that the political dimension seems much less important than the agony of a young man who must play his part in the family romance, that, in fact, the play's political resolution—with Fortinbras now ruler of Denmark—seems relatively unimportant.)

For O'Neill what happens in *More Stately Mansions* represents what has happened to America, and what *is* happening even as he is writing his history cycle, and what *will* happen as he looks into the future. (The future predicted in Shakespeare's history plays, we must remember, was always part of Shakespeare's past and, of course, the prophecies prove true. The future in O'Neill's histories is the product of O'Neill's dark speculations and, alas, they too have often proven true.) The past for O'Neill is always the present and the future too. And that past, as it is represented on stage in *Mansions* by a specific family between the years 1832 and 1842, tells the story of greed and power. Very early in the play (1.1) a "patriotic" note is struck in a dialogue between Sara and her mother. It seems that Simon, for sentimental reasons, foolishly bought the log cabin where he and Sara first made love, but Sara suggests that the business-foolish purchase may be "useful in the end."

> *Sara.* There's over two hundred acres, and he bought it for a song, and the little lake on it is beautiful, and there's grand woods that would make a fine park. With a mansion built on the hill by the lake, where his old cabin was, you couldn't find a better gentleman's estate.
> *Nora.* (*with admiring teasing*) Glory be, but you're sure av havin' your way!
> *Sara.* (*determinedly*) I am, Mother, for this is America not poverty-stricken Ireland where you're a slave! Here you're free to take what you want, if you've the power in yourself.
>   (3:305)

Notice the pride in an America where one is "free" to "take what you want." Sara here sounds the theme of greed and power connected with possessors. She recognizes that her husband is essentially a dreamer who writes poetry, who wishes to write a book to "show people how to change the Government and all the laws so there'd be no more poor people, nor anyone getting the best of the next one, and there'd be no rich but everyone would have enough" (3:305). But Sara has managed to "laugh" those foolish ideals "out of him," and Simon, who always has taken joy "in getting ahead," becomes the play's main possessor. He abandons the possibility of "a greedless Utopia" because he himself gets "the greatest satisfaction and sense of self-fulfillment and pride out of beating my competitors in the race for power and wealth and possessions!" (3:360). He epitomizes America's lost dream, a dream connected with freedom and wilderness and equality and charity, and represents America's spiritual death, a cynicism connected with ruthless power and huge greed. He and Sara live a life based on the principle that "the strong are rewarded, the weak are punished" (3:388). (Here the words of a fallen king-poet, Richard II, may come to mind, as he tells Bullingbrook: "they well deserve to have / That know the strong'st and surest way to get" [3.3.200–201].) As the play progresses, Simon and Sara are triumphant in all their business ventures, with Simon taking over his father's business and Sara replacing Deborah as the mistress of the Harford mansion. Eventually Simon, displaying all the negative qualities of American capitalism, wishes to create a monopoly that will control both production and consumption, even to the point where he will possess plantations in the South and have his own "nigger slaves," imported in "his own slave ships" (3:499). Simon wants nothing less than to completely control the business market, to attain, as he puts it, "the all-embracing security of complete self-possession" (3:432). But in the course of his ambitious endeavor to possess everything, Simon loses everything, including his self. He turns his wife into his whore, forcing her to believe that "life means selling yourself and... love is lust" (3:482–83). He coldly destroys his business adversaries, makes his own brother a victim of his callous cruelty, treats his mother contemptuously, even proposes that his wife and mother kill each other. He ultimately wants complete emotional possession of both wife and mother. In short, Simon Harford becomes what his mother calls him: a "greedy, soulless trader in the slave market of life" (3:525). He wants to be, to use Sara's phrase, "the King of America" (3:364), as well as the unconditional ruler of his family. But he must pay a price for his ruthlessness and greed. The possessor becomes dispossessed, the "more stately mansions" become a prison for the soul, the "garden of dreams" becomes "a battlefield of reality," in fact, the American dream becomes a nightmare of greed and materialism, just as the garden of his youth—mother's garden!—has become, according to O'Neill's stage directions, "*unnatural and repellently distorted and artificial*" (3:503). Simon and America have lost their innocence; the Garden of Eden has become polluted. Simon loses all, reverting to childishness, helplessly unable to enter his mother's summer house—an entering that would have fulfilled his Oedipal desires (and that reflects O'Neill's own Oedipal longings)—the victim of a fever in the brain. The play's Epilogue gives us a Simon who is whole again, perhaps the dreamer of the past with a touch of the poet, the "son" to Sara, the wife who now understands the importance of love, who seems content to live on a farm rather than in a stately mansion, but who revealingly indicates in her last speech (delivered while Simon is asleep in her arms, and therefore having all the force of a soliloquy) that her sons—"Fine boys, each of them"—will "take what they want from life, once they're men!" (3:559). The distorted American dream goes on, we see, and Sara's abrupt and guilty "No! To hell with your mad dreams, Sara Melody!" does not convincingly squelch her deeply felt thoughts. The Epilogue is O'Neill's device for pointing ahead to the plays that will come, in each of which one of the sons will play out his prescribed role in the big American story of material possession and spiritual loss. (*The Calms of Capricorn*—for which we have only the scenario and which is too spotty to allow assured discussion—presents the story of one of these sons.)

In *More Stately Mansions,* as in Shakespeare's history plays, the relationships within a family and the desires of individual members of the family reflect the condition of the nation. Both dramatists focus their attention on the personalities, on the psychology, of their players in history, with Shakespeare's royal players more importantly implicated than O'Neill's democratic players. In O'Neill the dramatic thrust seems to push more relentlessly toward the inner character, toward divided personalities and anguished souls, but all along the particular character's progress and regress stand for the progress and regress of a nation. Deborah's garden is not only her place of reclusiveness, not only the garden of lost innocence for Simon, the garden that represents the warmth of a mother's womb to an Oedipal man-child, it is also the garden associated with the land called America, the garden connected to the Temple of Liberty, the "garden of dreams"—read "American dreams" as well as the dreams of fantasy and childhood—the garden that becomes "distorted" and "unnatural" with the passing of time, that is, during the course of history. Traditionally, the garden carries obvious symbolic weight, which O'Neill is exploiting in *Mansions,* but in addition, I suggest, behind O'Neill's garden are the gardens found in Shakespeare's histories, not only the garden where the red and white roses are plucked to differentiate the warring families, but, more interesting and more influential, the garden in *Richard II,* the play that dramatizes the cause of all the troubles that follow. John of Gaunt's choric utterance on England—"This other Eden, demi-paradise, . . . this little world . . . This blessed plot, this earth, this realm, this England, / This nurse, this teeming womb of royal kings" (2.1.42–51)—attributes all that is precious and nurturing and triumphant to that garden-island England, a kind of "English dream" of beneficial power and greatness. But now, Gaunt states, now, because of Richard's wasteful kingship, England has become a place of "shame," a "dear land" that has lost its precious quality. The garden-nation symbolism is beautifully reenforced in 3.4, a *literal* garden scene in which onstage gardeners compare the commonwealth to the garden they are tending, complaining that the chief gardener of the land, Richard II, is not taking care of "our sea-walled garden"; the land is now "full of weeds" and "caterpillars." The ideal garden called England, like the garden of dreams called America, must endure "the battlefield of reality," to use Simon Harford's phrase. In Shakespeare a new gardener named Bullingbrook/ Henry IV will come along to prune his garden, to destroy the caterpillars, to make things grow again, but this will be temporary because the woes caused by a deposition will come in the near future, the wars of the roses will ensue, the paradisal garden will remain only a dream. With time, Shakespeare's view will darken to the point where not only England but the world will be "an unweeded garden / That grows to seed, things rank and gross in nature / Possess it merely" (1.2.135–37). The speaker will be a prince "sick at heart" because of an unbearable family situation, a Shakespeare character who seems to prod O'Neill's imagination in whatever genre he writes. Of course, the garden, like the mirror, is a unifying device in both Shakespeare and O'Neill; it forces the audience to pay attention to the specific even as it relates the specific to large historical and philosophical ideas; it invites the audience to think about the *repeated* image or idea or prop in newly emerging contexts, allowing it to generate larger meanings. I believe that in O'Neill the meanings become even larger because he is using, whether consciously or not, a Shakespearean image or idea or prop, thereby extending and deepening the effectiveness of the repetition.

Mansions projects a despairing view of American history, a vision darker than the one presented in *A Touch of the Poet* because unrelieved by the comic dimension of Con Melody's characterization. That Con Melody is dead strikes the dark note immediately in *Mansions,* just as the death of Falstaff emptied *Henry V* of its joy, just as the talk of death and sleep and disease informed the darker world of *2 Henry IV,* so different in tone from *1 Henry IV*. Both O'Neill and Shakespeare seem to work through their histories toward the bleaker view of tragedy. In this connection, the use of the Epilogue by both dramatists is instructive. Shakespeare's *2 Henry IV* ends with an Epilogue that promises another play that will "continue the story, with Sir John in it." That play is *Henry V,* but Falstaff does not appear. There have been many scholarly speculations on the reasons for his absence, but the best reason, I believe, is that the Falstaff so coldly rejected by the newly crowned Henry V in *2 Henry IV* would have clouded the glorious heroic accomplishments of Henry in a play devoted solely to him. Instead of the appearance on stage of Falstaff in all his bulk, we have the report of his death by Mistress Quickly, a report that perfectly captures the child-man who, to the very end, heard "the chimes at midnight." The Epilogue of *2 Henry IV* clearly functions as a link between plays, projecting a play to come, a kind of preview, but a play the dramatist had not as yet written. Now, the Epilogue to *More Stately Mansions* serves similarly as a link to the plays that O'Neill projected for the future, plays never completely written, eventually destroyed, with only the scenario to *The Calms of Capricorn* surviving. But O'Neill's Epilogue has another function, more important because it reveals his large attitude toward the history he is presenting. In it, as we noticed, Sara voices her hope for the future of her sons, men who will not be satisfied with "this little scrub of a farm," men who will persist in pursuing the American dream of power and possessiveness, men who, like their father, will smother whatever touch of the poet they may have in order to satisfy a greed that will drain them spiritually. A dark view of America's future. O'Neill's Epilogue in *Mansions* is closer in vision and tone not to the Epilogue of *2 Henry IV* but to the Chorus Epilogue of *Henry V*. *Henry V*, it is important to observe, is the last play of the second tetralogy, really the last of Shakespeare's history plays (if we discount, as we should in this connection, the much later *Henry VIII*), so that its Epilogue is the last statement Shakespeare is making about the histories that he wrote. Henry V has just won a remarkable victory over the French at Agincourt, and he has just won the hand of Katherine of France. The play ends triumphantly for England, and then the Chorus, as Epilogue, after verbalizing what we have witnessed—that Henry has won "the world's best garden"—tells us what every Elizabethan in the audience already knew: that Henry's son, "Henry the Sixt . . . lost France, and made his England bleed; / Which oft our stage hath shown." With this statement, the triumph of battle, the glory, the "comedy" of successful wooing, turns to something else, the picture darkens, and we are back to the first tetralogy in which Shakespeare had already shown the costly civil wars, the feuding families, his own bloodstained version of possessors dispossessed. Ultimately, both Shakespeare and O'Neill are realists who understand and disclose the thirst for power and the human limitations and losses that result from the exercise of that power. For both dramatists of their countries' histories, an Epilogue is not merely a pleasant closure, or a convenient link between plays, but a statement of dark continuities.

O'Neill and Shakespeare are *historical* dramatists in the sense that they dramatize a large sweep of events during the course of time, but their focus is on the *individual* who changes with time, the individual on whom time has an effect, an emphasis that seems to push both dramatists toward the writing of tragedy. For both O'Neill and Shakespeare the past controls the present and future, a truth that history reveals and that tragedy dwells on. Even so early a history play as *Richard III,* which completes Shakespeare's first tetralogy, gives us a scene that captures this important idea. In the artificial tent scene just before the Battle of Bosworth Field, ghosts appear in mechanical fashion to both Richard and Henry Richmond, telling the former, "Despair and die!" telling the latter, "Live and flourish!" These are the ghosts of Richard's past, those he had murdered in order to seize and keep the crown. At this crucial moment in the play, Richard's past has caught up with him, so to speak, and his nightmarish vision of ghosts of the past makes him awaken with "Have mercy, Jesu! Soft, I did but dream. / O coward conscience, how does thou afflict me!" He continues:

> The lights burn blue. It is now dead midnight.
> Cold fearful drops stand on my trembling flesh.
> What do I fear? Myself? There's none else by.
> Richard loves Richard, that is, I am I.
>
> (5.3.180–83)

His fearful soliloquy goes on to acknowledge his guilt, his villainy, and, most poignantly, I feel, his terrible aloneness: "I shall despair; there is no creature loves me, / And if I die no soul will pity me." Fear, pity, acknowledgment of guilt, aloneness, a figure trapped in time's deterministic net. History here is touching the tragic, even when the historical figure is so mechanically the villain as Richard is. A less mechanical villain will extract much more sympathy from us and will be more tragic when he is called Macbeth.

But perhaps a more interesting example, certainly a more complex example, of the past controlling the present and future in a history play and touching the tragic relates to the most important character of the second tetralogy, Prince Hal/Henry V. Hal's predicament in the *Henry IV* plays—in which a young man must confront the sins of his father, must live with them even as he establishes his own right to rule, must function in an historical world where his familial past is bound up with his country's future—Hal's predicament is a blueprint for Hamlet's, but in the tragedy the feelings seem more personal, the prince's consciousness is more closely examined, the audience's involvement is more intense. Time itself seems to be more tangible, as it is in O'Neill's late plays, dark plays that abandon the sweep of history projected in his "Tale of Possessors, Self-Dispossessed" in order to concentrate on individual lives trapped in time, in fact, trapped in the classical unities.

I do not know whether O'Neill, in writing his two formal history plays, meant the various Shakespearean echoes that I have discussed to be heard by audience or reader, nor do I know whether O'Neill himself heard these echoes in a conscious way. Because the connections are so diverse and at times so tentative they defy full analysis and prevent assured declarations of "influence." But surely O'Neill, the writer of a projected cycle of history *plays,* was not indifferent to the *plays* written by the greatest writer of history plays in a language they shared; surely the very process of writing such history plays forced him to tap a resource that was always lodged in his mind, with the word *mind* encompassing more than what is merely intentional. There are some affinities in aim and theme and tone and image and method between the history plays of O'Neill and Shakespeare, as I have suggested, and both dramatists share important large ideas: that family and nation are closely linked; that history is the story of the past that is really the story of the present, and the future too; that the *now* of the immediate theatrical experience of seeing a history play is the best way to teach the lessons of history, lessons which demonstrate, for both O'Neill and Shakespeare, the necessity of knowing the human story of people (in contexts monarchical or democratic) who are caught up in the politics of power and desire, who suffer the consequences, the psychological consequences, of such power and desire, and whose actions and thoughts reflect the present and future condition of a nation.

Chapter 6

Tragedy

"A Tale of Possessors, Self-Dispossessed" occupied O'Neill's mind for five years (1934–39), and he became increasingly impatient with it. "A devilish job, this Cycle!" he writes to Richard Dana Skinner in June 1939.[1] The more he works on it, the more it seems to "stand still," he complains. The deeper he wishes to delve into the motivations of his characters, the more he overreaches his medium. By the time he writes to Lawrence Langner, a month later, he is able to say: "The cycle is on the shelf, and God knows if I can ever take it up again because I cannot foresee any future in this country or anywhere else to which it could spiritually belong."[2] This seems a curious statement because the cycle insists on the spiritual emptiness of America, predicting the madness and destruction that can come from a nation's greed. O'Neill surely realized that his dark view of his country's history and future, as expressed in the cycle, was being substantiated by what was happening in the world. Such substantiation resulted not in O'Neill's satisfaction with his own clear-sightedness, but rather in despair. Putting the cycle on the shelf, thereby aborting his most ambitious project, he turned from the larger history of a nation to his more personal history. Perhaps that is what he wanted to do all along, as he traced the Harford-Melody family back further and further, and then projected that family into a future that would eventually touch *his* family. We already noticed that he was thinking of his own family even as he portrayed the Melodys and Harfords. Now, having worked through his history plays and having invested much of his creative energy on the idea of family, he was ready to confront his own family, his own life, more directly, and by so doing he writes his most enduring tragedies, *The Iceman Cometh* and *Long Day's Journey Into Night*. I believe the same could be said about Shakespeare, who worked through his history plays, containing family-nation relationships, before he entered his dark period of tragedy when he wrote plays that focus more intensely on family relationships, that touch the emotions so deeply that we are forced to believe that they reflect Shakespeare's personal life, although with Shakespeare we have no clear external verification for such a view.

There is no reason to doubt that O'Neill was thinking about *Iceman* and *Long Day's Journey* while he was writing the cycle, although it may be more accurate to say that his whole creative life *included* these autobiographical plays and that now he felt ready enough or ripe enough to confront them, now, when he was in despair because of his health and because of the war situation (his ear always "glued to the radio for war news"), when he had already dramatized his personal family relationships in many and different guises, when his dramatic art seems to have matured to its fullest extent. Simon Harford's words in *More Stately Mansions* clearly anticipate *The Iceman Cometh*. Perhaps speaking for O'Neill, Simon believes that men's lives "are without any meaning whatever—that human life is a silly disappointment, a liar's promise... a daily appointment with peace and happiness in which we wait day after day, hoping against hope, and when the bride or the bridegroom cometh, we discover we are kissing death" (3:528). The words describe the situation of *Iceman* and point to the play's title, *and* they uncannily anticipate the situation of Beckett's *Waiting for Godot* even as they touch Shakespeare. I wish to use Simon's words as a springboard for the following discussion of the first of O'Neill's two tragedies of his late period.

Simon Harford's phrase, "the bridegroom cometh," comes directly from the Bible: "While the bridegroom tarried, they all slumbered and slept. And at midnight there was a cry made, Behold, the bridegroom cometh" (Matthew 25:5–6). Because O'Neill gave special attention to his titles and seems to have gone out of his way to present what on first consideration is an awkward title, close attention must be paid to his choice of words. Dudley Nichols, a friend of O'Neill and himself a writer, offers this explanation:

> The iceman of the title is, of course, death. I don't think O'Neill ever explained, publicly, what he meant by the use of the archaic word, "cometh," but he told me at the time he was writing the play that he meant a combination of the poetic and biblical "Death cometh"—that is, cometh to all living—and the old bawdy story, a typical Hickey story, of the man who calls upstairs, "Has the iceman come yet?" and his wife calls back, "No, but he's breathin' hard." Even the bawdy story is transformed by the poetic intention of the title, for it is really Death which Hickey's wife, Evelyn, has taken to her breast when she married Hickey, and her insistence on her great love for Hickey and

his undying love for her and her deathlike grip on his conscience—her insistence that he *can* change and not get drunk and sleep with whores—is making Death breathe hard on her breast as he approaches ever nearer—as he is about "to come" in the vernacular sense. It is a strange and poetic intermingling of the exalted and the vulgar, that title.[3]

The archaic word *cometh* points to the Bible in the "Death cometh" phrase that Nichols presents, and, more likely and perhaps more significantly, in the "bridegroom cometh" phrase that Simon Harford uses. When the biblical bridegroom, Jesus, comes, death comes (and the possibility of resurrection). So too when the iceman in O'Neill's play comes, death comes, with the colloquial death phrases clinging to the iceman idea (like putting someone on ice) and with a host of crude sexual jokes surrounding the iceman (for whom the Frigidaire was not a substitute), including Hickey's iceman joke. The same kind of double entendre used by O'Neill in his title in connection with the word *come* was practiced by Shakespeare when he used the word *die*. King Lear's playful words, for example, provide an interesting echo in O'Neill's play: "I will die bravely, like a smug bridegroom" (4.2.198). This combination of the crude and the biblical mirrors the realistic-symbolic nature of the play, which an audience must confront immediately when Larry Slade, the only lodger in Harry Hope's place who is not asleep, offers the following description of the saloon:

> It's the No Chance Saloon. It's Bedrock Bar, The End of the Line Café, The Bottom of the Sea Rathskeller! Don't you notice the beautiful calm in the atmosphere? That's because it's the last harbor. No one here has to worry about where they're going next, because there is no farther they can go. (3:577–78)

At the play's outset O'Neill, we notice, is pointing the realistic toward the symbolic, as he did in his early plays, and the sea, ever present, provides the guiding metaphor.

It's a dying place, this saloon, containing sleepy men filled with booze and pipe dreams who are waiting for death to come. Little do they realize that Hickey, the son of a preacher who, Jesus-like, wishes to be their savior,[4] will be the "death" of them, just as he was the death of his wife, becoming the very iceman of his bawdy joke. Simon Harford's words bring together the bridegroom and the kiss of death, exactly what occurs in *The Iceman Cometh*. They also pinpoint the idea of *waiting*, exactly what Harry Hope's lodgers are doing in anticipation of Hickey who, they believe, will bring them a little "peace and happiness," again Simon's phrase. (The first three acts in this four-act play end with the word "happy," always uttered by Hickey.) "Waiting for Hickey" would have been an apt descriptive title for O'Neill's play, and once we think about the idea, we cannot avoid looking at O'Neill in a Beckettian context, with *Waiting for Godot* as an interesting focus for comparison,[5] with Beckett offering a revealing indirect route to Shakespeare.

Admittedly, the idea of placing O'Neill next to Beckett seems "absurd" at first glance. O'Neill thrives on expansiveness, a maximalist who wrote not only full-length plays but marathon plays, allowing for dinner breaks, and relying on the patience of his audience if not the fleshiness of their backsides. Robert Benchley, commenting on the notorious *Strange Interlude,* jokingly wondered what everyone was getting excited about; after all, it's "just an ordinary nine-act play."[6] And a reviewer of the massive *Mourning Becomes Electra* captioned his piece, "Evening Becomes Intolerable."[7] Samuel Beckett, on the other hand, thrives on minimalism, and with the passing years he offered less and less by way of stage time, reducing and simplifying, hardly giving his audience a chance to settle in before the play is over. Beckett told Peter Hall that "all true grace is economical,"[8] and he dedicatedly practiced that belief. To my knowledge, no one writing or talking about O'Neill ever used the words *grace* or *economical*.

Other basic differences come easily to mind. O'Neill's plays often seem old-fashioned, conventional, melodramatic, even somewhat crude at times. A realist, his stage settings usually offer what is recognizably found in real life. His characters are usually developed, and they belong to a particular time and place. His plots are traditional, and he has stories to tell. Beckett, called a postrealist, provides stage settings that are generalized, unlocalized, often bare. His characters are not full or round; they cannot be placed firmly in a specific time or place. He offers no plots, although he does have stories to tell. And if these differences are not enough to demonstrate the incongruity of placing O'Neill next to Beckett, then there is one big difference that clearly separates the two giants of drama—their language. Beckett's stage speech, when he offers speech, is spare, poetic, memorable. Always aware of the shortcomings of language, the basic inability of words to express the inexpressible, he pares his stage speech down, reaching for elemental and concrete things by a process of deverbalization, stripping. He seems to wish to escape from what Nietzsche called "the prison house of language." O'Neill's stage speech overflows the measure, and his characters usually come close to saying exactly what they mean. He offers few memorable lines or phrases. He too believed that language is a prison house, that words are unable to touch what one really means, but instead of trying to escape from the prison, instead of stripping down, O'Neill attempts to manipulate more and more words either to make his point or to release the desired emotion in his audience. He laments not the shortcomings of language, but his *own* shortcomings in using language. Nowhere is this shortcoming better stated—and here we do have some memorable O'Neill lines—than in Edmund's words to his father, James Tyrone, after his father gives him a rare compliment by saying that Edmund has "the makings of a poet."

> The *makings* of a poet. No, I'm afraid I'm like the guy who is always panhandling for a smoke. He hasn't even got the makings. He's got only the habit. I couldn't touch what I tried to tell you just now. I just stammered. That's the best I'll ever do. I mean, if I live. Well, it will be faithful realism, at least. Stammering is the native eloquence of us fog people. (3:812–13)

In this particular context, O'Neill, I believe and will attempt to demonstrate later, has Shakespeare in mind when he refers to a poet. If O'Neill had known Beckett's work, Beckett too would have qualified as a poet who does not stammer.

Before I discuss what is Beckettian about *Iceman,* a brief account of its reception will provide an interesting context. O'Neill's *Iceman* was written in 1939, but he did not want the Theatre Guild to present it on Broadway at that time, believing that America was not ready to accept its dark vision. It was performed in 1946, and that year marked the end of O'Neill's twelve-year absence from Broadway. The play was widely publicized and eagerly awaited. Its critical reception was mixed, with most detractors predictably complaining about its length and its prosaic language. Closing after a modest run of 136 performances, it was the last O'Neill play to be performed on Broadway during O'Neill's lifetime. Ten years later—in 1956, three years after O'Neill's death—*Iceman* began O'Neill's revival. José Quintero's production for the Circle-in-the-Square, in which Jason Robards, Jr., played Hickey, had the longest run of any O'Neill play ever, 565 performances. We cannot be sure exactly why the play was so successful this time around. Much credit must go to Quintero's brilliant direction and Robards's fine acting. Perhaps the intimacy of the theater helped; originally a Greenwich Village nightclub, the Circle-in-the-Square seated only two-hundred people: the kind of theater that allowed the hooks to go in, as Beckett would say. Perhaps the lapse of ten years made a difference, with America catching up to an O'Neill whose attitude toward life now seemed more acceptable because the ideas of such modern thinkers as Camus and

Sartre were being widely discussed. To this list of speculations about O'Neill's revival in 1956 I wish to add one more. Is it mere coincidence that 1956 is the year that *Waiting for Godot* came to Broadway? *Godot* opened on 19 April, *Iceman* on 8 May. So strong an impression did *Godot* make when it arrived in New York that when Richard Watts, Jr., of *The New York Post* reviewed the 8 May revival of *Iceman,* comparing it to the earlier 1946 production, he wrote the following:

> In those days, there was a tendency to compare it to Gorky, since its people are doomed misfits of the earth and its setting a saloon and lodging house of the lowest degree. Now the comparison is likely to be "Waiting for Godot," because it deals with lost mankind's search for dreams and illusions. Indeed, it may be said that "The Iceman Cometh" shows sardonically what happens when Godot arrives, for Hickey, the salesman whose coming is so eagerly awaited by O'Neill's exiles, does get there, and brings, not happiness, but the destruction of their dreams.

Godot has been in New York for only three weeks, and *Iceman* already is closer to *Godot* than to Gorky. The derelicts are now waiting for Hickey, and that very idea of waiting, always with us, takes on a resonance and significance it never had before. Beckett from the start was being used to describe another dramatist. *The Iceman Cometh,* written by that old-fashioned established realist who was thought to be worlds apart from that new avant-garde man in town, now seemed to be *contemporary* with *Waiting for Godot,* and, in fact, it was, having been written only ten years earlier. Both plays come out of a world climate shared by O'Neill and Beckett. They are both children of their century, which means that each in his own way had to confront the terrifying prospect that there are no firm values, no scientific absolutes, no ultimate meanings, that there is no God, that man's struggle against necessity is self-destructive. And O'Neill's last plays and Beckett's first plays belong to a post–World War II atmosphere of suffering and despair, of irrational demonic forces at work in man, of the possibility of catastrophic destruction. To *think* about the times, therefore, as both O'Neill and Beckett did, is to grope for some meaning behind events, and this finally places the thinker at the edge of uncertainty and despair. As O'Neill's hairy ape says, "Tinkin' is hard." In these circumstances, one has to be "a little in love with death," words that come from the mouth of Edmund Tyrone but also seem to belong to Didi and Gogo, who await "the last moment," a phrase said "*musingly*" by Didi. "The last moment."

Death and uncertainty and the predicament of living in a purposeless universe, ever darkening—these are the metaphysical concerns that bring together O'Neill and Beckett, giving O'Neill's last plays a Beckettian contemporaneity. Look at the denizens of Harry Hope's bar, for whom time is frozen. They fill their lives with pipe dreams and whiskey. They belong together, feed off each other, and, in fact, their sense of community sustains them as they join in refrains of song, tell stories of the past, and wait for the promising tomorrow that will never come. They also wait for Hickey, who will break some of the monotony of living. He is always good for a few drinks and more than a few laughs. They eagerly await him for almost all of the first act, talking about him, recalling his usual iceman joke—that he left his wife in bed with the iceman—and displaying such anxious anticipation of his coming that Hickey the salesman takes on a larger significance than can be attached to a mere mortal. Willie Oban, the most educated of the bums, says: "Let us join in prayer that Hickey, the Great Salesman, will soon arrive bringing the blessed bourgeois long green! Would that Hickey or Death would come!" (3:586). Hickey comes, and when he does, death enters the play. He will attempt to kill the pipe dreams of his buddies at Harry Hope's, and his illusion-destroying, salvationist activity converts Harry's place to a morgue. He puts all the derelicts on ice, so to speak, and Hickey becomes the iceman of death for them *and* the iceman of his own crude joke when he reveals that he murdered his sleeping wife, with the word *come,* as we already noticed, taking on its sexual overtones.

O'Neill so calculatingly delays the arrival of Hickey, builds up such expectation of that arrival, and invests his character with so dark a significance that one cannot avoid linking waiting for Hickey with waiting for Godot. In both plays the waiters are in a frozen, boundary situation. In both the waiters, forming a self-sustaining bond, fill up their time with sleep and repetitious talk and meaningless activity. In both plays the art of the dramatists makes both the waiting and the atmosphere of death reflections of the bedrock reality of human existence.

O'Neill and Beckett share the same metaphysical ground, it seems, and O'Neill's own words, in a rare press conference he gave before the 1946 opening of *The Iceman Cometh,* seem to be describing the kind of tragicomedy Beckett gives us in *Waiting for Godot.*

> It's struck me as time goes on, how something funny, even farcical, can suddenly without any apparent reason, break up into something gloomy and tragic.... A sort of unfair *non sequitur,* as though events, as though life, were being manipulated just to confuse us. I think I'm aware of comedy more than I ever was before; a big kind of comedy that doesn't stay funny very long. I've made some use of it in *The*

Iceman. The first act is hilarious comedy, *I think,* but then some people may not even laugh. At any rate, the comedy breaks up and the tragedy comes on.[9]

Comedy veering toward tragedy is an apt description of both *Iceman* and *Godot,* with both plays the objects of much critical debate partly because of the difficulty of that comic-tragic linkage. Yes, O'Neill's play, unlike Beckett's, can be labeled realistic; yes, it is long and lacks economy; yes, it has the trappings of a murder mystery, with Hickey's murder of his wife revealed in stages. Still, in the blending of the comic and the tragic, in tone and atmosphere, in the idea of happiness as a habitual irony of life linked to man's "hopeless hope," as well as in the hermetic quality of its closed situation, in the waiting, in the nihilism, and in the bond between people in the face of that nihilism, *Iceman* and *Godot* offer similar views of a modern existence that has lost its significance, with death the central preoccupation, whether we are stationary on a road with Didi and Gogo, moving on that road with Pozzo and Lucky, or at the end of the road with Harry Hope and company.

On that same metaphysical ground we find Shakespeare—and that is why I have taken this indirect Beckettian route, relying on the reader's patience—Shakespeare, whose work is so inclusive that he can be called Beckettian or O'Neillian or anything else, it seems. But when one looks closely at Shakespeare's tragedies—where roads come to an end—Shakespeare deeply resembles both Beckett and O'Neill in his preoccupation with death and in his insistent suggestion that "nothing" may be lodged at the center of our lives. Certainly his major characters at powerful moments in his tragedies express what Gogo says in his first utterance in *Waiting for Godot,* "Nothing to be done," words verified by the rest of that play. The tale of life is "told by an idiot" and signifies "nothing," Macbeth tells us. "Nothing will come of nothing," King Lear says, and that word *nothing* informs the play. Hamlet's thoughts will be "bloody," he exclaims, or "be nothing worth." Iago makes Othello "nothing of a man." Of course, any discussion of these specific phrases must be qualified by large discussions of the plays in which they appear. In Shakespeare these nothings lead to both nothing and everything.[10] The point I'm making is that the Beckettian O'Neill and the Beckettian Shakespeare often meet on the same ground because both O'Neill and Shakespeare are dramatizing a universal human problem connected with the fact of death and the fear of nothing.

When O'Neill states about *The Iceman Cometh* that the first act is comedy, "*I think,*" but that the tragedy comes on, he is confronting head-on the play's genre. I find his words especially interesting because of that revealing "*I think,*" as if O'Neill is not quite sure of the play's comic dimension or effect. His words present a more tentative O'Neill than we are accustomed to. Is it that he didn't altogether trust the comic side of his own essentially tragic nature? Is it that the idea of comedy gave him problems throughout his career and he was protecting himself now? (How *should* we take the *Anna Christie* ending? Why *does* O'Neill label *The Hairy Ape* "A Comedy of Ancient and Modern Life in Eight Scenes"? Do we ever laugh or even smile when reading, never seeing, *Lazarus Laughed*? What is the effect of the divinely happy ending of *Days Without End*?) In any case, in *The Iceman Cometh* the comedy, O'Neill asserts, breaks up and tragedy takes over.

The nature of this tragedy is pinpointed by O'Neill in another important statement about the play, made in a letter to Lawrence Langner (11 August 1940): "there are moments in it that suddenly strip the soul of a man stark naked, not in cruelty or moral superiority, but with an understanding compassion which sees him as a victim of the ironies of life and of himself. Those moments are for me the depth of tragedy, with nothing more that can possibly be said." His tentativeness about the comedy in his play is not found in this statement. He knows these men, he knows the need for the pipe dream, and he states his position boldly and feelingly. This position, coupled with his statement on the play's comedy, prods closer discussion of the play's genre.

This dark play contains almost every characteristic of comedy, O'Neill opening up all the stops on his comic pipe. He offers jokes of all kinds, especially sexual jokes, including that big joke about the iceman. He presents a wide range of comic wordplay: bickering, insults, boasting matches, wisecracks, funny stories, semantic differences (tart vs. whore), bawdy songs (rap, rap, rap), dialectal humor. He creates comic characters whose attributes cling to traditional comic types: the parasite (McGloin and Mosher), the drunkard (all of the derelicts and the doctor of Mosher's story), the prostitute, the trickster, the braggart soldier, the newspaper cartoon character (the way Hugo is described). The play contains comical physical activity, like brawls and threatening gestures. And it includes the clichéd comic participants in the battle of the sexes: the shrewish wife, the henpecked husband, the cuckold.

Now, as I've suggested in chapter 4, these various comedic elements were used by O'Neill throughout his career, more or less—more in his late plays. But what I find most interesting, in this connection, are the *large* ideas of comedy that O'Neill's drama has absorbed, ideas that complicate our response to this difficult play. For example, how exactly should we take Hickey? Is he the tragic protagonist, as many have claimed, or is he the comic catalyst? Of course, stating the question so baldly falsifies the complexity of this difficult character, and labeling him a *comic* character in a play as dark as *The Iceman Cometh* may seem perverse, as if we are playing with ideas rather than feeling what is happening in the play. Still, Hickey's comic dimension deserves attention.

O'Neill's stage directions allow us to picture a bald "*stout roly-poly figure*" who possesses "*a salesman's winning smile of self-confident affability and hearty good fellowship,*" whose eyes twinkle with humor even as they "*take you in shrewdly*" (3:607). Whatever Hickey symbolically represents—and we all seem to agree that he is the play's iceman, he's death, he's the anti-messiah—he remains the salesman who provides a comic exterior, singing a song, tapping a dance, quick with his verbal retorts and his glad hand, a touchy-feely kind of guy who can do a vaudeville turn with the best of them. Small wonder that the bums look forward to his arrival, as we in the audience do, and when he does arrive, he's singing in falsetto, "It's always fair weather, when good fellows get together." The good fellows, O'Neill tells us, "*roar with laughter at this burlesque which his personality makes really funny*" (3:607). Hickey, awaited a long time as we measure time on stage, comes to move the play along.

Certainly, Hickey's coming is the event that will resolve the plot, if plot is not too strong a word for the situation that we call *The Iceman Cometh*. Hickey comes, and comedy is in the air—in his appearance, in his manner and delivery, in his songs, in the laughter he provokes, and, perhaps surprisingly, in his function. For what have we? A character who enters a holiday world with a sobering sense of reality, with a moralistic drive that comes close to destroying the peace and security of the derelicts. The old Hickey once belonged to this holiday world; the new Hickey tries to change it by exposing its inhabitants to the truth of things. In this respect the new Hickey, the sober Hickey, is like Shakespeare's Malvolio, who, because he is virtuous, cannot belong to a "cakes and ale" world. Perhaps the phrases "holiday world" and "cakes and ale"—phrases that describe the festive atmosphere of Shakespearean romantic comedy—are too joyous to denote accurately where the inhabitants of Harry Hope's saloon dwell. But the phrases do suggest the hermetic quality of that saloon world: its security, boozy and dreamy; a world in which the dwellers comfortably accommodate one another. Whatever their reasons for escaping the everyday life, whatever their weakness in avoiding reality, they do belong together, they do make up a distinct, self-contained society. They carry on life with one another. They are a family.

Paradoxically, the character who comes on with a song and in the spirit of amiable affection (so unlike Malvolio in this respect) is trying to stop the music and disrupt the comedy, as did Malvolio. Hickey, in short, is functioning as the traditional blocking figure of comedy whose moralistic drive is rather frightening at times, almost demonic. His symbolic function, his close relationship with death, gives this son of a preacher an otherworldly quality. But part of his aura, I suggest, depends on his function as a conventional negative force in a comic world, a truth teller in a world that must be nourished by lies. In this sense, Hickey, like Malvolio, is the "mad" one, out of tune with the world of Hope and company. And he, again like Malvolio, must be thrust aside, removed, in order for the comic world to persist.

And that is exactly what happens at play's end. Not only does he leave the stage, but the derelicts latch on to the "mad" idea in order to convince themselves that his high-sounding truth telling was a manifestation of a sick mind. Hickey helps them come to this conclusion by going along with Harry Hope's lie about Hickey's insanity; and here, as throughout, Hickey's genuine affection for the bums is evident. He is no Malvolio after all, except in function; he wants them to be "happy," that haunting and troublesome word in this play and throughout O'Neill's career. Well, they *are* happy when he leaves, the only time the word *happy* doesn't end an act, the only time the word is translated into a stage action of "happiness" for the derelicts as they sing and drink the whiskey that is now alive.

I do not wish to push the idea of comedy too far in connection with Hickey, but I do believe that he, in part at least, is a character who belongs to a comic tradition. I also believe that Harry Hope and company inhabit what in many respects resembles a traditional comic world. When Hickey arrives with the words, "Hello, Gang!" and then sings his song about good fellows getting together, he is highlighting a basic characteristic of comedy—it thrives on company, on companionship, on having the guys together. Add whiskey and laughter to this society, as Hickey immediately does, and we have a traditional tavern world inhabited by everyday creatures who retain individual characteristics that include the comedic. So that Ed Mosher, for example, is a parasite, a practical joker, a teller of funny stories, the possessor of *"a round kewpie's face."* And Hugo Kalmar's head is *"much too big for his body"*; Hugo is a type of anarchist *"as portrayed, bomb in hand, in newspaper cartoons."* And Harry Hope is a *"softhearted slob"* given to tantrums (3:567, 565–66, 569). And so on. In this respect, Harry Hope's saloon is just up the road from the Boar's Head Tavern where Falstaff and company drink and thrive.

But more important than these individual comic characteristics is the group feeling, the family feeling, the *social* unity that they display—in their drinking, laughter, pipe dreams; in their sleepiness, inability to face reality, accommodation to one another; in their physical togetherness in that one saloon that is a haven for all of them; in their relationship to Hickey, and in their general function as chorus. Both the comic and the pathetic comprise their small lives, and if we were forced to place them in a distinct genre, I believe it would be comedy. It would not be tragedy, although O'Neill does want us to take a step closer to these men; we have a feeling for their pitiful condition; we clearly realize that the word *happy* cannot be attached to them without much qualification.

O'Neill, we remember, believed that the play strips the souls of these characters "stark naked," producing moments of "deep tragedy." He seems to be saying that all creatures are tragic, even these seemingly small men. My argument against their tragic status—a status that traditionally depends on the isolation of a character, aloneness, uniqueness, and a kind of height because of this uniqueness—depends upon the social togetherness of the gang, coupled with their survival at play's end. Survival is an idea that usually belongs to comedy, the genre that allows us to acknowledge continuity, preservation, harmony, a condition of "happily ever after." We may wish to discuss what survival really means in connection with Harry Hope and his friends, whose weakness and constant inebriation may lead us to ask, "What price survival?" But if we do discuss them in these terms we come dangerously close to moralistic judgment, perhaps discovering a little touch of Hickey in ourselves.

We begin the play with the bums existing, merely existing, in their self-contained tavern world. We live with them for four hours, a long time—a time that is necessary because O'Neill wants us to feel the sheer survival quality of these creatures who have come to the "last harbor." They are always on stage; their presence is felt throughout. They were there when the curtain rose, and they will be there after the curtain decends. At play's end they are where they were at play's beginning, only more jovial, singing and laughing, whereas in the beginning they were asleep. Hickey has shaken them up; Hickey has "happened" and made them unhappy "for a time"; but now they are back to their old selves, and they are carrying on. They will live in that comedy world of "happily ever after," although the word *happily* comes strangely to our lips, of course, because death hangs heavily in the play's atmosphere. A literal death has come to Parritt (we just heard the thud!); Hickey is going to his death; Larry is staring at death. But the survival of the others seems secure. It is not the survival of vitality, or of truth, but it is survival.

O'Neill himself said about them, "In some queer way they carried on." Well, not so queer when we acknowledge the life-giving power of their pipe dreams and the strength of their whiskey. And we should recognize that the whiskey and pipe dreams function the way the genre of comedy functions: comedy blurs reality to the point where it is acceptable; it allows one to laugh away a true awareness of self and mortality; it allows for life. (Is it mere coincidence that O'Neill's one unequivocal comedy, *Ah Wilderness!*, is his most deliberate lie about his own life, as we noticed in my chapter on comedy?) When the play ends, we hear the songs and laughter of the gang at Harry Hope's. "The End of the Line Cafe" it is, as Larry insisted, and the men can go no further. But they can go on where they are, in Hope's secure, comfortable, comedic tavern world.

Dudley Nichols said that "O'Neill himself delighted in the play's laughter." Some of this laughter persists to the end, even though the play itself is tragic. And that is why Larry Slade is so crucial a character in any discussion of the play's genre. Without Larry the play would be precariously lodged on the curve of tragicomedy; with Larry it settles into tragedy, but not without some complicating problems for the audience.

There is no need to rehearse all that has been written about Larry Slade, who for many, including myself, is the play's central character, certainly the most haunting character. What I wish to emphasize here is his changing *generic* role. It seems appropriate that this tortured creature who has been condemned to look at two sides of every question should himself occupy two generic worlds, moving from one to the other. Larry Slade, from the moment the curtain rises, is *the* critical commentator on what is happening on stage. The only one awake, his statements are naturally accepted by the audience. O'Neill invests his utterances with a prose rhythm and range of metaphor that indicates we are listening to an educated, intelligent man. O'Neill's physical description of Larry supports his role as spokesman: his eyes, always containing "*a gleam of sharp sardonic humor*" (3:566), are those of a mystic; his face is that of a weary priest. His first words on his fellow "inmates" offer a literary allusion to the Feast of All Fools, followed by references to the sea and ships. The two ideas come together in our minds as the traditional *Narrenschiff,* ship of fools, an indication that we may have entered a comic world, after all.

This reference to fools reverts to Larry himself, who is called the old "foolosopher," and who functions as the Fool—capital *F*—in this play. That is, like the Fool in comedy and tragedy, he is seemingly set apart, looking at the others in the play, commenting on them, allowing us to see the world through his eyes, which are clear and awake and contain a gleam of sardonic humor. He seems to be a kind of detached spectator, standing where Puck stands, or Feste, offering comments on human nature that we accept. (I say "seems to be" because we know Larry is more like the Fool in *King Lear,* who is *not* so detached, who feels deeply his master's agony.)

O'Neill gives him the important statements of the play, the most important uttered almost immediately: "To hell with the truth! As the history of the world proves, the truth has no bearing on anything. It's irrelevant and immaterial, as the lawyers say. The lie of the pipe dream is what gives life to the whole misbegotten mad lot of us, drunk or sober" (3:569–70). Larry Slade places himself—wrongly, we come to realize—where the Fool is placed traditionally, "in the grandstand of philosophical detachment," where he observes a dance of death.

Throughout he seems pleased with his own objective stance and his own ability to see the world more clearly than the others. There's something foolish about his smugness at times, and the others are right to mock "de old Foolosopher." In this respect Larry reminds us of Jaques, who is anxious to wear the motley of Touchstone in order to inveigh against the world with license, to philosophize in good set terms on how the world goes—"we ripe and ripe . . . we rot and rot." Larry's belief that the lie of the pipe dream gives *life* to the bums proves true, and, in fact, touches the very nature of comedy, which is the lie that affirms life, that represses the terror of death, that allows for a kind of "happiness." (O'Neill, in a letter to Macgowan, December 1940, said that the bums at play's end "must tell these lies as a first step in taking up life again.")

Larry Slade, in short, functions as the Fool, looking at two sides of every question, the critical commentator sporting a sardonic grin. We know, however, as Hickey knows, as the others know, that Larry is *not* an outsider, that he is involved, that he cannot sustain his role as objective looker-on, standing apart from the others, but must, because of his essential nature, take a step closer to them. His comic stance is his way of hiding from himself his tragic pity. He wishes merely to observe the dance of death, but he is dancing with the rest. This is his important discovery at the end of the play, thanks to Hickey and Parritt. As he himself states, he's "the only real convert to death Hickey made" (3:710). Jaques, who wanted to be Touchstone, has become Hamlet, contemplating the skull. We, the audience, have actively participated in his generic struggle throughout the play, and at play's end we participate in his accomplishment of realizing that he is finally facing the truth, which means death because in terms of the play only the lie can give life. A creature of comedy has become tragic, and we admire him and pity him, a combination of feelings that traditionally belong to the tragic hero.

In *Iceman* O'Neill seems to be staring directly at man's existence, with Larry Slade—who ends the play staring in front of him, "*oblivious*" to the "*racket*" of the others—O'Neill's representative. (*Staring* is an important stage gesture for O'Neill throughout his career; it carries great weight. Notice Ruth Mayo at the end of *Beyond the Horizon* or Anna and Matt at the end of *Anna Christie*. The gesture is equally important in Shakespearean tragedy—where, for example, the onstage onlookers in *King Lear* gaze at "the promis'd end"; where Iago in silence stares at the tragic bed. And Beckett's Krapp ends his play "staring before him" as the tape "runs on in silence.") We know that Larry Slade—like the other roomers who were based on real-life acquaintances and friends of O'Neill—was modeled after Terry Carlin, a good friend of the young O'Neill. Carlin was already sixty when O'Neill met him, and his ideas on anarchism, Nietzsche, and life in general had a profound influence on O'Neill, who considered the derelict a wise man, a philosopher of sorts. And there is no question that O'Neill, in addition to drawing from memory for his characters, was influenced, both generally and specifically, by Gorky's *The Lower Depths* and Ibsen's *The Wild Duck* and Strindberg's plays, which feature the battle of the sexes, influences well-documented by many scholars. But I wish to suggest, in addition, that in O'Neill's last plays Shakespeare comes more and more into play, with *Hamlet* once again providing the most interesting and pervasive echoes, and, in connection with *Iceman*, with Larry Slade Hamlet-like in so many ways. His are the darkest comments on human nature. He, like Hamlet, is filled with disillusionment bordering on cynicism. "What a piece of work is a man," Hamlet exclaims, as he offers a litany of high possibilities for mankind, only to end his speech with "And yet, to me, what is this quintessence of dust." Larry, who also saw high possibilities for mankind—when he was with the Movement—now no longer wishes "to communicate with the world" because of "its greedy madness" (3:580) (reminding us of the theme of greed in the history cycle). He sees mankind as "a mixture of mud and manure" (3:581). Like Hamlet, Larry Slade is a melancholic, filled with thoughts of suicide and death, and he even plays on the relationship between sleep and death. Like Hamlet's mind, Larry's is also split between opposing possibilities, with Larry "born condemned . . . to see all sides of a question" (3:580), including the most important question of to be or not to be. Like Hamlet, Larry is a role player, not putting on so antic a disposition as Hamlet but surely playing the old foolosopher and playing the man eager for death. Like Hamlet, Larry struggles against a mighty opposite who is a death dealer. Like Hamlet, Larry is "sick of life"; his words to Don Parritt almost place us in the graveyard scene in *Hamlet*:

> Honor or dishonor, faith or treachery are nothing to me but the opposites of the same stupidity which is ruler and king of life, and in the

end they rot into dust in the same grave. All things are the same meaningless joke to me, for they grin at me from the one skull of death. (3:636–37)

Hamlet in the graveyard literally held that skull of death; Larry will stare at it in his dark imagination when *Iceman* ends. Both characters have an intense awareness of mortality. For the young Hamlet, by the time he physically and emotionally confronts Yorick's skull near the play's end, death has become the most important condition of his felt experience—and of the audience's experience of the play. So too for the old Larry Slade, who is living a death in a bar that resembles a "morgue," who himself is called "Old Cemetery," who recognizes that those around him are doing "their death dance," and who finally realizes the deathly music is playing for him too. Hamlet, dying, says "the rest is silence." Larry, "the only real convert to death Hickey made here," silently stares in front of him. For both tragic actors, death is intrinsically bound up with a woman's sexuality—just as the Shakespearean word *die* combines the two ideas, as does O'Neill's title, *The Iceman Cometh*. We needn't rehearse Hamlet's obsession with his mother; his whole life is changed not only because of a father's death but also, what seems even more important, because of a mother's sexuality. His attitude toward mother, his love for mother—including a repressed incestuous love that perhaps reflects Shakespeare's own feelings and certainly anticipates the feelings of that later American playwright who seems obsessed with the Hamlet story—colors his behavior throughout the play. Larry Slade's life, we have no doubt, was changed because of the sexuality, the whorishness, of that freedom-loving woman, Rose Parritt, the "mother" that Larry has not forgotten despite his defensive words to Don, the woman who caused Larry to leave the Movement, who made Larry "sick of life," a Larry who could have said—if his creator had the language of Shakespeare—"How weary, stale, flat, and unprofitable / Seem to me all the uses of this world."

Larry's strained and disillusioning relationship to Rose is just one among many devastating man-woman relationships in *Iceman,* in all of which the woman is absent, so that we get to know her character from what is said about her.[11] O'Neill will use this technique—of allowing the audience to learn from onstage characters about characters who never appear on stage—in *Hughie,* a one-act play in a proposed group of plays collectively called "By Way of Obit." Interestingly, the absent women in *Iceman* are there "by way of obit" too, so to speak, because Evelyn Hickman is dead, Bessie Hope is dead, and Rose Parritt is incarcerated, a living death for this "free" woman. (As we have already seen, the absent woman, Eben

Cabot's mother, informs *Desire Under the Elms*.) Rose Parritt is the woman who connects Larry Slade to Don Parritt, a connection that Larry tries to avoid but cannot. O'Neill offers the tantalizing suggestion that Larry, one of Rose's many lovers, might be Don's father, so that when Larry, at play's end, tells Don to commit suicide it has the force of a father's command. In this respect, Don Parritt, who betrays his mother, who has a love-hate relationship with her—which reflects the love-hate relationship of Larry and Rose and, in fact, the love-hate relationship of all men and women, seen and unseen, in the play—seems Hamlet-like in his reactions to his mother and to women in general. His misogynistic streak stems from his feeling that his mother betrayed him. Her indiscriminate sexual activity, "all the guys she's had" (3:634), gave Don the feeling he was "living in a whorehouse" (3:635). He recalls Larry's last fight with Rose, saying he took Larry's side because Larry was "like a father" to him, agreeing with Larry who had told Rose, "I don't like living with a whore" (3:635). Because of his mother's promiscuity, Parritt considers all women to be whores, and he certainly has a deep aversion to the onstage "tarts." Like Hamlet, too, Don Parritt has a distinct death wish, and he believes he is a worse murderer than Hickey because Hickey's wife is dead, whereas Rose is still alive. For Don, as for Hamlet, it seems that death is "felicity" and life is drawing one's breath in pain. Merely a reflective character, as his name indicates, personally obnoxious and gathering to himself very little sympathy from O'Neill or the audience, the unattractive Don Parritt, so unlike the charismatic Hamlet, is sent to his death by his "father," as Hamlet is sent to his death by his ghostly father, the family romance forever feeding death in the tragedies of O'Neill and Shakespeare.

Of course, the play's most important love-hate relationship is Hickey's with his wife Evelyn. Anxious to destroy the pipe dreams of all the lodgers at Harry Hope's, genuinely interested in saving their lives and bringing them peace, Hickey badgers them to the point where they figuratively die, with even the whiskey no longer having a kick. Hickey, however, has his own pipe dream, that he loved his wife. It is while he is delivering his long confession, in which he reveals how he murdered Evelyn, that he blurts out that he laughed when he killed her and said: "Well, you know what you can do with your pipe dream now, you damned bitch!" (Harry Hope had previously used the word *bitch* when referring to his nagging wife Bessie, whom he claims he loves, but it's quite obvious that he hated her and is glad she's dead. And Parritt, who early in the play says, "I hate every bitch that ever lived!" will later call his mother a "damned old bitch!") For that moment Hickey's pipe dream is shattered; his love was a lie, it seems. He hated his wife for the guilt she made him feel. He killed her to rid himself of her forgiveness and love *and* his own guilt. Because he cannot face the truth of his hatred, because he must continue to believe that he loved Evelyn, he says, "Good God, I couldn't have said that! If I did, I'd gone insane! Why, I loved Evelyn better than anything in life!" (3:700). He leaves the stage—accompanied by police officers whom he called and who heard his confession—pleading insanity, not to escape punishment, as they seem to think, but because his pipe dream persists. Just as the derelicts return to their pipe dreams, latching on to Hickey's insanity as the reason for his strange behavior and his lies about them, so Hickey returns to his. For the derelicts, the whiskey has a bite again, and they can sink into the illusions about yesterday and tomorrow that they possessed in the play's beginning.

Hickey's act of killing Evelyn in her bed brings us back to Simon Harford's words in *More Stately Mansions,* for when "the bridegroom cometh, we discover we are kissing death." Hickey is the bridegroom-iceman bringing death, figuratively to the derelicts in Hope's saloon, literally to his wife.[12] The powerful combination of love and death, *liebestod,* so starkly presented in Hickey's confession of murder—he seems to be reliving the act of murder and love even as he speaks—should call to mind another murderer who kills a loving and devoted wife in bed, a wife who is wearing the nightgown she wore when her black bridegroom first slept with her, a wife who sings "Willow, willow, willow" and will soon be cool beneath the willow trees. Othello believes his murder to be a kind of sacrifice, and after the murder he connects the idea of madness to his murderous act, an act that he confesses and that leads directly to his death. I am suggesting that Hickey's murder of his wife calls to mind the bedroom scene of Desdemona's murder, a scene of love and death in which Othello literally kisses death. And what prods me to do so is the importance of a woman's chastity in both plays. Hickey, we know, wanted his wife to sleep with the iceman; her unfaithfulness would have relieved him of the guilt he always felt when he returned to her chaste bed, shamed by her loving forgiveness after he slept with other women. Othello too would have been relieved of his immense burden of guilt and shame if his wife were not the chaste Desdemona, and at one point he visualizes her as a prostitute to the army. In both plays men kill the women they think they love because their love is bound up with the feeling that their women are ideal. Certainly, the idea of a woman's purity and faithfulness is an important focus in *Iceman* (in relation to Evelyn, to Rose, to Jimmy Tomorrow's wife, and to Bessie Hope) and in *Othello* (in relation to Desdemona, to Emilia, and to the onstage prostitute Bianca). In both plays the atmosphere is charged with the idea that women will always sleep with the iceman. Chuck's belief—

"De minute your back is toined, dey're cheatin' wid de iceman or someone" (3:683)—is voiced by Iago in a more sophisticated idiom: you women, he tells Desdemona and Emilia, are "players in your huswifery, and huswives in your beds"; "You rise to play, and go to bed to work" (2.1.112,115). Hickey is so complex a character that critics have a difficult time trying to formulate him in a phrase. I have already discussed the comic dimension of the character that many believe to be the play's tragic protagonist. Having suggested that a Hickey-Othello connection can be felt in Hickey's murder of his wife, I will now complicate the suggestion by asserting that throughout the play *up to* the confession of murder, Hickey has Iago-like characteristics. He is a compulsive talker, he has a cynical attitude toward women, he is destructive of peace of mind, he is a man's man, drinking with the guys, ready with a song and sexual joke, he disturbs his environment, his words bring death, and he kills his wife. (I add parenthetically that Hickey is the only character in *Iceman* who has no specific living model that O'Neill knew personally, although there is much of Jamie O'Neill in Hickey. The Jamie-Iago connection will be discussed when we look at *Long Day's Journey*.)

The misogynistic view of women that informs Shakespearean tragedy informs O'Neill's plays as well, never more so than in *The Iceman Cometh*. Whether a woman is selfless and sweet and forgiving and loving, like Evelyn, or selfish and belligerent and independent and whorish, like Rose, the result is the same: the woman destroys. O'Neill's view is deeply colored by his relationship with his mother and three wives, and it is no exaggeration to say that his entire career is a working out or working through this relationship, especially his ambivalent attitude toward his mother. Louis Sheaffer goes so far as to say, and it's difficult not to agree with him, that in *Iceman* Hickey's murder of his wife and Parritt's condemnation of his mother to a living death reveal O'Neill's basic matricidal instincts, allowing the stage to give vent to his most private feelings of hatred and self-hatred.[13] O'Neill's creative activity, his writing of plays, perhaps the most public of arts, brings us to the private man, as many scholars and critics have demonstrated. We have much less external information about the private life of Shakespeare, but can we doubt that *Hamlet* and *Othello* and *King Lear* and *Macbeth*, to name only his four major tragedies, display his most private thoughts? Can we doubt that Shakespeare had the most turbulent private life of all? The destructive relationship between man and woman is an important part of all the Shakespeare tragedies mentioned and of O'Neill's important tragedies, *The Hairy Ape, Desire Under the Elms, Mourning Becomes Electra, Iceman,* and *Long Day's Journey*. I have been suggesting in this connection some possible analogues between Shakespeare's tragedies and O'Neill's, with the Shakespearean echoes sometimes powerful, sometimes weak, but usually giving O'Neill's art a richer density of meaning.

The end of *The Iceman Cometh* is emotionally charged, perhaps too charged for the reconciling closure we usually experience in witnessing tragedy or comedy. Too much happens in the end, and in a play that lasts four hours too much happens quickly and together. Hickey calls his murdered wife a "damned bitch," catches himself, pleads insanity; Harry Hope pounces on that idea in order to survive; Hickey understands the pouncing and goes along with it; Hickey leaves the stage declaring his love for Evelyn; Parritt declares his guilt, echoing Hickey's words; Larry sends Parritt to his death; Hope and the others are jubilant, the whiskey now alive again; the thud of Parritt's body is heard; Larry realizes he's Hickey's only convert to death; and Hope and the chorus, pipe dreams restored, sing and roar with laughter. An abundance of happenings within twenty minutes of playing time, maintaining a rhythm, a speed, that makes the ending of the play more *alive* than any previous dramatic segment. The same can be said about the theatrical activity at the end of *Hamlet:* swordplay, poison, treachery, the entrance of a marching army, the piling up of dead bodies, the carrying of a dead body offstage.

Certainly, Hope and company are more alive at play's end than they were in the play's beginning. Larry, in contrast, is now the dead one, *"oblivious to their racket,"* O'Neill tells us. He is looking directly at truth, at mortality, at the skull, at existence; in fact, Larry, now a tragic figure, is looking at what the genre of tragedy traditionally looks at: the truth of our existence, the terror of death, the vulnerability of mankind. The racket of the bums, their laughter, their togetherness, their survival, their ability to weather the storm and come to a safe harbor—last harbor though it is—all belong to a world of comedy. These two clashing ideas make the ending of *The Iceman Cometh* especially complex and troublesome. When O'Neill says that "the comedy breaks up and the tragedy comes on," he seems to be tracing the movement of Larry Slade, as I have attempted to describe it.

I believe, however, that some of the comedy remains to the very end, that Hope and his comrades are not as tragic as O'Neill maintains. He sees them as victims of life, and he treats them with "understanding compassion," as he states, but we leave them in the midst of life, poor life though it is, lacking the vivacity we associate with the soul of festive comedy, but carrying on, in illusion and drink. They live. Our last image before the curtain descends is an uneasy one. We look at the tragic Larry, alone, facing the truth of things; and we look at and hear Harry Hope and the gang carousing. We witness the death of illusion and the life of illusion, and we leave the theater recognizing that O'Neill's vision of life, tragic though it is, contains the important dimension of comedy, thereby offering his audience the deepest sense of reality, giving his play the kind of large inclusiveness that we associate with Shakespeare and with Beckett.

Many of the Shakespearean echoes that I hear throughout the play, and that I have attempted to pinpoint, perhaps were not consciously offered by O'Neill, and certainly the Beckettian qualities I have discussed could not have been in O'Neill's mind because O'Neill came before Beckett, not much before but before. However, all three dramatists share common ground, both tragic and comic, and for all three—for Shakespeare in tragedy, for Beckett in *Waiting for Godot* and *Endgame*, for O'Neill in *The Iceman Cometh*—death, despite the comic trappings, is the abiding reality, the condition the dramatists force into our minds insistently. Whatever other labels they may be given, all three are ultimate realists, approaching the truth of things and eliciting the deepest responses from their audiences. All three seem to have written their plays out of deep despair, but for all the very composing of plays seems to have been an answer to that despair.

We know that O'Neill, when he was writing his last plays, was sick at heart because of his ill health and because of what was happening in the world. Hitler was on the march. Germany invaded Poland in 1939, when *The Iceman Cometh* was being written. (In a very real sense, Hitler was the world's iceman.) Great Britain and France then declared war on Germany. America entered the conflict in 1941, the year O'Neill completed *Long Day's Journey*. The miserable state of the world was an important reason for O'Neill's twelve-year "silence." No new O'Neill play appeared on Broadway from 1934, when *Days Without End* was produced, to the 1946 *Iceman*. His despairing attitude is captured by Deborah Harford in *More Stately Mansions* when she hopes that "the Second Flood may come and rid the world of this stupid race of men and wash the earth clean." O'Neill's social pessimism during the years he wrote the cycle and the last plays is profound. His dark thoughts were expressed in numerous letters to his friends and in some public statements, and they are translated into plays that usually carry the stamp of the tragic.

We have no way of knowing, from external sources, Shakespeare's feelings about what was happening in his world when he wrote his tragedies, beginning with *Hamlet,* for him the breakthrough play, as we already observed, the play that begins a period of creativity based on a view that we must label tragic. We can merely speculate about his personal reasons for entering his dark period, but surely the writer who felt all things so deeply was profoundly affected by the momentously changing conditions in his time. He, like Donne, must have been looking at a dying world around the year 1600, with not only the "new philosophy" calling all in doubt, but with a queen, whether or not admired or loved by Shakespeare, literally dying and taking with her all that she symbolically represented. And, of course, the Reformation was changing the way Elizabethans were looking at life and death and God, with important ramifications for the drama, and especially for England's most sensitive dramatist. Here C. L. Barber's speculations are especially illuminating. He sees the drama as "a new organ of culture," as "an agency in the historical shift of the Renaissance and Reformation from a ritual and ceremonial view of life, with absolute assumptions about meaning and reality, toward a psychological and historical view."[14] Asking the important question, "Why was *tragic* form for the drama needed?" he answers it by discussing "the new religious situation brought on by the Reformation—or more precisely, the transition or break from Catholicism to Protestantism," a situation that demanded a "new theater," a "new place apart" for "the expression of impulses, profoundly disruptive both intrapsychically and socially."[15] In this new place, which substituted for the old place, the old "theater" called the Church, tragedy functioned as a substitute for religious worship, with important differences, of course. Instead of worshipping a divine Holy Family, the theater audience—and characters *in* the play—now "worship" the play's hero. Now the center of interest is the *human* family. Barber brilliantly pinpoints "a crisis of heritage" in Shakespeare's tragedies, beginning with *Hamlet,* which directly pertains to the problem of the protagonist's need to achieve "masculine identity" in relation to a woman who makes demands on him. This relationship between man and woman involves "worship or a dependency akin to worship; it regularly embodies an underlying wish to surrender the will, to lose or merge the self."[16] In short, for Barber Shakespeare's tragedies draw on "the same roots of infantile feeling that religion draws on" and they "exhibit family relations, or family-like relations, being made sacred or demonic or both."[17] After asserting that "the tragic heroes are vulnerable to the feminine," he suggests—again beautifully playing with the loss of Mother Church in England but the presence of an "idolatrous church . . . the mother of whoredom" in France—that the women who make demands on the hero are either saints or strumpets.[18] Even so scanty a summary of Barber's rich ideas reveals the remarkable closeness of Shakespeare's situation to O'Neill's. O'Neill also felt the loss of Catholicism, the absence of a Holy Mother, and the need to look for a lost mother. O'Neill, like Shakespeare, dramatizes what Barber calls "a post-Christian situation." O'Neill also looked for ways to make his theater a "Temple."[19] He too invests his most creative energies in the human *family* and gives us man-woman relationships that involve worship and the need "to lose or merge the self," a condition that Edmund Tyrone will feelingly express in *Long Day's Journey*. O'Neill also sees women as either saints or whores. The years in which both Shakespeare and O'Neill were writing their most tragic plays were turbulent ones for each. Although the turbulences which shook their creative imaginations were very different, they helped produce dramatic artifacts which share common characteristics.

O'Neill chose the year 1912 as the time in which his two tragic autobiographical plays take place; certainly 1912 is the most turbulent and important year of his life. In that year's winter of his discontent O'Neill attempted suicide at Jimmy-the-Priest's, a New York waterfront saloon that helped provide the setting for *The Iceman Cometh*. (Also helping were a bar in Greenwich Village called The Hell Hole and the bar in the Garden Hotel, located opposite the old Madison Square Garden.) Jimmy-the-Priest's also furnished O'Neill with the derelicts and friends who frequent Harry Hope's "end of the line" saloon. During that year O'Neill toured the West as a bit player in his father's vaudeville adaptation of Dumas's *The Count of Monte Cristo*, the play that provides an important focus of attention in *Long Day's Journey*. Shortly after that tour O'Neill's divorce from his first wife Kathleen Jenkins came through. (He had never seen their son Eugene O'Neill, Jr., now two years old, and would not see him for ten more years.) O'Neill spent the summer of 1912 in the family's Monte Cristo summer home in New London, Connecticut, a summer he will memorialize in *Long Day's Journey*. It was then that he learned that his chronic cold was really tuberculosis. On Christmas of that year he entered Gaylord Farm Sanatorium in Connecticut, commencing a six-month stay that gave him a chance to pause and think about his life "for the first time." "It was in this enforced period of reflection that the urge to write [plays] first came to me."[20] During that period he began to read seriously every play he "could lay hands on: the Greeks, the Elizabethans—practically all the classics—and of course all the moderns. Ibsen and Strindberg, especially Strindberg, [who] first gave me the vision of what modern drama could be."[21] At Gaylord Farm Sanatorium O'Neill decided "to be an artist or nothing," as he later writes to George Pierce Baker, in whose playwriting course he enrolls in Harvard in 1914.

O'Neill's two tragedies share the year 1912, and they also, it seems, came into his mind together. When he decides to give up the history cycle, he says in his work diary that he will make outlines of the two plays whose ideas appeal to him most, and there's no question that he was actively thinking about *Long Day's Journey* while he was writing *The Iceman Cometh*.[22] Both plays deal more directly with his personal biography than any play that came before, both are family plays, both obey the unities, both share themes and techniques, both can be discussed from a Beckettian point of view. And over both the ghost of Shakespeare hovers. But in *Long Day's Journey*, where O'Neill gets as close as he possibly can to his own family—the family of a famous actor, we must always remember—the ghost of Shakespeare does not merely hover. Shakespeare enters the play directly and importantly. Just as all of O'Neill's plays seem to be leading him to this one great outpouring of emotion-turned-to-art called *Long Day's Journey Into Night*, so all of the previous Shakespearean echoes and analogues and allusions and devices seem to gather in this autobiographical play that mentions Shakespeare by name eleven times (in only one other play is the name mentioned, *Ah, Wilderness!*, and there only once), and that has as its centerpiece a portrait of Shakespeare.

At a 1988 performance of *Long Day's Journey*, directed by José Quintero and starring Colleen Dewhurst as Mary Tyrone and Jason Robards as James Tyrone, I was struck, as I sat in the theater watching the darkening plight of the four haunted Tyrones, by the *centrality* of the portrait of Shakespeare in the living room, just above the bookcase containing those dangerous volumes of Nietzsche and Strindberg and Schopenhauer and Ibsen. One feels that James Tyrone must have furnished the room, giving Shakespeare that prominent position, but one also feels that his sons who fought with him about everything, including Shakespeare, did not object to that portrait. As I sat there watching, the portrait took on a large life, perhaps larger than O'Neill himself intended, because I thought about another room with another portrait, also a dying room, Ezra Mannon's study in *Mourning Becomes Electra,* in the house in which Lavinia would remain incarcerated for the remainder of her years, and these would be *many* years, since she begins that play at age twenty-three—in fact, the age of Edmund Tyrone. For me, O'Neill's earlier play, *Mourning Becomes Electra,* became part of the play I was seeing, not an inappropriate happening when we think of each of O'Neill's plays as part of a whole, and when we reflect on O'Neill's persistent belief that the past is the present. When we think of Shakespeare in the work of O'Neill, the past *is* the present, once again.

The exact position of Shakespeare's portrait in the Tyrone living room is part of O'Neill's specific stage directions; here, as always, he leaves little room for the independence of the director or stage designer. He wanted that portrait to be *"above"* the small bookcase *"containing novels by Balzac, Zola, Stendhal, philosophical and sociological works by Schopenhauer, Nietzsche, Marx, Engels, Kropotkin, Max Stirner, plays by Ibsen, Shaw, Strindberg, poetry by Swinburne, Rossetti, Wilde, Ernest Dowson, Kipling, etc."* The other bookcase, *"glassed-in,"* is up against the left wall of the living room; it contains *"sets of Dumas, Victor Hugo, Charles Lever, three sets of Shakespeare, The*

World's Best Literature in fifty large volumes, Hume's History of England, Thiers' History of the Consulate and Empire, Smollett's History of England, Gibbon's Roman Empire and miscellaneous volumes of old plays, poetry, and several histories of Ireland" (3:717). This bookcase contains the volumes that James Tyrone holds dear. Notice that Dumas begins the listing—it is the Fechter version of Dumas's *The Count of Monte Cristo* that proved to be the great success-failure of Tyrone's life—and histories of Ireland end the listing—the family's Irishness will be an important ingredient of the play. (O'Neill said, "one thing that explains more than anything about me is the fact that I'm Irish."[23]) In between Dumas and Ireland in Tyrone's "traditional" bookcase are the sets of Shakespeare. That these books are glassed in suggests their preciousness, although O'Neill insists that these volumes were *"read and reread."* As the play progresses we have little doubt that the Tyrone sons also read the volumes in Tyrone's bookcase, and we have no doubt that Tyrone read none or few of the books in that other bookcase, the smaller one, over which Shakespeare's picture hangs. The portrait of Shakespeare, it is important to observe, does not hang over the bookcase containing the volumes of Shakespeare; it hangs over Nietzsche and Strindberg and Shaw and Wilde and company. We must believe that the meticulous O'Neill had a reason for this specific arrangement. He is pointing in his stage directions to what will prove to be opposing beliefs in the continuous quarrel of sons and father. O'Neill, ever fond of counterpointing, of juxtaposition, of rhythms that engage and release our emotions—in this respect, ever fond of the techniques that Shakespeare used so remarkably before him—is underlining a conflict that will materialize as the play progresses. Here, as the curtain rises, the audience cannot *see* exactly which volumes are in the bookcases; this will be the focus of discussion by father and sons later in the play. Once again we observe in O'Neill the kind of careful attention to detail that a novelist employs and that seems superfluous when we think of an audience's experience of a play. Once again we must assume that O'Neill is painting as full a picture as he can for the reader and to guide those who will direct and act in the play.

With Shakespeare looking at us from that central position, it does not take long for the first Shakespeare quotation to be uttered: "The Moor, I know his trumpet." The quotation has a clear dramatic function. It perfectly fits the mood of the opening scene; it immediately reveals an important side of the character of Jamie Tyrone; it triggers the play's first argument between sons and father, establishing the pattern for all the confrontations to come. And it indicates O'Neill's deep acquaintance with *Othello* because the setting of the quotation in *Othello* and the setting of the quotation in *Long Day's Journey* are emotionally analogous, whether or not

O'Neill consciously wished to establish the connection. This quotation, like all the quotations in the play, deserves careful attention.

The first act of *Long Day's Journey* opens with sunshine coming through the windows in the Tyrone living room, and with James and Mary Tyrone entering *"together"* from breakfast, seemingly happy and rather playful. This will be the "happiest" time in the play. In the three remaining acts no member of the family will enter together with anyone else; each will experience terrible aloneness. And the sunshine of act 1 will become *"a faint haziness"* in act 2, an *"early dusk"* caused by the fog in act 3, dark midnight in act 4, when the wall of fog is densest. Perhaps we can say about *Long Day's Journey* what O'Neill said about *Iceman:* "the comedy breaks up and the tragedy comes on." At their entrance Tyrone gives his wife *"a playful hug,"* telling her she's "a fine armful now," pleased that she gained twenty pounds during her stay at the sanatorium. Mary thinks she's "gotten too fat," and the playful side of this first conversation between them—a conversation that also includes more serious remarks on Tyrone's foolish real-estate deals and Edmund's summer cold, as well as references to the fog that is now gone and the "awful foghorn" that kept Mary from sleeping well—culminates in Mary's teasing remark that Tyrone was "snoring so hard I couldn't tell which was the foghorn!" Laughing, she *"pats Tyrone's cheek playfully,"* but her reference to his snoring makes him a little testy: "Nonsense. You always exaggerate about my snoring" (3:719–21). When Jamie and Edmund enter together, they are chuckling over a story they will soon tell about Shaughnessy and the pigs. Mary's first words to her sons refer to Tyrone's snoring: "I've been teasing your father about his snoring," but then she adds that she also heard Jamie snoring "as bad as your father. You're like him." Edmund backs her up about "Papa's snoring. Gosh, what a racket!" and then Jamie, agreeing and *"putting on a ham-actor manner,"* offers the play's first Shakespeare quotation: "The Moor, I know his trumpet" (3:723–24). This clever linking of Tyrone's snoring and Othello's trumpet causes both Edmund and Mary to laugh, as it should, but Tyrone angrily retorts: "If it takes my snoring to make you remember Shakespeare instead of the dope sheet on the ponies, I hope I'll keep on with it" (3:724). This begins the first of many arguments in the play. But the quotation itself must give us pause. It was delivered as a joke in this sunniest scene of the play, with Jamie immediately revealing the clever cast of his mind, taking a quotation out of one context and placing it within another that jokingly fits the occasion and fits the object of the joke. That he delivers the line like an ham actor is meant to be a playful critical stab at his father, the actor who is always quoting Shakespeare, but his father doesn't appreciate the playfulness of the remark. We should note that the line is not one of the familiar quotations from Shakespeare; in fact, it is almost a throwaway line in *Othello*. But Jamie knows it. Indeed, he seems to know Shakespeare as well his father knows Shakespeare, perhaps even better, because Tyrone always offers the most familiar quotations. Jamie's impressive familiarity with Shakespeare, here used to poke mild fun at his father, actually binds him to the father he ostensibly hates. He is like his father in his snoring, as Mary said, in his physicality, as the stage directions inform us, in his being "a healthy hulk," as his father tells him, and in his closeness to Shakespeare. But his Shakespeare doesn't turn out to be his father's Shakespeare, for Jamie will force the Shakespearean quotations and allusions to serve his own, usually cynical, purposes. O'Neill's stage directions at Jamie's entrance mention Jamie's *"habitual expression of cynicism,"* and in this respect he resembles the Shakespeare character who is "nothing if not critical," who has a dark contempt for the world around him, who considers virtue a "fig," and who, in fact, utters the line, "The Moor, I know his trumpet" (and whose name is the Spanish translation of James). Jamie, the Iago of *Long Day's Journey*—and he will quote once more from Iago in his devastating confession to Edmund in act 4—here jokingly refers to his father as the Moor. In act 4 we will learn that Tyrone *was* the Moor, playing Othello better than Edwin Booth ever did. There is a remarkable appropriateness to all of Jamie's quoting from Shakespeare, and the darkening vision of this tragedy can be charted by comparing this early playful line about snoring in sunny act 1 with his later quotations in the fog-bound act 4.

The family's first discussion deals with Tyrone's snoring, and trivial as the subject is, the discussion provides the first indication of the divisions within the family and the first pattern of behavior that will be repeated throughout the play. Jamie offers a joke at his father's expense; his mother and brother laugh; his father scathingly answers him. Mary tells Tyrone not to be so touchy, Edmund tells him to "give it a rest"—the "it" being the constant criticism of Jamie's life-style and lack of ambition—and Jamie boredly states, "Let's forget it." Alliances are immediately established, but as the play progresses these will shift—here, sons against father, mother against father; later, mother against sons, brother against brother, and so on. Here, in act 1, especially in the later conversation between Jamie and Tyrone, tensions form around the question: who is to blame for Edmund's tuberculosis? But the tensions seem mild in this sunny beginning; as the day progresses into night the play's atmosphere will be charged with greater tension based on the question: who is to blame for Mary's drug addiction? The darkening day will produce many accusations and regrets, will reveal much hate and love. Here, in act 1, life, taking its cue from a sunny morning, seems brighter. And in this respect too the quotation from *Othello* seems appropriate, revealing O'Neill's fine understanding of the rhythm of Shakespeare's play. "The Moor, I know his trumpet" is uttered by Iago at the arrival of Othello's ship in Cyprus in act 2. Just before this, Iago expressed his views on the lustful antics of women in a playful conversation with Desdemona and Emilia in which he offered the line which describes him best, "For I am nothing if not critical" (2.1.119). Immediately after Iago's trumpet quotation, Othello enters to have his happiest scene with Desdemona. Desdemona is his "soul's joy," she is the calm after the "tempest" he has just experienced. Othello is absolute in his contentment: "If it were now to die, / 'Twere now to be most happy." They kiss. Shakespeare's remarkable ironies are forever at work. This short scene in Cyprus is filled with endearments, with sweet talk, with happiness. It is the calm after the storm that Othello has experienced at sea, but perhaps more importantly, it is the calm before the storm of the rest of the play. Shakespeare's play will move to the rhythm of passions and end in death and darkness for lovers not so happy. Now notice where Jamie's Shakespeare quotation is placed in *Long Day's Journey:* after a description of Jamie's cynicism, in the middle of a playful scene containing sweet talk between husband and wife, containing a kiss, in a period of calm because of Mary's return from the sanatorium. After this, chaos will come, and even during this scene shadows are beginning to fall which will completely darken the family picture by play's end, just as in *Othello,* even as Othello and Desdemona are together briefly in their sweet joy, Iago is already spinning the web to ensnare the couple and darken their journey. In short, Jamie's clever, seemingly trivial, quotation has surprising resonance; it testifies to O'Neill's deep acquaintance with Shakespeare's play, whether or not he calculatingly aimed for the resonance.

Like act 1, act 2 contains one Shakespeare quotation, this begun by Tyrone and completed by Edmund. The situation: Edmund is leaving the house to go to Doctor Hardy but needs carfare. Ready to begin "*a customary lecture*" on Edmund's always being broke, Tyrone, "*looking at his son's sick face,*" checks himself and "*pulls out a small roll of bills from his pants pocket and carefully selects one. Edmund takes it. He glances at it and his face expresses astonishment. His father again reacts customarily—sarcastically,*" saying, "Thank you." And then Tyrone quotes: "How sharper than a serpent's tooth it is," completed by Edmund's "To have a thankless child" (3:767). Tyrone assumes that his son is "thankless" when Edmund is actually "speechless," having received a ten-dollar bill instead of the one dollar he expected. Tyrone assumes thanklessness because he acts and reacts "*customarily,*" as O'Neill's stage directions insist, never expecting gratitude from his children, and usually offering this appropriate Shakespeare quotation to sum up the situation. The quotation from *King Lear* is so predictable and habitual a response from Tyrone that Edmund can easily complete it, with Shakespeare once again providing a link between a father and son. But a child's thanklessness *is* fleetingly evident when Edmund cynically wonders why his father is so uncharacteristically generous: "Did Doc Hardy tell you I was going to die?" A cruel question. The "serpent's tooth" hurts Tyrone, as Edmund immediately realizes: "No! That's a rotten crack. I was only kidding, Papa." He gives his father *"an affectionate hug,"* says he's "very grateful. Honest, Papa." The hug is returned by Tyrone with the phrase, "You're welcome, lad," said genuinely because Tyrone is *"touched"* (3:767). Between Tyrone's sarcastic "Thank you" and his warm "You're welcome," ordinary phrases of everyday life, we find the quotation from *King Lear*, which offers an attitude that is commonplace, helping to make James Tyrone, as it made Lear, a representative father. Of course, the quotation, when it first appeared in Shakespeare's play, had a freshness and a power it has since lost because of familiarity and repetition (true for all of Shakespeare's fresh phrases!), certainly lost to Edmund and Jamie Tyrone because their father habitually quotes the line. Mechanical as Tyrone's response is, however, he is expressing, through Lear, the pain and frustration of fatherhood. He does not have the ability to freshly articulate his feelings; he must appropriate Shakespeare's words, not an unusual thing for an actor to do. And he surely goes to the right place for quotation because nowhere in Shakespeare is the agony of fatherhood—and the mistakes of fatherhood—more powerfully dramatized than in *King Lear*. Lear's arrogance and foolishness and need for love *and* his realization that he is a man both sinned against and sinning are all wrapped up in Shakespeare's complex creation. These characteristics rub off on Tyrone, who quotes Lear—Shakespeare here helping O'Neill form a character—and the quotation itself touches the agony of all parents who feel, whether justifiably or not, the sharp-toothed pain of a child's ingratitude. In this respect—the quotation's aptness of phrase, its succinct expression of an abiding and representative parental emotion—the words that Tyrone the father recites brings him closer to the audience. But because the quotation comes so *"customarily"* to Tyrone's lips, because he's always the ham actor quoting Shakespeare, and because the familial situation in *Long Day's Journey* (a father giving his son carfare) seems so distant from the Lear situation (a father powerfully cursing his "degenerate" daughter with sterility because she turned away his hundred knights), the audience might be disposed to feel less sympathetic toward him. This emotional movement of the audience—getting close, stepping back—mirrors the movement of the characters in the play, with each member of the family coming close to, then moving away from, another member.

The togetherness of father and son in their physical embrace negates the alienation that the Shakespeare quotation encapsulates, but the soft interlude is suddenly interrupted by Mary's angry "I won't have it!" For a moment the audience might think that she is jealous of the father-son closeness (which she might very well be), but she goes on to say: "Do you hear, Edmund! Such morbid nonsense! Saying you're going to die! It's the books you read! Nothing but sadness and death!" She says that his morbidness is merely a pose, that he's making "a great to-do about nothing" (3:768). Unconsciously, for Mary Tyrone and perhaps for O'Neill, her words extend the *King Lear* atmosphere in which "sadness and death" hang heavy, and in which Shakespeare makes much ado about nothing, the word that triggers the play's action when Cordelia says it in the first scene, the word that is repeated throughout the play, pointing to the values connected with the play's world, giving the play a Beckettian stamp. (The word *nothing* occurs fifty-one times in *Long Day's Journey,* a much greater number than in any other O'Neill play except *Strange Interlude,* a nine-act play.)

No Shakespeare quotations are found in act 3 of *Long Day's Journey,* which is ostensibly Mary Tyrone's act. (It is interesting to note that Jamie Tyrone does not appear in this act.) While the men are away from the house, and as she goes *"deeper within herself,"* helped by the drugs, sometimes acting girlishly, sometimes cynically, Mary tells Cathleen about her past, her first meeting with James Tyrone, her love for him. When Cathleen leaves her, Mary at first stares *"fixedly at nothing,"* then she hears the foghorn, which prods her bitter soliloquy:

> You're a sentimental fool. What is so wonderful about that first meeting between a silly romantic schoolgirl and a matinee idol? You were much happier before you knew he existed, in the Convent when you used to pray to the Blessed Virgin. (*longingly*) If I could only find the faith I lost, so I could pray again! (*She pauses—then begins to recite the Hail Mary in a flat, empty tone.*) "Hail, Mary, full of grace! The Lord is with Thee; blessed art Thou among women." (*sneeringly*) You expect the Blessed Virgin to be fooled by a lying dope fiend reciting words! You can't hide from her! (*She springs to her feet. Her hands fly up to pat her hair distractedly.*) I must go upstairs. I haven't taken enough. When you start again you never know exactly how much you need. (3:779)

Even in her agitated state she has the intellectual honesty to realize that her prayer cannot be heard by the Blessed Virgin because Mary is "a lying dope fiend." Perhaps her soliloquy, a Shakespearean device, allows us to recall Claudius's in the prayer scene in *Hamlet*. He also could not pray because he realized what he really was. The echo may be faint, but I believe it is heard because so much of *Hamlet* finds its way into this play, as I shall soon demonstrate. Later in this act Edmund will express his deep disillusionment with his mother's behavior, her taking drugs: "God, it made everything in life seem rotten!" (3:787). The words could have been said by Hamlet, another son so disillusioned with his mother's actions that his attitude toward life is polluted. Of course, these Shakespearean echoes are not specific quotations, but there is an appropriateness to the absence of quotation in this act, which belongs to Mary. She is the only member of the family who does not quote Shakespeare, indicating one more aspect of her alienation. The men of the family are able to leave the house, to drink from the same whiskey bottle, to function together as observers of Mary's increasingly drugged condition—and they share Shakespeare. Mary Tyrone is alone and, more terrible, she realizes she lost the only support that she alone had, the Blessed Virgin. In the next and last act, when midnight comes, we will discover that her husband's loss of Shakespeare will mirror Mary's loss of the Virgin Mary, but here in act 3, as the fog begins to thicken, Mary seems isolated in her anguish.

The last act of *Long Day's Journey* displays the most persistent and revealing use of Shakespeare by O'Neill, appropriately so if my thesis is correct, because O'Neill's most autobiographical play in its powerful last movement insistently forces us to feel the ghostly presence of that other member of the family, Shakespeare. Midnight finds Tyrone alone playing solitaire. "*He is drunk,*" the stage directions tells us, but "*despite all the whiskey in him, he has not escaped,*" and he appears "*a sad, defeated old man, possessed by hopeless resignation*" (3:792). When Edmund stumbles into the scene, having collided with the hat stand because only one bulb was burning in the hallway, father and son have the first of several altercations, this one focusing on Tyrone's stinginess and ending with Tyrone's turning on the bulbs in the chandelier, what Edmund mockingly calls "a grand curtain." Tyrone asks where Jamie is, and when he learns that Edmund split the ten-dollar bill with his brother, he says: "Then it doesn't take a soothsayer to tell he's probably in a whorehouse." Then, "*contemptuously,*" he says, "It's the fit place for him. If he's ever had a loftier dream than whores and whiskey, he's never shown it." Edmund retorts: "Oh, for Pete's sake, Papa. If you're going to start that stuff, I'll beat it" (3:794–95). I call attention to this snippet of dialogue for three reasons. First, Tyrone's word *soothsayer* is an unusual word in family conversation, rather formal, even stuffy, but not an unexpected word from a Shakespearean actor, one who played in *Julius Caesar,* as we learn later in the act. Second, when Tyrone evaluates his son Jamie he uses the word *dream,* an idea important throughout the family's long day's journey into night. Third, Edmund's *stuff,* a rather weak, common word—a far cry from *soothsayer*—coming from the lips of a budding writer, will soon function in a more charged context.

After Edmund tells his father he walked home in the fog—"I loved the fog. It was what I needed"—he presents the act's first quotation, from Dowson, one of the poets in the bookcase containing his (and O'Neill's) favorite writers. The last stanza reads: "They are not long, the days of wine and roses: / Out of a misty dream / Our path emerges for a while, then closes / Within a dream" (3:795). Dowson's words prod Edmund's own revery:

> The fog was where I wanted to be. Halfway down the path you can't see this house. You'd never know it was here. Or any of the other places down the avenue. I couldn't see but a few feet ahead. I didn't meet a soul. Everything looked and sounded unreal. Nothing was what it is. That's what I wanted—to be alone with myself in another world where truth is untrue and life can hide from itself. Out beyond the harbor, where the road runs along the beach, I even lost the feeling of being on land. The fog and the sea seemed part of each other. It was like walking on the bottom of the sea. As if I had drowned long ago. As if I was a ghost belonging to the fog, and the fog was the ghost of the sea. It felt damned peaceful to be nothing more than a ghost within a ghost. (3:795–96)

And then, responding to his father's worried and irritated staring, he says, "Don't look at me as if I'd gone nutty. I'm talking sense. Who wants to see life as it is, if they can help it?" (3:796). The reality of life is unbearable to Edmund who, like his mother, wishes to be lost in the fog. Notice that his question—"Who wants to see life as it is?"—points to the idea of pipe dreams, already given dramatic life in *The Iceman Cometh.* It would not take a gigantic leap of the imagination to find Edmund as one of the roomers in Harry Hope's saloon, and perhaps he was there as Willie Oban. (A much shorter leap would find Jamie there.) Edmund's thoughts have gone from fog to Dowson's "dream" to fog again and sea, and to ghosts that seem to belong to a dream world. His father's mixed reaction is predictable, part of the love-hate rhythm of the play: "You have a poet in you but it's a damned morbid one!" Then, "Devil take your pessimism. I feel low-spirited enough. (*He sighs.*) Why can't you remember your Shakespeare and forget the third-raters. You'll find what you're trying to say in him—as you'll find everything else worth saying. (*He quotes, using his fine voice*) 'We are such stuff as dreams are made on, and our little life is rounded with a sleep'" (3:796). This is the first Shakespeare quotation of act 4, coming naturally and mechanically from the lips of Tyrone, using the "*fine voice*" that Shakespeare always seems to inspire in him. Edmund "*ironically*" counters with: "Fine! That's beautiful. But I wasn't trying to say that. We are such stuff as manure is made on, so let's drink up and forget it. That's more my idea." That may be more Edmund's idea, but his crude rephrasing seems to lack imagination. He cannot effectively say what he is trying to say—later he will tell us he can only "stammer"—nor does he (and here he resembles his father) adequately appreciate what Shakespeare's Prospero is saying, although he does perfunctorily exclaim "Fine! That's beautiful!" Edmund's appreciation is dismissive. He seems not to realize that Shakespeare's words may be closer to his idea than his own trite substitute of "manure" for "dreams."

Tyrone extracts Prospero's much-quoted words from the very familiar "Our revels now are ended" speech, spoken by Prospero when he precipitously interrupts the masque he has staged to bless the young lovers, Miranda and Ferdinand. The speech gives Shakespeare the opportunity to present a memorable theater image in this, his last play before retirement. Throughout his career Shakespeare has played with the idea of "play" and even incorporated plays within his plays. Here Prospero interrupts an incorporated play, supposedly because he suddenly remembers that Caliban is plotting against him, a rather weak narrative device, but surely because Shakespeare wants to present this self-reflexive speech, wants to bring together the ideas of theater and life from the perspective of his surrogate onstage, the artist-magician Prospero. Prospero's speech offers a commonplace idea so effectively that it gathers to itself the force of unequivocal truth.

> Our revels now are ended. These our actors
> (As I foretold you) were all spirits, and
> Are melted into air, into thin air,
> And like the baseless fabric of this vision,
> The cloud-capp'd tow'rs, the gorgeous palaces,
> The solemn temples, the great globe itself,
> Yea, all which it inherit, shall dissolve,
> And like this insubstantial pageant faded
> Leave not a rack behind. We are such stuff
> As dreams are made on; and our little life
> Is rounded with a sleep.
>
> (4.1.148–58)

The revels of play and life are over. The dissolving of "the great globe itself"—a glancing reference to Shakespeare's Globe Theatre—and the melting of the actors point to the end of play and life, with the pageant described as insubstantial, leaving not a trace behind when it is ended. The last sentence of the speech perfectly sums up all that came before. We are the "stuff" of dreams, passing, ephemeral. It serves as a positive aphorism for Tyrone, but it is not an intrinsically positive idea. Considered from a different angle, coming from a darker figure, "life" can be described as

> a poor player,
> That struts and frets his hour upon the stage,
> And then is heard no more. It is a tale
> Told by an idiot, full of sound and fury,
> Signifying nothing.
>
> (5.5.24–28)

For Macbeth life is a play as nightmare, for Prospero it is a play as dream, but both "actors" point to life's insubstantiality. Some of Macbeth's heavy resignedness resides in Prospero's "vision." Prospero is not tired in the same way that Macbeth is tired; he has not experienced the tedium of terror, he has not witnessed his own damnation. But Prospero has experienced much—if we think of Prospero as Shakespeare he has even experienced the creation of such a character as Macbeth—and his words touch truth.

Prospero's words are wonderfully appropriate to the immediate context in which Tyrone quotes them and are richly suggestive for the play as a whole. Tyrone wants to give his son a Shakespeare aphorism on "life," and he cleverly draws on a quotation that contains the idea of dreams, exactly what Edmund's prose and Dowson's poetry were stressing *and* what Tyrone himself referred to when he mentioned Jamie's "dream" of whores and whiskey, the "stuff" that Edmund didn't want him to talk about. Tyrone, believing that Prospero's words are positive, is offering a very familiar Shakespeare quotation to squelch the "pessimism" of his son. Well, the quotation is certainly not "morbid," but it contains a quality of resignedness that may appeal more strongly to the pessimist than to the optimist. That life is a fleeting dream, that death is sleep, that life, in fact, is "little life," with "little" pointing to both time and insignificance—these are ideas that should appeal to Edmund's darker sensibility; in fact, he voices them in a more prosy way and by way of quotation from his favorite "morbid" poets. Edmund doesn't appreciate the quotation because it comes from his ham-actor father and because he doesn't seem to understand its tone or implications, as his word *manure* suggests. I believe that O'Neill is pointing here to the limitations of Edmund Tyrone in his portrait of the artist as a young man, the dramatist perhaps judging himself as he was, suggesting that Edmund's point of view is as limited as his father's. Tyrone sees in Prospero's words what he wants to see: life as a pleasant dream. If he thought about it—"'Tinkin' is hard!"—if he confronted Shakespeare's words less mechanically, if he saw himself now as he really is, a *"defeated old man, possessed by hopeless resignation,"* he would be able to appreciate the resignation implicit in Prospero's speech. Tyrone doesn't see himself or life clearly. (It is only at the very end of his life that James O'Neill will say, "This sort of life—froth!—rotten—all of it—no good!")[24] Instinctively, unthinkingly, Tyrone quotes from the dramatist who contains "everything . . . worth saying," which means everything Tyrone wishes to be said. Tyrone finds in Shakespeare what he wants to believe, just as he wants to believe that Shakespeare was an Irish Catholic. Edmund, rejecting his father and his father's Shakespeare, is not able to find what he wants in Shakespeare, so he changes the words. An older and wiser Jamie Tyrone, we come to realize, would never change Shakespeare's words; he would use them to his own advantage, seeing possibilities in them that his brother and father cannot. In this respect, certainly, Jamie is closer to O'Neill, who not only understands the full implications of the Shakespeare quotations but manages to place them in contexts that fully exploit their dramatic and thematic possibilities. In short, Edmund cannot find in Shakespeare what he's "trying to say" because he is not wise enough to fully appreciate the poet who contains "everything." Tyrone does find what he wants to say in Shakespeare, aphorisms presented for moral instruction, but he doesn't recognize the implications of the quotations as they relate to his own life or to the life of the Shakespearean play from which he is quoting. One almost feels that Tyrone not only lost the ability to be a great Shakespearean actor but also the ability to understand the playwright he quotes so readily. Sadly, as we learn later in the act, he is forever quoting the dramatist who clearly represents his loss of soul.

Although he is himself *"possessed by hopeless resignation,"* Tyrone does not appreciate the tone of resignation in Prospero's words. When Edmund brings up his mother's condition as the reason for his getting drunk, Tyrone *"dully"* suggests, "All we can do is try to be resigned—again." Edmund has another suggestion, "Or be so drunk you can forget," after which he quotes from Baudelaire's prose poem, beginning with the words "Be always drunken." Tyrone's reaction, again predictable: "Pah! It's morbid nonsense! What little truth is in it you'll find nobly said in Shakespeare" (3:796–97). Since Shakespeare contains everything, he necessarily contains the "little truth" that Baudelaire can squeeze out. Little truths are what Tyrone is always offering his sons through Shakespeare. Edmund continues to quote Baudelaire, this time from his poetry, what for Tyrone is "morbid filth," followed by a quotation from Dowson. It is at this moment that Tyrone informs the audience about the books in the small bookcase that O'Neill listed in his initial stage directions, the bookcase above which is the portrait of Shakespeare.

> Where you get your taste in authors—That damned library of yours! (*He indicates the small bookcase at rear.*) Voltaire, Rousseau, Schopenhauer, Nietzsche, Ibsen! Atheists, fools, and madmen! And your poets! This Dowson, and this Baudelaire, and Swinburne and Oscar Wilde, and Whitman and Poe! Whoremongers and degenerates! Pah! When I've three good sets of Shakespeare there (*he nods at the large bookcase*) you could read. (3:799)

For Tyrone, his sons' pessimism about life, their morbidity and atheism, comes from the books in that smaller bookcase, books that provide the sons with quotations. Tyrone's quotations come from those "three good sets of Shakespeare" in the other, glassed-in, bookcase. But, as I've already observed, the portrait of Shakespeare, which the audience will always *see,* hangs over that smaller bookcase, as if Shakespeare, who contains everything, as we have been told, also contains the morbid and filthy poets—and, of course, he does. That is why Jamie and Edmund also quote Shakespeare, recognizing his comprehensiveness without acknowledging his greatness because Shakespeare is their *father's* idol. Tyrone appreciates only Shakespeare; the range of his sons' acquaintanceship with poetry and literature in general is wider. Edmund, needling his father, makes this comment: "They say he [Shakespeare] was a souse, too." To which an angry Tyrone replies: "They lie! I don't doubt he liked his glass—it's a good man's failing—but he knew how to drink so it didn't poison his brain with morbidness and filth. Don't compare him with the pack you've got in there. (*He indicates the small bookcase again.*) Your dirty Zola! And your Dante Gabriel Rossetti who was a dope fiend!" (3:799). Tyrone "*starts and looks guilty,*" his words bringing him and us back to Mary Tyrone, the dope fiend whom we will soon hear moving around upstairs. But not before Tyrone and Edmund discuss Shakespeare once more in a dialogue that briefly softens the father-son antagonism just witnessed. Shakespeare, we notice throughout, both divides and joins the male members of the family. Here is the exchange:

Edmund. You can't accuse me of not knowing Shakespeare. Didn't I win five dollars from you once when you bet me I couldn't learn a leading part of his in a week, as you used to do in stock in the old days. I learned Macbeth and recited it letter perfect, with you giving me the cues.

Tyrone. (*approvingly*) That's true. So you did. (*He smiles teasingly and sighs.*) It was a terrible ordeal, I remember, hearing you murder the lines. I kept wishing I'd paid over the bet without making you prove it. (*He chuckles and Edmund grins. Then he starts as he hears a sound from upstairs—with dread*) Did you hear? She's moving around. I was hoping she'd gone to sleep. (3:799)

This is a pleasant moment between father and son. Tyrone is pleased that Edmund learned Macbeth's part and recited the lines "letter perfect." His son met the father's challenge, proving that he could do what the actors did "in the old days." This was Edmund's way of competing with his father in his father's milieu, reflecting exactly what O'Neill did when he memorized the part of Macbeth, as his biographers tell us, and, more important, what he did when he became a playwright and transcended his father's accomplishment in the theater. This rivalry, not dissociated from Oedipal rivalry, takes a pleasantly comic turn when Tyrone says Edmund murdered the lines.[25] Shakespeare has brought father and son together for a brief exchange before a "*sound*" breaks the mood. A previous light moment between Edmund and his father was darkened by Mary, we remember. Now it's the sound of her moving around upstairs. That the sound fills Tyrone "*with dread*" perhaps carries a resonance from the play just mentioned, in which Shakespeare brilliantly orchestrates sounds that fill Macbeth with terror. That the dread is caused by a woman who is moving around instead of sleeping carries a more powerful resonance from *Macbeth*, one that will materialize as stage action when Mary later "*moves like a sleepwalker.*" O'Neill is in full control here, manipulating the Shakespeare references and quotations and echoes, not only giving them thematic relevance but also allowing them to color the atmosphere and modify the family relationships. The dramatic segment I have been describing—from Edmund's stumbling entrance into act 4 to this sound of Mary upstairs, which will begin a painful discussion of Mary's condition—is filled with Shakespeare and has as its verbal centerpiece Prospero's rich quotation. Of course, here as throughout, Shakespeare is looking at the Tyrone family and at us from that picture on the back wall.

Both Edmund and Tyrone hope that Mary will not come down to the living room. Edmund knows "she'll be nothing but a ghost haunting the past by this time." It's Mary's past that the two men discuss now, the past before Edmund was born. They attempt to play casino, but Mary's "ghost" hangs over the game. Edmund, in this segment, makes the following insightful comment on his mother: "The hardest thing to take is the blank wall she builds around her. Or it's more like a bank of fog in which she hides and loses herself. Deliberately, that's the hell of it! You know something in her does it deliberately—to get beyond our reach, to be rid of us, to forget we're alive! It's as if, in spite of loving us, she hated us!" (3:801). He describes her behavior perfectly. She wishes to get beyond the reach of the others, and she both hates and loves her family. But the description applies to *all* the members of the family, including Edmund—hating and loving is the dualism we witness throughout; wanting to escape is the desire of all. Mary, because of her morphine, sometimes succeeds in losing herself; the men, despite the considerable amount of whiskey in their blood, cannot get beyond the reach of the family. And "that's the hell of it" for all. In that living room, in that long day's journey, hell is a loving-hating family, frozen to its condition.

Tyrone and Edmund angrily pick on the sore of who's to blame for Mary's condition. Edmund says his father is to blame because of his stinginess, because he never gave Mary a proper home, because he "dragged her around on the road." His increasing anger forces him to blurt out, "Jesus, when I think of it I hate your guts!" Tyrone is both hurt and filled with rage; "*goaded into vindictiveness*" he puts the blame on Edmund: "if you hadn't been born she'd never . . . " O'Neill tells us "*he stops ashamed,*" and tries to deny what he said: "I only said that because you put me in such a God-damned rage, raking up the past, and saying you hate me" (3:803–4). As in all the family arguments, anger leads to shame, reinforcing the usual rhythm of the Tyrone family relationship, hate-love. Edmund tells his father he didn't mean it, then "*he suddenly smiles—kidding a bit drunkenly,*" and says, "I'm like Mama, I can't help liking you in spite of everything." Tyrone "*grins a bit drunkenly in return,*" saying, "I might say the same of you. You're no great shakes as a son. It's a case of 'A poor thing but mine own.'" At which point "*they both chuckle with real, if alcoholic, affection*" (3:804).

Here a Shakespeare "quotation" ends a dramatic segment, with Shakespeare bringing father and son together for a moment of affection before they present their long frank confessions about the past that makes the present what it is. Like all of Tyrone's Shakespeare quotations, this one is very familiar and fits the particular situation. (Did it come to O'Neill's mind because of the previous "great shakes"?) It gives a comic turn to the segment, gracefully allowing father and son to share a grin and a chuckle. In one way it could be compared to Jamie's "The Moor, I know his trumpet" because it's meant to be humorous, but it does not display the clever use of Shakespeare that Jamie exhibited. It is more straightforward and predictable, exactly right for Tyrone. But as with the other Shakespeare quotations that Tyrone recites, there may be more here than what seems obvious. First, it is interesting to observe that the quotation is a variation on Shakespeare's words, not an exact quotation. In the last scene of *As You Like It,* Touchstone presses in among "the country copulatives," those about to marry, to say that he wants to marry a country wench, Audrey: "A poor virgin, sir, an ill-favor'd thing, sir, but mine own." This has been reduced with time to "A poor thing but mine own." It seems a little surprising that Tyrone, the Shakespearean actor, does not utter the exact quotation. Perhaps O'Neill himself thought it *was* an exact quotation and presented it as such. Certainly, most people in the audience wouldn't recognize that words are missing. I bring up this possibility because earlier in the play, in act 1, when Tyrone was talking about the ingratitude of Jamie, he offers another convenient quotation, a line that Jamie says he saw "coming" because his father repeated it more than a "thousand times": "Ingratitude, the vilest weed that grows!" Because the line is in quotation marks, one must assume it comes from a specific text, but I have been unable to find a source for the line. It *sounds* like a Shakespeare quotation, and because Tyrone quotes only Shakespeare one can easily assume it *is* Shakespeare. But it isn't. Did O'Neill, hearing that line from his father thousands of times, also assume it was Shakespeare? Is that why he placed it in quotation marks? The line certainly fits the specific situation in the play, it comes easily to Tyrone's lips, and it prepares us for the later *King Lear* quotation, "How sharper than a serpent's tooth it is / To have a thankless child." But it is not Shakespeare. What we have is a non-Shakespearean quotation that seems Shakespearean. And with "A poor thing but mine own" we have an inexact quotation from Shakespeare that is not recognized as inexact. James Tyrone's knowledge of Shakespeare is somewhat spotty, it seems, although his love of Shakespeare cannot be disputed. He recites "Shakespeare" quotations to meet the demands of the moment, and he does so with great assurance and ease. O'Neill, controlling the situation and the quotations, allows the words to comment on the family relationships. "A poor thing but mine own" is meant to be amusing, and it comes from a comic Shakespearean context—in fact, it is the only quotation or near-quotation or allusion in the play that comes from a Shakespeare comedy. But the idea behind the words is heavily serious. Each member of the Tyrone family could recite that quotation about every other member. Each member clearly recognizes the deficiencies, the sins, the guilt, of the others, but each accepts the others as "mine own." Each picks the common sore of who's to blame for their terrible situation—hating, condemning, mocking—but each acknowledges connectedness with the others. They are *family,* and each member finds it impossible to disown family, although the thought of doing so is ubiquitous. They may be misbegotten—and we should fully acknowledge the deterministic force of family inheritance, as we did in *Mourning Becomes Electra*—but once begotten they are kin. Edmund is speaking for all the Tyrones when he later tells his father, "You have to make allowances in this damned family or go nuts!" (3:805). "Damned" they are, and each recognizes the hell every other member has helped to create, but all recognize they are bound together as family. "A poor thing but mine own" may be a convenient comic throwaway quotation, as Tyrone recites it, but it touches the very heart of this family tragedy.

The dialogue between Tyrone and Edmund continues while they play cards. As they go deeper into night, and as they consume more whiskey, they approach the time of frank confession. Tyrone tells the story of his past—his father's desertion of the family ("I hope he's roasting in hell"); his mother's sacrifice and endurance ("A fine, brave, sweet woman. There never was a braver or finer"); the years of poverty ("It was in those days I learned to be a miser"). More agonizing for him, it seems, and told to his son for the first time "tonight" because he is "heartsick" and feels "at the end of everything," Tyrone reveals the fact that he ruined his great talent as a Shakespearean actor when he found "that God-damned play" (*The Count of Monte Cristo,* never mentioned by name), and made "a great money success." Before that he was considered "one of the three or four young actors with the greatest artistic promise in America." And then he talks about Shakespeare, and when he does he becomes passionate, delivering his best speech of the play. Shakespeare, we hear, inspired him then, in the past, and even now, while talking about Shakespeare, he seems inspired. His simple declarative sentences come directly from the heart. A genuine moment for this ham actor who usually poses and offers easy quotations. His words on Shakespeare deserve lengthy quotation.

> I studied Shakespeare as you'd study the Bible. I educated myself. I got rid of an Irish brogue you could cut with a knife. I loved Shakespeare. I would have acted in any of his plays for nothing, for the joy of being alive in his great poetry. And I acted well in him. I felt inspired by him. I could have been a great Shakespearean actor, if I'd kept on. I know that! In 1874 when Edwin Booth came to the theater in Chicago where I was leading man, I played Cassius to his

Brutus one night, Brutus to his Cassius the next, Othello to his Iago, and so on. The first night I played Othello, he said to our manager, "That young man is playing Othello better than I ever did!" (*proudly*) That from Booth, the greatest actor of his day or any other! And it was true! And I was only twenty-seven years old! As I look back on it now, that night was the high spot in my career. I had life where I wanted it! And for a time after that I kept on upward with ambition high. Married your mother. Ask her what I was like in those days. Her love was an added incentive to ambition. But a few years later my good bad luck made me find the big money-maker. It wasn't that in my eyes at first. It was a great romantic part I knew I could play better than anyone. But it was a great box office success from the start—and then life had me where it wanted me—at from thirty-five to forty thousand net profit a season! A fortune in those days—or even in these. (*bitterly*) What the hell was it I wanted to buy, I wonder, that was worth—Well, no matter. It's a late day for regrets. (*He glances vaguely at his cards.*) My play, isn't it? (3:809–10)

What he is and what he could have been! A tragic moment that allows his son Edmund to understand his father's terrible disappointment with what life has done to him. In this confession Tyrone's prose reveals the inner man; he seems most alive when talking about Shakespeare, just as he was most alive when acting Shakespeare. The words—so well chosen by O'Neill, the dramatist whose stage prose was more effective than even he realized—the words allow us to feel both the joy Tyrone experienced as a Shakespearean actor and his great sense of loss. Talking about Shakespeare seems to change his very being and brings him closer to his son and to us. In contrast, when he quotes Shakespeare, the words, mechanically plucked from his mental repertoire, are not only less heartfelt (perhaps the usual fate of familiar quotation) but also are not fully understood by the speaker, as we already noticed and as we'll discover when Tyrone recites his next Shakespeare quotation. But a humorous piece of stage action comes between his painful confession and his easy quoting.

When the play's last act began, the stingy Tyrone, challenged by Edmund, turned on the bulbs of the chandelier, saying with "*dramatic self-pity*": "We'll have them all on! Let them burn! To hell with them! The poorhouse is the end of the road, and it might as well be sooner as later!" Edmund, appreciating the humor of the situation, affectionately says to his actor-father, "That's a grand curtain" (3:794). Now, after his confession to his son about his life's failure, Tyrone glances at the chandelier "*disapprovingly*" and stands up to click out one bulb after another. Edmund bursts out laughing, which hurts Tyrone. "What the devil are you laughing at?" The answer: "Not at you, Papa. At life. It's so damned crazy." Tyrone's growling retort: "More of your morbidness! There's nothing wrong with life. It's we who . . . " And then he recites what to him is the perfect quotation for the occasion: "The fault, dear Brutus, is not in our stars, but in ourselves that we are underlings" (3:810–11). But this mechanical moment is brief. A sad troubled Tyrone continues, bringing us back to the Tyrone who offered his painful confession: "The praise Edwin Booth gave my Othello. I made the manager put down his exact words in writing. I kept it in my wallet for years. I used to read it every once in a while until finally it made me feel so bad I didn't want to face it any more. Where is it now, I wonder? Somewhere in this house. I remember I put it away carefully" (3:811). To which Edmund adds with *"ironical sadness,"* "It might be in an old trunk in the attic, along with Mama's wedding dress." For a moment they continue playing cards mechanically until a sound is heard upstairs— Mary is moving around again, "a ghost haunting the past," according to Edmund. The sound ends this dramatic segment, which is charged with the idea of theater. Even Tyrone's question, "My play, isn't it?" which refers to their card playing, provides the proper closure to Tyrone's confession about "that God damned play" that changed his life. His putting out the lights, the only piece of stage action in the segment, punctuates his comments on playing Othello and casts an ironic shadow on Tyrone's activity because Othello, in the tragic climax of his painful journey, also put out the light before he "put out the light." We have no way of knowing whether O'Neill wanted that echo to be heard, but no matter. *Othello* is in the air, and Shakespeare informs the entire scene, the entire act, the play.

The specific quotation from *Julius Caesar* has a significance that goes beyond the dramatic moment and invites special attention. On one level it is a brief canned aphorism on life that comes easily to an actor-father's lips. On a deeper level it raises the idea of free will versus determinism that is crucial to any discussion of tragedy. Notice that even though Tyrone recites the quotation with easy acceptance of its truth, he had just revealed some confusion about his own relationship to life, which in the immediate context points to the idea of determinism. That is, when he played Othello to Booth's Iago, the highlight of his acting career, he had "life" where he wanted it, he claims. He must have felt at that time that he was controlling the stars. But then, with that box-office success, life began to control him; his wrong choice through an act of free will made him an "underling." However, that choice was determined by other forces—his family's poverty, a history of alienation because he is an Irishman, his psychological makeup, which produced not only the need to act in a great romantic part but an ego that believed he could do it better than anyone else. And his love for his wife also determined his choice. Mary's love and his ambition were linked, we heard in his confession, just as Booth's note to him and Mary's wedding dress belong together in the same attic, according to Edmund. When Tyrone says to Edmund, "There's nothing wrong with life," he seems to be contradicting what he had just said about life. And when he quotes what Cassius says to Brutus, he is as misguided as Cassius, who doesn't fully understand the forces at work behind the decisions of individuals, the "Force behind," to use O'Neill's phrase. Tyrone *feels* the force of determinism, what life does to us, but goes to a Shakespeare quotation that gives exclusive power to the individual, no power to the stars. On the other hand, Mary Tyrone, throughout the play and in her quiet way, is the most eloquent exponent of determinism. She believes that she made some wrong choices and she pinpoints some of these—marrying the actor James Tyrone, listening to Mother Superior, leaving Jamie with little Eugene—and she feels others have made decisions that profoundly affect her, but she also presents larger statements about "life" in order to absolve herself and those around her of guilt. Life does things to us, she claims repeatedly, and although this idea seems an easy excuse for her own and her family's shortcomings, it carries the conviction of truth, perhaps touching what we all finally believe.

Mary on Jamie:

> But I suppose life has made him like that, and he can't help it. None of us can help the things life has done to us. They're done before you realize it, and once they're done they make you do other things until at last everything comes between you and what you'd like to be, and you've lost your true self forever. (3:749)

Again, on Jamie:

> It's wrong to blame your brother. He can't help being what the past has made him. Any more than your father can. Or you. Or I. (3:751)

To Tyrone:

> James! We've loved each other! We always will! Let's remember only that, and not try to understand what we cannot understand, or help things that cannot be helped—the things life has done to us we cannot excuse or explain. (3:764)

To Tyrone, who tells her to "forget the past":

Why? How can I? The past is the present, isn't it? It's the future, too. We all try to lie out of that but life won't let us. (3:765)

Like all writers of tragedy, O'Neill confronts the conflict of free will versus determinism, and like all great writers of tragedy he offers no clear answer as to which is unequivocally responsible for man's plight. John Henry Raleigh asserts that "O'Neill's characters are both free and unfree, depending on one's angle of vision,"[26] an idea supported by Judith Barlow, who sees O'Neill's characters as both accountable and not accountable for their actions.[27] I would qualify their arguments. Although in O'Neill, as in Shakespeare, the tragic characters are both free and determined, the scales, I believe, tilt more heavily toward determinism. Large powerful forces are at work, forces difficult to name, although we are forever naming them—God, gods, fate, passion, blood, time, the stars—with the most accurate, because the most dark, name pinpointed by O'Neill when he calls it "Mystery," thereby touching another Irishman's phrase for this shadowy phenomenon, "the secret cause," what James Joyce's Stephen Dedalus believes is the essence of tragic terror. Forces that reach beyond his individual responsibility push Brutus Jones on his journey toward his origins and his self. The same is true for Yank Smith's tragic journey toward death. In *Desire Under the Elms* we witness the tragic journeys of all three characters, Abbie, Eben, Ephraim, controlled by that sinister force called Mother, with the Freudian pattern clear and powerful. In *Mourning Becomes Electra,* the play possessing the greatest tragic depth of O'Neill's first career, O'Neill successfully meets his self-imposed challenge of finding a "modern psychological approximation of Greek sense of fate." In his last plays the characters seem to be "misbegotten" rather than active actors in their own lives' journeys. The word is used by Larry Slade to describe the denizens of "The End of the Line Cafe," but it applies as well to all the members of the Tyrone family, and it will provide the title for O'Neill's last play, which treats one member of that family. In *Long Day's Journey* the birth of Edmund Tyrone helped to determine the present condition of Mary Tyrone and the resultant agony of the entire family. One cannot control one's being born—whether it's an Edmund Tyrone, who should have been "a sea gull or a fish," or a Hamlet who was "born to set things right." Of course, other reasons for the family's agony are presented, some caused by the free actions of the members of the family, but Mary Tyrone's words seem closer to the truth than the many accusations of guilt found throughout the play: "None of us can help the things life has done to us." The idea clearly rubs against Cassius's words about "the stars" and "ourselves," but even Tyrone who quotes Cassius—and remember he played Cassius to Booth's Brutus *and also* Brutus to Booth's Cassius—is enveloped by the truth of Mary's large statement of determinism. Here I disagree with Richard Sewall, a rare disagreement, who places more emphasis on "the exercise of the will" than on determinism. He takes O'Neill's word "haunted," which can be explained as "the facts of inherited temperament," as merely a partial explanation of the Tyrone situation, carrying nothing like the force of the curse on the house of Atreus, and he uses Tyrone's quotation from *Julius Caesar* to assert that "O'Neill makes it clear that the fault is not in their stars."[28] I, on the other hand, believe that the quotation is there precisely to point up Tyrone's easy acceptance of a conventional idea that must be qualified and ultimately rejected. I find the Tyrone family to be more cursed than free, and *haunted* is a word that carries great force for O'Neill, a word that touches the idea of "Mystery."

Tyrone's quotation from *Julius Caesar* is his last quotation of the play. The next two Shakespeare quotations and the last Shakespeare allusion belong to Jamie, so that father and sons, in act 4 as throughout, are connected by Shakespeare but also, when we consider the tenor of Jamie's quotations, separated by Shakespeare. Before Jamie enters the act, O'Neill gives Edmund his long revelation about his memories, "all connected with the sea," a time when he was "set free," when he "belonged" to "Life itself." At that moment he saw "the secret."

> For a second you see—and seeing the secret, are the secret. For a second there is meaning! Then the hand lets the veil fall and you are alone, lost in the fog again, and you stumble on toward nowhere, for no good reason! (*He grins wryly.*) It was a great mistake, my being born a man, I would have been much more successful as a sea gull or a fish. As it is, I will always be a stranger who never feels at home, who does not really want and is not really wanted, who can never belong, who must always be a little in love with death! (3:812)

For Edmund—and for O'Neill, it seems—the journey of life is a stumbling toward nowhere, with death a desired end. (Soon, Jamie will stumble on to the scene and talk about roads that "get you nowhere fast . . . nowhere.") Despite the morbidity of Edmund's thought, Tyrone compliments his son: "Yes, there's the makings of a poet in you all right." The poet Tyrone probably has in mind is the one who, from Tyrone's limited perspective, lacked morbidness, the one whom he is so quick to quote throughout his life, throughout the play, Shakespeare. Edmund may also have Shakespeare in mind as the poet when he "*sardonically*" picks up his father's phrase:

> The *makings* of a poet. No, I'm like the guy who is always panhandling for a smoke. He hasn't even got the makings. He's got only the habit. I couldn't touch what I tried to tell you just now. I just stammered. That's the best I'll ever do. I mean, if I live. Well, it will be faithful realism, at least. Stammering is the native eloquence of us fog people. (3:811–12)

Ironically, this is the best use of language by the young man who claims he can only stammer. (There is no question that the statement reflects O'Neill's own belief that he lacked a language to express his characters' deepest feelings.) At this moment Jamie, drunk and stammering, comes stumbling in, complaining that there should be a lighthouse out on the porch because the fog is so thick. (O'Neill here is using the Shakespearean device of telegraphing the entrance of an offstage character by an onstage character's words, which ostensibly have no connection to the entrance. In *Macbeth,* for example, Duncan talks about his mistaken judgment of the traitor Cawdor: "He was a gentleman on whom I built / An absolute trust. [*Enter* Macbeth.] O worthiest cousin!") With whiskey serving as a prod to revelations and truth telling, Jamie is drunk enough to offer his confession to his brother, the climactic confession of the play, in which he reveals his deep-seated jealousy of Edmund. Throughout the play—and throughout the life of Jamie O'Neill—Jamie tries to reach for his mother who is the secure center of his shiftless life. She draws away from him, as she does from her other two men, James and Edmund. But he seems to need her most. With painful sincerity, brought on by his advanced state of drunkenness and by his sure knowledge of his mother's return to morphine, Jamie warns his brother against himself. During this confession, in which he admits he calculatingly attempted to corrupt his brother, he utters Iago's famous line to Roderigo: "Therefore put money in thy purse." This quotation should remind us of the clever use of Shakespeare that Jamie displayed in act 1 when he proclaimed Iago's "The Moor, I know his trumpet." Here he is humorously suggesting to Edmund, who is on his way to a tuberculosis sanatorium and perhaps to death, that it's important to have money to bribe the judge at the Last Judgment. The Iago resonance fits the occasion perfectly, O'Neill summoning Shakespeare to help us see Jamie for the corrupter he really is, as his parents claimed. Jamie's poisoning of his brother's mind, making him his monster—"I made you! You're my Frankenstein!" (3:819)—was based in part on his jealousy. Iago, in part spurred on by jealousy, poisoned the mind of Othello, we recall, making him a monster. (Desdemona's wish, "Heaven keep the monster from Othello's mind!" does not, alas, come true.) But Jamie's hatred of his brother goes deeper than jealousy, as does Iago's hatred of Othello. "And it was your being born that started Mama on her dope. I know that's not your fault, but all the same, God damn you, I can't help hating your guts—!" (3:820). Jamie's words allow us to return to the free will versus determinism debate. Jamie recognizes that Edmund had no control over his being born but still irrationally condemns him for ruining the mother to whom Jamie is so closely tied. The irrational side of Iago's hatred of Othello, his "motiveless malignity," has received too much critical discussion to need repeating here. Of course, Jamie negates his Iago image when he goes on to declare his love for his brother, warning him that he will continue to try to make him fail, so watch out. His confession is agony for Edmund who is forced to confront the jealousy and hatred behind his brother's love and companionship. His brother's confession allows Edmund to discover bitter truths behind appearances. Othello must discover his own truths, with Iago remaining silent to the very end. Although described as "Mephistophelian" in countenance, Jamie has redeeming qualities; Iago is Satan incarnate. But Jamie does share Iago's cynicism, especially in his attitude toward women. For both characters, who are nothing if not critical, love is a minor branch of lust, and all women are whores. For Jamie even his mother has become one because he "never dreamed before that any women but whores took dope!" (3:818). In addition, Jamie enjoys getting Edmund drunk, as Iago enjoyed getting Cassio drunk. And, of course, the Iago who hates Othello is the Jamie who hates his father who played Othello better than Edwin Booth did, the father who puts out the lights, causing Jamie to comically stumble on to this very scene.

Having made his confession, Jamie's passion is spent. Taking "that last drink—the old K.O.," he falls into a *"drunken doze."* (3:821). Tyrone enters the room to sadly voice his disgust with his eldest son: "A waste! A wreck, a drunken hulk, done with and finished!" He takes a drink from the bottle of whiskey that gave Jamie the knockout, the whiskey that prods the three Tyrone men to make their important revelations. At that point Jamie opens his eyes, points his finger at his father, and *"recites with dramatic emphasis"*:

Clarence is come, false, fleeting, perjured Clarence,
That stabbed me in the field by Tewkesbury.
Seize on him, Furies, take him into torment.

(3:822)

This, the act's second Shakespeare quotation, comes from Clarence's dream (1.4.53–55) in *Richard III,* producing ominous overtones and a rich network of association. On the most obvious level, Jamie—who hates his father, who mocks his father at every opportunity, who criticizes his father's profession (which, incidentally is Jamie's profession too), who will soon criticize Edwin Booth's acting, knowing how close Tyrone is to the great Booth who gave Tyrone's acting such high praise—is insulting his father, who has just come into the room, asking the Furies to "take him into torment." That he uses a Shakespeare quotation to insult his father is meant to be especially annoying to Tyrone, a case of turning his father's idol against him, as he did more mildly in the Moor-trumpet quotation. And notice that O'Neill wants Jamie to quote Clarence's lines with "*dramatic emphasis,*" thereby mimicking his father's ham-actor style. But the quotation is a strange one, rather forced, I believe, if it is meant only to show a son's hatred of a father. In fact, the only real point of connection here—again, on the most obvious level—is that Jamie is awakening from his drunken doze and Clarence has awakened from his dream, which he is in the process of describing. We must examine further to understand the reasons for O'Neill's selection of this particular quotation.

Clarence has his dream while he is prisoner in the Tower of London. Soon murderers sent by his brother Richard will kill him, as the audience knows. Clarence's dream, which he relates to the Keeper of the Tower, is a rhetorical indulgence containing motifs that Shakespeare stresses throughout the play. Death informs Clarence's dream, as does night and the sea. In the dream itself Clarence is with his brother Richard on a ship, and as they pace along "Upon the giddy footing of the hatches, / Methought that Gloucester stumbled, and in falling / Strook me . . . overboard / Into the tumbling bellows of the main" (1.4.17–20). This clearly foreshadows the action to come, for Richard will cause the death of his brother and will himself eventually fall. O'Neill, we must observe, is using a quotation that has as its Shakespearean context the betrayal of a brother, and this, of course, is the focus of Jamie's confession to Edmund, which immediately preceded the drunken doze from which Jamie is now awakening. We can say, therefore, that Jamie is not only connected to the villainous Iago but also to the villainous Richard III who forces his brother to lose his footing and to drown. "O Lord, methought what pain it was to drown!" Clarence's word "stumbled" and his dream of being with his brother on a ship at sea allow us to recall Edmund's revelation to his father in *this* act, in which he talks of losing himself in the sea and must "stumble on toward nowhere" once he returns to reality. The big difference, of course, is that Edmund's "drowning" is a positive mystical experience for him, a moment of freedom, "a saint's vision of beatitude." Clarence's drowning is a nightmare: "What sights of ugly death within my eyes!" But surely the very ideas of death and sea and the dream action of a brother causing a brother to fall (and, I add parenthetically, the fact that a drunken Jamie is quoting a character who will soon be drowned in the malmsey-butt) reflect closely the immediate situation in *Long Day's Journey*. We *should* be thinking of the rivalry between brothers and the fall of Edmund because of Jamie, what Jamie revealed just before the Shakespeare quotation. Still, even this does not fully exploit the rich implications of the quotation.

In Shakespeare Clarence's dream is the nightmare of a man who betrayed his family, who went to the side of the Lancastrians during the civil wars and then returned to York during battle. His horrible visions of hell and death are the products of a guilty conscience that, in dream, must confront the ghosts of the past. In fact, in his dream he is already dead, having passed across "the melancholy flood" (Styx) and entered "the kingdom of perpetual night," where one of the ghosts—Prince Edward, the son of Henry VI, whom Clarence killed—shrieks aloud the quotation that Jamie recites. Jamie Tyrone, like Clarence, is living a nightmare in a play that emphasizes night and dream, and he is uttering words (coming from the mouth of the ghost Prince Edward) that apply to himself. Jamie's finger is pointing at his father, and the Clarence dream is pointing up the sibling rivalry of Clarence and Richard, but the quotation's important emphasis is on the self-torment of a betrayer, a man who is blaming himself for his past actions, in fact, a man who is "dead"—Jamie told Edmund, "think of me as dead"—but even death cannot erase "the tempest to my soul" (Clarence's words). In short, Jamie, not his father, is Clarence, and the Furies have already seized him. (We may wish to think back to another father-hater and mother-lover, Orin Mannon, and his living death, pursued by Furies.) Very early in *Long Day's Journey*, when his father tells Jamie that he sneers at everything "except yourself," Jamie replies: "That's not true, Papa. You can't hear me talking to myself, that's all." Jamie's quotation from Shakespeare's *Richard III* indicates how deeply felt is his sneering at self. His torment is excruciating and abiding. He suffers because of his Iago-like corruption and Richard-like betrayal of a brother, because of his Iago-like hatred of his father (Othello), because his dope-filled mother is lost to him, and because he sees himself as dead, "finished," to use his father's word. In case his quotation from Clarence's dream of death does not make the last point clear, Jamie goes on to quote from one of his favorite poets, Dante Gabriel Rossetti: "Look in my face. My name is Might-Have-Been; / I am also called No More, Too Late, Farewell" (3:822). These words apply equally to Tyrone, on stage at this moment, also a "might-have-been," a betrayer of his histrionic gift, as his heartrending confession revealed—and once again father and son are connected.

The quotation from Clarence's dream is perfectly placed, not only relating to what came before in Jamie's confession to Edmund but also extending the important idea that came from another Shakespeare quotation at the beginning of this climactic act, "We are such stuff as dreams are made on," and serving as an effective bridge to the climactic "dreaming" of Mary Tyrone, who now enters the last act to give the play its remarkable curtain. When Mary enters—deep in her dope-induced past, carrying her old-fashioned wedding gown *"neglectfully"*—the three Tyrone men stare at her, frozen in silence. It is Jamie who once again goes to Shakespeare to help him voice his deep disgust. His "The Mad Scene. Enter Ophelia!"—the last Shakespeare reference in the play—shatteringly breaks the silence. The Shakespeare allusion—notice that it is not a Shakespeare quotation, as if Jamie is so familiar with Shakespeare that he can create his own Shakespearean stage directions—has powerful resonances.

The charged entrance of Mary Tyrone, like the remembered entrance of Ophelia, impresses itself vividly upon the mind. A fragile woman, deep within herself, enters a room, takes center stage, becomes "the observed of all observers," talks of loss and death and of a past that will never come again and perhaps never was. An image presented so hauntingly that we cannot escape the feeling that it came from deep within the hidden chambers of O'Neill's mind. Biographies of O'Neill tell us about his mother's condition and how it affected his entire life. In writing *Long Day's Journey*, in facing his dead, the image of his dope-filled mother entering a room of helpless men was inescapable. Less inescapable, but still compelling, is O'Neill's allusion to the entrance of Ophelia.

Shakespeare's Ophelia, according to Quarto 1, enters act 4, scene 5 *"playing on a lute, and her hair down, singing."* Her first song laments a dead lover who went to his grave showered with flowers and tears. Claudius believes she is referring to her father Polonius, recently killed by Hamlet. But, in her deranged mind, Father blends with Hamlet, her lover now gone, and her next song unmistakably alludes to Hamlet. It is a bawdy St. Valentine's Day ballad that unveils Ophelia's sexual repression—"Young men will do't, if they come to 't / By cock, they are to blame." The two songs reveal Ophelia's aloneness, her frailty, her true inner feelings, what she has always kept within and can only come out in madness. The plucked strings of the lute vibrate to chords within, and the disheveled hair is an external sign of her madness, her loss of control over her self. (The Russian Grigori Kozintzev worked wonders with the Ophelia of his film version of *Hamlet*. Up to her madness, Ophelia, a cool, blond beauty, is always wearing her hair tight in a bun, always corsetted and meticulously attired, always the proper young daughter who will "obey" her father. When she is mad, she appears loose gowned, long hair wild and hanging loose, distracted, no longer *contained,* and therefore able to utter the truth of her soul.) What is within Ophelia comes out in madness.

What is within Mary Tyrone comes out in the dope-induced dream of the past. Modern drama's equivalent to Elizabethan madness as a revealer of truth is drink or dope. Before Mary's entrance she too was playing an instrument, the piano; and her hair is hanging *"over her breast."* Her outward appearance has been transformed by the dope she just took. Her eyes glisten; her face appears youthful; she wears, according to O'Neill, *"a marble mask of girlish innocence"* (3:823). When she speaks, it is to herself, recalling her "good and generous" father who paid for her piano lessons. She distractedly gives James Tyrone the wedding gown she has been carrying— "It's very lovely, isn't it? . . . But I don't know what I wanted it for. I'm going to be a nun"—and then ends the play with a long poignant monologue on her past: her desire to be a nun and her meeting with James Tyrone "in the spring," when she fell in love and "was so happy for a time." She, like Ophelia, talks—to herself, in her own world—about father and lover. And she wanted to get to the nunnery to which Ophelia was sent by Hamlet.

Tyrone's reaction to Mary's condition is: "It's the damned poison. But I've never known her to drown herself in it as deep as this" (3:827). Claudius's reaction to Ophelia: "Oh, this is a poison of deep grief." (Ophelia literally drowned herself.) When Ophelia returns to the scene to give out flowers, her brother Laertes weeps. Jamie Tyrone sobs to see his mother in her condition. Laertes calls Ophelia "rose of May," alluding to her youth and beauty and innocence. Mary is wearing a mask of girlish innocence, and she refers to the spring of her life. Ophelia's prop, flowers, are given for remembrance; Mary's prop, the wedding gown, also prods remembrance. Ophelia's parting words have a religious flavor, often mentioning God. Mary talks of the Blessed Virgin and Holy Mother and of her desire to enter a nunnery. In her last song, Ophelia sings:

And will a' not come again?
And will a' not come again?
No, no, he is dead,
Go to thy death-bed,
He never will come again.

(4.5.190–94)

Ophelia's song, blending memories of dead father and sexual lover ("come"), points to a past that controls the present mood, that causes the grief and loneliness of that moment. Mary's last speech recalls the past that is lost and that controls her present moment, a past that, as she herself says in a previous act, "causes you to lose your true self forever." Ophelia leaves the stage to go to her watery deathbed. Mary will go deeper into her night.

Jamie's "The Mad Scene. Enter Ophelia!" is a *conscious* O'Neill allusion to Shakespeare's *Hamlet;* however, many of the parallels I have mentioned are probably not conscious. Some of the echoes are subtle, some are transformed, some may be coincidental, but all point to an important relationship between *Long Day's Journey* and *Hamlet*. In writing *Long Day's Journey* O'Neill, as his dedication to Carlotta insists, found the courage "to face my dead at last." In meeting his ghosts of the past, he is most influenced by that Shakespearean ghost play, *Hamlet*. The connection between the two tragedies helps to explain the remarkable resonances that affect us on the deepest emotional level. A ghost returns to Hamlet, insisting that he be remembered; the young prince must appease that ghost before both the ghost and he can rest in peace. O'Neill's ghosts haunt his mind, and he must appease them before they and he rest in peace.

Family relationships are crucial to *Hamlet* and *Long Day's Journey*, especially the relationship of a son to his father and, even more important, to his mother. The fathers are difficult taskmasters. Old Hamlet gives his son a momentous task; he writes a play in which his son must act the role of avenger in killing a murderous uncle without harming an incestuous mother. James Tyrone, not a king and not involved with murder and incest, wants his sons to play more modest roles, wants them to be dutiful, to drink less, to waste less money, to be less bitter about life, more religious, *and* to be kinder to mother. The mother in each play is important to all the men in her life: Gertrude controls the lives of Claudius, Hamlet, and Old Hamlet, even to the point where a betrayed Old Hamlet orders his son not to "taint" his mind against his mother; Mary is the source of life for James, Jamie, and Edmund, who are happy when she is normal, who are devastated when she returns to her drugged state, who are aware of her every movement in that other, darker room. The bitterness and cynicism of the sons stem in large part from the nature of their relationship to mother. In this respect, the affinity of Jamie Tyrone and Hamlet (and, by extension, O'Neill and Hamlet) deserves especially close examination.

We, like Rosencrantz and Guildenstern, will never be able to search out the heart of Hamlet's mystery, but surely much of his cynicism and melancholy is caused by the shattering of his illusions. That he should return from Wittenberg to find his idealized father dead is devastating to him. Death was never before confronted by Hamlet; now his life will deal only with death. The image of Hamlet holding a skull is emblematic of his new condition. But even more devastating for this son, it seems, is what he has learned about mother. Must he remember how she doted on his father, how his father loved her and protected her? Is it possible that she is now sleeping with his satyrlike uncle, that she, in fact, rushed like an animal to those incestuous sheets? What he thought she was and what she is—the difference betweeen innocent illusion and crass reality—causes his heart to break and his attitude toward life to turn sour: "How weary, stale, flat, and unprofitable / Seem to me all the uses of this world!" These thoughts come before he learns the details of his father's murder, and when he does learn the details, "O most pernicious woman!" comes before "O villain, villain, smiling, damned villain!" But Hamlet must hold his tongue until the climactic bedroom scene, when he relieves himself of his sexual nausea by condemning his whorish mother, by purging himself of his feeling of disgust for her, but revealing as well how his condition is inextricably bound with hers: "would it were not so!—you are my mother." It *is* so, and he must suffer for it. It *is* so, and all his illusions are shattered, leading to cynicism and heartsickness, leading to the belief that all women are frail and all basic human affections are false. Hamlet's need to have his mother pure, not the harlot she has become in his diseased mind, prompts him to urge her to repent. And only after she is dead, having drunk from the poisoned cup meant for him, can Hamlet finally accomplish his deed of vengeance. In short, Hamlet's life is so bound up with his mother that we're forced, with Ernest Jones, to account for many of Hamlet's actions and reactions by going to the Oedipus complex.[29] Hamlet is so devoted to his mother, so dependent on her love and affection, that her sexual frailty colors his entire attitude toward life. His unwillingness to share her affection with anyone—both father and uncle—helps to account for his motivation for revenge and his delay.

Jamie Tyrone is O'Neill's Hamlet in *Long Day's Journey*. Bitter and cynical, his whole life revolves around the condition of his mother. His are the most terrible comments on his mother's dope addiction, as his reference to the mad Ophelia indicates, because he, more than his father and brother, has the greatest dependence on her. His love is greatest and therefore his disappointment is greatest. That she has come to this! The woman he is forever reaching out to grasp, to hold as the secure center of his shiftless life. He reaches out, and she withdraws—true for James and Edmund as well, and, in fact, the very dynamism of the play: movement toward a loved one, retreat of that loved one. Jamie's heavy drinking is linked to his mother's addiction. He tells Edmund, "This time Mama had me fooled. I really believed she had it licked.... I suppose I can't forgive her—yet. It meant so much. I'd begun to hope, if she'd beaten the game, I could, too"

(3:818). His sobbing, horrible because it is sober, causes Edmund to cry out, "Stop it, Jamie!" Jamie's retort reveals the painful realization by a young man of a mother's frailty: "I've known about Mama so much longer than you. Never forget the first time I got wise. Caught her in the act with a hypo. Christ, I'd never dreamed before that any women but whores took dope!" Not only does the shattering of Jamie's illusion remind us of Hamlet's situation, but the mother-whore combination points directly to both Hamlet's and Jamie's agonizing dilemma. For Hamlet, his mother has become a whore; she wears the blister of the harlot; because of this, all women are whores. The nunnery to which he sends Ophelia is a brothel as well as a convent. For Jamie, mother and whore also meld together. His interest in prostitutes is the substitute for his Oedipal interest in his mother. This is made crystal clear by O'Neill when we hear about Jamie's relationship with Fat Violet. Feeling sad, and "ready for a weep on any old womanly bosom" (3:816), Jamie chooses Fat Violet rather than any of the other whores of Mamie Burns's stable. He says he felt sorry for her because she was going to be let go by Mamie. It seems that she's been going on "drunks" and therefore has not been able to play the piano, the only reason she's in Mamie's house, since she is too gross for sexual companionship. When we realize that Mary Tyrone is worried about getting fat, that she too plays the piano, that her dope, like Fat Violet's drunks, incapacitate her, we can understand why Jamie picked Fat Violet's ample bosom to weep on. And he does engage in sexual intercourse with her. Characteristically, the experience leads him to a humorously cynical conclusion: "This night has opened my eyes to a great career in store for me, my boy! . . . I'll be the lover of the fat woman in Barnum and Bailey's circus!" The cynicism, however, cannot hide his disgust with himself and the world around him. For him, with mother returned to dope, the road of life is weary, all is "finished now—not a hope!" Fittingly, Jamie sings this snatch from a ballad:

> If I were hanged on the highest hill,
> Mother o'mine, O mother o' mine!
> I know whose love would follow me still.
>
> (3:817)

Thoughts of death and mother and whores, wrapped in world-weariness and cynicism. Jamie Tyrone is as close to Hamlet as any character in modern drama.

Jamie's wish to die—he *saw* himself as a dead man, as the Clarence quotation suggested—is stronger than his wish to live. True for Hamlet too, and true for O'Neill, who put more of himself into Jamie than into Edmund, the ostensible portrait of himself as a young man. This accounts in part for the more neutral characterization of Edmund Tyrone. One can say, hopefully without succumbing to the temptations of easy psychology, that O'Neill could not face his ghosts, especially his love for his mother, directly, giving to his brother his own unconscious feelings.[30] We know a great deal about O'Neill the man, and everything we know—up to his last dying days when he called his wife Carlotta his "mama"[31]—points to O'Neill's unresolved Oedipus complex. It has become virtually impossible for a critic to approach O'Neill without some discussion of Freud (as my own discussion clearly demonstrates), without some recognition that O'Neill was unable to present pure love without thinking of mother, and sexual love without thinking of prostitutes, but often combining the two, blurring the two, in his plays, thereby creating his most emotionally charged scenes. O'Neill's personal unresolved tensions produce the richest complexity in his art. Keeping in mind O'Neill's Oedipus complex, his wish for death, his bouts with melancholy and cynicism, and his deep interest in the ghosts of the past that haunt the present, it is difficult to believe that Shakespeare's Hamlet was not exerting pressure on his creative imagination. How could he avoid the psychic consequences of his knowledge of *Hamlet*? The portrait of Jamie Tyrone suggests that he could not.

That the past controls the present is the strongest thematic link between O'Neill's *Long Day's Journey* and *Hamlet*. The return of ghosts of the past, the shattering of illusions, the disappointment with what life has become, the sense of what could have been—these are common to the two plays. As a result, the characters long for death, as do Hamlet and Jamie and Edmund, or for death in life, as do James Tyrone in drink and Mary Tyrone in dope. That is, all are journeying to a night, and their journeys are filled with anguish.

Outside of the action, but important to the meaning, we find ships at sea. Hamlet goes on a sea voyage, supposedly to death, but actually to a miraculous escape and a return to Elsinore. Hamlet suffers a mysterious sea change; in the graveyard of Elsinore he seems to have become a different man. He realizes that heaven is now directing the revenge play in which he is the main actor, and he understands that "the readiness is all." Edmund Tyrone's contact with the sea has its dimension of mystery; in the sea he too was "set free," as he tells his father. In the sea he "dissolved"—should we hear the echo of Hamlet's "Oh, that this too too sallied flesh would melt, / Thaw, and resolve itself into a dew"? (1.2.129–30)—and "belonged without past or future, within peace and unity and a wild joy, within something greater than my own life, or the life of Man, to Life itself! To

God, if you want to put it that way" (3:812). Hamlet and Edmund, two young men connected with the sea's mystery, are strangers in their own homes, "can never belong," and are, like Jamie and O'Neill himself, "a little in love with death!"

Even one of the most important differences between O'Neill's plays and *Hamlet* furnishes an interesting similarity. O'Neill is not like Shakespeare in dealing with time and place. Shakespeare is expansive, allowing months to transpire before Hamlet takes his revenge. O'Neill is restrictive, allowing his characters' onstage journeys to take a short time, from 8:30 A.M. to midnight in *Long Day's Journey*. Shakespeare sets his major scenes on the battlements of Elsinore, inside the castle, and in the graveyard nearby. O'Neill sets all of *Long Day's Journey* in a living room. Although O'Neill obeys the classical unities more strictly than the Elizabethan Shakespeare, Elsinore and the Tyrone living room release surprisingly similar emotions in us. Each place is a brooding center, to which people come and from which people go. Each place is isolated, taking on the moods of its inhabitants. Each touches darkness and mystery—a ghost hovers in the shadows of Elsinore, fog thickly surrounds the Tyrone living room. In each play we experience an action so highly unified and intense that it broadens to include the world outside and deepens to include what is happening within.

It seems that O'Neill in his most autobiographical play, the one he *had* to write, could not avoid the psychic pressure exerted by his knowledge of *Hamlet*. Shakespeare's play—which, as we have seen, it was psychologically necessary for Shakespeare to write—gave O'Neill a deeper view of the reality of his personal situation. Admittedly, the only *specific Hamlet* allusion in *Long Day's Journey* is Jamie's shocking "The Mad Scene. Enter Ophelia!" but that allusion broadens out to lead directly to a consideration of character and theme and texture and purpose, all linking *Long Day's Journey* to *Hamlet*. O'Neill wrote his ghost play in the shadow of Shakespeare's ghost play, I have no doubt, but, of course, as we have already observed, other Shakespeare plays find their way into *Long Day's Journey*.

I return to the entrance of Mary Tyrone, which prodded Jamie's Shakespeare allusion. At the same time that we hear the Ophelia echoes, we are reminded of another woman in Shakespeare, Lady Macbeth in her sleepwalking scene—mad, lost in her past, entering a scene that causes the onlookers to freeze at her sight. In girlish fright, afraid of the dark, previously unable to kill Duncan herself because he looked like her father, she re-creates the entire murder scene in horror. A vulnerable woman, a she-man who displays a fragility she never thought she possessed, Lady

Macbeth utters, "What's done cannot be undone," a sentiment similar to Mary Tyrone's "The past is the present, isn't it? It's the future too." In her dreamlike state, Lady Macbeth talks to her absent husband, asking him to "come" to that sterile bed they both have contaminated. Of course, the Macbeth world is more nightmarish, more filled with terror, than the world of *Long Day's Journey,* but the *Macbeth* echo, I believe, sends its distinctive tragic chill through the audience at that moment of Mary's entrance, the Mary who *"moves like a sleepwalker"* (3:826), according to O'Neill's stage directions. (Parenthetically, it is interesting to note that when O'Neill read aloud the manuscript of *Long Day's Journey* to Katina Paxinou, the great Greek actress, when she visited his home, he made a mistake and read "The Mad Scene: Enter Lady Macbeth!" instead of "Enter Ophelia!" I should also point out that Carlotta Monterey at that moment was lurking in the hallway while he was doing the reading.)

The one tragedy of Shakespeare's big four that does not specifically come into this last act by way of quotation or allusion is *King Lear*.[32] O'Neill gives us a specific *Lear* quotation in the second act when Tyrone talked of the serpent-tooth ingratitude of children, and, of course, O'Neill is treating parent-child relationships, the important thematic concern in Shakespeare's *King Lear*. But, surprisingly, he offers no specific *King Lear* quotation or allusion in an act filled with Shakespeare. Nevertheless, I believe that *King Lear* exerts a powerful influence on the play's ending. I wish to stress an analogy that is less conclusive or verifiable than the others I've discussed, but perhaps more interesting: the way both O'Neill and Shakespeare manipulate their audiences in order to produce two of the most effective endings in all drama.

In *King Lear* and *Long Day's Journey* Shakespeare and O'Neill make an incredible investment of creative energy on the idea of family. Both playwrights write family values into their plays, both powerfully dramatize the destructive side of family relationships, but they also allow the positive side to temper our despair. Although all of Shakespeare's sources for *King Lear* allow Cordelia to live, Shakespeare kills her, offering an ending almost unrelievedly excruciating in its feeling of tragic loss. I say "almost" because some light does manage to penetrate the darkness. We know that Lear and Cordelia belong together, even though it is in death. Each finally did not give up on the other. Love and loyalty and family affection have a place in their story, although the terror remains. The howls of King Lear, as he enters the last scene with the dead Cordelia in his arms, cannot be muted in our minds; it *is* "the promised end."

This approaches the feeling that O'Neill gives us at the end of that long night with the four Tyrones. The three men are sitting in that ever-darkening living room, sharing the death of hope, the agony of loss, as they helplessly watch the center of their lives, Mary, enter the room. In her dope dream—notice that O'Neill tells us she stares *"dreamily"* before her as she gives her last speech, allowing us to recall all the dreams of the play, including Clarence's dream and Prospero's comment on life—in her dope dream she is completely separated from the men, as she recalls her past, and ends the play with the by-now famous words: "That was in the winter of senior year. Then in the spring something happened to me. Yes, I remember. I fell in love with James Tyrone and was so happy for a time." At that moment, before the final curtain, O'Neill's stage directions tell us that *"Tyrone stirs in his chair"* while *"Edmund and Jamie remain motionless."* Tyrone stirs, of course, because he was directly involved in that past. The sons remain completely frozen because they were not part of that particular past when "something happened" to Mary. But all are involved *now,* as they helplessly and frozenly watch this precious woman who is taking leave of them. They watch. They endure. They do not leave the room that has imprisoned them, and we the audience—the extended family, if I can put it that way—also remain frozen in that larger room, the theater, as we also helplessly watch the three Tyrone men watch the lost Mary. The dramatic moment, the theatrical stage action, takes in actors and audience—exactly what happens at the end of *King Lear,* where the lookers-on can only stand mute as witnesses to the final agony. The endings display both Shakespeare's and O'Neill's fondness for the circle. *King Lear* begins with a father and three daughters and it ends with a father and three daughters, all now dead, with the two evil daughters dragged back *on* stage to complete the circle, the very opposite of the Elizabethan practice of dragging bodies *off* stage. *Long Day's Journey* begins in a sunny morning with Mary the center of attention of the three men, a Mary not yet overwhelmed by her addiction, trying to joke about her husband's snoring and concerned that she's getting fat, and now at play's end, enveloped by night after a long day, she remains the center of their attention in a world no longer sunny. In both endings, we witness a suffering that goes beyond words and that takes in the audience as well as the actors. The human bond seems to transcend the stage, and this feeling, this personal feeling, that we are participating in the agony of the Tyrones and the agony of Lear and Edgar and Kent and Albany, responding in pity and fear, but unable to do anything, touches the very heart of tragedy, an effect that both O'Neill and Shakespeare, by similar theatrical means, are striving for and accomplish.

Did O'Neill learn from Shakespeare the importance of the final stage image that gathers to itself the meaning of a play, which forces us at that moment—because drama is an immediate experience—to feel all that came before it? In both *King Lear* and *Long Day's Journey*, so close is the intimacy between actor and audience, between stage life and real life, that we may wonder whether we are experiencing "the promised end" or witnessing "the image of that horror," only a play. I know of no modern play whose ending comes closer to the ending of *King Lear* in its sheer power of feeling than *Long Day's Journey*.

That last family tableau in *Long Day's Journey* haunts the imagination, and touches not only Shakespeare but also Beckett, with the three dramatists occupying the same tragic ground, as I have suggested in my discussion of *The Iceman Cometh*. That remarkable O'Neill curtain at play's end, offering a stage picture of the frozen despairing human condition, is clearly Beckettian. But so too is the frozen situation of the entire play, with the four Tyrones enclosed in a room, surrounded by fog, waiting for day to end in night. For four hours we hear talk about a past that has so profoundly influenced the present that "the past is the present," as Mary Tyrone expresses it, thereby pinpointing another frozen situation. The family's physical entrapment within the confines of a room is intensified by its temporal entrapment within the confines of a day—a heightened day in which Mary returns to her dope addiction and Edmund Tyrone learns he has tuberculosis—and both the physical and temporal are related to their emotional entrapment, since each Tyrone is a member of *that* family, unable to leave it, tied to it by ropes of guilt and hatred and dependence and love. Waiting is the play's nonactivity, with Mary waiting for her morphine to begin working its soothing magic, with the three Tyrone men playing a waiting game, hoping that Mary did not return to her habit but finally recognizing how hopeless hope really is. In her dope-induced state, Mary returns to her youth, leaving her three men in the agonizing present. As we watch them forever watching her, we are very close to Didi's "At me too someone is looking . . ."

Mary's word *happy* in her last speech—like the *happy* that ends three of the four acts of *Iceman*—takes on a Beckettian irony and serves to remind us of the comic moments in the play. Comedy blending with tragedy, as in *Iceman* and *Godot* and *King Lear*. Beckettian too—in addition to the single set, the darkening atmosphere, the minimum of props, the repetitions, the separations and bondings of characters, the rhythm of hate/love—is the play's self-reflexive quality, the self-conscious gestures of O'Neill's theatrical family, the recited quotations, the awareness that an audience is watching. Of course, this self-reflexivity touches the kind of metatheater that we associate with Shakespeare, who also looks *out* at the world around him and *in* to the world of the play, exploring the very idea of *play*, as we observed in the "Our revels now are ended" discussion.

In *Long Day's Journey* especially, but also in *Iceman,* O'Neill plunges deeper into himself than ever before. In this he is helped by the dramatist who plunged deepest of all, the dramatist who was a member of the family, a companion in creativity. Lacking the verbal eloquence of Shakespeare (who doesn't?), aware that he could only "stammer," O'Neill's dramatic eloquence depends in part on the Shakespearean echoes I have been discussing. O'Neill's use of Shakespeare is most pervasive and potent when he is writing the two tragedies of his last period, as if his more direct autobiographical plays allow him to release fully the poet he has so deeply absorbed. This is the natural consequence, I believe, of Shakespeare's important presence in O'Neill's personal biography. But perhaps more important, in writing tragedy O'Neill is sharing a deeply felt vision of life that belongs to both Shakespeare and the Greek dramatists. The single vision that informs most of O'Neill's work is the tragic, as his own statements make clear. Very early in his career, in 1921, O'Neill said, "To me, the tragic alone has that significant beauty which is truth. It is the meaning of life—and the hope."[33] And the truth of life as he saw it and felt it was always the essential beginning in his process of composition, with language and form and technical devices following from that essential idea. The "truth," he said in 1922, "goes deep. So it reaches you through your emotions."[34] A dramatist of the emotions, searching for truth, by nature and nurture closer to the dark view of things, "misbegotten" and haunted, O'Neill was profoundly influenced by the playwright whose plays most successfully dramatized the tragic condition. O'Neill's oft-repeated statement about tragedy could have been said by Shakespeare, certainly more poetically but not more seriously:

> I'm always acutely conscious of the Force behind—Fate, God, our biological past creating our present, whatever one calls it—Mystery certainly—and of the one eternal tragedy of Man in his glorious, self-destructive struggle to make the Force express him instead of being, as an animal is, an infinitesimal incident in its expression.[35]

The celebration of mystery, the pressure of the force behind, the sense of fated frustration and sadness, the nobility of man's struggle or endurance, the dramatization of the question mark of our lives, the knowledge that no answers to life's important questions can ever be found—these are the characteristics of tragedy that allow us to talk of a tragic tradition, of which Shakespeare and the Greek dramatists are powerful representatives, certainly models of inspiration for the American dramatist whose sensibility was intrinsically and essentially tragic.

Chapter 7

Tragicomedy

Unquestionably, O'Neill's highest achievements are the two tragedies of his last period, *The Iceman Cometh* and *Long Day's Journey Into Night,* his most personal *and* universal dramatizations of man's losing but courageous battle against the "Force behind," of man's existential condition. These autobiographical plays reveal O'Neill's inherently tragic view of life; at the same time they belong to a tragic tradition, sharing characteristics with, and receiving echoes from, the best tragedies produced by the Greeks and Shakespeare. This is just another way of saying that the forms of tragedy in the Western tradition change because of time and place but that the substance of tragedy remains essentially the same. Tragicomedy—the designation I wish to apply to O'Neill's last play, *A Moon for the Misbegotten,* the designation that best describes Shakespeare's last plays as well—is a genre without a firm basis in tradition. Always a troublesome term, shifting its meaning through the ages, the word itself must be examined. When Plautus first used the term in his prologue to *Amphitryon,* he was alluding to the mingling of gods (who belong to tragedy) and low characters like slaves (who belong in comedy). The Renaissance latched on to this "mingling" as the essence of tragicomedy, an irregular genre that blurred the neat classical distinctions between tragedy and comedy. When such a classicist as Sir Philip Sidney referred to the genre, he did so with contempt. For him, "mingling kings and clowns" produced "mongrel Tragi-comedy."[1] A formal definition was given to the term by John Fletcher in his letter "To the Reader," which prefaced *The Faithful Shepherdess:* "A tragi-comedy is not so called in respect of mirth and killing, but in respect it wants deaths, which is enough to make it no tragedy, yet brings some near it, which is enough to make it no comedy."[2] This definition points to the importance of endings. Classically, a tragedy ends sadly, a comedy happily; a tragedy ends in death, a comedy in marriage. The tragicomedy that Beaumont and Fletcher wrote was tragic along the way but ended as comedy. And with the years this kind of tragicomedy has been cultivated, with the greater emphasis placed on *how* exactly to manipulate a happy ending from seemingly tragic situations, an emphasis clearly recognizable in eighteenth-century sentimental comedy as well as in modern James Bond melodrama. But this is not the tragicomedy that modern dramatists are writing, nor do those modern writers who use the term take any cognizance of Plautus or Sidney or Fletcher. Ionesco, for example, says that in modern times "the comic is tragic, and . . . the tragedy of man is pure derision." He claims that for him there is no difference between "the comic and the tragic."[3] Friedrich Dürrenmatt, who labels his *The Visit* a tragicomedy, believes that in our time the tragic comes out of the comic, that comedy, in fact, brings forth the tragic "as a terrifying moment, as an abyss that opens suddenly."[4] His words *terrifying* and *abyss* traditionally belong to tragedy and indicate how difficult it is to state with any sense of exactness what modern tragicomedy is. Perhaps the best example of this difficulty is Beckett's use of the term when he calls the English edition of *Waiting for Godot* a "tragicomedy." Beckett's play contains much comedy—vaudeville turns, clever language, pratfalls, Laurel and Hardy routines—and laughter is evoked. But the effect of a reading of *Godot,* of a performance of the play, is tragic, I believe. Beckett's play, like the plays in the tragic tradition, prods the ultimate questions, evokes the secret cause, forces us to face the fact of mystery, the "Force behind." The tragic and the comic are tied together throughout—as strongly as Lucky is tied to Pozzo—but the tragic eventually sucks the comic into itself.[5]

Conceding the fact that the term *tragicomedy* is difficult, I still find it useful as a descriptive label for Shakespeare's last plays and for O'Neill's last play, *A Moon for the Misbegotten.* In their last plays Shakespeare and O'Neill share some of the characteristics that have been absorbed by this mongrel genre. What strikes me as especially interesting and perhaps ultimately unexplainable is the need for some tragic dramatists—for all artists, perhaps—to create toward the end of their careers works of art that reach for the symbolic and mystical, for light, for a safe harbor in the fog, to use an O'Neillian image. In *Oedipus at Colonus*—the last of Sophocles' more than one hundred plays, the conclusion of the story of Oedipus, whose career remains to this day a paradigm of the tragic tradition—Sophocles presents Oedipus as a sick, old, angry man, a blind beggar who is finally lifted to the gods, a blessed creature. The tone of the plays of Ibsen's last period, plays that are powerfully symbolic and mystical, is best characterized by one of the play's titles, *When We Dead Awaken.* The last efforts of Beethoven and Yeats also reach for heights that seem to touch the gods. And Shakespeare in his last plays, like O'Neill in *Misbegotten,* seems to emerge from the darkness of tragedy to give his audience a different dramatic experience, exploring a genre that both plummets the depths, like tragedy, and reaches for the sun and sky, like comedy, a genre that allows a mysterious daylight to filter through the clouds of darkness.

Most scholars agree that Shakespeare's last plays, *Pericles, Cymbeline, The Winter's Tale, The Tempest,* form a distinct group,[6] and that the group, although distinct, holds threads of connection to the plays that come before, affirming once again that all of Shakespeare's plays can be woven together to make one carpet.[7] Scholars do not agree on what to label these plays, with "romances" or "tragicomedies" the usual epithets, with "the last plays" or "the last phase" used by scholars who find the other labels to be misleading, therefore opting for the vaguer, less restrictive but perhaps less useful designations. Frank Kermode believes that the last plays can "with some accuracy" be called romances, and he clearly pinpoints the characteristics that make them romances: "All the romances treat of the recovery of lost royal children, usually princesses of great, indeed semi-divine, virtue and beauty; they all bring important characters near to death, and sometimes feature almost miraculous resurrections; they all end with the healing, after many years of repentance and suffering, of some disastrous breach in the lives and happiness of princes, and this final reconciliation is usually brought about by the agency of beautiful young people; they all contain material of a pastoral character or otherwise celebrate natural beauty and its renewal."[8] This is a useful statement. But the word *romances* suggests ideas and even traditions that do not apply to Shakespeare's plays. It is a term that demands the kind of pointed, qualifying discussion that Kermode offers. The reason we have a problem with the label is that the plays under question received no satisfactory label from Shakespeare's contemporaries. In the First Folio of 1623 *Cymbeline* was put with the tragedies, *The Winter's Tale* and *The Tempest* with the comedies. *Pericles* was not included. Because Shakespeare did write tragedies and comedies, because he played with the tragic and the comic in all his plays, because the word *romance* was never, to my knowledge, used in his time to describe his plays, and because the term *tragicomedy was* used (but used to describe more accurately the plays of Beaumont and Fletcher), I find the label tragicomedy to be more satisfying and useful. When writing his last plays Shakespeare had his tragedies behind him, tragedies in which the last minutes attempted a kind of reconciliation or renewal, sometimes only a token gesture, usually not enough to lead us too far out of the darkness. In his tragicomedies the darkness is always there, but finally the renewal or restoration or rejuvenation is strong enough to dispel it. The weight of each tragicomedy falls on the comic side of the tragic/comic balance. The same can be said about O'Neill's last play, which, although a romance in that it deals with lovers and moonlight, can be described as tragicomedy, and which displays threads of connection to Shakespeare's last plays, especially to *The Winter's Tale* and *The Tempest*.

A Moon for the Misbegotten, written in 1943, first produced in 1957, is the last play O'Neill completed. Like *Iceman* and *Long Day's Journey,* it is intensely personal, it observes the classical unities, it focuses on family, and it is both tragic and comic. Unlike the other two, its setting is out-of-doors and, most important to the present discussion, it is not a tragedy. There is every reason to consider it a kind of epilogue to *Long Day's Journey,* which suggests that O'Neill could not rest easy with the fixed tableau of the haunted Tyrones at the final curtain of that play. In *Misbegotten* he continues the story of Jamie, now James Tyrone, Jr., (called Jim and designated "Tyrone" in the script), which seems to be his primary reason for writing the play, as if he didn't say enough about Jamie or didn't give him all the "deep pity and forgiveness and understanding" that he mentions in his dedication of *Long Day's Journey* to Carlotta. But it also seems clear that he had to say more about the other members of the family, including himself. Jim is now like his father—hence, the "Tyrone" designation, I believe—and he still has mother to contend with and relate to. So too is Phil Hogan in many ways like O'Neill's father, Josie Hogan like his mother. And O'Neill himself can be found, here as always, in the portrait of his brother (and at times in Josie too). The autobiographical underpinning of *Misbegotten* has been documented by some of our best O'Neill scholars; it need not be reviewed here.[9] Whatever were the specific psychological pressures on O'Neill to write the play, it is clear that he had to continue the story of Jamie and he had to soften its tragic implications. The pain that he felt in writing *Misbegotten,* also well documented, does not prevent the play from offering a sense of peace and reconciliation and "forgiveness." It is more positive than the tragedy for which it serves as epilogue.

It is interesting, perhaps important, to observe that O'Neill had already, in his one-act play *Hughie* (written 1940), offered a kind of epilogue to his other tragedy, *Iceman,* as if there too he couldn't break away from his subject or wished to offer a positive closure. *Hughie* was part of a projected six-play cycle of one-act plays, to be collectively called "By Way of Obit." In each play of the cycle the main character would talk about a recently dead person to a listener who usually remains silent. By means of what is essentially a monologue by the main character the audience would get a full picture of the dead person "by way of obit" *and* of the narrator—and, by means of stage directions, the audience would learn about the person listening. *Hughie* is a natural extension of *The Iceman Cometh* in that contact between men, in this play between the talker Erie Smith and the listener Charlie Hughes, must be made and illusions shared in order for man to endure. The play extends the tragic implications of *Iceman* because the audience feels the terror of loneliness and the need for a dream, but it ends with a sense of union between men, a sharing of a dream, a veritable return from death to life. Both Erie and Charlie will get through the night, at least. The play offers a delicate blending of the tragic and the comic throughout, but the positive ending allows it to be considered a tragicomedy, if one is searching for a label for this one-act play.

Misbegotten takes place in the autumn of the year of Jamie O'Neill's death, 1923, eleven years after the summer of 1912, when the four Tyrones, locked in their living room and tied to each other, gave voice to their frustrations and dreams. The day of that play began on a sunny morning and ended in dark, fog-dense night, the movement of day and play relentlessly tragic. In *Misbegotten* the noon of a hot sunny day, in which comedy is the prevalent mode (act 1), turns into a moonlit night, filled with a dark, tragic lyricism (acts 2 and 3), which dissolves into the dawn of a new day (act 4)—from act 2 a tragicomic progression. The play begins in laughter, a special laughter stemming from the Irishness of the three main characters. In fact, this play is more Irish than any other O'Neill play, which is saying much because Irishness touches everything O'Neill wrote. O'Neill himself said, "One thing that explains more than anything about me is the fact that I'm Irish."[10] Both Josie Hogan—"*The map of Ireland is stamped on her face*"— and her father Phil Hogan—who likes his whiskey and speaks "*with a pronounced brogue*" (3:857,862)—are proud of their Irishness, especially happy to confront the Yankee, T. Steadman Harder, in a scene filled with broad Irish humor, both physical horseplay and rhetorical mockery. The comic writing here—as in the many confrontations between short, snub-nosed Phil Hogan and his large daughter—is worthy of Synge; it captures the Irishman's earthiness and linguistic playfulness. Jim Tyrone thoroughly enjoys witnessing how cleverly the Hogans overwhelm Harder; after all, Jim is an Irishman, his father's son. When "*he smiles without sneering,*" O'Neill tells us in his stage directions, Jim "*still has the ghost of a former, youthful, irresponsible Irish charm,*" but this doesn't happen too often. More characteristic is "*his habitually cynical expression,*" and he still has the "*Mephistophelian quality*" that the younger Jamie possessed in *Long Day's Journey* (3:875). He drinks like an Irishman and he engages in witty verbal battles with Phil Hogan, but he lacks an Irish quickness of spirit in this play. Even in the midst of all the comedy in act 1, we know we're looking at a "dead" man. When Josie first sees him walking up the road to their house, she says pityingly, "Look at him when he thinks no one is watching, with his eyes on the ground. Like a dead man walking slow behind his own coffin" (3:874). The description is an apt one. Jim is spiritually dead and literally drinking himself to death because of a great burden of mind, one that he will reveal to Josie, one that relates to his dead mother. (Perhaps the echo is too faint to catch, but the first time we see Hamlet he too, according to his mother, has eyes that are downcast, looking for his "noble father in the dust," carrying a burden that relates to his mother.) Act 1 is marked by the realism of earthy behavior, laughter both crude and mocking, whiskey. In it we witness the genuine affection Jim and Josie have for one another, even though both put on masks and play roles—Jim the Broadway cynic, Josie the wanton whore.

When moonlight comes, the play's tone changes. The earthy comedy disappears; an atmosphere of tender lyricism begins to form. Traditionally, night is meant for lovers, and the encounter between Jim and Josie—designed to be a plot by Josie to snare Jim as a husband, what is conventionally a comic plot—becomes the most special love experience for both. After many false starts—in which Jim sometimes sees Josie as one of the many whores in his dissolute life, in which Jim seems confused about what he really wants from Josie, and Josie seems equally confused about what she wants from Jim—they reveal who they are. Under the moon, sitting on the steps of the dilapidated farmhouse, his head on Josie's ample breast, a guilt-ridden Jim Tyrone makes his agonizing confession to Josie. The story he tells is the only part of the play that holds autobiographical truth. When Mary Ellen O'Neill gave up her dope, Jamie, who lived with her in California, gave up his whiskey. As we recognized in *Long Day's Journey,* his fate was truly tied to his mother's fate. When she was dying, he returned to drink, something his dying mother discovered, which filled him with guilt. When she died, Jamie brought her body back on a train from Los Angeles to New York City, and on that train carrying his mother's coffin—and this causes Jim Tyrone's deepest guilt—he slept every night with a $50-a-night blond whore, for "revenge" against his mother for leaving him, it seems, but also perhaps for darker Oedipal reasons. Jamie O'Neill desperately needed his mother's forgiveness, but she was dead. Jim Tyrone—and now we come to the part of the play that is imaginary, that O'Neill fabricates—has a sympathetic listener in Josie Hogan, no, more than that, he seems to have his mother in Josie, and even more than that, the Blessed Mother, the Virgin Mary, the spiritual prop for Mary Tyrone, as we learned in *Long Day's Journey,* the personage who, in fact, helped O'Neill's mother break her drug habit.

The story Jim tells Josie repels her at first, but then, recognizing Jim's desperation and understanding her role in this loving relationship, she gives him the forgiveness he needs: "I do forgive!... As *she* forgives, do you hear me! As *she* loves and understands and forgives!" (Echoes of the parlour scene in that other New England farm play, *Desire Under the Elms,* can be heard clearly.) Josie then *"bends over him with a brooding maternal tenderness"* as he cries his *"heart's repentance against her breast."* She hugs him tightly, stopping his sobbing with the poetical words that even surprise her, as she speaks of a dawn that "will wake in the sky like a promise of God's peace in the soul's dark sadness" (3:933). Amusedly she says, "Sure, love is a wonderful mad inspiration!" But then she looks down to see Jim asleep, eyes closed, face pale in the moonlight, *"calm with the drained, exhausted peace of death."* As she looks up at the sky, she closes act 3 with these *"self-derisive"* words: "God forgive me, it's a fine end to all my scheming, to sit here with the dead hugged to my breast, and the silly mug of the moon grinning down, enjoying the joke!" (3:933–34) A stunning and memorable stage image. O'Neill has plucked the strings of comedy and then tragedy to come to this remarkable moment, thereby creating his own version of Pietà. He has pushed his play toward the symbolic, with Josie acquiring mythic proportions in keeping with her largeness of size. Josie—grounded in reality, strong and sensitive, the virgin playing the whore, lover and mother, Fat Vi and the Virgin Mary—is O'Neill's most powerful imaginative creation of a woman. She makes the tragic discovery that her lover is really dead, that there is no possibility that theirs could be the usual "love" situation. Jim's confession is his salvation.[11] Because of Josie, Jim has the possibility of rebirth even as he lay dying. Without losing its earthy dimension—after all, what we *see* is a big-breasted farm woman holding a tired drunkard—the scene takes on a mystical and symbolic dimension. We can never forget that O'Neill's Irishness contains Catholicism (of which the confessional is an important ingredient), and although we are not dealing with the supernatural, what O'Neill presents does force us to *think* in those terms, to *see* Mother and Child and all that such a charged Christian image represents.

Dawn comes with act 4 and with Josie and Jim *"in the same position,"* a frozen Pietà—Josie still holding a sleeping Jim, her face displaying *"resigned sadness,"* his face *"the same exhausted deathlike repose."* O'Neill's stage directions tell us that *"the two make a strangely tragic picture in the wan dawn light—this big sorrowful woman hugging a haggard-faced, middle-aged drunkard against her breast, as if he were a sick child"* (3:935). Phil Hogan—coming from the outside world, himself a comic figure, entering to consummate a "comic" marriage plot against Jim Tyrone—breaks our concentration on that *"tragic picture."* According to Josie, he has come to witness "a great miracle": "A virgin who bears a dead child in the night, and the dawn finds her still a virgin. If that isn't a miracle, what is?" (3:936). Hogan wonders if his daughter has "gone mad in the night," but Josie articulates her recognition that Jim had "died already—that it was a damned soul coming to me in the moonlight, to confess and be forgiven and find peace for a night" (3:937) After she sends Hogan into the house, thereby leaving the lovers on stage alone again, Josie *"with a maternal tenderness"* says: "I hate to bring you back to life, Jim, darling. If you could have died in your sleep, that's what you would have liked, isn't it?" She then awakens Jim, who denies at first what happened to him during the miraculous evening, who reverts to his characteristic cynicism, even saying, as he looks at the *"exceptionally beautiful sunrise,"* that "God seems to be putting on quite a display. I like Belasco better. Rise of curtain, act-Four stuff." But finally he says he remembers: "I—I'll never forget it—here with you" (3:942). Recalling the tortured details of his confession, he is filled with guilt again, but Josie pleads that he remember her love which gave him "peace for a while." He tells her he'll never forget her love and kisses her—"Never! (*kissing her again*) Never, do you hear! I'll always love you, Josie. (*He kisses her again.*) Good-bye—and God bless you!" (3:944) He leaves the stage walking *"quickly"* down the road, much different from the man who came into the play "like a dead man, walking slow behind his own coffin." He is leaving to die, still following his own coffin—and, of course, following the coffin of the mother he will soon join in death, the coffin that was the focus of his confession and of the refrain of the song he couldn't erase from his mind. But now he moves quickly, a reborn child, leaving a "mother" to go to a mother, at peace with himself, journeying from womb to tomb which is womb again. The play ends—after a lively reconciliation between Josie and her father—with Josie's words, as she looks down the road Jim was walking: "May you have your wish and die in your sleep soon, Jim, darling. May you rest forever in forgiveness and peace." Gentle words of benediction. Then she goes into the house as the curtain falls. Lavinia, at the end of her play, entered a house to confront the ghosts of the past. Josie, at the end of her play, enters a house to continue life with a feisty father, carrying with her the remembrance of her strange interlude with a lover called Jim Tyrone whom she sent to death with peace and forgiveness. O'Neill entered the Mannon house with Lavinia in order to face his ghosts and write out his story, the plays of his second career. In the last of his late plays O'Neill allowed Josie Hogan, his most sympathetic portrait of a woman, to voice his benediction over a dead brother, in fact, over all the O'Neills, including himself, satisfying a deep need in himself, allowing his art to make substantial a wish that had no relationship to autobiographical reality. His brother Jamie died in a sanatorium of cerebral apoplexy, nearly blind and mad from too much alcohol. His father died slowly of cancer, uttering as his final words, as we noticed in the last chapter, "This sort of life—froth!—rotten—all of it—no good!"[12]—words that he would have criticized the cynical Jamie for saying, probably rejecting them with an appropriate Shakespeare quotation. (Phil Hogan tells Josie at the end of the play that he wasn't cursing Jim—"It was life I was cursing—.") His mother had several strokes before her death, with the entire right side of her body paralyzed, and just before her death she despairingly realized that Jamie had returned to heavy drinking. O'Neill himself, at the time he was writing the play, was struggling with his body as well as his tortured mind. His hands could not stop shaking, which prevented him from writing, and when he couldn't write his life was empty. Of course, he could not be sure that *Misbegotten* would be his last play, but it seems so right *as* his last play, and the last words of Josie seem so perfect as marking O'Neill's departure from stage and from "life"—even though O'Neill would live for ten more years—that perhaps his body was responding to impulses of the soul that were deeper than O'Neill could have realized.

In the movement toward a final affirmation, toward a rebirth, toward a sense of forgiveness, with death as a strong focus of the play, O'Neill's last play duplicates the movement of Shakespeare's last plays. Both O'Neill and Shakespeare are manipulating the delicate balance between the tragic and the comic. O'Neill, in a letter to Dudley Nichols, referring to *Misbegotten*, calls it "a fine unusual tragic comedy."[13] He also called it a "strange combination comic tragic" work.[14] Notice that he is not consistent in placing one genre before the other when referring to the play. But in writing it he, like Shakespeare in his tragicomedies, tilts the balance toward the comic. It isn't that we return in *Misbegotten* to the boisterous Irish comedy of Phil and Josie Hogan, although this kind of comedy will inform the rest of their lives. Rather, we emerge with an affirmation that rests on comedy in the large sense, a re-creation, the kind of comedy that Dante called divine, but that we can view as restorative without the need for the supernatural, although suggestions of miracle and magic and the mystical, as we have seen, are unavoidable in such an affirmation of life in the face of death, especially within a Christian context. Both O'Neill and Shakespeare do not allow us to forget death even as they turn our attention to life. The crucial words of the Shepherd in *The Winter's Tale* produce the key passage in that richly suggestive play, but they apply to all of Shakespeare's tragicomedies and to *A Moon for the Misbegotten:* "Heavy matters, heavy matters! But look thee here, boy. Now bless thyself: thou met'st with things dying, I with things new-born" (3.3.112–14). The newborn will help to qualify the dying, and that's a blessing, but it will not erase the dying, and that's the truth about life. A dead Jim Tyrone becomes a newborn child in his mother's arms; restored to peace, forgiven, he is ready to die. (The readiness *is* all!) In *The Winter's Tale* the newborn child Perdita will help to make the winter's tale a spring's tale. But Shakespeare does not allow us to forget that another child, Mamillius—a "gallant child; one that, indeed, physics the subject, makes old hearts fresh" (1.1.38–39)—is dead. In the last act, when Florizel and Perdita have arrived in Sicilia from Bohemia, about to see Leontes, Paulina recalls "our prince, / Jewel of children," Mamillius, who, were he alive, would be the same age as Florizel. Leontes would rather not hear Paulina speak of Mamillius: "Prithee, no more; cease. Thou know'st / He dies to me again when talk'd of" (5.1.119–20). That is precisely why Shakespeare mentions him here, as the play winds to its miraculously positive conclusion. He wants Mamillius to die again even as the young lovers, Florizel and Perdita, make old hearts fresh, bringing "the spring to th' earth." Shakespeare is playing with our emotions, mixing sadness with the sense of jubilation resulting from the restorations and reconciliations. Stanley Cavell asks the important questions about the death of Mamillius, questions that Shakespeare forces us to ask; otherwise Shakespeare wouldn't have "talk'd" about him again for him to die again:

> Shall we say that the absent boy is meant to cast the shadow of finitude or doubt over the general air of reunion at the end of the play, to emblematize that no human reconciliation is uncompromised, not even one constructible by the powers of Shakespeare? Or shall we say that in acquiring a son-in-law the loss of the son is made up for? Would that be Hermione's—the son's mother's—view of the matter? Or shall we take the boy's death more simply symbolically, as standing for the inevitable loss of childhood? Then does Perdita's being found mean that there is a way in which childhood *can,* after all, be recovered? But the sixteen years that Perdita was, as it were, lost are not recovered. Time may present itself as a good-humored old man, but what he speaks about in his appearance as Chorus in this play is his lapse, his being spent, as if behind our backs. Then is the moral that we all require forgiveness and that forgiveness is always a miracle, taking time but beyond time?[15]

All of Cavell's questions have weight but the last is absolutely applicable and important not only to *The Winter's Tale* but also to *The Tempest* (as I shall soon suggest) *and* to *Misbegotten.* Jim Tyrone, like O'Neill, like all of us, requires forgiveness, and the play dramatizes the miracle of forgiveness, with Josie Hogan its loving instrument; she even uses the word *miracle,* we noticed, when she refers to herself as "the virgin who bears a dead child in the night" and remains a virgin. The magical moonlit moment when we find Josie holding Jim, then Jim awakening to a different dawn than he has ever experienced before, produces emotions in the audience that are close to those felt when we witness the coming to life of the "statue" of Hermione at the end of *The Winter's Tale*. That moment demanded silence—"I like your silence," Paulina tells the assembled onlookers, talking to audience as well as players—as does O'Neill's frozen Pietà. In *The Winter's Tale* too, forgiveness is tightly connected to a "miracle" on stage, life emerging from death, with the help of a strong woman, Paulina, whose very name seems to touch the Christian story of death and resurrection. It is Paulina who guided the repentance of Leontes and who now offers the miracle of the "statue." Although *The Winter's Tale* is too rich a play to be categorized as symbolic in Christian terms only, although Shakespeare is not systematic, as was his great predecessor Dante, in offering Christian allegory, it is impossible not to remark on the Christian analogues, the echoes from that larger religious story. The play opens with an image of the world before the fall, a time of "innocence," when Polixenes, the speaker, and Leontes were "two lads that thought there was no more behind / But such a day to-morrow as to-day, / And to be boy eternal," (1.2.63–65), a time when no one knew or dreamed of "the doctrine of ill-doing." But "temptations" come along, especially connected with women ("devils"), and sins abound, and innocence is lost. After these charged references in a seemingly casual conversation about boyhood between Polixenes and Hermione, Leontes' jealousy erupts, unmotivated, it seems. He offers a passionate aside filled with vile thoughts; his knowledge is evil and it is filled with sexual repulsion, reminiscent of Hamlet and Lear. His diseased imagination, like Othello's, produces the tragic part of *The Winter's Tale,* and his accusations eventually lead to the death of Mamillius and the "death" of Hermione. Witnessing death, Leontes suddenly repents, and vows to visit the dead in the chapel: "tears shed there / Shall be my recreation" (3:2.239–40). He asks Paulina to lead him "to these sorrows." And it is Paulina who will lead him out of his sorrow sixteen years later, arranging the statue scene after the arrival of the lost daughter, Perdita—recreating Hermione and thereby re-creating Leontes. In act 2 Mamillius was about to tell a winter's tale about "a man" who "dwelt by a churchyard," a tale interrupted by the entrance of a deranged Leontes. Well, Leontes is the man who dwells by the churchyard for sixteen years, a time of "sorrows" and deep repentance. He is the main character of his son's tale of winter. But spring eventually comes in the person of a glorious daughter, as "sacred" as her mother, and it comes in the coming to life of a statue, an onstage miracle—and the only time Shakespeare in all of his thirty-eight plays does not work with audience awareness, so that the resurrection, the surprise, is felt by the audience as well as the players. Music awakens the "statue," Hermione has life again, Leontes is forgiven in the embrace of his wife, the "heavens directing" the miracle. Separation has led to reunion; the pattern of reconciliation is complete; tragedy has become comedy.

Even so brief and limited a description of *The Winter's Tale* suggests the play's connections with *Misbegotten,* whether or not O'Neill consciously recognized the connections. Jim Tyrone's knowledge, like Leontes', has infected his imagination. He, like Leontes, has "drunk and seen the spider," producing a passionate misogyny. That "blonde pig who looked more like a whore than twenty-five whores" fills his mind and repulses him (3:931), as do all the whores he detests when he awakens to the dawns of his usual days. He, like Leontes, believes he caused the death of the woman he loved most. He, like Leontes, needs forgiveness, and receives it from a woman in a scene touched by stage magic and informed by Christian ideas. Most interesting, perhaps, he, like both Leontes and Polixenes, would like to have remained "boy eternal," living in a time of innocence before woman caused temptation and eventual revulsion. During that time the "boy" was with the one woman who nourished him, the one woman he was connected to in the most loving and positive way, his mother. Mamillius and Hermione have such a relationship, and when Hermione is taken away from him, Mamillius pines. Their separation produces such anxious thoughts ("conceit and fear") that Mamillius dies. This is what happens to that other "boy," Jim—separation from mother produces terrible thoughts and eventual death. In this connection Coppelia Kahn's belief that "Shakespeare makes Mamillius a symbol of the union of male and female," that the name Mamillius connects him "with the maternal function of nursing" is wonderfully suggestive, leading her to the assertion that "it is fitting that Leontes," when he clasps Hermione's hand, "characterizes the reunion with her in terms of the most primitive, elemental human activity, begun at the mother's breast: 'O, she's warm! / If this be magic, let it be an art / Lawful as eating.'"[16] This provocative image of a man "nursing" from a warm nurturing woman points directly to O'Neill's Pietà in *Misbegotten* and, in fact, allows us to assert unequivocally that for both Shakespeare and O'Neill the image of a mother with child at her breast is the most precious and affirmative possible. In *Antony and Cleopatra,* the play that Shakespeare wrote before the tragicomedies, the play that can be considered a link between Shakespeare's tragedies and tragicomedies, we find the same potent image in Cleopatra's last scene, in which Shakespeare brilliantly converts the poisonous asp to a nursing baby: "Peace, peace! / Dost thou not see my baby at my breast / That sucks the nurse asleep?" (5.2.308–10). Here the usual symbol of evil and pure sexuality is transformed to an instrument of peace and easeful death. Cleopatra will join Antony in death, a death that is welcome. Coming so unexpectedly in the dramatic context, no other image, one must believe, could have served Shakespeare so well as that of a mother nursing a child. In the tragedy he wrote just before *Antony and Cleopatra* Shakespeare has Lady Macbeth deny her nurturing womanhood by using the same powerful image in attempting to persuade Macbeth to kill Duncan:

> I have given suck, and know
> How tender 'tis to love the babe that milks me;
> I would, while it was smiling in my face,
> Have pluck'd my nipple from his boneless gums,
> And dash'd the brains out, had I so sworn as you
> Have done to this.
>
> (1.7.54–59)

For Shakespeare, a baby nursing at a mother's breast represents the most positive connection between two people. So too for O'Neill.[17] He plays with the idea at different times in his career and in different ways—consider, as examples, Eben with Abbie, Orin with Christine, Simon with Deborah—but nowhere in O'Neill is the image more powerful, more lyrical, more affirmative, more miraculous, than Josie with Jim under moonlight in *Misbegotten*. Josie has given birth to a dead child in the night, as she tells us, but the child is able to feed at his mother's breast, becoming alive enough and wise enough to seek and recognize a mother's forgiveness and love, only to return once more to death, an easier death, a better death.

In *The Winter's Tale* and *Misbegotten*, as we have observed, sadness is mingled with joy, the play's large comedy absorbing but not erasing the tragic. The same is true for Shakespeare's last play, *The Tempest*, in which the main character, who moves toward restoration in the spirit of forgiveness, reminds us at play's end that "every third thought shall be my grave" (5.1.312). Prospero had already told us that life, like the "revels" of a play, is ephemeral, that its actors dissolve into "thin air," that we are the "stuff" of dreams, that the sleep of death is our inevitable closure—thoughts that are more despairing than both James Tyrone and Edmund Tyrone realized in *Long Day's Journey*, as I have suggested in the previous chapter. Forgiveness and death are also important themes in *Misbegotten*, and although I do not wish to assert that these universal ideas found in Shakespeare are direct influences on O'Neill, I do hear echoes from Shakespeare's last play in O'Neill's last play.

The spirit of forgiveness, the sense of compassion and charity, overrides Prospero's desire for revenge against those who took away his title in Milan. They are "at his mercy," in his power, we hear, and *mercy* becomes the operating word. Perhaps Ariel taught him to be more "human" when that airy creature displayed pity for Prospero's enemies; it's difficult to know from the words in the text. But Prospero does take pity on them, recognizing that "the rarer action is / In virtue than in vengeance." A large statement, bringing us into a tragicomic world. In Shakespeare's tragedies, beginning with *Julius Caesar,* revenge was the important theme or an important theme, driving or helping to drive the plays to their conclusions. In Shakespeare's tragicomedies revenge is an important element in the plays, but one that is subdued or absorbed by the more powerful ideas of forgiveness and pardon. This spirit of forgiveness is the large idea in *Misbegotten* too, as we have observed, so large that it is easy to forget that the idea of revenge is also present in the play. Josie, angry because she believes that Jim betrayed her and her father by selling the farm, wishes to avenge herself by tricking Jim into sleeping with her, with the result that an honorable Jim would propose marriage. This is the comic plot of her father, so that Josie is playing in her father's play, as Hamlet was asked to play in his father's play, the difference being the genres in which the fathers operate. But Josie's better nature recognizes the desperate need of Jim for forgiveness. Hers is "the rarer action." Revenge comes into the play in another plot, closer to the spirit of tragedy. Jim, in his confession to Josie, tries to explain why he slept with the blond whore in the train carrying his dead mother: "The blonde—she didn't matter. She was only something that belonged in the plot. It was as if I wanted revenge—because I'd been left alone—because I knew I was lost, without any hope left—that all I could do would be drink myself to death, because no one was left who could help me" (3:932). The blond whore is Jim's revenge on mother for leaving him, an act of vengeance that fills him with enormous guilt, relieved only when his "mother," in the person of Josie Hogan, gives him the forgiveness needed to release him from despair and life. Josie, squelching a comic plot, acts like a forgiving Prospero rather than a vengeful Prospero. Josie, in the more tragic plot, acts like the Prospero who, recognizing "heart sorrow," saves his enemy Alonso from despair. Josie does not have the magical power of Prospero, but her inclusive nature, her earthiness and sanctity, her mythic status, allow her to imitate his role.

Of course, in respect to the idea of death, Jim, not Josie, is closer to

Prospero. More than every third thought is his grave; in fact, all thought is his grave. And, most interesting in this connection, the magician Prospero, like the drunkard Jim Tyrone, has to be forgiven in order to find "release"—for Jim, release to die; for Prospero, release to return to Milan, where he will think about death; and for the actor playing Prospero release from an audience by means of applause, as we learn in the Epilogue to *The Tempest,* where the vital connection between forgiveness and freedom is made for the last time. Prospero speaks the Epilogue:

> Now our charms are all o'erthrown,
> And what strength I have's mine own,
> Which is most faint. Now 'tis true,
> I must be here confin'd by you,
> Or sent to Naples. Let me not
> Since I have my dukedom got,
> And pardon'd the deceiver, dwell
> In this bare island by your spell,
>   But release me from my bands
> With the help of your good hands.
> Gentle breath of yours my sails
> Must fill, or else my project fails,
> Which was to please. Now I want
> Spirits to enforce, art to enchant,
> And my ending is despair,
> Unless I be reliev'd by prayer,
> Which pierces so, that it assaults
> Mercy itself, and frees all faults.
>   As you from crimes would pardon'd be,
>   Let your indulgence set me free.

Prospero, having given up his magic, having drowned his book, needs help to return to Milan. He needs a gentle breath to fill his sail, far different from the tempest that began the play. He needs the breath of pardon to release him from his bonds, and the actor playing Prospero is asking for the breath of gentle hands clapping to release him from his role. The potent rhyme of *despair* and *prayer* points to the spiritual movement of the play—the movement in *Misbegotten* too, and, in fact, the movement of tragicomedy. Mercy leads to freedom for those who need forgiveness—like Alonso and Sebastian and Antonio and Jim Tyrone—and for those who give forgiveness— like Prospero and Josie Hogan. Josie, we must understand, is set free when she releases Jim from his burden of guilt, just as Prospero is set free when he releases his enemies from their burdens. But Prospero *and* the actor playing Prospero still need the "pardon" of the audience to be released from island *and* theater. And in this gesture of theatrical self-consciousness we are reminded of the "Our revels now are ended" speech and of all the moments in this play and his other plays, especially his late plays, when Shakespeare gives his audience the strong sense that what they are seeing is being performed, that it is illusory, that theatrical representation is artifice, but at the same time that the play is a metaphor for life, and that the play metaphor helps us to understand the nature of reality.[18] Prospero, before he steps into the Epilogue as mere actor, was the master artist, the dramatist, in full control of his cast of characters. They played in his play and, in addition, he put on other plays for their edification—like the banquet scene, interrupted by Ariel as Harpy, who told his enemies they were "men of sin," that they would suffer "ling'ring perdition" if they did not display "heart's sorrow"; like the masque of Juno and Ceres as a blessing for the forthcoming marriage of Miranda and Ferdinand, a masque also interrupted, this time by Prospero, so that the "Our revels now are ended" speech can be delivered, a speech which so effectively expresses the play-life idea. The metatheatrical dimension of *The Tempest* is strong, and it takes on even more significance because we know—and Shakespeare knows—that this is Shakespeare's last play, tempting us to see it as his farewell to his art. But the theatrical self-consciousness is important to *The Winter's Tale* too, a play filled with theater imagery, a play that calculatingly blurs the distinctions between life and play, that, in fact, mocks life with art and mocks art with life in the remarkable statue scene, already discussed. At play's end, Leontes reminds us that we were seeing a play:

> Good Paulina,
> Lead us from hence, where we may leisurely
> Each one demand, and answer to his part
> Perform'd in this wide gap of time, since first
> We were dissever'd.
>
> (5.3.151–55)

The dissevering took place in the tale of winter; now, because of the part each character has performed, we have a tale of spring. We have experienced tragicomedy that, even as it balances tragedy and comedy, balances life and art, reality and illusion. As Shakespeare's career develops, as he writes his tragedies—let us say, from *Hamlet* on—Shakespeare's art seems to be reaching deeper and deeper inside himself. Certainly *Hamlet* and

Othello and *King Lear* and *Macbeth,* to name only his four major tragedies, seem to touch deeper sources within Shakespeare than he ever plummeted before. (Similarly, O'Neill in his two late tragedies, *Iceman* and *Long Day's Journey,* goes deeper within himself than ever before.) As Shakespeare's career develops further, his art in his last plays, the tragicomedies, seems to sound itself, plummeting the very medium he is using. Both *The Winter's Tale* and *The Tempest* are deliberately self-conscious in different ways. Notice, for example, how self-consciously *expansive* Shakespeare is in his use of Time in *The Winter's Tale,* giving us the sixteen-year gap, with the figure of Time holding an hourglass, delivering a speech of thirty-two lines, turning the glass over on line sixteen. Notice how self-consciously *restrictive* Shakespeare is in his use of Time in *The Tempest,* with a sense of urgency that Prospero perform his magic in three hours, the exact time for the performance of the play, making us too aware of the unity of time. Shakespeare's last plays call attention to themselves as plays even as they reflect life's tragicomic reality.

In this respect, too, O'Neill's last play bears a discussable resemblance to Shakespeare's last plays. *A Moon for the Misbegotten* is the most theatrically self-conscious of O'Neill's plays, with *Long Day's Journey,* for which *Misbegotten* is a kind of epilogue, also highly metatheatrical. Of course, it is not surprising that O'Neill's autobiographical family plays should contain many references to the theater. We are, after all, dealing with the family of a famous actor who is proud of his profession if not the choices he has made within that profession, an actor whose profession dictated the life-style of his family, for worse or better. It is natural that James Tyrone should quote from Shakespeare in *Long Day's Journey,* that his sons, in revolt against father, should mock or change the quotations, that his sons—one an actor, the other the future dramatist writing the play—should *think* in terms of theater. For example, Edmund, we found, responds teasingly and spontaneously to his father's large gesture of turning on the bulbs: "That's a grand curtain." His father, just as naturally, carries on the idea: "That's right, laugh at the old fool! The poor old ham! But the final curtain will be in the poorhouse just the same, and that's not comedy!" Here, as throughout *Long Day's Journey,* the male members of the family are conscious of the roles they play, the quotations they recite, the theatrical gestures they make, even the dramatic genres within which they place their gestures. It is precisely because the family is so vitally connected to theater that the metatheatrical dimension does not seem so self-conscious as Shakespeare's theater allusions, which, in fact, often break the illusion of theater. O'Neill does not break the illusion in *Long Day's Journey,* but he is toying with the idea. In *Misbegotten,* however, O'Neill is most metatheatrical, forcing his audience to see theater as theater even as he uses theater to depict the "truth" about life.[19]

O'Neill's last play contains many references to acting, staging, theatrics in general; it moves from comic vaudeville to a tragic confessional and a sacred Pietà scene. It has as its protagonist an actor, but here in *Misbegotten* Jim Tyrone calls more attention to his "ham actor" status than in *Long Day's Journey.* Throughout he considers himself "a third-rate ham," but his agonizing contempt for himself as an actor—"Once a ham, always a ham!"—is most deeply felt when he puts on a show for those who expect him to display grief for his dead mother:

> So I put on an act. I flopped on my knees and hid my face in my hands and faked some sobs and cried, "Mama! Mama! My dear mother!" But all the time I kept saying to myself, "You lousy ham! You God-damned lousy ham! (3:931)

Jim, Josie, and Phil Hogan play many roles during the course of the play. When Phil tells Josie—significantly, after she tells how, as a young girl, Hogan dressed her up to meet James Tyrone, "a true Irish gentleman" and a "rich and famous" actor, in order to "soften his heart" before Tyrone asked for the rent money—when Phil tells Josie, "You should have gone on the stage," he is speaking about the three actors in *Misbegotten.* They are all "on the stage" because they wear many masks and perform many parts *and* because they are on the stage now as they speak, and O'Neill wants us to be aware of this. Josie is the most versatile actor on stage because she can play virgin and whore and lover and mother and daughter, some of them against her instinctive nature. When she most wants to be a lover, for example, filled with sexual desire for Jim, she must play the role of mother, subduing her desire for the man in order to become mother to the boy—and eventually playing not just mother but her most important role, Holy Mother in a Pietà scene. That she plays the role so well is a tribute to her love and understanding. Phil Hogan, as Raleigh observes, is "a consummate actor, switching his roles easily and rapidly." Raleigh, believing that *Misbegotten,* in addition to pronouncing "a benediction on Jamie O'Neill," furthers "the absolution of his father," clearly identifies Hogan with James O'Neill.[20] Certainly an important reason for such an identification, added to his peasant vitality and Irish nationalism and whiskey drinking, is Hogan's role playing, his ability as an actor.

Jim Tyrone, as we saw, despises himself for being a ham and shrewdly observes himself while playing his roles. He is his own most alert audience, observing and criticizing. Nowhere is this more evident than in act 4 when O'Neill has Jim "(... *face the east, where the sky is now glowing with all the colors of an exceptionally beautiful sunrise. He stares, drawing a deep breath. He is profoundly moved but immediately becomes self-conscious and tries to sneer it off—cynically*) God seems to be putting on quite a display. I like Belasco better. Rise of curtain, act-Four stuff. (*Her face has fallen into lines of bitter hurt, but he adds quickly and angrily*) God damn it! Why do I have to pull that lousy stuff? (*with genuine deep feeling*) God, it's beautiful, Josie! I—I'll never forget it—here with you" (3:942). Jim, talking about God's display, is reminding us that the theater technician is in charge of the stage magic. Playing his role as drunken cynic, Jim prefers Belasco, the great showman of the American theater at the turn of the century, to that other showman God, and he reminds us—for a moment breaking the illusion that realistic drama wishes to create—that we are *in* act 4 of a play, an artifice that gave us effective stage moonlight in act 3 and is giving us effective stage sunrise in this act, now. But then the "real" Jim (who is still an actor in a play but no longer seems to be acting), observing the Jim who *plays* the cynic, relents, and the deep feeling of his utterance, "God, it's beautiful, Josie!" brings us back to reality, to the truth of things, with God—here, perfectly placed by O'Neill—no longer a Belasco, and with Josie the presence that makes the moment beautiful and memorable. This is a precious stage moment, all the more precious because O'Neill, like Shakespeare before him, plays with the ideas of illusion and reality, theater and life, forcing an audience to confront both the distinction between the two and the lack of distinction.

After the first two acts, which offer unabashed Irish comic realism, *A Moon for the Misbegotten* glows with artifice even as it presents the genuine agony of two souls caught in moonlight and sunrise. The artifice—or, rather, O'Neill's calling attention to the artifice—perhaps is O'Neill's way of revealing to the audience and to himself that what happened to Jim Tyrone in *Misbegotten*, his last play, is make-believe, a lie, as much a wish fulfillment as the comedy that began his second career, *Ah, Wilderness!* As if *Long Day's Journey*, that seering play that makes you feel the pressure of autobiography, *needs* an epilogue that allows artifice to temper biography, to change tragedy into something else—not the comedy that *Ah, Wilderness!* is, but the tragicomedy that *Misbegotten* is, offering a final blessing to his brother and the rest of the family. After his tragedies, Shakespeare could not return to the kind of comedy we have in *As You Like It* and *Twelfth Night;* he wrote the kind of comedy we have in *The Winter's Tale* and *The Tempest,* his tragicomedies. Perhaps Shakespeare, like O'Neill, had to temper his tragic vision without erasing it, had to transcend the terror and offer his own final blessings. For O'Neill we know the facts; for Shakespeare we can only speculate, allowing the plays to give us the man. But both dramatists, in their last efforts, write plays that seem profoundly self-conscious, plays that belong to a genre that blends tragedy and comedy. Both seem, in these last plays, to be more intensely interested in exploring the relationship of artifice to reality, with artifice reflecting reality even as it calls attention to itself as artifice. For a moment in time a dead man lying against a woman's breast under stage moonlight finds salvation. For a moment a statue comes alive, and the woman, the real woman (as "real" as an actress can be when playing a part), flesh and blood, is more miraculous than the remarkable piece of sculpture, although the "statue" was necessary for the true appreciation of the "woman." For a time, three hours, an island experience, magical, containing earthy creatures and airy spirits, leads to reconciliations and the finding of self before a return to a world that is neither brave nor new—but a world that will be experienced anew because of that island experience. Artifice, art, play, refreshes life in these last plays even when the dramatists want us to be aware of play as play, even though life means thoughts of death. O'Neill may not have had Shakespeare's last plays consciously in mind while he was writing *Misbegotten*, but the resemblances—and these, we noticed, include, in addition to the metatheatrical dimension, the blending of the tragic and comic, the movement of tragedy toward comedy, the tonal similarities, the Christian analogues and trappings, the mother-child relationships, both the misogyny and the identification of woman as nurturing and divine—the resemblances tease me into thinking that Shakespeare was not too far from O'Neill's mind.

I am on firmer ground, of course, when confronting the three specific Shakespeare allusions in *Misbegotten:* a reference to Hamlet in act 4, a quotation from *Othello* in act 3, a phrase from *Cymbeline* in act 2. In all three instances Jim Tyrone, appropriately, is the speaker; he, we noticed in *Long Day's Journey*, often had Shakespeare on his lips. He delivers two of the allusions in a mocking tone, reminiscent of his tone in *Long Day's Journey*. The one straightforward reference, almost given as a piece of information, said neutrally, is when he mentions Hamlet in act 4. Josie is helping him recall the night before, "the romance of the moon." She tells him he was "mostly quiet and sad—in a kind of daze, as if the moon was in your wits as well as whiskey" (3:941). Jim then says:

> I remember I was having a grand time at the Inn, celebrating with Phil, and then suddenly, for no reason, all the fun went out of it, and I was

more melancholy than ten Hamlets. (*He pauses.*) Hope I didn't tell you the sad story of my life and weep on your bosom, Josie. (3:942)

Jim is melancholy, so the reference to Hamlet comes easily and naturally to mind. We feel none of the bitterness and anguish that his "The Mad Scene. Enter Ophelia!" revealed. The bitterness is gone because he has already made his confession; he has told his "sad story" and wept on his "mother's" bosom. He is calm; his misogyny is muted. But he remains a Hamlet figure, as he was in *Long Day's Journey,* Oedipally connected to mother. Even his evenings with the blond whore—his revenge on mother—is, on the deepest level, evenings with his mother. Notice that his mother's body in the coffin, "with her face made up," looked "young and pretty like someone I remembered meeting long ago." (Do we catch an echo of Hamlet's "Let her paint an inch thick . . . "?) The "blonde pig," also made up, had "a face like an overgrown doll." Jim thought that sleeping with her would make him forget his mother "in the baggage car ahead." But, of course, as Jim says, he "didn't seem to want to forget." The whore was mother, and the virginal Josie, who played whore, is also mother. And only when Jim comes to terms with mother is he able to die in peace. In *Misbegotten,* as in *Long Day's Journey,* Jim Tyrone is a tortured Hamlet, world-weary, cynical, thinking of death and whores and mother. But in O'Neill's last play, purely a wish fulfillment, as I have suggested, the Jamie Tyrone of *Long Day's Journey,* that play's most lost character, the most dead corpse in the house he calls a morgue, becomes the Jim Tyrone who receives benediction, who goes gentle into that good night.

Josie's suggestion to Jim, just before his reference to Hamlet, that "the moon was in your wits" directly points back to the quotation from *Othello* "*he recites mockingly*" toward the end of act 3.

> It is the very error of the moon:
> She comes more nearer earth than she was wont,
> And makes men mad.
>
> (3:933)

Jim had just confessed that he slept with the blond whore for revenge on his mother, that he kept hearing the last two lines of "a lousy tear-jerker song"—"And baby's cries can't waken her / In the baggage coach ahead"—that he was too drunk to go to his mother's funeral. Josie is repulsed by what she hears, but then her "*horror*" ebbs as "*her love and protective compassion*" return. Jim also displays mixed emotions, as he says: "She'd understand and forgive me, don't you think? She always did. She was simple and kind and pure of heart. She was beautiful. You're like her deep in your heart. That's why I told you. I thought—(*Abruptly his expression becomes sneering and cynical—harshly*) My mistake. Nuts! Forget it. Time I got a move on. I don't like your damned moon, Josie. It's an ad for the past" (3:932). He then recites the *Othello* quotation. Genuine feeling abruptly changes to cynicism, just as later, cynicism—"Act-Four stuff"—will abruptly turn to genuine feeling—"God, it's beautiful, Josie!" In act 4, as we already noticed, the stage light produces sunrise; here in act 3 the stage light is the moon, the play's most important prop and symbol. Josie and Jim meet under moonlight, as lovers traditionally do. But this is a moon for the misbegotten. For Jim the moon is a "damned moon," "an ad for the past," and, of course, it is the past, a tortured past, that Jim had confronted in his confession to Josie, a story told, O'Neill insists in his stage directions, while Jim is staring into the moonlight. At the moment that he recites the quotation he feels the confession had no result, that Josie will not forgive him, that he made a mistake in revealing his agony to her. The quotation, therefore, is an appropriate comment on what has just happened on stage. Jim feels it was a kind of madness in him to make the confession, or a kind of madness to think that he could be forgiven. In order to make the connection between moon and madness, Jim goes to Shakespeare and, as he did in *Long Day's Journey,* he offers a quotation that shimmers with implications. The *Othello* quotation forces Shakespeare's play into the dramatic context of *Misbegotten,* and the first observation to make is that Jim is quoting Othello himself, not Iago, the character he quoted twice in *Long Day's Journey.* This suggests that the role of Jamie Tyrone changed when he became the Tyrone of *Misbegotten.* O'Neill is now concentrating on his brother as tragic hero or tragic victim, not as the poisonous corrupter, the Mephistopheles, of the previous play. By quoting Othello, Jim is clearly connected to his father—also "Tyrone"—who played Othello so brilliantly that he received praise from Booth. (This adds further support to the idea that O'Neill wrote his play as a benediction to his brother *and* to his father, who share many qualities in *Misbegotten.*) The Othello who presents the quoted lines in Shakespeare's play had just killed Desdemona, the pure wife he believes to be a whore. Jim Tyrone is obsessed with the death of his mother, whom he connects to the whore on the train. Revenge is the motive for the actions of both protagonists. Both men kill the women they love: Othello literally kills Desdemona, Jim indirectly kills his mother when she realizes he has returned to the bottle. Desdemona miraculously "returns" from death in order to absolve Othello of his crime—"A guiltless death I die . . . Commend me to my kind lord. O, farewell." Jim's mother "returns" from death in the person of Josie Hogan to forgive his sin. Both Othello and Jim Tyrone are self-dramatizers, and each seeks death at play's end. Othello kills himself, knowing he will be roasting in sulphur, going to hell; Jim walks toward the grave he will soon occupy, his tomb the womb of earth, a union with mother. The last, of course, is the difference between tragedy and tragicomedy.

Blaming planetary influence for the behavior of men, Othello invests great power in the moon's ability to make men mad, especially when it comes "nearer" the earth. Shakespeare wants us to think of Othello's madness here, the madness of killing Desdemona, presented in a scene of both love and death, with Othello kissing his wife before he kills her and himself dying upon a kiss as he joins her in the bed they shared. The moon always seems nearer the earth when lovers meet; in *Othello* the moon also seems nearer when lovers kill, thereby coloring the *liebestod* idea with the brush of madness. Shakespeare had already told us about lovers and madmen in *A Midsummer Night's Dream*, another moon play but a pure romantic comedy. In *Othello*, a tragedy, the moon brings madness and death. In *Misbegotten*, a tragicomedy, the moon again seems nearer the earth, producing another kind of madness, in fact, producing a miracle related to love and death. As a conventional symbol and stage prop, the moon had been exploited by O'Neill throughout his career, beginning with the early sea play, *The Moon of the Caribees*, in which the moon represented love for Smitty, produced a kind of madness in the sailors, and, when connected to the chant, evoked death and mystery for all, including the audience. The moon acquires every dimension of significance in O'Neill's last play, its importance highlighted by its presence in the title.

As we have already observed, O'Neill took great care in selecting the titles of his plays. Originally, *A Moon for the Misbegotten* was called "The Man of Other Days" or "The Moon of Other Days." Judith Barlow reads the manuscript words as the latter, Virginia Floyd as the former.[21] Floyd's reading suggests that O'Neill wanted Jim Tyrone as the main character with the play concentrating on the revelation of his guilt. Barlow's reading gives the moon the important emphasis, although it's difficult to understand exactly what "The Moon of Other Days" means in relation to the play. (Was a former moon worse or better than this one? Is that former moon ever mentioned in the play? Is it the "other days" of the moon or of the main characters?) O'Neill's next title, "The Moon Bore Twins," gives equal status to Jim Tyrone and Josie Hogan as main characters; it also includes the moon, which metaphorically gives birth to Jim and Josie. In O'Neill's work notes, we hear Josie tell Jim that the two of them were "born of the sadness of beauty . . . in the dark night."[22] These words do not appear in the final version of the play, but in the final version, as we saw, "a virgin" bore "a dead child in the night," connecting moon and virgin and mother. This title is functional and interesting, but somewhat awkward. Then the play's title was changed to "Moon of the Misbegotten," the "of" suggesting that the moon belongs to Jim and Josie, that it was *their* moon, and also introducing the important idea of misbegotten for the first time. Now *misbegotten* invites many interpretations,[23] including some emphasis on the physical—Josie being "*so oversize for a woman that she is almost a freak*" (3:857)—but most important, I believe, is that the word suggests that Jim and Josie were born doomed, that fate played the main part in their birth, that they were "star-cross'd lovers." Then came "Moon for the Misbegotten," which indicates that the misbegotten are being served by the moon, that it doesn't belong to them, as the previous title suggested, but that it is given to them, a gift that they can use or appreciate. The "A" is added to the final version of the title, perhaps suggesting it is just one moon among many possible moons. And many moons *are* possible, or, to put it another way, the moon offers many possibilities of interpretation in *A Moon for the Misbegotten*. Traditionally connected with romantic love, the moon has shed its light on many a lover in story and play. (Recall the adolescent Richard and Muriel spooning under moonlight in *Ah, Wilderness!*) In *Misbegotten* the lovers Jim and Josie meet in moonlight, Josie anticipating a night of sexual love. At the same time, the moon represents different kinds of femininity. It is the chaste moon that we associate with Diana, "the cold fruitless moon" that we encounter in *A Midsummer Night's Dream,* the wanton inconstant moon that Juliet would rather Romeo not swear by, the pale moon that brings peace and dreams (Jim's "*dissipated face looks like a pale mask in moonlight*" [3:927]), the moon of another side of Diana who, chaste though she is, remains the goddess of childbirth, a universal mother (Josie is both "chaste" and "mother"), the moon of Christianity that represents the Virgin Mary (Josie again, the sympathetic listener to Jim's confession, feeling the presence of Jim's mother "in the moonlight, her soul wrapped in it like a silver mantle" [3:933]). In addition it is, of course, the moon of madness, the *luna* of lunacy, that causes strange behavior, like murdering a pure wife, as we witness in *Othello,* like miraculous forgiveness, as we witness in *Misbegotten*. It is a powerful entity, the moon, controlling men's behavior even as it controls the tides, its light shedding love and forgiveness and peace and revery *and* penetrating men's imaginations to make them mad. It may be treated mockingly, as when Jim Tyrone rejects moonlight in favor of "one light on Broadway," as when Josie talks of "the silly mug of the moon grinning down" on her and Jim—despite all of its feminine associations, the moon at times is masculine, the man in the moon a kind of joke—but finally the moon's sheer beauty and mystery and power, the heavy pressure of its traditional associations, have to be acknowledged. Moonlight bathes the climax of O'Neill's last play, O'Neill exploiting every aspect of its significance. Jim Tyrone's quotation from *Othello* adds to the importance of the moon even as it allows Shakespeare's tragedy to enter O'Neill's tragicomedy with a rich suggestiveness.

The play's first Shakespeare allusion occurs in moonlight close to the end of act 2. This, like the quotation from *Othello*, is said "*mockingly*" by Jim, and it is directly connected to a specific quotation from Keats. The exact sequence of presentation is importantly relevant to my thesis. Phil Hogan has just left Josie and Jim alone, and as he recedes from the scene he sings a "*mournful Irish song*"—"Oh, the praties they grow small, Over here, over here"—which "*continues to be heard at intervals*" for a few minutes. Josie leads Jim to the steps of her bedroom with these words: "Come on now and we'll sit on my bedroom steps and be romantic in the moonlight, like we planned to" (3:908). Sitting on the top step, with Jim on the step beneath her, "*she puts her arms around him and draws him back till his head is on her breast.*" Jim closes his eyes; Josie stares at his face "*with a passionate, possessive tenderness.*" Then, after a pause—O'Neill working effectively with pauses and silences in his last plays—we hear Hogan's "*mournful song*" drifting back "*through the moonlight quiet.*" Jim "*rouses himself*" and "*mockingly*" says: "Hark, Hark, the Donegal lark! 'Thou wast not born for death, immortal bird.' Can't Phil sing anything but that damned dirge, Josie?" When she doesn't reply, Jim "*goes on hazily*": "Still, it seems to belong tonight—in the moonlight—or in my mind." And then he quotes Keats:

> Now more than ever seems it rich to die,
> To cease upon the midnight with no pain,
> In such an ecstasy!

Having recited this "*with deep feeling,*" he then "*sneers*" and says, "Good God! Ode to Phil the Irish Nightingale! I must have the D.T.'s" (3:909). Notice here, as throughout this play and *Long Day's Journey*, Jim's quick changes of emotion and tone. The mocking tone is connected to the Shakespeare allusion—"Hark, Hark, the Donegal lark!"—and to the Keats line, "Thou wast not born for death, immortal bird." O'Neill does not put the Shakespeare phrase in quotation marks, indicating that the educated Jim Tyrone, very familiar with Shakespeare, realizes it is not a direct quotation. (The same, we remember, was true of his "The Mad Scene. Enter Ophelia!") The Keats line, a direct quotation, *is* in quotation marks. The Shakespeare phrase comes from *Cymbeline*, the second of Shakespeare's four late tragicomedies, specifically from a song that belongs to an "aubade" tradition, a morning or dawn serenade of a lover, in this case sung by Cloten, the villain and fool, asking Imogen to arise from bed:

> Hark, hark, the lark at heaven's gate sings,
>   And Phoebus gins arise,
> His steeds to water at those springs
>   On chalic'd flow'rs that lies;
> And winking Mary-buds begin to ope
>   their golden eyes;
> With every thing that pretty is, my lady
>   sweet, arise:
>   Arise, arise!
>
> (2.3.20–26)

Jim is cleverly playing with Shakespeare's phrase, bringing in the Irish Hogan with "Donegal" not only because an Irishman is now singing a song but also because the song is an *Irish* song, an authentic Great Hunger song about potatoes, that Irish staple. The "here" of the song refers to Ireland, but it can also signify that Irish hardships continue here in America. (The song reminds us that James O'Neill, like Phil Hogan, comes from Irish peasant stock, both immigrants in a not-altogether-receptive country.) The lark, of course, is a morning bird, naturally connected with the aubade tradition, but one must wonder how appropriate the allusion is at this moment in *Misbegotten,* when moonlight bathes the stage—the sun will not rise until act 4—and when Hogan's song is referred to as a "dirge." Perhaps that is why Jim immediately quotes the Keats line, which gives us a night bird and which introduces death. Then, again, Jim was roused from his reverie when he heard Hogan's song, and the scene does feature lovers. And *Cymbeline,* like *The Winter's Tale* and *The Tempest* which come after it, is a play that gives us miraculous restorations and reconciliations, so that in this respect too it has a connection to *Misbegotten.* Still, Jim's quick switch from lark to nightingale must give us pause. Perhaps it's a natural sequence, going from one bird to another, from lark to nightingale, and going from one poet to the next, from Shakespeare to Keats. What is striking, however, is the mocking tone connected with the lark and with the first mention of the nightingale, and then the *"deep feeling"* connected with the nightingale when Jim continues to quote from Keats, until Jim catches himself, sneers, and, as is his wont, makes a cynical remark about his own genuine feelings. The Keats quotation touches Jim's heart's core; it is the key to understanding his attitude toward death. Sleeping with his head on Josie's breast, in a state of peaceful contentment, with death belonging to moonlight and mind, he is roused by a sad song, he mockingly alludes to a dawn song and a morning bird, quickly switches to the bird and quotation that come closer to his genuine feelings, feelings connected with love and death, dying in ecstasy, "now." I wish to suggest that in moving so quickly from Shakespeare to Keats, Jim Tyrone does not leave Shakespeare behind, and, in fact, that Shakespeare directs the move from lark to nightingale.

Where, we may wish to ask, do we have the most memorable dramatic treatment of the aubade idea? Few would disagree that act 3, scene 5 of *Romeo and Juliet* presents the idea in its most exquisite form. Romeo and Juliet have only one night of wedded love, and when morning comes Romeo, having been banished, must part from Juliet. The scene begins with the sound of a bird and then Juliet's words:

Wilt thou be gone? it is not yet near day.
It was the nightingale, and not the lark,
That pierc'd the fearful hollow of thine ear;
Nightly she sings on yond pomegranate tree.
Believe me, love, it was the nightingale.

(3.5.1–5)

Romeo knows his bird sounds, it seems: "It was the lark, the herald of the morn / No nightingale." It is morning, and he must leave his love if he wants to live. Juliet, wanting her lover to remain, insists, "Yond light is not day-light, I know it, I." Romeo, quickly deciding to remain with Juliet, changes his mind—"Come, death, and welcome!"—causing Juliet to change *her* mind: "Hie hence, be gone, away! / It is the lark that sings so out of tune, / Straining harsh discords and unpleasing sharps." A remarkable give-and-take, a fresh variation on the aubade, perfectly capturing the urgency and poignancy of young love. As Romeo is descending from the balcony, Juliet has a premonition of death; she sees him "as one dead in the bottom of a tomb. / Either my eyesight fails, or thou lookest pale" (3.5.56–57). This is the last time the lovers are together before they both die in the Capulet tomb.

I believe that this scene from *Romeo and Juliet* exerts pressure on O'Neill's lark-nightingale scene in *Misbegotten*, perhaps without O'Neill being aware of it. The allusion to the lark of the morning song in *Cymbeline* naturally brings to mind the lark in the dramatic treatment of the aubade in Shakespeare's young tragedy. Jim's switch from lark to nightingale echoes the switch from one bird to the other in Shakespeare. That the Shakespeare scene contains lovers who must part after their only night of love, that it contains the idea that death is "welcome," that it even presents a lover who is "pale" with death and an image of morning as "the pale reflex of Cynthia's brow"—these give added weight to my suggestion that there is a clear relationship between the quoted phrase from *Cymbeline* and the scene in *Romeo and Juliet*. And Shakespeare's nightingale sings the same song and evokes some of the same emotions as Keats's nightingale. Jim Tyrone's move from Shakespeare to Keats is no great leap of the imagination. Keats is the most "Shakespearean" of the Romantic poets, having been influenced by Shakespeare in almost every poem he wrote, and strongly influenced in *Ode to a Nightingale*.[24] I am suggesting that Shakespeare is absorbed by O'Neill even in O'Neill's taste for Keats. Jim Tyrone's genuinely deep feelings when he recites the lines from Keats's *Ode to a Nightingale* stems, in part, from Jim's (and O'Neill's) closeness to Shakespeare's Hamlet. Jonathan Bate asserts that the ode is "haunted by the language of *Hamlet*," from the first phrase—"My heart aches"—to the "Adieu"s of the last stanza.[25] Jim goes to stanzas 6 and 7 for his Keats quotations. His first quotation, the first line of stanza 7—"Thou wast not born for death, immortal bird"—needs no discussion; it is said in the same mocking tone as "Hark, Hark, the Donegal lark!" But stanza 6 deserves some attention. It directly reflects Jim Tyrone, and more than Jim Tyrone. Jim's three lines of quotation come from the stanza's middle. Interestingly, it is not an accurate quotation in that it omits a line. Keats gives us this:

> Now more than ever seems it rich to die,
> To cease upon the midnight with no pain,
> While thou art pouring forth thy soul abroad
> In such an ecstasy.

Jim omits "While thou art pouring forth thy soul abroad," perhaps because O'Neill didn't remember that the line should be there, but more likely because he wanted the "ecstasy" to be Jim's, not the nightingale's; he wanted the ecstasy to depend solely on what is happening now onstage— Jim held by Josie, his head against her breast. The time of death, that is, *when* one dies, is important to Keats in his poem and to O'Neill in writing his play about the death of his brother. Both the poet and Jim want to die at the moment of greatest happiness, for Keats sensuous happiness, listening to the nightingale sing in such an ecstasy, for Jim peaceful happiness in the arms of a forgiving "mother." Both Keats's poet and Jim Tyrone desire death—true for Hamlet too, and for Edmund Tyrone in *Long Day's Journey*. Here the lines in Keats's stanza 6 that *precede* the quoted words prove interesting:

Darkling I listen; and, for many a time
I have been half in love with easeful Death,
Called him soft names in many a mused rhyme,
To take into the air my quiet breath.

The Hamletian Keats of this remarkable ode offers reflections on mortality throughout. Mourning becomes him, as it does O'Neill and those characters in his plays, especially the late autobiographical plays, who seem to represent him, like Edmund and Jamie (and Jim) Tyrone. The connection between the poet's "I have been half in love with easeful death" and Edmund's insistence that he "must always be a little in love with death" seems more than merely coincidental. Whether or not O'Neill is conscious of such connections, we do not know. But we do know that his mind is filled with thoughts of death, that—perhaps stemming from such thoughts—the play *Hamlet* has always exerted pressure on his creative imagination, that the ghost of Shakespeare hovers close by (even as the portrait of Shakespeare hangs in the Tyrone living room), that here in *A Moon for the Misbegotten* the Romantic poet who is closest to Shakespeare, who offers an ode filled with Hamletian thoughts and echoes, provides O'Neill with an important quotation that allows us to penetrate Jim Tyrone's deepest self. Jim is always listening "darkling"—a Shakespeare word!—attentive to the moment that will bring him easeful death, a moment that is approaching because he is *now* in position (Pietà), the now when death will be most "welcome" (to use the word from the aubade scene in *Romeo and Juliet*), when death is an ecstasy. In this connection I catch one other Shakespeare echo, coming from *Othello,* the play that will provide Jim Tyrone with the important direct quotation on the moon and madness in the next act. When Othello meets Desdemona in Cyprus after the storm—in the scene already examined when I discussed Jamie Tyrone's "The Moor! I know his trumpet"—he is ecstatic and expresses himself this way: "If it were now to die, / 'Twere now to be most happy." *When* one dies, the now of death for Shakespeare and Keats and O'Neill, is an idea that haunts the three writers and binds them. At the least, it speaks for what we call "tradition," the notion of continuity or influence flowing from one writer to the next, whether consciously or not. Certainly, as I have suggested here and throughout, a thread connects O'Neill to Shakespeare (and in *Misbegotten* to Keats, himself connected to Shakespeare). Whether or not the thread is subliminal, whenever O'Neill appropriates Shakespeare his drama becomes deeper and richer.

It was imperative that O'Neill write *A Moon for the Misbegotten* in order to relieve himself of the dark thoughts, the tragic terror, that we found in his family tragedy, *Long Day's Journey Into Night*. In his tragicomedy he not only allows us to hear echoes from the plays of Shakespeare, the dramatist who has always been with him and always been a part of his family, but in the *writing* of this tragicomedy—which becomes his last play—O'Neill follows the pattern of Shakespeare's development. Shakespeare ends his career with plays that emphasize reconciliation and restoration, always acknowledging the darkness of truth, the power of death and determinism, but allowing that knowledge to be absorbed by a more generous vision, perhaps a vision impossible to contemplate without the help of miracle and magic. To the very end of his career, Shakespeare remains with O'Neill. Shakespeare's words, his characters, his conventions, his methods of presentation, his tragic vision, his emphasis on family, his compassion for mankind, the curve of his development—all become part of O'Neill's lifeblood. And Shakespeare was a member of the family when O'Neill was growing up in his father's house. I have no doubt that Shakespeare was a major unacknowledged influence on O'Neill. I like to think that I have demonstrated that the word *influence* is more than quotation and allusion and imitation and inspiration, all of which it includes. *Influence* points to an organic relationship. One writer *flows into* the other, as the word suggests, infuses the other. So that the title of this book, *O'Neill's Shakespeare,* points to the Shakespeare that O'Neill *uses* in his dramatic art, but it also suggests that O'Neill *contains* Shakespeare. As Iago says to Othello at the end of the temptation scene, but with better results: "I am your own for ever."

Notes

Introduction

1. Peter Brook, *The Empty Space* (New York: Avon, 1969), 87.
2. Marjorie Garber, *Shakespeare's Ghost Writers* (New York: Methuen, 1987), 176.
3. *Selected Letters of Eugene O'Neill*, ed. Travis Bogard and Jackson R. Bryer (New Haven: Yale University Press, 1988), 24.
4. Quoted in Ulrich Halfmann, *Eugene O'Neill: Comments on the Drama and the Theater* (Tübingen: Narr, 1987), xxvii.
5. Harold Bloom, *The Anxiety of Influence: A Theory of Poetry* (New York: Oxford University Press, 1973).
6. Bloom, *Anxiety*, 91.
7. Bloom, *Anxiety*, 96.
8. Bloom, *Anxiety*, 76.
9. Bloom, *Anxiety*, 31.
10. Roland Barthes, *Mythologies* (London: Paladin, 1972).
11. Eric Bentley, *Thinking About the Playwright* (Evanston Ill.: Northwestern University Press, 1987), 302.
12. Francis Fergusson, *The Idea of a Theater* (New York: Doubleday, 1949), 239.
13. Bert O. States, *Great Reckonings in Little Rooms* (Berkeley and Los Angeles: University of California Press, 1985), 82.
14. *Samuel Johnson on Shakespeare*, ed. W. K. Wimsatt, Jr. (New York: Hill and Wang, 1960), 25.
15. Norman Rabkin, *Shakespeare and the Common Understanding* (New York: Free Press, 1967), 18. Rabkin footnotes Claude Levi-Strauss, *Tristes Tropiques* (New York, 1961).
16. Stephen Greenblatt, *Shakespearean Negotiations* (Berkeley and Los Angeles: University of California Press, 1988), vii.

Chapter 1

1. The statement is found in the playbill O'Neill wrote for the Provincetown Players' production of Strindberg's *The Spook Sonata*, 3 January 1924.
2. *Bound East for Cardiff* in Eugene O'Neill, *Complete Plays 1913–1920*, 195. All quotations from O'Neill's plays will come from the three-volume *Complete Plays*,

edited by Travis Bogard, published by the Library of America, New York, 1988. Citations will appear in the body of the book, specifying volume number and page number. Volume 1 contains the plays from 1913–20; volume 2 1920–31; volume 3 1932–43.

3. This important statement is found in a letter O'Neill wrote to Arthur Hobson Quinn. It was first published in Quinn's *A History of the American Drama,* vol. 2, 1945. It is reprinted in Oscar Cargill, N. Bryllion Fagin, and William J. Fisher, eds., *O'Neill and His Plays* (New York: New York University Press, 1961), 125, hereafter cited as Cargill, *O'Neill and His Plays.*

4. The metaphorical nature of Shakespeare's theater is brilliantly discussed in States, *Great Reckonings* 56–63.

5. All references to Shakespeare's plays will come from *The Riverside Shakespeare,* ed. G. Blakemore Evans (Boston: Houghton Mifflin, 1974). References are to act, scene, and line.

6. Louis Sheaffer, *O'Neill: Son and Playwright* (Boston: Little, Brown, 1968), 430–31.

7. Michael Manheim, *Eugene O'Neill's New Language of Kinship* (Syracuse: Syracuse University Press, 1982), 18.

8. C. L. Barber and Richard Wheeler, *The Whole Journey: Shakespeare's Power of Development* (Berkeley and Los Angeles: University of California Press, 1986), 39–47.

9. On kinship in O'Neill see Manheim, *New Language of Kinship* and Bennett Simon, *Tragic Drama and the Family* (New Haven: Yale University Press, 1988), 177–211.

Chapter 2

1. Louis Sheaffer, *O'Neill: Son and Artist* (Boston: Little, Brown, 1973), 28.

2. Travis Bogard, *Contour in Time: The Plays of Eugene O'Neill* (New York: Oxford University Press, 1972), 136–37.

3. Sheaffer, *Artist,* 28.

4. For example, John Shand, in an otherwise negative review, applauds Robeson: "Mr. Robeson's voice, intelligence, physique, and sense of the stage immediately made me want to see him in *Othello.*" "The Emperor Jones," *The New Statesman,* 19 September 1925, 628–29.

5. Martin B. Duberman, *Paul Robeson* (New York: Knopf, 1988), 278.

6. Sheaffer, *Artist,* 35.

7. Sheaffer, *Artist,* 37.

8. Duberman, *Paul Robeson,* 588.

9. Duberman, *Paul Robeson,* 622.

10. Duberman, *Paul Robeson,* 274.

11. Duberman, *Paul Robeson,* 275.

12. In *Eugene O'Neill* (New York: St. Martin's, 1982), 64–69, I discuss the differences between *Jones* and *Ape,* offering the opinion that *Ape* is America's first existential tragedy and first important play of social criticism.

13. See Sheaffer, *Artist,* 134–44, and Duberman, *Paul Robeson,* 57–67.

14. Duberman, *Paul Robeson,* 64.

15. Sheaffer, *Artist*, 135.
16. Ludwig Lewisohn, "All God's Chillun," *Nation*, 4 June 1924, 664.
17. See Sheaffer, *Artist*, 118; Arthur and Barbara Gelb, *O'Neill* (New York: Harper and Row, 1962), 534–35; and Manheim, *New Language of Kinship*, 30–34.
18. Sheaffer, *Artist*, 118.
19. Sheaffer, *Artist*, 119.
20. Philip C. Kolin, "*All God's Chillun Got Wings* and *Macbeth*," *The Eugene O'Neill Newsletter*, 12 (Spring 1988): 55–61.
21. T.S. Eliot, review of *All God's Chillun*, reprinted in Cargill, *O'Neill and his Plays*, 169.
22. This idea is convincingly discussed in Barber and Wheeler, *Whole Journey*, 13 and passim.

Chapter 3

1. See Bogard, *Contour*, 200–203, for a fine discussion of O'Neill's possible indebtedness to Sidney Howard.
2. Sheaffer, *Artist*, 174.
3. Sheaffer, *Artist*, 190.
4. Sheaffer, *Artist*, 174.
5. Ernest Jones, *Hamlet and Oedipus* (New York: Doubleday, 1949), 118.
6. Barber and Wheeler, *Whole Journey*, 238.
7. Sheaffer, *Artist*, 130.
8. Emil Roy, "O'Neill's *Desire* and Shakespeare's *King Lear*," *Neueren Sprachen* 65 (1966): 1–6.
9. The phrase is Philip Weissman's, cited in Gelbs, *O'Neill*, 538.
10. I am indebted to C. L. Barber's provocative observations on this idea in Barber and Wheeler, *Whole Journey*, 291–97.
11. Kenneth Muir, "The Singularity of Shakespeare," in *Shakespeare: Pattern of Excelling Nature*, ed. David Bevington and Jay L. Halio (Newark: University of Delaware Press, 1978), 74.
12. Every discussion of Shakespeare's complementarity is indebted, as mine is, to Rabkin's *Shakespeare and the Common Understanding*.
13. Jean Howard, *Shakespeare's Art of Orchestration* (Urbana: University of Illinois Press, 1984), 53.
14. The idea is found in O'Neill's "Memoranda on Masks," in Cargill, *O'Neill and His Plays*, 121.
15. Ronald H. Wainscott, *Staging O'Neill* (New Haven: Yale University Press, 1988), 165.
16. Wainscott, *Staging O'Neill*, 161.
17. Kenneth Macgowan, *The Theatre of Tomorrow* (New York: Boni and Liveright, 1921), 248.
18. Leonard Chabrowe, *Ritual and Pathos—The Theater of O'Neill* (Lewisburg: Bucknell University Press, 1976), 20.
19. Cargill, *O'Neill and His Plays*, 126.
20. Cargill, *O'Neill and His Plays*, 121.
21. Macgowan, *Theatre of Tomorrow*, 243.

22. Robert K. Sarlos, *Jig Cook and the Provincetown Players* (Amherst: University of Massachusetts Press, 1982), 124.
23. Bogard, *Contour*, 266–67.
24. Cargill, *O'Neill and His Plays*, 116.
25. Bogard, *Contour*, 307.
26. Peter Egri, *The Birth of American Tragedy* (Budapest: Tankonyvkiado, 1988), 72.
27. Sheaffer, *Playwright*, 277.
28. Bernard Beckerman, *Dynamics of Drama* (New York: Knopf, 1970), 125.
29. Frederic I. Carpenter, *Eugene O'Neill* (Boston: Twayne, 1979), 120.
30. Bogard, *Contour*, 301.
31. Manheim, *New Language of Kinship*, 61.
32. Sheaffer, *Artist*, 306.
33. Virginia Floyd, *Eugene O'Neill at Work* (New York: Frederick Ungar, 1981), 143.
34. Sheaffer, *Artist*, 463.
35. Gelbs, *O'Neill*, 698.
36. "The Theatre We Worked For," ed. Jackson R. Bryer (New Haven: Yale University Press, 1982), 190
37. Work Diary, in *Eugene O'Neill: Three Plays*, ed. Normand Berlin (London: Macmillan, 1989), 28.
38. Work Diary, 25.
39. *Selected Letters*, 350.
40. St. John Ervine, in Berlin, *Eugene O'Neill: Three Plays*, 74.
41. *Selected Letters*, 354.
42. Horst Frenz and Martin Mueller, "More Shakespeare and Less Aeschylus in Eugene O'Neill's *Mourning Becomes Electra*," *American Literature* 38 (March 1966): 85–100.
43. Manheim, *New Language of Kinship*, 79.
44. See Frederick Wilkins's "The Pressure of Puritanism in Eugene O'Neill's New England Plays," in *Eugene O'Neill: A World View*, ed. Virginia Floyd (New York: Frederick Ungar, 1979), 237–44.
45. The father-son relationship in *Hamlet*, as it reflects Shakespeare's personal family situation, is convincingly discussed in Barber and Wheeler, *Whole Journey*, 237–72.

Chapter 4

1. Floyd, *O'Neill at Work*, 240.
2. Bogard, *Contour*, 357.
3. Croswell Bowen, in Cargill, *O'Neill and His Plays*, 67.
4. Hamilton Basso, "The Tragic Sense," *New Yorker*, 6 March 1948, 46.
5. Sheaffer, *Playwright*, 101.
6. Gelbs, *O'Neill*, 762.
7. John H. Raleigh, *The Plays of Eugene O'Neill* (Carbondale: Southern Illinois University Press, 1965), 79–83; Bogard, *Contour*, 358–59.
8. Carpenter, *Eugene O'Neill*, 142.

9. I have presented these similarities and differences in *Eugene O'Neill*, 118–19.

10. The reactions of reviewers to *Ah, Wilderness!* are succinctly summarized in Jordan Y. Miller, *Eugene O'Neill and the American Critics* (Hamden, Conn.: Archon Books, 1973), 222–27.

11. *Selected Letters*, 204.

12. *Selected Letters*, 424.

13. C. L. Barber, *Shakespeare's Festive Comedy* (Princeton: Princeton University Press, 1959), 9.

14. See Raleigh's discussion of the songs in *Ah, Wilderness!* in *Plays of Eugene O'Neill*, 77–79.

15. Sheaffer, *Artist*, 405.

16. *Selected Letters*, 432.

17. Cargill, *O'Neill and His Plays*, 118.

18. *Selected Letters*, 433.

Chapter 5

1. Raleigh, *Plays of Eugene O'Neill*, 34–36.

2. Egri, *Birth of American Tragedy*, 114; Jean Chothia, *Forging a Language: A Study of the Plays of Eugene O'Neill* (Cambridge: Cambridge University Press, 1979), 225.

3. Barrett H. Clark, *Eugene O'Neill: The Man and His Plays* (New York: Dover, 1967), 162.

4. Gelbs, *O'Neill*, 938.

5. Bogard, *Contour*, 369.

6. Floyd, *O'Neill at Work*, 184.

7. Travis Bogard offers the clearest reconstruction of the cycle in *Contour*, 380–94. Peter Egri's account is admirably full in *Birth of American Tragedy*, 99–106.

8. *The Calms of Capricorn* (New Haven: Yale University Library) was published as a play by Donald Gallup in 1981. Volume 1 contains O'Neill's scenario "transcribed by Donald Gallup"; volume 2 contains the play "developed by Donald Gallup."

9. An interview with O'Neill by J. S. Wilson in *PM*, 3 September 1946, 18.

10. *Selected Letters*, 447.

11. Norman Rabkin, *Shakespeare and the Problem of Meaning* (Chicago: University of Chicago Press, 1981), 86.

12. Lawrence Stone, *The Family, Sex, and Marriage in England, 1500–1800* (New York: Harper, 1977).

13. Sheaffer, *Playwright*, 441.

14. I treat this idea more fully in *The Base String: The Underworld in Elizabethan Drama* (Rutherford: Fairleigh Dickinson University Press, 1968), 174–92.

15. Travis Bogard makes perceptive and lively use of the "mirror" idea throughout *Contour in Time*.

16. Manheim, *New Language of Kinship*, 106–7; Virginia Floyd, *The Plays of Eugene O'Neill* (New York: Frederick Ungar, 1985), 440–45.

17. Chothia, *Forging a Language*, 210.

18. Manheim succinctly articulates the autobiographical dimension of *Mansions* in *New Language of Kinship*, 118.

19. O'Neill's debt to his father's theater is convincingly discussed in John H. Raleigh's seminal essay, "Eugene O'Neill and the Escape from the Chateau d'If," in *O'Neill: A Collection of Critical Essays,* ed. John Gassner (Englewood Cliffs, N.J.: Prentice-Hall, 1964), 7–22.

20. Barber and Wheeler, *Whole Journey,* 40–56.

21. In *New Language of Kinship,* 118–19, Manheim pinpoints the important connection between Mary Tyrone and Deborah Harford.

Chapter 6

1. *Selected Letters,* 488.
2. *Selected Letters,* 510.
3. Gelbs, *O'Neill,* 831.
4. The biblical underpinning of the play is discussed by Cyrus Day, "The Iceman and the Bridegroom: Some Observations on the Death of O'Neill's Salesman," *Modern Drama* 1 (May 1958): 3–9.
5. Much of the following discussion of the Beckett-O'Neill connection can be found in my two journal articles: "The Beckettian O'Neill," *Modern Drama,* 31 (March 1988): 28–34, and "O'Neill and Comedy: *The Iceman Cometh,*" *Eugene O'Neill Newsletter,* 12 (Winter 1988): 3–8.
6. Robert Benchley, "All about *Strange Interlude,*" *Life,* 16 February 1928, 21.
7. J. George Frederick, *Vanity Fair,* January 1932, 46–7.
8. *Peter Hall's Diaries: The Story of a Dramatic Battle,* ed. John Goodwin (New York: Harper, 1984), 127.
9. Gelbs, *O'Neill,* 871.
10. My objection to Peter Brook's stage production of *King Lear* in 1961 is that he did not allow Shakespeare's inclusiveness to emerge. He dwelled on "nothing," on nothing but "nothing," making *King Lear* a less rich play than Shakespeare wrote. See my "Beckett and Shakespeare," *French Review* 40 (April 1967): 647–51.
11. The idea of "absence as presence" is effectively presented by Bette Mandl, "Absence as Presence: The Second Sex in *The Iceman Cometh,*" *Eugene O'Neill Newsletter* 6 (Summer-Fall 1982): 10–15. See also James A. Robinson, "Ghost Stories: *Iceman's* Absent Women and Mary Tyrone," *Eugene O'Neill Newsletter* 12 (Winter 1988): 14–19.
12. Winifred Frazer treats this important idea in *Love as Death in "The Iceman Cometh"* (Gainesville: University of Florida Press, 1967).
13. Sheaffer, *Artist,* 499–500.
14. Barber and Wheeler, *Whole Journey,* 19.
15. Barber and Wheeler, *Whole Journey,* 20.
16. Barber and Wheeler, *Whole Journey,* 13.
17. Barber and Wheeler, *Whole Journey,* 21.
18. Barber and Wheeler, *Whole Journey,* 32.
19. Eugene O'Neill, "A Dramatist's Notebook," *American Spectator,* January 1933, excerpted in Cargill, *O'Neill and His Plays,* 121.
20. Quoted in Halfmann, *Eugene O'Neill,* 1.
21. Quoted in Halfmann, *Eugene O'Neill,* xxvii.
22. Floyd, *O'Neill at Work,* 260.

23. Quoted in Halfmann, *Eugene O'Neill*, 147.

24. Sheaffer, *Artist*, 22.

25. Bennett Simon sees irony in the fact that the play is *Macbeth* "and the son 'murders' the lines" because Shakespeare's play is about "the murder of *dynastic* 'lines,'" with Macbeth doomed not to have children. For Simon this is "a painful subliminal reminder of how fragile is this father-son rapprochement" because the Tyrone family line will not be continuing. (*Tragic Drama and the Family*, 202).

26. Raleigh, *Plays of Eugene O'Neill*, 159.

27. Judith E. Barlow, *Final Acts: The Creation of Three Late O'Neill Plays* (Athens: University of Georgia Press, 1985), 105–8.

28. Richard B. Sewall, *The Vision of Tragedy* (New York: Paragon House, 1990), 174.

29. Jones, *Hamlet and Oedipus*.

30. A fine discussion of this point is found in Bogard, *Contour*, 440–44.

31. See Sheaffer, *Artist*, 669.

32. Tragedies other than the big four come into *Long Day's Journey*, but more spottily, I believe. John H. Astington offers a lively discussion of the influence of *Antony and Cleopatra* on the play in "Shakespeherian Rags," *Modern Drama* 31 (March 1988): 73–80.

33. Cargill, *O'Neill and His Plays*, 104.

34. Mary B. Mullett, "The Extraordinary Story of Eugene O'Neill," *American Magazine*, November 1922, 34.

35. Cargill, *O'Neill and His Plays*, 125.

Chapter 7

1. Sir Philip Sidney, *An Apologie for Poetry* (1595), in *European Theories of the Drama*, ed. Barrett H. Clark (New York: Crown, 1918), 105.

2. John Fletcher, *The Faithful Shepherdess* (1608), in *Elizabethan and Stuart Plays*, ed. C. R. Baskerville, V. B. Heltzel, and A. H. Nethercot (New York: Holt, Rinehart and Winston, 1965), 1147.

3. Eugene Ionesco, *Notes and Counter-Notes* (New York: Grove, 1964), 27.

4. Friedrich Dürrenmatt, *The Marriage of Mr. Mississippi* and *Problems of the Theatre* (New York: Grove, 1966), 32.

5. I offer an extended discussion of the tragic aspects of *Waiting for Godot* in *The Secret Cause: A Discussion of Tragedy* (Amherst: University of Massachusetts Press, 1981), 96–107, and in "The Tragic Pleasure of *Waiting for Godot*," *Beckett at 80/ Beckett in Context*, ed. Enoch Brater (New York: Oxford University Press, 1986), 46–63.

6. Almost every important critic of Shakespeare has discussed this distinct group of Shakespeare's last plays. I find especially interesting the following books: Frank Kermode, *Shakespeare: The Final Plays* (London: Longmans, 1963); G. Wilson Knight, *The Crown of Life* (New York: Barnes and Noble, 1966); Robert G. Hunter, *Shakespeare and the Comedy of Forgiveness* (New York: Columbia University Press, 1965); Rabkin, *Shakespeare and the Common Understanding;* Joan Hartwig, *Shakespeare's Tragicomic Vision* (Baton Rouge: Louisiana State University Press, 1972); Howard Felperin, *Shakespearean Romance* (Princeton: Princeton University

Press, 1972); Barbara A. Mowat, *The Dramaturgy of Shakespeare's Romances* (Athens: University of Georgia Press, 1976).

7. Francis Fergusson convincingly demonstrates this idea in *Shakespeare: The Pattern in His Carpet* (New York: Dell, 1958). He gets his title from T. S. Eliot, who says the following in his essay on Dante (1929): "We do not understand Shakespeare from a single reading, and certainly not from a single play. There is a relation between the various plays of Shakespeare, taken in order; and it is the work of years to venture even one individual interpretation of the pattern in Shakespeare's carpet." Eliot's statement is equally true for the plays of O'Neill.

8. Kermode, *Final Plays*, 7.

9. See, especially, Manheim's discussion in *New Language of Kinship*, 191–208.

10. O'Neill's statement is quoted in Croswell Bowen, "The Black Irishman," in Cargill, *O'Neill and His Plays*, 65. John Henry Raleigh offers the clearest and most convincing discussion of O'Neill's Irishness in "O'Neill's *Long Day's Journey Into Night* and New England Irish-Catholicism," in Gassner, *O'Neill*, 124–41. See also the discussion of O'Neill's "connections" to Ireland in Edward L. Shaughnessy, *Eugene O'Neill in Ireland: A Critical Reception* (Westport, Conn: Greenwood Press, 1988), 1–50.

11. See John Henry Raleigh's fine discussion of the confessional in "The Last Confession: O'Neill and the Catholic Confessional," in Floyd, *Eugene O'Neill*, 212–28. Also see Laurin Porter's perceptive discussion in *The Banished Prince: Time, Memory, and Ritual in the Late Plays of Eugene O'Neill* (Ann Arbor: UMI Research Press, 1988), 97–103.

12. Sheaffer, *Artist*, 22.

13. Virginia Floyd, *The Plays of Eugene O'Neill* (New York: Frederick Ungar 1985), 580.

14. Floyd, *Plays*, 581.

15. Stanley Cavell, *Disowning Knowledge* (Cambridge: Cambridge University Press, 1987), 193.

16. Coppelia Kahn, "The Providential Tempest and the Shakespearean Family," in *Representing Shakespeare*, ed. Murray M. Schwartz and Coppelia Kahn (Baltimore: Johns Hopkins University Press, 1980), 233.

17. See Manheim, *New Language of Kinship*, 206–8, for a sensitive discussion of the mother-infant image.

18. The "play" metaphor in Shakespeare and Shakespeare's "metatheater" have received much attention from Shakespeare critics. For fine discussions of this important dimension of Shakespeare's art, see Ann Righter, *Shakespeare and the Idea of the Play* (London: Chatto and Windus, 1962); James L. Calderwood, *Shakespearean Metadrama* (Minneapolis: University of Minnesota Press, 1971); and Thomas F. Van Laan, *Role-Playing in Shakespeare* (Toronto: University of Toronto Press, 1978).

19. A number of critics have discussed the "metatheatrical" O'Neill. See, especially, Robert Ready, "The Play of the Misbegotten," *Modern Drama* 31 (March 1988): 81–90, and Michael Hinden, "Desire and Forgiveness: O'Neill's Diptych," *Comparative Drama* 16 (1982): 238–50.

20. John Henry Raleigh, "The Irish Atavism of *A Moon for the Misbegotten*," in Floyd, *Eugene O'Neill*, 231–33.

21. Barlow, *Final Acts,* 184–85; Floyd, *O'Neill at Work,* 372.

22. Floyd, *O'Neill at Work,* 376.

23. See Bogard, *Contour,* 453–54, for a discussion of the word *misbegotten* that does not include my "star-cross'd" idea.

24. An excellent discussion of Shakespeare's influence on Keats can be found in Jonathan Bate, *Shakespeare and the English Romantic Imagination* (Oxford: Clarendon Press, 1986), 175–201. Bate finds fifty Shakespearean analogues in "Ode to a Nightingale," an eighty-line ode.

25. Bate, *English Romantic Imagination,* 195.

Index

Aeschylus: *Oresteia*, 102, 103, 105, 107, 109
Ah, Wilderness!, 57, 115–29, 131, 132, 133, 177, 188, 243, 248
American Mercury, The, 46
"And Give Me Death," 137
Anna Christie, 42, 74, 173, 179
Antony and Cleopatra, 22, 42, 74, 94–97, 236–37
Appia, Adolph, 83
As You Like It, 121, 122, 178, 202–4, 243

Baker, George Pierce, 3, 187
Barber, C. L., 25, 66, 119, 186
Barlowe, Judith, 208, 247
Barrymore, John, 3
Barthes, Roland, 6
Bate, Jonathan, 252
Baudelaire, Charles, 199–200
Beaumont, Francis, 225, 227
Beckerman, Bernard, 91
Beckett, Samuel, 1, 7, 8, 168, 169, 170, 171, 172, 185, 223; *Endgame*, 185; *Krapp's Last Tape*, 179; *Waiting for Godot*, 166, 168, 170, 171, 172, 185, 223, 226
Beethoven, Ludvig van, 226
Belasco, David, 243
Benchley, Robert, 168
Bentley, Eric, 6
Beyond the Horizon, 57, 81, 144, 179
"Blessed Sisters, The," 137, 138, 143
Bloom, Harold, 4, 5
Bogard, Travis, 28, 86, 89, 97, 115, 136

Booth, Edwin, 47, 191, 206, 207, 208, 209, 211, 212
Bound East for Cardiff, 11–16, 19, 23, 29
Brady, Alice, 112
Brecht, Bertolt, 1
Brook, Peter, 3
Bryant, Louise, 97
Byron, George Gordon, 144
"By Way of Obit," 180, 228

Calms of Capricorn, The, 135, 138, 159, 161
Camus, Albert, 169
Carlin, Terry, 179
Carpenter, Frederic, 93, 116
Cavell, Stanley, 234
Chabrowe, Leonard, 83, 84
Chekhov, Anton, 1
Chothia, Jean, 135, 153
Chris Christophersen, 75
Clark, Barrett, 135
Cocteau, Jean, 31
Conrad, Joseph, 1, 18, 23, 27; *The Heart of Darkness*, 27; *The Nigger of the Narcissus*, 18
Cook, George Cram, 83, 84
Count of Monte Cristo, The, 47, 153, 187, 189, 204
Craig, Gordon, 83; *The Theater Advancing*, 27
Crouse, Russell, 99
Cymbeline, 227, 244, 249–52

Dante, 7, 131, 233
Days Without End, 18, 98, 99, 115, 116, 117, 118, 129, 130, 131–33, 173, 185

DeQuincey, Thomas, 151
Desire Under the Elms, 15, 48, 57–82, 84, 85, 90, 94, 97, 98, 100, 101, 102, 104, 105, 106, 107, 109, 110, 115, 135, 154, 181, 183, 208, 231, 237
Dewhurst, Colleen, 188
Dickens, Charles, 135
Donne, John, 185
Dowson, Edward, 196, 198, 200
Dumas, Alexander, 189
Durrenmatt, Friedrich, 226
Dynamo, 82, 97–98, 99, 130

Egri, Peter, 89, 135
Eliot, George, 135
Eliot, T. S., 25, 55
Emperor Jones, The, 24, 27–42, 43, 44, 47, 49, 55, 74, 88, 91, 100, 147, 208
Ervine, St. John, 102
Euripides, 1; *Hippolytus*, 58–59, 61, 68, 109
Experimental Theater, The, 84

Fechter, Charles, 189
Fergusson, Francis, 6
Fletcher, John, 225, 226, 227
Floyd, Virginia, 143, 247
Fountain, The, 85, 132, 133, 135
"Four Brothers, The," 138, 143
Frenz, Horst, 102
Freud, Sigmund, 4, 57, 58, 82, 83, 86, 87, 97, 105, 107, 219
Frye, Northrop, 118

Garber, Marjorie, 3
Gaylord Farm Sanatorium, 3, 4, 20, 187
Gelb, Arthur and Barbara, 117
Gilpin, Charles, 32, 41
Gorky, Maxim: *The Lower Depths*, 179
Great God Brown, The, 74, 82, 85–87, 88, 89, 93, 99, 111
"Greed of the Meek, The," 137
Gruenberg, Louis, 42

"Hair of the Dog," 138
Hairy Ape, The, 15, 17, 42–46, 47, 48, 49, 51, 55, 88, 91, 98, 173, 183, 208
Hall, Peter, 168

Hamilton, Gilbert, 58
Hamlet, 3, 7, 22, 24, 29, 57, 58, 60–68, 69, 73, 76, 77, 78, 80, 84, 89, 90, 97, 98, 103–12, 120, 121, 123, 125, 126, 128, 142, 152, 153, 155–56, 160, 162, 172, 178, 179, 180, 181, 183, 184, 185, 186, 195, 208, 214–20, 230, 235, 240, 244–45, 252, 253
Harvard University, 3, 187
Henry VIII, 161
Henry V, 140, 141, 142, 149, 150, 160, 161
Henry IV, 90, 136, 141, 142, 148, 149, 152, 153, 154, 160, 162
Henry VI, 139, 140, 141, 150, 161
Hitler, Adolf, 185
Homer, 7; *The Iliad*, 59
Howard, Jean, 78
Howard, Sidney: *They Knew What They Wanted*, 57
Hughie, 15, 75, 180, 228–29
Hugo, Victor, 135
Huston, Walter, 75

Ibsen, Henrik, 1, 4, 5, 20, 28, 187, 188; *Peer Gynt*, 28; *When We Dead Awaken*, 226; *The Wild Duck*, 179
Iceman Cometh, The, 17, 18, 75, 115, 135, 153, 165, 166–85, 187, 196, 208, 223, 225, 228, 229, 241
Ionesco, Eugene, 226
Ives, Burl, 75

Jenkins, Kathleen, 187
Johnson, Etta, 48
Johnson, Jack, 48
Johnson, Samuel, 7
Jones, Ernest, 58, 66, 217
Jones, James Earl, 38
Jones, Robert Edmond, 81, 82, 84, 112
Jonson, Ben, 118, 119
Joyce, James, 208; *Ulysses*, 89
Julius Caesar 22, 24, 29, 41, 74, 84, 153, 196, 206–9, 238
Jung, Carl, 82, 83, 86, 87

Kahn, Coppelia, 236
Kaiser, George, 49

Keats, John, 249-53
Kermode, Frank, 227
Kierkegaard, Soren, 5
King Lear, 41, 43, 68-73, 77, 78, 80, 91, 92, 126, 167, 172, 175, 179, 183, 192-94, 203, 221-23, 235, 241
Kolin, Philip, 53
Kozintzev, Grigori, 214
Krutch, Joseph Wood, 99, 101, 102

Langner, Laurence, 118, 165, 173
Lazarus Laughed, 82, 83, 87, 88, 93, 131, 132, 133, 135, 173
Levi-Strauss, Claude, 7
Lewis, Sinclair, 85
Light, Jimmy, 58
London, Jack: *The Call of the Wild*, 28
Long Day's Journey Into Night, 3, 5, 7, 8, 17, 18, 22, 25, 47, 67, 75, 83, 101, 110, 115, 117, 127, 128, 135, 153, 154, 165, 166, 169, 183, 185, 187-224, 225, 228, 229, 230, 237, 241, 242, 243, 244, 245, 246, 249, 252, 253, 254
Long Voyage Home, The, 19
Loren, Sophia, 75
Love's Labor's Lost, 37

Macbeth, 3, 16, 24, 29, 30, 31, 41, 46, 50-54, 74, 78, 80, 109, 138, 150, 151, 172, 183, 198, 201, 210, 220-21, 237, 241
Macgowan, Kenneth, 82, 83, 84, 89, 100, 117, 178; *Masks and Demons*, 86; *Theatre of Tomorrow*, 84
Manheim, Michael, 25, 97, 104, 143, 154
Marco Millions, 74, 82, 85, 87, 88, 93, 131, 135
Melville, Herman, 18, 23
Memoranda on Masks, 84, 86, 87, 89, 130
Merchant of Venice, The, 3, 37
Midsummer Night's Dream, A, 119, 121, 122, 129, 177, 247, 248
Moeller, Philip, 112
Moon for the Misbegotten, A, 15, 64, 105, 135, 225, 226, 228-54
Moon of the Caribees, The, 19, 247
More Stately Mansions, 135, 136, 138, 139, 143, 145, 149, 150, 152-61, 166, 182, 185, 237
Mourning Becomes Electra, 3, 15, 25, 48, 74, 82, 84, 88, 94, 98, 99, 100-112, 115, 117, 118, 129, 135, 154, 168, 183, 188, 204, 208, 213, 232, 237
Mueller, Martin, 102
Muir, Kenneth, 76

Nathan, George Jean, 102
Nazimova, Alla, 112
Nichols, Dudley, 166, 167, 177, 233
Nietzsche, 1, 4, 5, 84, 85, 86, 89, 168, 179, 188, 189; *The Birth of Tragedy*, 83; *Thus Spake Zarathustra*, 88

Olivier, Laurence, 39, 65, 77
O'Neill, Carlotta Monterey, 17, 100, 115, 136, 216, 219, 221, 228
O'Neill, Edmund, 67
O'Neill, Ella Quinlan, 25, 47, 48, 57, 143, 154, 214, 228, 230
O'Neill, Eugene, Jr., 187
O'Neill, James, 3, 4, 47, 48, 57, 67, 68, 69, 143, 153, 228, 233, 250
O'Neill, Jamie, 3, 48, 57, 210, 228, 229, 230, 232
Othello, 22, 28, 31-42, 43, 44-46, 47, 48, 50, 53, 54, 55, 77, 172, 182, 183, 189-92, 203, 206, 210-11, 212, 213, 235, 241, 244, 245-49, 253, 254

Paxinou, Katina, 221
Pericles, 22, 227
Plautus, 119, 225, 226
Polanski, Roman, 78
Princeton University, 3
Provincetown Players, 11, 13

Quintero, Jose, 169, 188

Rabkin, Norman, 7, 140
Racine, Jean, 1
Raleigh, John Henry, 116, 135, 208, 242
Reed, Jack, 97
Reinhardt, Max, 83
Richard II, 140, 141, 142, 146-47, 148, 153, 158, 159, 160

Richard III, 24, 79, 140, 141, 142, 145, 146, 161–62, 211–14
Robards, Jason, Jr., 169, 188
Robeson, Paul, 32, 38, 41, 42, 45, 46, 55
Rolland, Romain: *Jean-Cristophe*, 135
Romeo and Juliet, 22, 74, 153, 248, 251–52, 253
Rope, The, 57
Rossetti, Dante Gabriel, 213
Roy, Emil, 68

Sam, Guillaume, 27
"Sara and Abigail," 138
Sartre, Jean-Paul, 170
Schopenhauer, Arthur, 188
Scott, Adam, 28
Scott, Sir Walter, 135
Sea Mother's Son, 18
Sewall, Richard, 209
Shaw, George Bernard, 1, 189
Sheaffer, Louis, 4, 25, 27, 47, 48, 58, 67, 89, 129
Sheeler, Charles, 27
Sidney, Sir Philip, 225, 226
Simonson, Lee, 85
Sisk, Robert, 139
Skinner, Richard Dana, 165
Smith, Joe, 28
Sophocles, 7, 57, 107; *Oedipus Rex*, 110, 156; *Oedipus at Colonus*, 226
Spenser, Edmund, 20

States, Bert, 7
Stone, Lawrence, 141
Strange Interlude, 13, 14, 52, 82, 88–97, 98, 99, 111, 129, 168, 194
Strindberg, August, 1, 4, 5, 20, 28, 76, 179, 187, 188, 189; *The Play*, 28; *The Spook Sonata*, 84
Synge, John Millington, 229

"Tale of Possessors Self-Dispossessed, A," 135–36, 141, 148, 162, 165
Tempest, The, 21, 22, 118, 197–99, 214, 227, 228, 234, 237–41, 243, 250
Terence, 119
Theatre Guild, 82, 112, 139, 169
Titus Andronicus, 37
Tolstoy, Leo: *War and Peace*, 135
Touch of the Poet, A, 135, 136, 138, 139, 143–52, 153, 160
Twelfth Night, 22, 121, 122, 123–26, 129, 174, 175, 177, 243

Watts, Richard Jr., 170
Where the Cross Is Made, 23–25, 28
Wilde, Oscar, 189
Winter's Tale, The, 22, 227, 228, 233–37, 240, 241, 243, 250
Winther, Sophus K., 131

Yeats, William Butler, 226